Witchcraft and Masculinities in Early Modern Europe

Palgrave Historical Studies in Witchcraft and Magic

Series Editors: **Jonathan Barry, Willem de Blécourt and Owen Davies**

Titles include:

Edward Bever
THE REALITIES OF WITCHCRAFT AND POPULAR MAGIC IN EARLY MODERN EUROPE
Culture, Cognition and Everyday Life

Julian Goodare, Lauren Martin and Joyce Miller
WITCHCRAFT AND BELIEF IN EARLY MODERN SCOTLAND

Jonathan Roper (*editor*)
CHARMS, CHARMERS AND CHARMING

Alison Rowlands (*editor*)
WITCHCRAFT AND MASCULINITIES IN EARLY MODERN EUROPE

Rolf Schulte
MAN AS WITCH
Male Witches in Central Europe

Forthcoming:

Johannes Dillinger
MAGICAL TREASURE HUNTING IN EUROPE AND NORTH AMERICA
A History

Soili-Maria Olli
TALKING TO DEVILS AND ANGELS IN SCANDINAVIA, 1500–1800

Laura Stokes
THE DEMONS OF URBAN REFORM
The Rise of Witchcraft Prosecution, 1430–1530

Palgrave Historical Studies in Witchcraft and Magic
Series Standing Order ISBN 978–1403–99566–7 Hardback 978–1403–99567–4 Paperback
(outside North America only)

You can receive future titles in this series as they are published by placing a standing order. Please contact your bookseller or, in case of difficulty, write to us at the address below with your name and address, the title of the series and the ISBN quoted above.

Customer Services Department, Macmillan Distribution Ltd, Houndmills, Basingstoke, Hampshire RG21 6XS, England.

Witchcraft and Masculinities in Early Modern Europe

Edited by

Alison Rowlands
Senior Lecturer in European History, University of Essex

palgrave
macmillan

First published 2009 by
PALGRAVE MACMILLAN

Palgrave Macmillan in the UK is an imprint of Macmillan Publishers Limited, registered in England, company number 785998, of Houndmills, Basingstoke, Hampshire RG21 6XS.

Palgrave Macmillan in the US is a division of St Martin's Press LLC, 175 Fifth Avenue, New York, NY 10010.

Palgrave Macmillan is the global academic imprint of the above companies and has companies and representatives throughout the world.

Palgrave® and Macmillan® are registered trademarks in the United States, the United Kingdom, Europe and other countries

ISBN: 978–0–230–55329–3

This book is printed on paper suitable for recycling and made from fully managed and sustained forest sources. Logging, pulping and manufacturing processes are expected to conform to the environmental regulations of the country of origin.

A catalogue record for this book is available from the British Library.

A catalog record for this book is available from the Library of Congress.

10 9 8 7 6 5 4 3 2 1
18 17 16 15 14 13 12 11 10 09

Printed and bound in Great Britain by
CPI Antony Rowe, Chippenham and Eastbourne

Contents

List of Figures and Tables vii

Preface ix

Series Foreword x

Notes on the Contributors xi

1 Not 'the Usual Suspects'? Male Witches, Witchcraft, and Masculinities in Early Modern Europe 1
Alison Rowlands

2 Male Witches in the Duchy of Lorraine 31
Robin Briggs

3 Men as Accused Witches in the Holy Roman Empire 52
Rolf Schulte

4 Witch-Finders, Witch-Hunters or Kings of the Sabbath? The Prominent Role of Men in the Mass Persecutions of the Rhine-Meuse Area (Sixteenth–Seventeenth Centuries) 74
Rita Voltmer

5 Why Some Men and Not Others? The Male Witches of Eichstätt 100
Jonathan Durrant

6 Giandomenico Fei, the Only Male Witch. A Tuscan or an Italian Anomaly? 121
Oscar Di Simplicio

7 Men and the Witch-Hunt in Scotland 149
Julian Goodare

8 Masculinity and Witchcraft in Seventeenth-Century England 171
Malcolm Gaskill

9 The Werewolf, the Witch, and the Warlock: Aspects of Gender in the Early Modern Period 191
Willem de Blécourt

10 Possession and the Sexes 214
Sarah Ferber

Index 239

Figures and Tables

Figures

2.1 Bewitchments attributed to Lorraine witches: data from trials of 96 men and a sample of 96 women 40
3.1 Duchy of Carinthia: Witchcraft persecutions by sex, 1540–1729 (numbers accused) 57
3.2 Duchy of Carinthia: Witchcraft persecutions by sex, 1540–1729 (percentage) 57
3.3 Bishopric of Bamberg: Witchcraft persecutions by sex, 1610–1635 (numbers accused) 60
3.4 Bishopric of Bamberg: Witchcraft persecutions by sex, 1610–1635 (percentage) 60
3.5 Duchy of Holstein and Saxony-Lauenberg: Witchcraft persecutions by sex, 1530–1730 (numbers accused) 63
3.6 Duchy of Holstein and Saxony-Lauenberg: Witchcraft persecutions by sex, 1530–1730 (percentage) 63
6.1 Number of cases of *Maleficia* and magic tried before the Inquisitorial Tribunal in Siena, 1580–1721 125

Tables

3.1 Proportion of men accused in Witch-Trials in the Holy Roman Empire, by region (1480–1760) 55
3.2 Proportion of men involved in Witch-Hunts in selected territories of the Holy Roman Empire 56
3.3 Proportion of men accused of Witchcraft in selected Catholic and Protestant territories of the Holy Roman Empire (by percentage) 66
6.1 Numbers of men and women investigated by the Inquisitorial Tribunal in Siena for love magic, 1580–1721 126
6.2 Numbers of men and women investigated by the Inquisitorial Tribunal in Siena for conjuration, 1580–1721 126
6.3 Numbers of men and women investigated by the Inquisitorial Tribunal in Siena for invocation of the Devil, 1580–1721 126

6.4 Numbers of men and women investigated by the Inquisitorial Tribunal in Siena for therapeutic magic, 1580–1721 126
6.5 Ages of women investigated on charges of Witchcraft by the Inquisitorial Tribunal in Siena, 1580–1721 127
6.6 Marital status of women investigated on charges of Witchcraft by the Inquisitorial Tribunal in Siena, 1580–1721 127
6.7 Occupations of women investigated on charges of Witchcraft by the Inquisitorial Tribunal in Siena, 1580–1721 128
6.8 Targets of the *Maleficia* of women investigated on charges of Witchcraft by the Inquisitorial Tribunal in Siena, 1580–1721 128

Preface

This book is the result of a conference, Witchcraft and Masculinities in the Early Modern World, held at the University of Essex from 21–23 April 2006. All the chapters in the book were presented on that occasion. The conference would not have been possible without financial support from the Arts and Humanities Research Council, the German History Society, and the Department of History at Essex University: my grateful thanks to them all. I would also like to express particular thanks to my co-organizer, Jenni Grundy, without whom the conference would have been much harder (and much less enjoyable) to plan; to Jenni, Herbert Eiden and Cathryn Wilson for acting as session chairs during the conference; and to all the paper-givers and conference participants for their lively input. Many thanks also to Belinda Waterman for technical assistance in preparing the manuscript.

The cover illustration is reproduced by courtesy of the Satdtbibliothek in Trier, and shows a detail from the so-called *Witches' Sabbath in Trier*, an engraving attached to Thomas Sigfrid, *Richtige Antwort auff die Frage* (Erfurt, 1593: 1594 edition), Signatur 1/34 8°.

This book is for Herbert, Susannah, and Sebastian (who thankfully waited until just after the conference to be born!)

ALISON ROWLANDS
Wivenhoe, September 2008

Palgrave Historical Studies in Witchcraft and Magic

Series Foreword

The history of European witchcraft and magic continues to fascinate and challenge students and scholars. There is certainly no shortage of books on the subject. Several general surveys of the witch trials and numerous regional and micro studies have been published for an English-speaking readership. While the quality of publications on witchcraft has been high, some regions and topics have received less attention over the years. The aim of this series is to help illuminate these lesser-known or little studied aspects of the history of witchcraft and magic. It will also encourage the development of a broader corpus of work in other related areas of magic and the supernatural, such as angels, devils, spirits, ghosts, folk healing and divination. To help further our understanding and interest in this wider history of beliefs and practices, the series will include research that looks beyond the usual focus on Western Europe and that also explores their relevance and influence from the medieval to the modern period.

Contributors

Willem de Blécourt is an historical anthropologist and an Honorary Research Fellow at the Huizinga Institute and the Meertens Institute, both in Amsterdam. His research interests include the histories of witchcraft, shape-shifting, popular culture, folk- and fairy-tales, irregular healers, and deviant sexuality. He is the co-author (with R. Hutton and J. La Fontaine), of *The Athlone History of Witchcraft and Magic in Europe. Volume 6: The 20th Century* (London, 1999); ed. (with O. Davies), *Beyond the Witch Trials. Witchcraft and Magic in Enlightenment Europe* (Manchester and New York, 2004); ed. (with C. Usborne), *Cultural Approaches to the History of Medicine* (Basingstoke, 2004); ed., *Sisters of Subversion: Histories of Women, Tales of Gender* (Amsterdam, 2008); and *Werewolves*, which was not published (London, 2005). He refrains from eating meat.

Robin Briggs is a Senior Research Fellow at All Souls College, Oxford. His research interests centre on the social and religious history of France under the ancien régime. Major publications include *Early Modern France, 1560–1715* (Oxford, 1977; 2nd edn 1998); *Communities of Belief* (Oxford, 1989); *Witches & Neighbours. The Social and Cultural Context of European Witchcraft* (London, 1996; 2nd edn Oxford, 2002); *The Witches of Lorraine* (Oxford, 2007). He was elected to a Fellowship of the British Academy in 2009.

Oscar Di Simplicio, a former Professor of Modern History at the University of Florence, has published extensively on the history of Italian witchcraft. Major publications include *Inquisizione, stregoneria, medicina* (Siena, 2000), and *Autunno della stregoneria. Maleficio e magia nell'Italia moderna* (Bologna, 2005). His new book, *La stregoneria in Italia. I caratteri originali (secc. IX–XVIII)* will be published in 2010.

Jonathan Durrant is a Senior Lecturer in Early Modern History at the University of Glamorgan. He is the author of *Witchcraft, Gender and Society in Early Modern Germany* (Brill, 2007) and editor of the Witchcraft Bibliography Project Online. His other research interests include masculinity and warfare in the seventeenth century, and the representation of early modern history on screen.

Sarah Ferber is Associate Professor of History at the University of Wollongong. She is the author of *Demonic Possession and Exorcism in*

Early Modern France (London and New York, 2004) and was a contributor to the 2006 ABC-Clio *Encyclopedia of Witchcraft*, edited by Richard M. Golden.

Malcolm Gaskill is a Reader in Early Modern History at the University of East Anglia. He is the author of *Crime and Mentalities in Early Modern England* (Cambridge, 2000), *Hellish Nell: Last of Britain's Witches* (London, 2001), and *Witchfinders: a Seventeenth-Century English Tragedy* (London, 2005). He is currently writing *Witchcraft: a Very Short Introduction* for Oxford University Press.

Julian Goodare is a Reader in Scottish History at the University of Edinburgh. He works on government, finance and politics in early modern Scotland, and the witch-hunt in Scotland and Europe. He is the author of *State and Society in Early Modern Scotland* (Oxford, 1999) and *The Government of Scotland, 1560–1625* (Oxford, 2004); his edited books include *The Scottish Witch-Hunt in Context* (Manchester, 2002) and *Witchcraft and Belief in Early Modern Scotland* (Basingstoke, 2008) (as co-editor with Lauren Martin and Joyce Miller). He was Director of the Survey of Scottish Witchcraft, which went online in 2003.

Alison Rowlands is a Senior Lecturer in European History at the University of Essex. Her publications on the history of witchcraft in early modern Germany include *Witchcraft Narratives in Early Modern Germany: Rothenburg, 1561–1652* (Manchester, 2003) and several articles. She is currently writing *Witch Hunts in the Early Modern World* for Blackwell. Other research interests include gender in early modern Europe, and representations of early modern witchcraft in modern tourism and public histories.

Rolf Schulte is a Teaching Fellow at the University of Kiel. His research interests include early modern witch-hunts, and German and European history of the nineteenth and twentieth century. His publications include *Hexenmeister. Die Verfolgung von Männern im Rahmen der Hexenverfolgungen von 1530 bis 1730 im Alten Reich* (Frankfurt, 2000; 2nd edn, 2001); ed. (with B. Schmidt), *Hexenglauben im modernen Afrika. Hexen, Hexenverfolgung und magische Vorstellungswelten/Witchcraft in Modern Africa. Witches, Witch-Hunts and Magical Imaginaries* (Hamburg, 2007); *Man as Witch. Male Witches in Central Europe* (Basingstoke, 2009).

Rita Voltmer is a Senior Lecturer in Medieval and Pre-Modern History at the University of Trier. Her research interests include the European witch-hunts; urban history; the history of criminality; and medieval and pre-modern communication media. Her publications include: ed. (with F. Irsigler), *Hexenwahn. Ängste der Neuzeit* (2002); ed. (with H. Eiden), *Hexenprozesse und Gerichtspraxis* (Trier, 2002); ed., *Hexenverfolgung und Herrschaftspraxis* (Trier, 2005); (with W. Rummel), *Hexen und Hexenverfolgung in der Frühen Neuzeit* (2008).

1

Not 'the Usual Suspects'? Male Witches, Witchcraft, and Masculinities in Early Modern Europe

Alison Rowlands

I

Historical analysis of the gendering of early modern witch-trials has been dominated by the complex question of why the majority of people who faced trial for witchcraft were women. To an extent, of course, this is as it should be: 75–80 per cent of all those tried as witches in early modern Europe were female and in some areas the proportion was even higher, standing at 90 per cent or above in Hungary, the Bishopric of Basel, the County of Namur, the English county of Essex, and the Wielkopolska region of Poland.[1] Historians have suggested various responses to the 'why were most witches women?' question. Some of these responses are more obviously influenced by feminism than others, but all construct a figure of the early modern witch that re-affirms rather than problematizes her gendered identity as female.[2]

Certain historians interpret witch-persecution as a means by which contemporaries identified and eliminated women who were perceived as a threat to the patriarchal order of early modern society, either because of their sexuality, their status as single, their problematic economic position, or the 'illicit' medical knowledge they supposedly possessed as midwives or 'wisewomen'. More radical feminists stress that the persecution was the work of men who held judicial power that they exercised with particular savagery (through torture) on the bodies of female victims.[3] A second historiographical approach situates witchcraft accusations in a social context of female competition for status and a psychological context in which the witch was imagined as the inverse of the ideal role of the early modern lay-woman, that of the good mother and housewife. Witches were thus more likely to be women, it is argued, because they were accused by other women who were fearful of the witch's malevolent power to attack their households, but who also sought to increase their own status within the community by labelling other women as bad housewives/witches.[4] Other historians take age as well as gender into account, and argue that older women were particularly vulnerable to witchcraft accusations. In the early 1970s, Keith Thomas and Alan Macfarlane suggested that it was the poverty and unwelcome dependence of old women that rendered them vulnerable to accusation by wealthier neighbours.[5] More recently, Lyndal Roper has argued that old women were the main victims of witch-hunts because, in a society that venerated fertility, the shrivelled bodies of post-menopausal women were regarded as poisonous and dangerous, and because old women who could no longer bear children were expected to be jealous of (and thus willing to harm) younger, still fertile women and their children.[6] Diane Purkiss also makes a link between anxieties about witchcraft and ways of imagining the female body, suggesting that the early modern witch was a fantasy-image of a leaky, polluting, and threateningly boundless maternal body.[7]

The problem with these approaches is that they (explicitly or implicitly) downplay the presence of men amongst the accused in witch-trials, despite the fact that men constituted 20–25 per cent of all of those tried for witchcraft in early modern Europe, and a majority of the accused in some areas (Iceland, Normandy, Estonia, and Russia, for example).[8] How, for instance, can men be incorporated into an explanatory framework that has the reproductive female body at its centre? This sidelining of men as accused witches within the historiography means that there is a relatively meagre list of publications devoted to the subject, including only four monographs. In the early 1990s, two (German) case studies of individual male witches were published. One is a brief analysis of the trial of a nine-year-old boy-witch from seventeenth-century Bamberg by Hans Sebald; the second, by Wolfgang Behringer, is an excellent study of the late-sixteenth-century case of Chonrad Stoeckhlin, a horse-wrangler and shaman who was forced into making a confession of witchcraft by the authorities.[9] Neither author was primarily concerned with the maleness of the accused, however. Sebald was mainly interested in the phenomenon of child-witches, while Behringer used the Stoeckhlin case as a way of exploring beliefs about night-flying spirits.

The first of two books to deal explicitly with male witches was Rolf Schulte's ground-breaking *Hexenmeister,* a detailed analysis of men as accused witches in the Holy Roman Empire, published in German in 2000.[10] *Hexenmeister* is a hugely important contribution to the historiography, given that around half of all executions for witchcraft and sorcery in early modern Europe took place within the Empire. The second book, *Male Witches in Early Modern Europe* (2003), by Lara Apps and Andrew Gow, contains few specific examples of men who were accused of witchcraft, but is, instead, valuable for the authors' critique of the dominant explanations for the gendering of witch-persecution and exposure of 'the historiographical structures and politics that exclude [male witches] as historical subjects'.[11] Apart from a couple of examples from the 1970s, articles and essays devoted to case studies of individual male witches or to regions that had a preponderance of male witches also began to be published only from 1990, with a steady trickle of such publications dating from the late 1990s onwards.[12]

The growing literature on male witches has raised a series of questions that are still far from being answered definitively. Were ideas about the practice of magic and witchcraft imagined along gendered lines? How many men were accused of witchcraft in any particular area, and why did the ratio of female to male accused vary regionally? Were men accused of witchcraft in their own right, or as the relatives of female witches? Were men accused on the basis of longstanding communal reputations for witchcraft, or dragged into trials only when persecution escalated in 'panic' episodes? Were some men more vulnerable to accusation than others and, if so, why? And what do trials involving men as accused witches and witch-hunters tell us with regard to broader expectations about masculinities and masculine behaviour? The aim of this volume is to give leading scholars the chance to reflect on some of these questions, and make their own contributions to the debates. The rest of this introduction will set the chapters in historiographical context, consider how much closer we are to a gender analysis of witch-hunts that is genuinely inclusive of both male and female, and suggest lines of enquiry for future research.

II

The compilation of reasonably accurate statistics is the starting point for any gender analysis of witch-persecution. The gender of an accused individual can usually be identified from his or her name, and is thus much easier to establish than anything else that the historian of witchcraft would – ideally – like to know about the accused, such as age, marital status or socio-economic status. Unnamed victims of witch-trials should not necessarily be assumed to be female, however, while poor survival of trial records can make meaningful statistical analysis of any kind problematic, if not impossible. Another problem, as far as comparative gender analysis is concerned, is that historians do not always agree about what constitutes a case of 'witchcraft'. Werewolves are a case in point in relation to the statistics on male witches. In Chapter 9, for example, Willem de Blécourt shows clearly that 'werewolves and male witches...occupied different conceptual niches' in the early modern world-view, and that (unlike male witches) 'werewolves usually did not bewitch anything, neither were they accused of enriching themselves in unbecoming ways'.[13] At the same time, however, de Blécourt shows how ideas about werewolves could be introduced into witch-trials involving men and boys, while Schulte's analysis of Carinthian male witches in Chapter 3 suggests that there was a thin dividing line in the region between beliefs about werewolves (men thought capable of changing into wolves) and *Wolfbanner* (men imagined as able to magically command wolves to do harm).

The problem of categorizing male witches for the purpose of counting is also highlighted in a recent article on male witches in England and New England, in which Elizabeth Kent increased the number of cases involving male witches in early modern Essex from the 23 identified originally by Alan Macfarlane to 86, by including not only men accused at the assize courts of *maleficium* (the working of harmful magic), but also men accused at assize and non-assize courts of a range of other magical acts. These included enchanting, conjuring, charming and sorcery, although Kent does not give a definition of sorcery, or clarify how it differs from *maleficium*.[14] The contributors to this volume tend to use a definition of witchcraft as the practice of *maleficium*, which often (but not always) involved an imagined liaison between the witch and the Devil, or a demonic being such as a familiar. Oscar Di Simplicio takes the process of categorization furthest in Chapter 6, where he provides a detailed gender analysis of various types of magic as they were defined and tried by the Inquisitorial Tribunal in early modern Siena: in this region *maleficium* emerges as an almost exclusively female magical power. Generally, we need to be sensitive to early modern terminology for different kinds of magical practices and practitioners and the degree to which this terminology was gendered in different languages, and careful not to subsume early modern nuances of meaning within modern linguistic categories. A final important point, made by Rolf Schulte in Chapter 3, is that we should try to count not only witch-trials that ended in execution, but also those that ended in acquittal or non-capital punishment, as even such apparently positive outcomes could have physically, socially and economically damaging effects on the accused. The consideration of allegations of witchcraft that did not end in death (or even in a formal trial) for the accused can help us paint a more detailed picture of the processes of persecution and provide more concrete answers to the question of whether it was easier for men than women to escape the worst legal consequences of a witchcraft accusation or denunciation.[15] Jonathan Durrant makes an important contribution to these debates in Chapter 5, where he discusses why the witch-commissioners in the German Prince-Bishopric of Eichstätt were more reluctant to prosecute men who had been denounced as witches by other suspects than they were to prosecute denounced women. Durrant also asks why some of the denounced men (but not others) were singled out for trial as witches – a question that needs to be explored in greater depth for other areas that experienced large-scale witch-hunts.

Statistical analysis also needs a chronological dynamic in order to show whether the proportion of men amongst the accused in any particular region changed over time. If the number of male witches increased, when did this happen and why? New ideas about witchcraft, and especially the witches' sabbath, were of particular importance in drawing men into trials in ever-larger numbers, especially when they were coupled with coercive legal procedures in which torture was used to force confessions and denunciations of other supposed witches from suspects who were already in custody. For example, men made up 37 per cent of those tried for witchcraft in the German Duchy of Westphalia between 1508 and 1732, but this proportion increased from 17.4 per cent of the total in the 1570s to 58.3 per cent in the 1680s. Peter Arnold Heuser links this increase to changes in the way that the sabbath was imagined in the Duchy from the 1590s. As the elite view of the sabbath was influenced by popular accounts of it as similar to a village festival, men – who played key organizational and especially musical roles in real village festivities and dances – could be more easily imagined as sabbath attendees.[16] In Chapter 4 of this volume, Rita Voltmer also demonstrates how the development of new ideas about the sabbath had a relatively rapid impact on the gendering of witch-trials in an area experiencing large-scale persecution. She describes how the boy-witch, imagined as a piper or drummer at the sabbath, was the first category of male witch to be created in the mass trials of the Rhine-Meuse area in the late sixteenth century, thereby confirming the idea of the 'dual-gendered' sabbath at both the popular and elite level, and making the denunciation and conviction of growing numbers of men of all ages and social status for witchcraft more likely.[17]

Erik Midelfort was one of the first historians to analyze the phenomenon of an increase in the number of male witches during large-scale trials in his 1972 publication, *Witch Hunting in Southwestern Germany, 1562–1684*. Midelfort suggested that increasing numbers of men (and children) were drawn into mass trials in the region after the stereotype of the witch as a woman (and often an older woman) broke down. Midelfort argued that this stereotype initially functioned to keep witch-persecution within 'acceptable' limits, because it enabled society 'to hunt its hidden enemies [that is, witches] without inviting social chaos'.[18] The 'breakdown of the stereotype', and the 'social chaos' this threatened, helped to end witch-trials, according to Midelfort, because local communities (and especially the men in charge of the courts) suffered a 'crisis of confidence' in the legal procedures available for trying witches once too many non-stereotypical witches (that is, men and children) were accused. This was particularly the case if the accused men were of high socio-economic or political status. Midelfort's emphasis on the significance of change over time in the social profiles of accused witches was extremely valuable, but his 'crisis of confidence' theory is by no means universally applicable, and needs to be tested on a region-by-region basis. Voltmer's discussion of the witch-trials of the Rhine-Meuse area in Chapter 4 and Heuser's analysis of witch-trials in the Duchy of Westphalia show that it was perfectly possible for the courts in some regions to see a significant increase in the number of men executed for witchcraft without any comment being made, let alone a 'crisis' suffered. Heuser suggests that any potential 'crisis' of judicial confidence was averted in Westphalia because the jurists who presided over witch-trials there came from a small circle of the Duchy's elite families and thus provided continuity and cohesion in terms of legal practice and ideas about witchcraft.[19]

We should not, moreover, assume that men were only accused of witchcraft during large-scale 'panics', or that the numbers of men accused necessarily increased at such times. In Chapter 2, Robin Briggs shows that the Duchy of Lorraine produced a significant proportion of male witches (28 per cent of all those tried) despite having only one concentrated episode of large-scale panic, while in Scotland the number of male witches dropped sharply during the largest witch-hunts.[20] We should also not assume that witch-persecution always started with women and gradually or rapidly incorporated men, even if this was a relatively common pattern of change across early modern Europe. In Finland, 60 per cent of those accused and 75 per cent of those convicted of witchcraft in the sixteenth century were men, many of whom were professional sorcerers. It was not until the 1660s that women outnumbered men amongst the accused, a change that Antero Heikkinen and Timo Kervinen argue resulted from the spread of western European witch doctrine, with its emphasis on a sexual pact between the Devil and the witch, across Finland.[21] Gender ratios amongst the accused could thus change in different ways or remain relatively constant, a point that needs to be acknowledged and explored at the regional level.

To test more rigorously the extent to which large-scale panics affected the gendering of persecution, we could usefully adopt Willem de Blécourt's suggestion that 'we should…differentiate between witches produced locally and those unfortunates who only acquired the label through judicial procedures which allowed for denunciations as sufficient indication of devil-worship'.[22] We need to tread carefully in drawing this distinction, however, regardless of the gender of the 'witches' involved. One danger in differentiating between these two types of witches is that it can encourage us to attach value judgements to them, with the result that we see the locally-produced witches as somehow more 'real' and deserving of historical attention than those who had no longstanding communal reputation for witchcraft, and who faced trial as a result of denunciations during large-scale panics.[23] We should remember that this latter type of witch must have seemed equally 'real' to the people who persecuted them, and that they also suffered the same (and sometimes more severe) rigours of imprisonment, torture and execution. We should also remember that large-scale panics did not take place in isolation from 'local' witchcraft beliefs, but could act as catalysts for the emergence of new ideas about witchcraft that could then influence witchcraft beliefs at the communal level. In Chapter 4, Voltmer shows how the mass trials of the Rhine-Meuse area generated new ideas about male witches that affected not only the processes of prosecution in that region, but also, by means of dissemination in influential demonologies, witch-trials in other Catholic parts of Germany. For Westphalia, Heuser has shown how the emergence of new ideas about a dual-gendered sabbath in the course of witch-trials was accompanied by a general shift to more gender-neutral ways of imagining the acquisition and exercise of harmful magical powers amongst the Duchy's inhabitants.[24]

III

Were popular beliefs about magic, and particularly harmful magic, gendered in significant ways? Historians of witchcraft are beginning to explore this question in increasing depth in the context of regional studies. In her groundbreaking article on the German Saar region, Eva Labouvie suggests that women were linked with magical powers perceived as more mysterious and harmful than those associated with men: powers to contact the world of spirits and demons, to cast spells, mix poisons, perform black magic, and fly through the air. These traditional beliefs, coupled with women's roles within the agrarian economy as housewives and mothers, meant that they were imagined as more likely than men to practice harmful magic connected with childbirth, death and love. By contrast, Labouvie suggests that men's magic was more practical and tied to the reality of everyday life because it was defined by a division of labour which deemed men primarily responsible for ensuring 'the preservation of the family, its members, the food and other goods needed to maintain life, livestock, fields, pastures and woods'.[25] Men were thus associated more strongly than women with harvest and weather spells; the magical healing of disease (in both livestock and humans), either as professional healers or as household heads who sought out the services of such healers; and for all measures involving the maintenance, increase and recovery of material goods. 'Magical techniques that served the actual increase of material wealth ... were the exclusive domain of men', Labouvie comments.[26] Willem de Blécourt reaches similar conclusions in his work on the gendering of popular witchcraft beliefs in the Dutch Republic: here, the male witch stereotype was the 'profit-making' man, who was 'the epitome of individual gain and achievement in a surrounding that valued the communal', while women were more strongly associated with the working of harmful magic.[27] However, de Blécourt argues that there was flexibility in the application of these stereotypes, noting that 'men could be classified under the female stereotype and women under the male one'.[28] In the eastern regions of the Dutch Republic, for instance, the label of the profit-making male witch could be attached to entire families (including the female members) defined by the male line. This shows how important the concept of the 'witch family' (discussed in section IV) is to our understanding of popular witchcraft beliefs, as it blurs what, at first glance, seem to be distinctly gendered witch-stereotypes.

Other historians who have tested Labouvie's ideas on their own regions of study tend to conclude that popular beliefs about magic were gendered to an extent, but not as distinctly as Labouvie suggests for the Saar region, especially as far as the practice of non-malevolent magic and healing was concerned. The chapters by Briggs (on the Duchy of Lorraine) and Di Simplicio (on Tuscany) in this volume make important contributions to this debate, as does Katrin Moeller in her study of witch-persecution in the German Protestant Duchy of Mecklenburg. Moeller acknowledges that there were folk-magic techniques that tended to be practised more by one gender than the other in Mecklenburg. She identifies soothsaying; the magical acquisition of riches; rituals designed to protect individuals against the violence of war, or to bring luck in hunting and shooting; and beliefs about werewolves as more male, and love magic; magical techniques aimed at improving milk and butter yields; and magical practices connected with pregnancy and childbirth as more female. However, Moeller notes that the boundaries between male and female practices were fluid and flexible, rather than rigid; that magical enrichment was a concern for women (through the use of butter and milk magic) as well as men; and that men could even be imagined as responsible for something as apparently female as *maleficium* aimed at newborn babies. She concludes that none of the magical techniques was practised exclusively by one gender, while the field of magical healing was also relatively undifferentiated by gender. Moeller agrees with Labouvie that women were more strongly associated with harmful magic, and with more threatening forms of harmful magic, than men, however. Allegations of *maleficium* were made against women in around half of all the witch-trials involving women in Mecklenburg (the comparable figure for men was 37 per cent), while women were also significantly more likely than men to be accused of killing people by magical means.[29]

A stronger popular association of women with the practice of *maleficium* doubtless forms some part of the answer to the 'why were most witches women' question. This association was by no means gender-exclusive to women, however, and the fact that (as de Blécourt points out) men could be identified in practice under the female witch-stereotype allowed for men to be imagined and prosecuted as workers of *maleficium* across Europe. They even formed a majority of those so prosecuted in certain areas. In Iceland, between 1604 and 1720, for example, 120 witch-trials with a primary focus on *maleficium* occurred: 110 of them involved men, and 21 of the 22 victims executed were also male.[30] Even in areas where men formed a minority of those prosecuted for *maleficium*, case studies of individual men thus prosecuted (the Englishman William Godfrey, the Tuscan Giandomenico Fei, and Michael Würth from the German imperial city of Rothenburg ob der Tauber, for example) show that they were imagined as behaving in much the same way as female workers of harmful magic.[31] This supports Malcolm Gaskill's conclusion that, despite the existence of gendered 'folkloric stereotypes' of witches, 'specific circumstances, relationships, and above all, the fear of maleficium took precedence over an unqualified appreciation of the sex of the suspect in the mind of the accuser'.[32] Moreover, the distinctiveness of gendered witch-stereotypes at the village level could diminish over time as a result of more gender-neutral ideas about witches that might be fostered and disseminated through trials and executions; preaching about witchcraft; and written and visual representations of witchcraft in popular print media, such as pamphlets. Such processes of change over time were doubtless facilitated by the flexibility with which the 'folkloric stereotypes' could be applied in the first place.

How gendered was witchcraft belief amongst the educated elites? For demonologists, was it 'literally unthinkable...that witches should be male', as Stuart Clark argues, because the intellectual system of dual classification within which they operated meant that they could not help but map women onto the negative side of any pair of polar opposites (good/evil, God/Devil and so on)?[33] Or did elite men find it harder to imagine men as witches because of demonologists' emphasis on the witch's pact with the Devil as sealed by sexual intercourse, and the general belief that women were naturally more lustful than men? These are complex questions that need to be explored more systematically at the level of demonological writing and the level of trial practice, where the beliefs of the men involved in implementing the law were shaped not only by demonologies, but also by educational experience, legal precepts and precedents, and the popular beliefs they encountered. In their books on male witches, Schulte and Apps and Gow criticize Clark's conclusion that the male witch was 'literally unthinkable'. Apps and Gow demonstrate that demonologists wrote about witches using both masculine and feminine terminology, and conclude that 'one can interpret early modern witchcraft theory as sex-specific only by ignoring a considerable body of evidence to the contrary'.[34] In his more detailed analysis, Schulte also shows that early modern demonologists imagined and discussed men as witches, to produce ideas about witchcraft that were more gender-ambivalent and heterogeneous than Clark's conclusions imply. This was particularly the case when demonologists accepted the reality of the witches' sabbath, with its potentially dual-gendered membership, and discussed it at length.[35] Demonological positions on the gendering of witchcraft varied according to confessional allegiance, however, and, in Chapter 3 of this volume, Schulte explains why Catholic elites in the Holy Roman Empire were more likely than their Lutheran counterparts to take the male witch seriously.

The willingness of elite men to imagine male witches in sexual relationships with demons varied on a regional basis as well, perhaps also in relation to confessional differences. Of male witches in Presbyterian Scotland, for example, Julian Goodare notes in Chapter 7 that 'their demonic pact was undramatic, and they almost never had sex with the Devil'.[36] Elsewhere, however, it was possible for men to construct (and be forced to construct) narratives of seduction by female demons under interrogation. Robert Walinski-Kiehl makes this point in his analysis of the trial for witchcraft of Johannes Junius, mayor of the Catholic German city of Bamberg, noting that Junius linked his initial introduction into witchcraft to sexual seduction by a demon in the guise of a young woman. Walinski-Kiehl suggests that the link between sexual gratification and diabolic seduction made by Junius and most other male and female witch-suspects during the Bamberg witch-trials of the late 1620s 'may have reflected some of the intense moralism characteristic of invigorated counter-Reformation Catholicism'.[37] This Counter-Reformation moralism was also at work in other German Catholic territories that experienced large-scale witch-persecution in the late sixteenth and early seventeenth centuries,[38] while Catholic demonologists listed men's aggressive sexuality as one of the sins by means of which they could fall prey to the Devil.[39]

Physical interaction between humans and the diabolic in early modern Europe was imagined in ways other than acts of sexual intercourse between supposedly willing 'witches' and demons or the Devil, of course. In England, this interaction was imagined most often and in greatest detail through narratives of the witch's familiar, a demonic imp that took the form of a small domestic or quasi-domestic animal that did the witch's malevolent bidding in return for sustenance suckled from unnatural marks or teats on the witch's body. These ideas became particularly prominent during the East Anglian witch-trials of 1645–47, discussed in Chapter 8 by Malcolm Gaskill, when self-styled witch-finders Matthew Hopkins and John Stearne placed unprecedented emphasis on the practice of searching (a physical, often highly invasive examination of a suspect's body for teats) as a method of identifying witches. The importance of suckling to the witch – familiar relationship has led some historians to interpret suckling as a literal and symbolic example of maternal inversion. Deborah Willis, for instance, suggests that English villagers:

> represented the witch as a malevolent mother who used her power to suckle, feed, and nurture a brood of childlike demonic imps in order to bring sickness and death to the households of other mothers.[40]

Men also told stories of suckling familiars that were accepted as plausible by contemporaries, however – a fact that has encouraged other historians to suggest more gender-neutral interpretative approaches.

Jenni Grundy suggests that the key point about the witches' mark or teat was not that it symbolized a demonized female breast but, rather, that it was a mark of the unnaturalness of a human body that was 'characterized by a fundamental and deeply disturbing ambiguity and fluidity' precisely because it could be too easily conflated with the body of an animal. Searching for these marks thus 'represented an attempt to manage' the anxieties aroused by this ambiguity and 'to grasp at the only physical evidence available of the witch's concealed identity'.[41] In Chapter 8, Malcolm Gaskill also suggests that the imagined intimacy between witch and familiar that was expressed through narratives of feeding needs to be read along a 'definitional axis ... [that] was not just male–female but human–beast'.[42] The idea that early modern people could imagine – and be troubled by – human bodies that intersected with the bodies of animals (and the implications of this for gender analysis) are explored in greatest depth in an intriguing discussion of werewolves and a third gender by Willem de Blécourt in Chapter 9.

Demonic possession was the other significant theme around which early modern people articulated ideas about interactions between humans and the diabolic, with the crucial difference being that demoniacs (unlike witches) were characterized as the unwilling recipients of diabolic attention who worked no *maleficium*. In Chapter 10, Sarah Ferber offers a wonderfully nuanced analysis of the ways in which demonic possession and the practice of exorcism were imagined along gendered lines, particularly in the 'limelight' possession cases that reached wide audiences through public exorcisms and/or texts written for public consumption. Ferber uses two limelight cases involving possessed adult men from seventeenth-century France in order to explore how they differed from those involving women, and offers some intriguing ideas about the connections between gender and volition on the part of the possessed. Ferber also insists on the importance of integrating bodies as fully as possible into the analysis. For Ferber, this includes not just the physically contorted body of the demoniac, which was the focus of so much contemporary attention, but also the bodies of the male exorcists, which were, by contrast, conspicuous by their absence from accounts of exorcisms.

The final point to note about witchcraft beliefs is that we can only make them do so much work in explaining the gendering of witch-persecution in any particular region. Beliefs never operated in a vacuum, and other factors influenced the decision to make a witchcraft accusation against a particular individual and the willingness of courts to take accusations seriously. An accusation against an individual might well be part of an ongoing social conflict between entire families, with women rather than men singled out for accusation as a strategy in such conflicts in certain areas by villagers who quickly 'learned' what sort of accusation (and against whom) was most likely to succeed at the local court, and thus cause maximum damage to their local rivals.[43] In many regions, women, especially if they were poor, might simply have been seen as easier targets than men for witchcraft accusations by neighbours, because they lacked the social, financial and educational resources to mount effective strategies in their own defence. This idea does not operate along neatly gendered lines, however: poor men also lacked such resources, while in certain circumstances wealth, status, and education were not enough to protect individual men (such as the Suffolk cleric, John Lowes; the mayor of Bamberg, Johannes Junius; or Dietrich Flade, one of the most powerful men in late-sixteenth-century Trier) from execution as witches.[44] Elite handling of witchcraft accusations could similarly be shaped by strategic concerns as well as witchcraft beliefs. The councillors of the German Lutheran city of Rothenburg ob der Tauber were not keen to take serious legal action against men suspected of witchcraft, a fact that can be linked to the tendency within Lutheranism to associate women more readily than men with witchcraft. However, their lack of enthusiasm for arresting and torturing urban craftsmen suspected of dubious magical practices was also linked to legal, political, and socio-economic considerations that had nothing to do with witchcraft; they were generally unwilling, for similarly pragmatic reasons, to let witchcraft suspicions against either men or women escalate into large-scale trials.[45]

IV

What sorts of men were accused of witchcraft in early modern Europe? The obvious answer to this question is 'those believed to have been witches by their accusers', but even this apparently straightforward response is complicated by the fact that some men were involved in cases where accusers utilized the opportunity offered to them by witch-persecution to target opponents for financial reasons, or for reasons of social or political rivalry. This idea is discussed by Di Simplicio in relation to the Fei case in Chapter 6, and by Voltmer in Chapter 4. Work by Voltmer and Walter Rummel on the witch-persecutions that occurred in the German territories bounded by the Rhine, Meuse, and Moselle rivers has shown the extent to which male witch-hunters, at all levels of the judicial process, sought to pursue a variety of interests by means of witch-prosecutions. Members of village witch-hunting committees used their power to target local rivals, territorial lords used witch-trials to assert their claims to legal power, while individual officials used the opportunities offered by persecution to advance themselves socially and financially.[46] This use of witch-hunting to further personal, familial, or political interests was as likely to target women as it was men, however, as a husband and whole family could be stained with a reputation for witchcraft through a wife. The German word *Instrumentalisierung* (instrumentalization) is a better term for this process than 'malicious prosecution', as the former implies that deliberate calculation (up to and including the complete fabrication of accusations) and genuine belief in witchcraft could be intertwined, albeit to varying degrees in different cases. It was probably all too easy to believe that one's bitterest rival was also a witch.

Did male witches from different regions fall into any discernible social and occupational categories, or exhibit any shared patterns of behaviour that are significant? In Chapter 2, Briggs argues that it was the heterogeneity of the male witch-suspects that was significant for the Duchy of Lorraine, noting that one of the few things they had in common was that they 'so often derived their reputation from a family history of previous accusations'.[47] This phenomenon of reputation by familial association for male witches has also been identified for other parts of Europe, although its significance for the gendering of persecution has not yet been analyzed adequately.[48] As Apps and Gow argue, historians tend to assume that such men were accused primarily because they were related to female witches (rather than for any other reasons), and to regard them as less important than their female counterparts as a result.[49] The concept of the witch-family – a group of people related by blood or marriage, amongst whom the ability to work magic was imagined as being passed on from one generation to the next – is important because it puts the family, rather than gender, at the centre of the analysis: being born into such a family was one of the most important factors dictating whether a person of either gender gained a reputation as a witch as an adult. We need to ask more detailed and consistent questions of witch-trial data that uncover familial links between suspects. Were women always the main bearers of reputation within such families, or was it possible for the men of related pairs or groups of alleged witches to be more feared locally? Were female members of such families accused formally because they were easier targets than the men? Did villagers and demonologists believe that witchcraft was passed down only along the maternal or paternal line or from both parents to all children? And did ideas about the transmission of occult power within witch-families change over time to become more or less gender specific?

Semi-professional male practitioners of various types of non-malevolent magic – usually aimed at healing and protecting people and animals, finding lost and stolen property, soothsaying and divination, identifying evil-doing witches, and communicating with the spirit world – emerge as distinct groups of the accused in witch-trials in certain parts of early modern Europe. They often came from occupations (herdsmen, blacksmiths, and clerics, for example) or ethnic groups (such as the Sami people of the northern Norwegian region of Finnmark) that were traditionally associated with the practice of magic and magical healing.[50] In Normandy, where 75 per cent of all witches prosecuted were men, 'shepherds composed a majority of ... men charged with witchcraft whose occupations can be identified', followed in prominence by clergymen and blacksmiths.[51] Male sorcerers and healers also figured significantly amongst those prosecuted for witchcraft in Estonia, where men constituted 60 per cent of the total prosecuted; Finland, where men constituted around half the total prosecuted; Iceland, where 110 out of 120 trials, and 21 out of 22 executions involved men; and Russia, where witch-trials mainly targeted men and 'folk healers comprised a ... sizable subset of the accused'.[52] Cunning men – including herdsmen, blacksmiths, and clerics – also figured in regions (such as the Duchy of Holstein, discussed in Chapter 3, and the Rhine-Meuse area, discussed in Chapter 4) where male witches were in an overall minority of the accused.

Cunning men and village sorcerers were usually accused of *maleficium* by dissatisfied clients who became annoyed when healing or other non-malevolent magical rituals failed or went wrong. The Reformation and Counter-Reformation provided a more general context in which the judicial and spiritual elites took a tougher line in condemning all magic as diabolic, however, a stance that put pressure on local authority figures (such as parish priests, village officials and local courts) in some regions to redefine the magical powers of cunning men as *maleficium*, and to prosecute them as witches. The idea that male workers of non-malevolent magic were prosecuted for witchcraft as part of a missionary programme instigated by central authorities interested in establishing religious orthodoxy and state power has been argued most forcefully for certain relatively weakly Christianized territories on the European peripheries. For example, Juhan Kahk suggests that the Estonian witch-trials occurred in the context of the attempt by the ruling Swedish state to abolish heathen idolatry and superstition, and to impose serfdom in Estonia.[53] Kirsten Hastrup suggests a similar context for the witch-trials in Iceland, where the political status of Iceland as part of the Kingdom of Denmark made it the object of new moral standards and legislation, under which the practise of magic was no longer tolerated, while Rune Hagen argues that the male Sami shamen prosecuted for witchcraft in the Finnmark region were the victims of Norwegian missionaries.[54]

Similar, albeit less overtly politicized, processes were also at work in central European regions, however, where concerns about religious orthodoxy were heightened in the late sixteenth and first half of the seventeenth centuries. William Monter has suggested that the preponderance of herdsmen and clerics amongst the male witches of Normandy might have been due to an increased concern with apostasy (understood as the misuse of sacred objects by male workers of magic) on the part of the authorities, especially after 1615 when the proportion of male witches increased.[55] In Chapter 4, Voltmer shows that the prosecution of cunning men in the Rhine-Meuse region was influenced by preaching campaigns undertaken by the Jesuits that condemned popular superstition and propagated new ideals of Counter-Reformation piety. This suggests that, while in many parts of Europe villagers were keen to keep their cunning folk out of the hands of the authorities, and were able to maintain meaningful conceptual distinctions between good and bad magic,[56] in certain regions, and at certain times, a new religious context could be established within which local practitioners of non-malevolent magic were more readily diabolized. Cunning women were also vulnerable to such processes, of course, and the question of whether men or women predominated amongst the practitioners of non-malevolent magic who were tried as witches needs to be examined on a regional basis.

Male vagrants emerge as another distinct group amongst the male witches of some regions. In Chapter 3, Schulte demonstrates that male vagrants featured significantly in witch-trials in Carinthia (where men constituted 68 per cent of all witches tried between 1540 and 1729), and explains their vulnerability to accusation in terms of the socio-economic context and the gendered structure of vagrant groups, which meant that male vagrants were much more mobile than their female counterparts. The victims of the *Zauberer-Jackl* (Sorcerer Jack) witch-trials that took place in late-seventeenth-century Salzburg were mostly young, male vagrants: between 1675 and 1681, two thirds of those executed were under the age of 21, and around two thirds were male.[57] Norbert Schindler suggests that the Salzburg witch-trials were the result of:

> a strategy for the social marginalisation of begging...adopted by the state authorities, but above all by the Counter-Reformation church to deepen the chasm between the population and inconvenient marginal groups.[58]

Beggars were extremely vulnerable to this strategy: unwilling alms-givers found it all too easy to believe that the beggars' threats and mumblings were malevolent curses, while vagrants themselves might have confessed to *maleficium* under interrogation as a way of articulating fantasies of revenge against those who had turned them away empty-handed. Like Schulte, Schindler attributes the preponderance of male youngsters amongst the Salzburg witches to the structure of vagrant groups, noting that more poor boys than girls were allowed to wander the roads without adult supervision.[59] The mobility of male vagrants, as much as their aggressive stance whilst begging, was enough to render them vulnerable to suspicions of witchcraft in some regions. In her study of male witches in seventeenth-century Russia, Valerie Kivelson shows that a significant sub-set of the accused were wanderers of various sorts (including vagrants and folk-healers), and suggests that they raised anxieties in an age 'when state and society were directing a large part to their energy toward fixing the population in rank and place'. Kivelson identifies itinerancy as one of four primary risk factors in rendering people vulnerable to witchcraft accusation in Russia: as the itinerant population was predominantly male, this affected men much more than women.[60]

Some historians of witchcraft suggest that, rather than belonging to any distinct social or occupational groups, a significant proportion of male witches were perceived to have contravened norms of masculine behaviour. As Walinski-Kiehl summarizes for Germany:

> male suspects' behaviour often violated expectations of masculinity embodied in the ideal of the honest, reliable, married household head ... they tended to display the following negative social and moral characteristics: bringing the family into debt, involvement in questionable business practices, theft, drunkenness, gambling, bigamy, and adultery.[61]

In Chapter 4, Voltmer identifies the 'rogue', who contravened the social and sexual behaviour expected of the pious household head, as one of six categories of male witch in the Rhine-Meuse region, while Labouvie concludes that all male witches in the Saar region 'had violated masculine roles and patterns of behaviour in some way', including the wealthy villagers who were perceived to have amassed their wealth unfairly.[62] Elizabeth Kent argues along similar lines for male witches in England and New England, concluding that they 'were masculine others, whose poor practice of patriarchy cut across paradigmatic idealization of masculine virtue'. These 'poor practices' included economic aggression and self-interest, intense competitiveness and/or litigiousness, the misuse of institutional power or mismanagement of a household, and outbursts of excessive rage.[63]

By no means were all men who contravened masculine norms accused of witchcraft, of course, and for each individual male 'witch' we must look at the many other factors (age, social status, personality, quality of social relationships with potential accusers, relationship to other suspected witches, sheer bad luck, and so on) that rendered him vulnerable to accusation. The idea is attractive, however, because it seems to offer us the best opportunity of integrating male witches into the same analytical frameworks within which female witches are so often situated, and which I outlined at the beginning of this chapter, and also the best opportunity for developing the sophistication of these analytical frameworks. We can, for example, regard a man who violated masculine norms and then stood trial for witchcraft as a 'victim' of institutionalized patriarchal power in the same way that female witches were: the bearers of patriarchal authority within early modern society were (at some level, at least) using witch-trials as a means of policing behavioural norms for both genders.[64] Far fewer men than women were tried as witches overall because men were the dominant bearers of patriarchal authority at communal and state level, while women were excluded from the formal exercise of judicial power at all social levels. However, early modern European men were divided significantly in terms of their socio-economic status; access to power and resources; and familial, financial, and religious interests. It was, thus, eminently possible for some men (as witch-hunters) to prosecute other men as witches (in some regions, in relatively high numbers), as long as the fundamental patriarchal order of society was not jeopardized in the process. By looking at the ways in which men persecuted other men as witches, then, we can begin to think about how judicial power was exercised by individuals and groups in early modern witch-trials in more nuanced ways.[65]

The idea of the male witch as the inverse of the good household head and all that this role entailed – a masculine 'other', to use Kent's term – is also attractive because it constitutes a neat counterpoint to Diane Purkiss's suggestion that female witches were imagined by early modern people as the inverse of the good housewife and mother.[66] The implication of both ideas is that unacceptable behaviour on the part of men and women ran the risk of being diabolized by neighbours made increasingly anxious about perceived social deviance during times of social tension, economic hardship, or religious change – particularly after the Reformation and Counter-Reformation, as ecclesiastical authorities attempted to set new standards of sexual, social, and religious behaviour amongst their flocks. In this context, all witches were 'bad neighbours' in the eyes of their accusers and, arguably, also in the eyes of the judicial elites, even in large-scale panics fuelled by the process of denunciation rather than long-standing social conflicts within local communities. The witch was, after all, imagined by the elites as a Christian who had made a pact with the Devil and rejected his or her faith and all that it stood for – and this included being a good neighbour, who strove to live in peace and charity with others. The witch as 'bad neighbour' (in both a theological and practical sense) is thus a potentially more useful conceptual category than that of the masculine or feminine 'other', because it is broad enough to incorporate a wide range of expectations about Christian communal living, some of which were less distinctly gendered than others.

In addition to constituting a 'masculine other' in terms of his behaviour, Kent also argues that the male witch could represent 'a masculine counterpart to the leaky boundless body of the female witch'.[67] Kent makes this point in her discussion of John Godfrey, who was tried for witchcraft in late-seventeenth-century Massachusetts. Godfrey was prone to excessive outbursts of emotion (particularly anger) and unpredictable, aggressive behaviour. In a society where emotional control and self-mastery were regarded as essential to the successful exercise of patriarchal authority, Kent implies that such 'uncontrolled' behaviour on the part of a man raised anxieties about an 'uncontrolled' and potentially boundless male body that could be in two places at once. Instead of the 'polluting fluids of the maternal body', however, 'the body of the male witch leaked envy and anger, aggression and revenge, malice and spite'.[68] Kent's willingness to integrate the bodies of male witches into her discussion is extremely valuable, but the maternal female body still dominates her analysis. If the bodies of both men and women could be imagined as potentially and threateningly boundless and polluting in early modern culture, then perhaps it is these shared characteristics and the ways in which they were inflected by gender, rather than the maternal body, that should be the starting point for any analysis of the unnatural body of the witch. Why it was easier to imagine men's bodies in this way in some contexts (witch-trials) than others (possession cases) also needs to be explored in greater detail.

V

The gendering of witch-persecution was clearly shaped to the significant disadvantage of women by the fact that they were excluded from the exercise of formal legal power. Women could participate in witch-trials as accusers and witnesses, while a small number played more formal roles as searchers for unnatural marks on the bodies of accused witches (in England) and – disguised as men – as prickers of such marks (in Scotland).[69] In continental Europe, midwives might also be asked to search the bodies of accused women, to ascertain whether they were still virgins, for instance.[70] Beyond this minimal involvement, however, the judicial apparatus of witch-hunting was exclusively in the hands of men: the local committees, assemblies, and officials who gathered pre-trial evidence; the judges, jurors, and interrogators who conducted trials and reached verdicts; the hangmen who tortured, and often ultimately executed, witch-suspects; the scribes and notaries who kept the trial-records; and the lawyers, theologians, and physicians to whom courts looked for advice in problematic cases.[71] Central authorities might establish additional judicial mechanisms – such as witch-commissioners in parts of Germany, or the Court of Oyer and Terminer in Salem – to expedite the prosecution process.[72] However, individuals or groups with new, semi-autonomous claims to judicial power as witch-hunters could also emerge at certain times and in certain places when anxiety about witchcraft was heightened and centralized control of local witch-hunting initiatives weak. The many (exclusively male) witch-hunting committees that formed amongst the villagers of the Rhine-Meuse region of Germany to become the driving force behind witch-persecution there fall into this category, as do self-styled witch-finders such as Matthew Hopkins and John Stearne, minor gentlemen who played key roles in the East Anglian witch-hunts of 1645–47.[73]

Given the importance of their roles in shaping witch-persecution, we know relatively little about individual witch-hunters, and even less about how their witch-hunting activities might have been linked to particular articulations of masculinity. Scholarly literature on them is sparse and patchy. This is because modern scholars have found it emotionally and morally easier to try to understand the victims rather than the perpetrators of the witch-hunts, and because the type of research necessary to construct detailed life histories of such men (beyond what the witch-trial records themselves tell us) is very painstaking and time-consuming, even assuming the relevant records have survived. There are only three modern book-length studies that make witch-hunters their focus. In 2003, Verena Perlhafter published a brief comparison of three seventeenth-century witch-hunters (Matthew Hopkins, New England cleric Cotton Mather, and German physician Adam Lebaldt von Lebenwaldt), while 2005 saw the publication of *Judge Sewall's Apology*, an account by Richard Francis of the life of the Salem judge who was unique amongst early modern witch-hunters for publicly recanting his involvement in the trials, and Malcolm Gaskill's *Witchfinders*, an excellent account of the roles played by Hopkins and Stearne in the East Anglian witch-hunts of 1645–47.[74] Of all early modern witch-hunters, Hopkins is arguably most notorious, at least in the English-speaking world, because he entered the popular public consciousness in a distinctive way after being made the subject of a novel and horror film in the late 1960s.[75] Gaskill provides a welcome analysis of Hopkins's role in the context of competing early modern codes of masculinity in Chapter 8 of this volume.

In terms of article-length studies, Claudius Musiel, one of the officials responsible for the exceptionally severe witch-hunt that occurred in the German territory of the Imperial Abbey of St Maximin in the late sixteenth century, is the subject of an excellent life history by Rita Voltmer. The detailed *Witch Register* drawn up by Musiel has also been published.[76] The executioners of Biberach, who exerted immense personal influence on witch-trials in the German southwest in the late sixteenth century, and jurist Daniel Hauff and witch-commissioner Franz Buirmann, who were notorious for their severity in witch-trials in Esslingen and Electoral Cologne respectively, are also the focus of specific studies.[77] Beyond these individuals, only witch-hunters who wrote demonologies as a direct consequence of their personal experience of hunting-witches (such as Henri Boguet, Heinrich Kramer, Pierre de Lancre, and Nicolas Rémy),[78] and territorial rulers who displayed a significant personal enthusiasm for witch-hunting (such as James VI of Scotland or the Catholic 'witch-bishops' – German ecclesiastical rulers who oversaw some of the most severe witch-hunts of the early modern period) have garnered much scholarly attention.[79] Research on the witch-hunting activities of village committees and local lords in certain parts of Germany is beginning to flesh out and complicate our picture of early modern witch-persecution, however, by demonstrating that in some areas local initiatives flourished that involved men of much lower social status, and which also exposed the difficulties faced by the territorial state in maintaining a monopoly of judicial power in witch-trials.[80]

What sort of men were the witch-hunters, and what drove them to hunt witches? The best attempt to explain the psychological motivation of judges and interrogators is made by Lyndal Roper in her study of witch-trials in the German territories of Würzburg, Augsburg, Nördlingen and Marchtal. Roper allows that a degree of sadism and sexual prurience on the part of such men was undoubtedly involved, particularly insofar as they sanctioned and oversaw the stripping, searching, and torturing of predominantly female witch-suspects. However, Roper also argues that they had a genuine sense of themselves as godly crusaders against the forces of evil and, in an age of elite obsession with paternal authority, as patriarchs responsible for the spiritual and social well-being of their subjects. For them, witches were malevolent and destructive tools of the Devil, an imaginative stance that enabled them to believe that their hunting of witches sprang not from ruthlessness, but from sympathy – for the suffering of the witch's victims and for the good of the witch's own soul, which could be saved only by her renunciation of the Devil and execution. In this context, Roper suggests that the psychology of persecutors was characterized by 'a strict separation of good and evil, an inability to admit to feeling envy, anger or hostility, and the conviction that these emotions were deeply destructive', all of which produced a 'rigid moralism' that 'failed to integrate the mixture of good and bad elements that are part of human life itself'.[81]

Roper's ideas are fascinating and worthy of further investigation: the notion of godly mission, which is almost always underpinned by the type of rigid moralism she highlights, was clearly shared by witch-hunters in many parts of Europe. However, Roper underemphasizes the degree to which much more prosaic concerns could also fuel the zeal of witch-hunters, as work on the 'instrumentalization' of witch-perscution and painstaking reconstruction of the life histories of specific witch-hunters is beginning to demonstrate. For example, by setting her study of Claudius Musiel's witch-hunting activities in the broader context of his family and career history, Rita Voltmer is able to show that Musiel used the opportunity offered by the witch-persecution as one of a bundle of available strategies (including the acquisition of offices and property, and the forging of links through advantageous marriage-making) in an ongoing, and ultimately highly successful, endeavour to further his career and improve his family's social and financial position. Here, of course, Musiel was fulfilling one of the key duties of the early modern father, that of securing the well-being of his children. The St Maximin trials (and, in particular, the lengthy *Witch Register* drawn up by Musiel) were also part of the abbot of St Maximin's efforts to assert – by means of frequent executions and masses of written documentation – the judicial autonomy of St Maximin vis-à-vis Electoral Trier. Thus, while Musiel was unusually conscientious and ambitious in performing his witch-hunting role, this was just one facet of the judicial duties he had to perform by virtue of his position as an official – and, thus, loyal servant – of the abbot and various other neighbouring territorial lords.[82]

We need, therefore, to combine the insights of psychoanalytic theory with the detail of prosopographical research in order to develop more sophisticated modes of explaining the motivation of witch-hunters that can incorporate both the prosaic and psychological, acknowledging that self-interest and opportunism were not incompatible with (or could, at least, be more comfortably justified by) the idea of commitment to a godly mission. We also need much more systematic comparison of witch-hunters from across Europe (preferably lodged in some sort of centrally managed database), so that common or divergent factors in their lives, education, careers, and witch-hunting activities can be identified, explained, and linked more effectively to the developing literature on gender and masculinities in the early modern period. Did motive differ according to the particular role a man occupied within the judicial framework of witch-hunting, his socio-economic position, level of education and religion? Is it possible to distinguish different witch-hunting 'profiles' (the anxious patriarch who used the hunts to master his fears, the career opportunist, the brutal sadist, the godly zealot, the reluctant hunter who participated under pressure, for example), or could one individual combine these different stances in a single witch-hunting 'career'?[83] Julian Goodare outlines an approach along these lines in his discussion of men and witch-hunting in Scotland in Chapter 7, in which he suggests that we need to distinguish between men who were involved in witch-trials simply as one aspect of a broader range of judicial duties, and 'serial witch-hunters' who showed a marked, specific, and repeated enthusiasm for pursuing witches at law. Goodare's chapter is also fascinating because it demonstrates the extent to which anxieties about witchcraft in Scotland were shaped by concerns about the proper exercise of patriarchal authority that extended to the person and power of King James VI himself. A better overall understanding of the varied motivations of witch-hunters as individuals and groups will help us to explain the dynamics of persecution in different regions, and also why the judicial power to hunt witches could be directed against other men – even former witch-hunters themselves – as well as women.[84] The actions of most witch-hunters seem to have been underpinned (to some extent, at least) by the sense of public duty and responsibility – to God, one's subjects, one's overlord, one's fellow villagers, or one's family – that was integral to early modern codes of masculinity. This might help explain why many men found it hard to oppose the horrors of witch-hunting, either in writing or reality.

VI

We are still working towards fuller answers to the questions about the gendering of witch-hunting outlined at the beginning of this chapter, an ongoing endeavour that must be rooted in detailed, regional studies of patterns of witch-prosecution. As Valerie Kivelson points out, we should not begin such studies with 'assumptions about the gender of evil', but should instead ask ourselves 'what particular kinds of people seemed likely to embody the witch in a given society'.[85] This immediately enables us to incorporate men and women within the same analytical framework, and also emphasizes the importance of the local context. Differing beliefs about the practice of magic and witchcraft, differing types of socio-economic, religious, or political tensions and (once witch-trials had started) differing traditions of persecution and interactions with the judicial and ecclesiastical elites, thus shaped perceptions about who was a witch (and who might be most successfully prosecuted as such) on a regionally varied basis. Instead of assuming that anxieties about witchcraft were linked to gender-specific spheres of influence within early modern society and culture that immediately exclude men from any analysis (such as housewifery or motherhood), I would argue, rather, that early modern people's beliefs about witchcraft were linked to anxieties that coalesced especially around the practices of parenthood, neighbourliness, and Christianity – categories that included both men and women, even if they were clearly inflected in different ways according to gender. Crucial to the whole analysis of witch-persecution, however, is the exercise of power. Witches everywhere were the victims of processes of social interaction (before a formal accusation was made) and then of law (in the course of formal trials) in which they usually became ever more disempowered at the hands, first, of neighbours and accusers, and then of the men who exercised formal judicial power over them. We need to know more about the gendering of persecution, not merely in terms of bald statistics, but also in terms of the dynamics of familial interaction amongst neighbours; the socio-economic divisions that enabled certain individuals or groups to assert the authority to define communal norms, and to stigmatize as witches those who deviated from them; and the mentalities and masculinities of the witch-hunters.

Notes

1. See the statistics on the gendering of witch-persecution given by B. P. Levack, *The Witch-Hunt in Early Modern Europe* (3rd edn, Harlow, 2006), 142; Lara

Apps and Andrew Gow list only Basel and Hungary as having 90 per cent or more female witches, see *Male Witches in Early Modern Europe* (Manchester and New York, 2003), 45.

2. For an excellent recent summary of the literature, see C. Opitz-Belakhal, 'Frauen- und geschlechtergeschichtliche Perspektiven der Hexenforschung', in G. Gersmann, K. Moeller and J. M. Schmidt (eds), historicum.net, URL: http://www.historicum.net/no_cache/persistent/artikel/5654/ (accessed 25 January 2008).
3. My brief summaries do a huge disservice to the length and sophistication of the debates on this question: apologies to all concerned. For a summary of feminist approaches, see E. Whitney, 'International trends: The witch "she"/the historian "he": Gender and the historiography of the European witch-hunts', *Journal of Women's History*, 7(3) (1995), 77–101; for a critique of radical feminist interpretations, see D. Purkiss, *The Witch in History. Early Modern and Twentieth-Century Representations* (London and New York, 1996), ch. 1.
4. See especially Purkiss, *Witch in History*, ch. 4. Willem de Blécourt advances the debates considerably in 'The making of the female witch: Reflections on witchcraft and gender in the early modern period', *Gender & History*, 12 (2000), 287–309.
5. A. Macfarlane, *Witchcraft in Tudor and Stuart England. A Regional and Comparative Study* (London, 1970; 2nd edn 1999), chs 10–16; K. Thomas, *Religion and the Decline of Magic* (London, 1971), chs 16–18.
6. L. Roper, *Witch Craze. Terror and Fantasy in Baroque Germany* (New Haven and London, 2004); *idem*, *Oedipus and the Devil. Witchcraft, Sexuality and Religion in Early Modern Europe* (London and New York, 1994), ch. 9. For a critique of these ideas, see A. Rowlands, 'Witchcraft and old women in early modern Germany', *Past & Present*, 173 (2001), 50–89.
7. Purkiss, *Witch in History*, ch. 5.
8. See Levack, *Witch-Hunt*, 142.
9. H. Sebald, *Der Hexenjunge. Fallstudie eines Inquisitionsprozesses* (Marburg, 1992); W. Behringer, *Chonrad Stoeckhlin und die Nachtschar: Eine Geschichte aus der frühen Neuzeit* (Munich, 1994). This was translated by H. C. E. Midelfort and published as *Shaman of Oberstdorf. Chonrad Stoeckhlin and the Phantoms of the Night* (Charlottesville, 1998).
10. R. Schulte, *Hexenmeister. Die Verfolgung von Männern im Rahmen der Hexenverfolgung von 1530–1730 im Alten Reich* (Frankfurt am Main, 2000; 2nd edn, 2001). Citations in this chapter are from the second edition. A revised edition is available in translation as *Man as Witch. Male Witches in Central Europe* (Basingstoke, 2009).
11. Apps and Gow, *Male Witches*, 5.
12. From the 1970s, see J. Demos, 'John Godfrey and his neighbors: Witchcraft and the social web in colonial Massachusetts', *William and Mary Quarterly*, 27 (1976), 258–65; R. Zguta, 'Witchcraft trials in seventeenth-century Russia', *American Historical Review*, 82 (1977), 1187–207. Most of the post-1990 literature is discussed later in this chapter. For a short summary of key publications, see W. Monter, 'Male witches', in R. M. Golden (ed.), *Encyclopedia of Witchcraft. The Western Tradition* (hereafter *EOW*), vol. III (Santa Barbara, 2006), 711–13.
13. See Chapter 9 of this book, p. 208.

14. E. J. Kent, 'Masculinity and male witches in old and New England, 1593–1680', *History Workshop Journal*, 60 (2005), 69–92, at 70–1. Kent concludes, rather unhelpfully, that 'Male witchcraft might be maleficium, but it could also be quite different and still be regarded as "witchcraft" by early modern complainants and courts in Essex', *ibid.*, 71.
15. I try to do this for the Rothenburg witch-trials, see A. Rowlands, *Witchcraft Narratives in Germany: Rothenburg, 1561–1652* (Manchester and New York, 2003), appendix.
16. P. A. Heuser, 'Die kurkölnischen Hexenprozesse des 16. und 17. Jahrhunderts in geschlechtergeschichtlicher Perspektive', in I. Ahrendt-Schulte, D. R. Bauer, S. Lorenz and J. M. Schmidt (eds), *Geschlecht, Magie und Hexenverfolgung* (Bielefeld, 2002), 133–74, at 135–42, 169–71.
17. Men were also initially incorporated into fantasies of the sabbath as musicians in the German town of Horn, again because men really did play the pipes, drum or lute at village festivities and dances, see I. Ahrendt-Schulte, 'Die Zauberschen und ihr Trommelschläger', in *idem et al.* (eds), *Geschlecht, Magie und Hexenverfolgung*, 123–31, at 124–5.
18. H. C. E. Midelfort, *Witch Hunting in Southwestern Germany, 1562–1684* (Stanford, 1972), 121–63, 178–90 (quotation at 179).
19. Heuser, 'Kurkölnische Hexenprozesse', 173–4. The chronological dynamic of the gendering of witch-persecution is discussed for German trials by Schulte, *Hexenmeister*, 87–106; Midelfort's model is evaluated at 89–93.
20. C. Larner, *Enemies of God. The Witch-hunt in Scotland* (Oxford, 1983), 92.
21. A. Heikinnen and T. Kervinen, 'Finland: The male domination', in B. Ankarloo and G. Henningsen (eds), *Early Modern European Witchcraft. Centres and Peripheries* (Oxford, 1990; paperback edn 1993), 319–38, at 321–2.
22. De Blécourt, 'Making of the female witch', 302.
23. Use of the labels 'primary' and 'secondary' for different categories of male witches, a practice established by Rolf Schulte in *Hexenmeister*, 215–43, also risks implying that certain male witches were more 'witch-like' than others, something I think we need to guard against, especially as there is no recognized practice of categorizing female witches in this way.
24. Heuser, 'Kurkölnische Hexenprozesse', 163, 169.
25. E. Labouvie, 'Men in witchcraft trials: Towards a social anthropology of "male" understandings of magic and witchcraft', in U. Rublack (ed.), *Gender in Early Modern German History*, (Cambridge, 2002), 49–68, quotation at 54. This was first published in German as 'Männer im Hexenprozess. Zur Sozialanthropologie eines männlichen Verständnisses von Magie und Hexerei', *Geschichte und Gesellschaft*, 16 (1990), 56–78.
26. *Ibid.*, 55. See also *idem*, *Zauberei und Hexenwerk. Ländlicher Hexenglaube in der frühen Neuzeit* (Frankfurt am Main, 1991), and 'Perspektivenwechsel. Magische Domänen von Frauen und Männern in Volksmagie und Hexerei aus der Sicht der Geschlechtergeschichte', in I. Ahrendt-Schulte *et al.* (eds), *Geschlecht, Magie und Hexenverfolgung*, 39–56.
27. De Blécourt, 'Making of the female witch', 299.
28. *Ibid.*, 298.
29. K. Moeller, *Dass Willkür über Recht ginge. Hexenverfolgung in Mecklenburg im 16. und 17. Jahrhundert* (Bielefeld, 2007), 228–31.

30. K. Hastrup, 'Iceland: Sorcerers and paganism', in Ankarloo and Henningsen, *Early Modern European Witchcraft*, 383–401, at 386.
31. For Godfrey, see M. Gaskill, 'The devil in the shape of a man: Witchcraft, conflict and belief in Jacobean England', *Historical Research*, 71 (1998), 142–71; for Fei, see Chapter 6; for Würth, see Rowlands, *Witchcraft Narratives*, 164–8.
32. Gaskill, 'Devil in the shape of a man', 161.
33. S. Clark, *Thinking With Demons. The Idea of Witchcraft in Early Modern Europe* (Oxford, 1997; paperback edn, 1999), 106–33, quotation at 130. Clark first argued this point in 'The "gendering" of witchcraft in French demonology: Misogyny or polarity?', *French History*, 5 (1991), 438–50.
34. Apps and Gow, 95–117, quotation at 112.
35. Schulte, *Hexenmeister*, 165–70.
36. See Chapter 7 of this book, p. 155.
37. R. Walinski-Kiehl, 'Males, "masculine honour", and witch hunting in seventeenth-century Germany', *Men and Masculinities*, 6 (2004), 254–71, at 259.
38. W. Behringer, *Witchcraft Persecutions in Bavaria. Popular Magic, Religious Zealotry and Reason of State in Early Modern Europe* (translated by J. C. Grayson and D. Lederer, Cambridge, 1997), 224–9.
39. Schulte, *Hexenmeister*, 167.
40. D. Willis, *Malevolent Nurture. Witch-Hunting and Maternal Power in Early Modern England* (Ithaca and London, 1995), 65.
41. J. Grundy, 'The male witch, the familiar and diabolic bodies', unpublished paper presented at the *Witchcraft and Masculinities in the Early Modern World* conference, University of Essex, 21–23 April 2006.
42. See Chapter 8 of this book, p. 178.
43. This happened in Mecklenburg (see Moeller, *Dass Willkür über Recht ginge*, 229) and Electoral Cologne (see Heuser, 'Kurkölnische Hexenprozesse', 172–3). The 'instrumentalization' of accusations is discussed in further detail later in this chapter.
44. Lowes is discussed in Chapter 8; Junius in Chapter 3; Flade in Chapter 4. Over 80 per cent of the male witches from the Saar territories were either property-less or poor, see Labouvie, 'Men in witchcraft trials', 59.
45. Rowlands, *Witchcraft Narratives*, 24–33, 161–4.
46. See, for example, W. Rummel and R. Voltmer, 'Die Verfolgung eigener Interessen durch Untertanen, Funktionäre und Herrschaften bei den Hexenjagden im Rhein-Maas-Mosel-Raum', in H.-G. Borck and B. Dorfey (eds), *Unrecht und Recht. Kriminalität und Gesellschaft im Wandel von 1500–2000* (Koblenz, 2002), 297–339; R. Voltmer, 'Hexenprozesse und Hochgerichte. Zur herrschaftlich-politischen Nutzung und Instrumentalisierung von Hexenverfolgungen', in H. Eiden and R. Voltmer (eds), *Hexenprozesse und Gerichtspraxis* (Trier, 2002), 475–525; W. Rummel, ' "So mögte auch eine darzu kommen, so mich belädiget". Zur sozialen Motivation und Nutzung von Hexereianklagen', in R. Voltmer (ed.), *Hexenverfolgung and Herrschaftspraxis* (Trier, 2005), 205–27. All the essays in the latter volume deal with witch-persecution in relation to the practice of lordship in various different territories. See also Section V on witch-hunters.
47. See Chapter 2 of this book, p. 50.

48. This phenomenon has also been identified for Scotland (see Larner, *Enemies of God*, 94), Würzburg (see Roper, *Witch Craze*, 264), and Rothenburg (see Rowlands, *Witchcraft Narratives*, 150–61), for example.
49. Apps and Gow, *Male Witches*, 43.
50. On the Sami, see R. Hagen, 'Traces of shamanism in the witch trials of Norway: The 1692 trial of the Sami shaman Anders Poulsen', in H. de Waardt, J. M. Schmidt, H. C. E. Midelfort, S. Lorenz and D. R. Bauer (eds), *Dämonische Besessenheit. Zur Interpretation eines kulturhistorischen Phänomens* (Bielefeld, 2005), 307–25, and 'Female witches and Sami sorcerers in the witch trials of Arctic Norway (1593–1695)', *Nordic Yearbook of Folklore*, 62 (2006), 123–42. On the links between shamanism and the prosecution of men for witchcraft, see also Behringer, *Shaman of Oberstdorf*, and C. Ginzburg, *The Night Battles. Witchcraft and Agrarian Cults in the Sixteenth and Seventeenth Centuries* (trans. J. and A. Tedeschi, London, 1983); first published in Italian as *I Benandanti* (Turin, 1966).
51. W. Monter, 'Toads and eucharists: The male witches of Normandy, 1564–1660', *French Historical Studies*, 20 (1997), 563–95, quotation at 580.
52. See M. Madar, 'Estonia I: Werewolves and Poisoners', in Ankarloo and Henningsen, *Early Modern European Witchcraft*, 257–72; Heikinnen and Kervinen, 'Finland'; Hastrup, 'Iceland'; V. A. Kivelson, 'Male witches and gendered categories in seventeenth-century Russia', *Comparative Studies in Society and History*, 45 (2003), 606–31, quotation at 620.
53. J. Kuhak, 'Estonia II: The Crusade against Idolatry' in Ankarloo and Henningsen, *Early Modern European Witchcraft*, 273–84.
54. Hastrup. 'Iceland'. On the Sami, see note 50.
55. Monter, 'Toads and eucharists', especially 588–92.
56. This was the case in Tuscany, for example (see Chapter 3). On the general unwillingness of the lower orders to accuse cunning folk of witchcraft, see W. Rummel, '"Weise Frauen und "weise" Männer im Kampf gegen Hexerei. Die Widerlegung einer modernen Fabel', in C. Dipper, L. Klinkhammer and A. Nützenadel (eds), *Europäische Sozialgeschichte. Festschrift Wolfgang Scheider* (Berlin, 2000), 353–76.
57. N. Schindler, *Rebellion, Community and Custom in Early Modern Germany* (translated by P.E. Selwyn, Cambridge, 2002), 236–92, at 238. This was first published in German as *Widerspenstige Leute. Studien zur Volkskultur in der frühen Neuzeit* (Frankfurt am Main, 1992).
58. *Ibid.*, 282.
59. *Ibid.*, 261.
60. Kivelson, 'Male witches', quotation at 618. This was strikingly different from early modern England, where poorer women settled within a community (rather than mobile poor men) were often the target of witchcraft accusations, see note 5.
61. Walinski-Kiehl, 'Males, "masculine honor", and witch hunting', 265.
62. Labouvie, 'Men in witchcraft trials', 57–65, quotation at 60 (157 men were prosecuted and 130 executed for witchcraft in the Saar region between 1575 and 1634). Around half of the 26 male witches in Lippe had also committed sexual sins, see Ahrendt-Schulte, 'Die Zauberschen', 129–30. Dietrich Flade (discussed in Chapter 4 by Voltmer) was also a classic example of a profit-making male witch.

63. Kent, 'Masculinity and male witches', quotation at 86.
64. Cf. Walinski-Kiehl, 'Males, "masculine honour", and witch hunting', 266; Labouvie, 'Men in witchcraft trials', 60–3.
65. See Section V on witch-hunters.
66. For Kent, see note 63; for Purkiss, note 4.
67. Kent, 'Masculinity and male witches', 85.
68. *Ibid.*, 83–5, quotation at 85. On the ways in which early modern commentators imagined men's bodies as leaky and polluting, see Roper, *Oedipus and the Devil*, chs 5 and 7.
69. These searchers and prickers are discussed in Chapters 7 and 8. In Germany, the hangman's wife could occasionally be given this searching role (usually performed by the hangman) to preserve the 'modesty' of accused female witches, see J. Nowosadtko, 'Meister zahlreicher Hexenprozesse. Die Scharfrichter Johann Volmar und Christoph Hiert aus Biberach', in S. Lorenz and J. M. Schmidt (eds), *Wider alle Hexerei und Teufelswerk. Die europäische Hexenverfolgung und ihre Auswirkungen auf Südwestdeutschland* (Ostfildern, 2004), 464–83, at 472.
70. See for example Rowlands, *Witchcraft Narratives*, 115.
71. This discussion does not include demonologists who wrote in favour of witch-hunting, unless they also participated personally in witch-hunts as judges, inquisitors or advisors in specific legal cases.
72. Witch-commissioners operated in Eichstätt (see Chapter 5); on Salem, see P. Boyer and S. Nissenbaum, *Salem Possessed* (Cambridge, MA and London, 1974), 7.
73. See Chapter 4 on the committees (which were formed, in the first instance, so that the financial risk of bringing a witchcraft accusation was spread collectively rather than borne by one individual) and Chapter 8 on Hopkins and Stearne.
74. V. Perlhafter, *Die Gestalt des 'Hexenjägers' des 17. Jahrhunderts und sein gesellschaftliches und politisches Umfeld* (Frankfurt am Main, 2003); R. Francis, *Judge Sewall's Apology. The Salem Witch Trials and the Forming of a Conscience* (2005); M. Gaskill, *Witchfinders. A Seventeenth-Century English Tragedy* (London, 2005).
75. The novel, *Witchfinder General* by Ronald Bassett (London 1966), was made into a film of the same name in 1968, directed by Michael Reeves, starring Vincent Price as Hopkins and co-produced by Tigon British Film Productions and American International Pictures. It was released in America as *The Conqueror Worm*.
76. R. Voltmer, 'Claudius Musiel oder die Karriere eines Hexenrichters. Auch ein Beitrag zur Trierer Sozialgeschichte des späten 16. Jahrhunderts', in G. Franz and F. Irsigler (eds), *Methoden und Konzepte der historischen Hexenforschung* (Trier, 1998), 211–54; R. Voltmer and K. Weisenstein (eds), *Das Hexenregister des Claudius Musiel* (Trier, 1996).
77. See Nowosadtko, 'Meister zahlreicher Hexenprozesse'; G. Jerouschek, 'Der Hexenprozess als politisches Machtinstrument. Der mysteriöse Tod des Hexeninquisitors lic. jur. Daniel Hauff und das Ende der Hexenverfolgung in Esslingen', *Esslinger Studien*, 30 (1991), 103–14; T. P. Becker, 'Buirmann, Franz (ca.1590–ca.1667)', in Golden (ed.), *EOW*, vol. I, 149.
78. See W. Monter, 'Boguet, Henri (ca. 1550–1619)', in Golden (ed.), *EOW*, vol. I, 133–4; G. Jerouschek, 'Kramer (Institoris), Heinrich (ca.1430–1505)', in

Golden (ed.), *EOW*, vol. III, 612–13, and W. Behringer, G. Jerouschek and M. Tschacher (eds), *Der Hexenhammer* (2nd edn, Munich, 2001), introduction by Behringer and Jerouschek, 9–98; J. L. Pearl, 'Lancre, Pierre de (1533–1630)', in Golden (ed.), *EOW*, vol. III, 622–3; E. Biesel, 'Rémy, Nicolas', in G. Gersmann, K. Moeller and J.-M. Schmidt (eds), *Lexikon zur Geschichte der Hexenverfolgung*, historicum.net, URL: http://www.historicum.net/no_cache/persistent/artikel/1670/ (consulted 02/09/2008). Jurist Benedict Carpzov can also be added to this list, although the extent of his personal role in witch-trials is unclear, see G. Jerouschek, 'Carpzov, Benedict (II) (1595–1666)', in Golden (ed.), *EOW*, vol. I, 170–1.

79. On James, see L. Normand and G. Roberts, *Witchcraft in Early Modern Scotland* (Exeter, 2000); Willis, *Malevolent Nurture*, ch. 4; and Chapter 7 of this volume. On the witch-bishops, see W. Behringer, 'Witch-Bishops (Holy Roman Empire)', in Golden (ed.), *EOW*, vol. IV, 1217–20.
80. See note 46.
81. Roper, *Witch Craze*, ch. 2, quotation at 63. For a less convincing approach that argues for the need to integrate psychoanalytical theories about anal fixation into historical research on the mentality witch-hunters, see W. Behringer *et al.* (eds), *Der Hexenhammer*, introduction, 78–81 ('Zur Psychologie Heinrich Kramer').
82. Voltmer, 'Claudius Musiel'. Voltmer notes that Musiel was just one of several men who advanced themselves and their families as a result of their involvement in the St Maximin witch-trials: all were 'treusorgende Familienväter' ('faithful and caring family fathers', 253).
83. On the witch-hunter as anxious patriarch, see Roper, *Witch Craze*, 61. For a more convincing interpretation, see L. Yeomen, 'Hunting the rich witch in Scotland: High-status suspects and their persecutors, 1590–1650', in J. Goodare (ed), *The Scottish Witch-Hunt in Context* (Manchester, 2002), 106–21, at 120–1.
84. See Chapter 4 for examples of former witch-hunters who were accused of witchcraft.
85. Kivelson, 'Male witches', 623.

2
Male Witches in the Duchy of Lorraine

Robin Briggs

Men were often found on trial for witchcraft in the Duchy of Lorraine, comprising some 28 per cent of the suspects for whom trial documents survive. Altogether, between 500 and 600 men probably faced such charges, with no perceptible change in the male–female balance over the period of the major persecution: there is such an abundance of information about a large sample of them that even a lengthy chapter in my recent book had to omit a great deal.[1] These figures should be understood with reference to the broader contours of the Lorraine persecution, as described in that book. In the sixty years between, approximately, 1570 and 1630, the ducal officials probably oversaw around 2000 trials, full records for some 400 of which still survive. When set against a population of around 300,000, this stands out as one of the most intense persecutions in Europe – at a level only exceeded, among territories of any size, in the neighbouring Duchy of Luxembourg and in the Electorate of Cologne. Apart from one set of trials in the late 1620s that produced at least 50 victims, there was no concentrated witch-hunt in Lorraine, so these trials were distributed widely in both time and space. The legal system in use essentially followed French practice, but there was no appeal to a higher court; torture was routinely employed, and produced a conviction rate of 79 per cent in the fully recorded cases, with very little difference by gender. Most of those convicted had local reputations for witchcraft stretching back for a number of years, sometimes two or three decades. A large majority of charges seem to have emanated from the local community (although these were mediated by ducal officials), and another large group of cases followed on from denunciations by those convicted. The accusations made by witnesses suggest a pervasive belief that witches were responsible for a wide range of sicknesses and misfortunes; they also show that most individual suspicions were dealt with by counter-magic and informal means, with the suspects often persuaded to make conciliatory gestures towards healing their alleged victims. Trials commonly represented the moment at which this routine pattern broke down. Witchcraft was a constant threat to good health and fertility, which linked into an unexpected form of therapy provided by the witches themselves, because only they were believed capable of removing the illnesses and other problems they had caused.

I

One rather paradoxical result of working with an exceptionally rich archive, such as that for Lorraine witchcraft, is that generalization becomes more difficult as information accumulates. The more one learns about those who fell victim to the persecution, the more they take on sharply defined individualities that burst out of any interpretative straitjacket. Although there was no shortage of elderly widows among the female accused, for example, they certainly did not form a majority, neither were their circumstances notably similar, overall. If anything, the picture is even more confusing with the male witches. With some 110 cases for study, this is an impressive sample, quite large enough to reveal general patterns, if any such are to be found. When it is compared with Eva Labouvie's study of male witches in the neighbouring Saarland, however, it lends little support to her identification of the suspects with particular forms of deviant behaviour that violated masculine roles.[2] Neither do the men in Lorraine trials usually resemble the shepherds and healers of Normandy investigated by William Monter; although we find a group of herdsmen among them, the odd animal healer, and a couple of notable *devins* (magical healers), these people only represent small, if significant, minorities.[3] The most striking result from an analysis of the whole group was that nearly half of them had a family member previously condemned as a witch, a considerably higher proportion than for women.[4] In that sense, at least, it would seem that witchcraft suspicions had a tendency to begin with women and be transmitted to men. It does not take much reflection, however, to see that this is unconvincing as any kind of general explanation. Only a small proportion of the kin of those executed suffered the same fate, while the details of the trials suggest that most of the male accused had behaved in ways that contributed very significantly to their problems. A rather surprising finding is that the men charged before 1600 were just as likely to have family reputations as those put on trial later, while the same proportion (about 30 per cent) had been named as accomplices by convicted witches. This is one of several respects in which the pattern of accusations remained remarkably stable through the half-century between 1580 and 1630, when it might have been expected to change as numerous trials created their own dynamic.

The link between suspect families and accusations also emerges in the much-touted notion that many male witches were dragged down by association with a suspect wife. In the Lorraine sample, there are only 12 cases where both partners in a marriage were accused, and in some of them it seems that the husband was more vehemently suspected than the wife.[5] It is rather surprising that the predictable link between witchcraft and serving as a village herdsman or shepherd shows up in a mere 14 cases; this could also be a transient occupation, so not all of the men concerned were still active in the role at the time of their trial.[6] Otherwise, it is hard to discern any meaningful way of forming the male suspects into clusters of any size. The two cases from the Saarland that Eva Labouvie cites in her article, those of Augustin Mattheis and Schneider Augustin, both involved men with a long history of extra-marital womanizing.[7] Although she does not give any figures, she implies that this was quite a common pattern in the Saarland. In Lorraine, such charges were remarkably rare. Two men were accused of witchcraft in conjunction with a range of sexual offences; both of them were tortured and put to death, but neither ever admitted to being a witch, and one of them, Jean Aulbry, blamed witchcraft by others for his misbehaviour.[8] In 1631, the *curé* (parish priest) of Vomécourt-sur-Madon, Dominique Gordet, was in trouble for his sexual misdemeanours as well as for his dubious exorcisms, and he had been identified as a witch by the servant he had apparently impregnated.[9] The case against Jean Goeury rested heavily on charges of bestiality, which he made little attempt to deny, while this theme made a very marginal appearance in the evidence against Anthoine Didier Valdexey.[10] Two men admitted incest, although in both cases this had apparently gone completely unsuspected until they confessed under torture to misbehaviour a long way in the past, so it had played no part in creating their reputations.[11] Jean Coinsse was tried for rape and witchcraft after allegedly trying to rape an 11-year-old girl; her story sounded very convincing, but there were no direct witnesses and he resisted the torture.[12] Altogether, this is a meagre haul of men with a reputation for sexual irregularities, when set against the levels we might expect from the rural societies of this epoch. It would look even less impressive if the two men with really lurid records were not counted as witches at all, on the grounds that the main charges against them concerned violence and immorality, with witchcraft as an ancillary charge to which they never admitted. In both cases, the trial was precipitated by an assault on a woman: Jean Gerardin attacked an elderly widow, later claiming that she had insulted him; while Jean Aulbry's victim was his own wife, subjected to a terrifying sexual ordeal.

Both these sexual predators can be linked to some other characteristics found in a small group of male witches, and Gerardin was one of many men among the accused whose family was suspect, with three witnesses giving special emphasis to this, including a specific story about his father. They certainly belonged to the category of men identified with anti-social conduct, alongside Claudin Clerget [084], Bastien Stablo [254], Jean Gregoire Mathis [240], and Noel Purel [032]. Aulbry, in particular, had also indulged in some rash talk on forbidden subjects, suggesting the kind of illicit knowledge that was readily given a diabolical significance. Here, it might not be quite appropriate to cite the *devins* Antoine Grevillon [022] and Nicolas Noel le Bragard [120] as parallel cases, since these magical practitioners were virtually obliged to engage in a degree of self-promotion, not to say mystification. For several other men, one must suspect a tendency to boasting and self-assertion, as with Jean Demenge le Clerc [188], Mengeon Clement Thiriat [068A], François Marion [212], Jean Jacques Gerardin [269], Nicolas Claudon [300], Gaspard Didier [307], and Nicolas Pairson [258]; all of these found their unwise claims to special knowledge or powers cited against them once they were on trial. In most of these cases, however, this element only formed one part of a complex set of accusations. With Nicolas Adam [066], the talk seems to have been more an expression of his despair as he realized how suspicions of witchcraft were accumulating against him, while the witnesses themselves were inclined to think that Jacquot Colin's wild remarks reflected some kind of mental disturbance [138]. When the thousands of witness statements suggest that there was so much gossip about witches and their deeds, we might again feel a certain surprise that relatively few of the accused had left themselves open to charges of this type. Another small group can be associated with aggressive behaviour in the economic sphere, perhaps a specific version of anti-social tendencies, although surely a very common one that would only be linked to witchcraft in very specific circumstances. So, if the village usurer Bastien Jean Viney [352] sounds like a lesser version of the celebrated Jean Didier Finance *alias* Babey, how many other local profiteers of this type never fell under suspicion?[13] Jean Diez [143] and George de Hault [156] attracted attention through their self-assertiveness, with claims that they would end up better placed than some richer neighbours; a similar allegation was made about Colas Gerard [226], whose reputation also suffered from his marriage to the niece of Jean Babey, and who was said to have enriched himself considerably. Mengeon Claude Perrin [208], Mengeon Clement Thiriat [068A], and Jean Lallemand [194] were all quite prosperous peasants who sound to have been fairly tough in defence of their interests, perhaps leaning towards sharp practice at times, but all these were complex cases that do not lend themselves to any simple interpretation. Demenge Mathis [288] was plainly an unpopular figure at Entre-deux-Eaux, as another man who was comfortably off, but had been detected stealing a sheep and engaging in frauds over the tithe. One neighbour who had been a tithe-collector with him commented:

> that he had found the accused very harsh, and devoid of conscience, towards those with whom he had dealings, and he had told the witness that they should add one of the sheaves they had already collected to those in the fields of other men, to catch them out cheating on their tithe when they were quite innocent of this.

There must be a strong presumption that most of these stories about deviant behaviour took their place in a package of charges against someone who was primarily identified as a witch, rather than being at the origin of the accusation. That would not be incompatible with the idea that village feuds were a major factor in accusations against men in particular, since the organizers of any such conspiracy would have had every reason to maximize the circumstantial evidence, and to represent their target as behaving in just the tiresome ways one would expect from a witch. This did, indeed, happen with Mengeon Clement Thiriat [068A], the one man who was quite clearly set up by a group of enemies – fellow villagers who briefed witnesses and sought support from local officials and power-holders.[14] This exceptional case is, however, a very poor reason for suspecting that similar manipulations underlay other trials, and were successfully concealed. The activities of Noel Gerardin and his associates in promoting the charges against Thiriat attracted so much comment, and were telegraphed in so many ways, that one has to conclude it was very hard to get away with such an operation and go unnoticed. Even though many of the accused appear to have been too confused or terrified to defend themselves effectively, everyone should have known that hostile witnesses could be challenged at the confrontations on the grounds that they deposed out of long-standing enmity.

Bastien Stablo [254] was less specific when he advised his neighbour Claudette Mengin to assert that the witnesses were not worthy people: when on trial himself, he said that several of those who gave evidence against him were thieves, but could not name any witnesses to support his claims. Jean Coinsse [081A] blamed his 'capital enemy' Mengin Remy for the rape and witchcraft charges against him, alleging that Mengin was after his property, so he seems to have felt no inhibition about using this defence and did, in fact, claim that two other witnesses held grudges against him.[15] Here, however, the evidence – which includes an accusation from Jean's own sister – would suggest that he had a reputation for witchcraft dating back more than a decade, which would have been quite sufficient foundation for a trial. One other man who could feel he had been victimized in a special fashion was Claudon Jean Gerardin [055A].[16] Although Gerardin clearly had a local reputation, largely derived from other suspects in his family, his trial looks to have been precipitated by the local *seigneur* (lord) M. d'Haraucourt, on whose behalf Claudon had previously been involved in the illegal seizure of a herd of cattle. It might well have been the resentments and threats deriving from this affair that led the *seigneur* to dispose brutally of an agent who had become a danger.

II

There is no obvious reason to think that the process of accusation was significantly different for men and women, except that the talk that mobilized local opinion would have been concentrated in the relevant gender groups. A number of the trial records for men include brief references to activity of this type. A couple of months before Chrétien Pierre was arrested in December 1601, according to Jean Huillier, 'he and some other men from Moriviller were talking of the witches who did so much harm every day, which led the witness to speak up and draw attention to the reputation this Chrétien had of being a witch, adding that this seemed very likely when his own mother had accused him of that crime' [209]. When he was interrogated, Chrétien admitted that he tried to sell his goods and flee 'because he foresaw that if he were accused no-one would want to talk with him', a further comment on the power of the community, which in this case we can be sure was that of the male householders. Indeed, all but one of the 18 witnesses was a man, nearly all of them being heads of households in the village. This case did, however, cut across gender boundaries in one striking respect, because Lienard Jean Lienard deposed that Chrétien had been very hostile to him because of a dispute over some shared fruit trees; later, it emerged that he might also have blamed Lienard for his mother's conviction as a witch the previous summer. Chrétien had come to the house at Easter time, then approached Lienard's wife Barbon, who was sitting by the fire holding her newborn baby, and insisted she took a coin, despite her attempt to refuse. The infant fell ill immediately, becoming so thin that it was skin and bones, although it was feeding normally. This continued for at least 10 weeks, and no remedy could be found. Finally, Lienard went around saying in public that his child and his animals had been bewitched and, if those responsible did not cure them, he would have them taken and burned. He claimed that Chrétien had heard about this, and that the infant had then recovered in two days. Although this scenario would have been a classic element in the charges against a woman, it is unusual (although not unique) to find a man held responsible for the illness and recovery of a baby. Chrétien, who never admitted this particular crime, said, in connection with the illness of another man, that he had cured him with a white powder his devil Napnel provided, a much more typical feature of these cases. He seems to have caused some disquiet when he named three of those who deposed against him as accomplices at the sabbath – persisting, despite suggestions that he held a grudge against them; it looks as though these charges were never followed up.

In this instance, at least, the accused failed to conform to the patterns identified by Eva Labouvie, when she sets out a series of putative dividing lines between male and female magic. A few examples would not disprove her arguments, however, and there is much in the Lorraine trials to confirm the general proposition that magical powers, whether to harm or to heal, had a tendency to be gendered. A marginal social group of herdsmen, knackers, and executioners does emerge from these records, with these men providing various kinds of protective magic, and claiming the ability to detect witchcraft. A number of male witches were alleged to have sought economic gain in a fashion not found with their female counterparts, unless one includes resentment at other beggars who received more in alms. It is no surprise that men were particularly involved in treasure hunting, or exchanged spells to hunt and shoot better, and to protect themselves from swords and bullets. The clerics involved in possession cases, or found acting as witch doctors, were men almost by definition, while one would naturally expect men to have made the long journeys to consult such experts or other *devins*. Where doubts really set in is with Labouvie's rather ill-defined notion of male and female magical spheres, with some activities being shared and others reserved to one sex. The central distinction, in her words, runs as follows:

> The magical domains and activities dominated actively and passively by men were far more strongly oriented towards everyday rural life and the experiential horizon of village and familial society than those that belonged to women. Thus 'men's magic' tended to be a more practical and circumscribed than a demonic and mysterious means of interpreting the world and mastering everyday life, and men's magical abilities depended more often on elements of the natural rather than the supernatural world, which had been rendered magical by ritual.[17]

Although there is an intuitive appeal to these claims, the attempt to apply them to a substantial body of evidence fails to clarify their precise meaning, while male witches in Lorraine seem to have been fully as demonic as their female counterparts. The material that Labouvie herself deploys in justification would seem to be better explained by another of her arguments, that men regarded female magic as more ambivalent than their own, partly because women were supposed to have easier access to the spirit world. Such masculine suspicions and fears towards women, coupled with the male domination of all forms of institutional and repressive power, would seem quite sufficient to explain not only many gendered aspects of witchcraft persecution, but also a broader hostility towards female magical practices among the ruling groups.

Another claim that seems wholly at odds with the Lorraine evidence is that 'magical practices that served the healing of human beings and animals were dominated by men', because they 'corresponded to a socially fixed male area of responsibility', while women were merely expected to provide nursing.[18] The very full records for the town of Saint-Nicolas-de-Port reveal a flourishing network of female healers, a pattern that is also implied by the much scrappier material available for other Lorraine towns.[19] Four of the six really active magical practitioners from elsewhere in the Duchy who ended up on trial for witchcraft were female, and women also predominate among the other similar figures who are only identifiable at second hand. If the male *devins* Nicolas Noel le Bragard and Antoine Grevillon did make rather showier claims about their range of abilities and the sources of their special knowledge than their female counterparts, that suggests a rather different pattern, with such men both hoping and pretending to access a world of elite magical knowledge that involved literacy, travelling, and wider contacts. We must also note that the female healer Barbe la Grosse Gorge [119] supposedly collected fern seeds in almost exactly the way Grevillon had done, and made a client a spell for good luck when gambling. The therapeutic element was so strong in the vast majority of Lorraine cases, and perhaps even more for women than for men, that any gender distinction in this area would seem absurd where human sicknesses are concerned. The picture does look rather different for animals, with herdsmen, blacksmiths, and knackers as regular practitioners on a scale no women are known to have matched, while a few male witches had strong reputations as animal healers. Even here, the general belief that witches, and only they, could remove the evils they had inflicted meant that female suspects were regularly invited to inspect sick animals, with the clear implication that they were expected to do something to heal them. These ideas were reinforced by the stories confessing witches told about the issue of healing powders by the Devil, or about his grudging agreement to help remove the effects of witchcraft.

III

Witchcraft accusations occupy a rather strange area, uneasily poised between fact and fiction. In consequence, these materials are hard to handle in any very logical fashion. When witnesses told their stories, they were putting a very strong slant on past events, however sincere their opinions might have been, which in many cases it is impossible to penetrate. The standard pattern linked a dispute to a subsequent misfortune, then in a significant number of cases to an apparent move to obtain a cure, whether successful or not. What the historian cannot reliably detect is how overt this process was at the time: were both accusers and suspect fully aware of the game they were playing out, or was most of the significance added in retrospect? While there is enough internal evidence to show that some encounters fell into the first category, most are located at an indeterminate point along the spectrum. This might link into one curious feature of the cases: even when witches proved ready to confess to an impressive number of crimes, they frequently denied some specific charges, presumably wanting to deny the ill-will perceived by the witnesses. Behind this, there is the crucial point that the charges were overwhelmingly determined by the intersection between two factors: the social world that made quarrels much likelier with some people than others, and the imaginary world of witchcraft beliefs that provided signs by which to judge behaviour. Both of these were certainly gendered, as well as mutually self-reinforcing; but it might be that, in Lorraine, the beliefs were not very clearly polarized according to gender. One rather crude way to test this is to count up allegations against male and female suspects, always remembering the cautionary remarks made above, which imply that there is something deeply ambiguous about the 'events' being counted (see Figure 2.1). Even in their own terms, there is a major difference between a widely shared belief that a suspect had killed a specific individual, reported by many witnesses, and a rather vague suspicion to that effect found in one or two depositions. The extreme (and quite common) case is that of witnesses who described some misfortune in terms that clearly implied the witch might have done it, while disclaiming any such belief. In the attempt to generate some statistical material, these last statements have not been counted, but all other charges have been treated as equal.

The calculations have been limited to the afflictions of people and animals. Other forms of misfortune are extremely rare in Lorraine witchcraft records; there are a few charges about hail that fell on some fields while sparing the crops of the suspects, and the odd case of broken machinery or an inability to get some process to work. Domestic activities such as butter-making only feature in the odd claim about unnatural success, rather than about mysterious failures. A few deaths or disabilities were the result of accidents, still attributed to specific malice by the witch, and these have been included with the other deaths and illnesses. Around 10 per cent of the bewitchments of animals recorded in the trials did not result in death; since this figure is remarkably

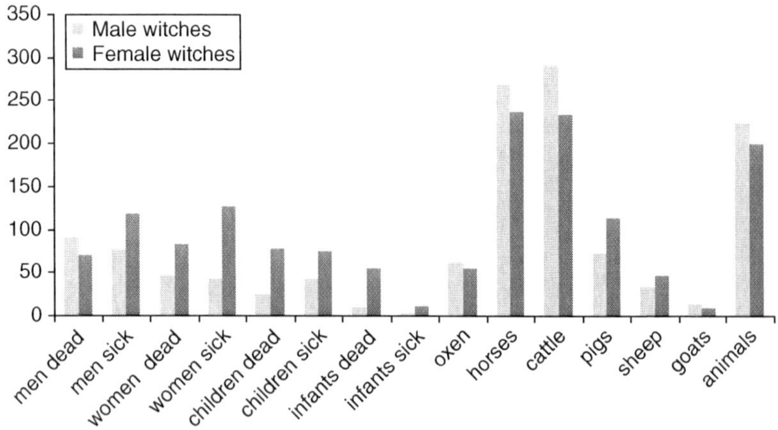

Figure 2.1 Bewitchments attributed to Lorraine witches: data from trials of 96 men and a sample of 96 women

constant across the sample, this complication has been ignored in subsequent calculations, with total numbers for bewitchments used as the comparator.[20] Some trials are too poorly recorded to be usable in this exercise, so the sample of male witches includes 96 cases. These have been set against the trials of 96 women, approximately one third of the total sample, chosen to give a good spread by both date and location. The results are astonishing in one respect because, outside a few predictable categories, Lorraine witchcraft seems hardly to have been gendered at all. Men bewitched other men almost as much as the women did men, and were held responsible for rather more male fatalities. Women were slightly more than twice as likely to be blamed for the sufferings of other women; even here, however, the disparity is less than might have been expected, as it is with children. One of the biggest surprises is to find that only 80 accusations involved infants (defined here as those under two years of age), in the context of the high rates of infantile mortality and the stereotypical nature of charges in this area. The figure would have been substantially lower if the sample had not included the supposedly murderous midwife Jennon Petit [241], blamed for the deaths of 16 babies. It is equally surprising that 13 of these charges were against men, 10 of them involving infant deaths. The female predominance where other women and children were supposedly bewitched does produce an overall difference, with men only thought responsible for 55 per cent of the human sickness attributed to women. Of course, one should remember that, if all the women in the sample were included, then their numerical preponderance would be reflected by much larger numbers of charges in every area. A comparison in terms of age and wealth does suggest that a higher proportion of the men among the accused came from the upper strata of peasant society; although this might be connected to economic or factional rivalries, only a very few cases seem to fit these patterns. The figures for women are probably influenced downwards, in this respect, by the large numbers of widows and the elderly poor among those brought to trial.

There are some small disparities at the margins: nine men were charged with harming animals, whereas only one woman fell into this category; two young boys (both much younger than any female accused) were thought responsible for harming a single person, apart from whom there were five men and three women whose alleged victims were all humans. When it came to healing capacities, most of the herdsmen and a couple of other men were thought to have special expertise in dealing with sick animals; blacksmiths also crop up in this connection, but the handful of smiths among the accused do not seem to have had any special reputation in this field, neither were any of the knackers who sometimes identified witchcraft apparently prosecuted as witches. Didier Pierrat [177] tried to defend himself by telling his judges that if they enquired throughout the *prévôté* (administrative district) of St Dié about the people and animals he had healed by the prayers he had recited, they would find he had cured 'for more than his weight in gold, and we should really have regard for this.' They were having none of it, retorting:

> we do not believe for a moment that this prayer could have the power to cure indiscriminately all those people and animals who were ill, and that it was far more likely that he cured them by the aid of the devil.

Pierrat's disconsolate response was 'in that case his father had taught him the prayer to his misfortune, and that if he was a witch they should burn him'. A dangerous mixture of claims was attributed to Jean Pierron Geliat [248] by one witness, Chrétien Brabant, who said:

> that since he occupies himself widely in healing animals, the witness has heard that he takes hours or days to collect up herbs, and that he performs many ceremonies around the animals, and indeed he wanted to give the wife of the witness a healing drink when she was suffering from hysteria, but this would have prevented her conceiving again, and since he did not trust him he declined.

Overall, it does seem that men were prominent when it came to treating sick animals, while they were much less likely than women to become involved with human illnesses. Male witches were, however, almost as likely as their female counterparts to be thought to have removed the harm they had inflicted; one sign of this was that 19 men talked about using healing powders given by the Devil, as against 28 of the women. The sicknesses of animals were ascribed to both sexes on a remarkably equal basis, the most notable discrepancy being that pigs were rather more likely to be bewitched by women, presumably because they were, in a sense, household animals. Overall, the men were blamed for an average of just under 14 bewitchments each; the women just under 16.

IV

As we have seen, some men seem to have strengthened the suspicions against them by claiming special knowledge. One of these was the blacksmith Gaspard Didier [307], a man of 38 living in the Grand Faubourg of Raon, who found himself on trial in January 1620 after being named as an accomplice by the pig-herder Jean Colin [303]. There was a long chain behind this, because Jean Colin had previously been identified by Jennon le Maire [302], herself the daughter of a convicted witch. Colin, whose own first wife was also said to have been convicted some years earlier, had confessed his guilt as soon as he was confronted with Jennon, perhaps justifying the remark by one of the witnesses that he had never seen 'a more cowardly man'. The 28 witnesses against Gaspard (who included four other blacksmiths) mostly put his reputation for witchcraft at somewhere between three and six years; apart from one dead horse, three human deaths and three illnesses were attributed to him in the recent past. Jean Piernille seems to have been a previous business partner, with whom there had been disagreements about their respective shares of the common stock. He testified that two years before they had attended a fair together, where Gaspard asked him what was being said of him. Jean would say nothing, but his brother told him he was being talked about as a witch; the brother then became strangely ill, talking of 'the foolish words that I used' until his death, making him suspect that he had caused this if he were a witch. He had once told Gaspard that he did not know how he managed to enrich himself all the time, while he himself worked hard for no gain, to receive the reply 'that he should go to Strasbourg where they sold familiar devils and these would give him some money'. When Jean suggested that anyone who did this would be damned, he answered 'not so, and when he had enough money he should get rid of the spirit, by putting it into the hands of a male child, which would prevent him being damned'. The idea here was apparently that the familiar could be passed on to a child to avoid any penalty falling on the previous owner – perhaps the child would also escape punishment as an innocent party. There was another report that, 12 years earlier, he had said 'that even if it cost him his life he would have some necromancer's books so that he could discover what necromancy was.' Babelon Parisot also spoke of that time, when he had been reading a large book, and told her that according to the book she would become well-off after a period of difficulties. Gaspard later agreed 'that in truth he consulted a book of the planets also called a calendar ... but he did not have much faith in it'.

Gaspard himself was clear that he blamed Demenge Pottier and Mongeotte Demenge for his reputation. All that is recorded of Pottier, who did not testify, is that he had said in the tavern that Gaspard was a witch and ought to be burned. Mongeotte described how, after a great quarrel with him and his wife three years earlier, her child had burned his hand outside his house, then developed a great contusion on his neck. Within three days he lost the use of his senses, dying three weeks later. She tried to get him to visit on various pretexts in the hope he would take pity on the child, but he would not come until a day or two before his death, then he merely made a remark about children being very tiresome and hard to get free from. She had obtained bread, salt, and ashes from his house in order to make a soup, which the child finished when he had been eating nothing else, but this did not prevent his death. Unlike the ideas about using magical means of enrichment, all this could equally as well have been a charge against a female witch. Another witness, Demenge Thiery, described how, when he was cutting up a horse the previous summer, which the carter concerned suspected Gaspard had bewitched, Gaspard asked him if there was any sign of witchcraft, so Demenge had shown him a ball of hair that he had found mixed with something resembling ink, whereupon Gaspard left without saying anything. There was some evidence that Gaspard had been aware of the developing rumours, because he had spoken about the claims by the late Nicolas Girard Michel that he was a victim of Gaspard's witchcraft, saying he would remember this all his life. Gaspard also agreed that he had visited the *curé* to ask him to remonstrate with Jean Colin, but denied offering him any money. Although Gaspard was severely tortured, including the strappado with a 50-pound weight for 15 minutes, he held out bravely and was released. It looks as though there might have been some mixture of professional jealousy and previous ill-feeling behind the charges, combined with Gaspard's evident enthusiasm in his twenties for necromancy and astrology, which had left him rather vulnerable to an accusation of the type made by Jean Colin.

Another blacksmith among the suspects had an unusual life history. Claudin Clerget [084] claimed to be about 50, and in his youth had moved about serving various masters in Nancy, Mirecourt, and Mattaincourt. He had settled at Mattaincourt during his first marriage, but when his wife died after 12 years (which must have been around 1572/3) he joined the company of M. de Clermont d'Antraigues near Paris, serving as a smith, and went to Poland with Henri de Valois, the future King Henri III of France. He returned some months later to Mattaincourt, where he met Jean Gilbert and Jean Ferry of la Neuveville-sous-Châtenois. He and Ferry then accompanied M. de Bouzey and some other gentlemen on an '*entreprinse*' (enterprise), without knowing what it was, until they were arrested at Chaumont. This adventure seems likely to have been an attempt to intervene in the religious conflicts in France, or to take advantage of them for some private purpose. After they had been released, Ferry persuaded him to come back to la Neuveville with him and marry his sister Margueritte, widow of Jean Lietard. This had been 10 years before, and he had since lived at la Neuveville with his wife, by whom he had four children. He had to admit that, six years earlier, he had been involved in a quarrel and killed a man from Vomécourt by throwing a stone, for which he had received letters of remission from the Duke. Claudin was dragged into a trial, starting in early July 1586, that also involved three women from la Neuveville, when some inhabitants of the village asked the *prévôt* of Châtenois to act against the witches whom they blamed for many deaths and sicknesses among their animals.[21] Two women were named at this stage, one of whom, Margueritte Gallier, promptly confessed her guilt when interrogated by the *prévôt*, naming Claudin and another woman as accomplices. She was soon followed by the other original suspect, Hanriotte des Boeufs, who named the same group, adding that, at the sabbath, Claudin was 'the boldest and was the cook': 14 men and 16 women then gave evidence against all four, with 19 out of the 30 speaking wholly or partly about Claudin. There were two major charges against him, concerning the deaths of three people, three other stories about horses that had died, and one accusation from a woman who thought he had made her ill. A striking story came from Dedier Liermey, who claimed that he had been harvesting at the nearby village of Sandaucourt five years earlier, about an hour after dawn, when he saw Claudin sit by a spring and strike the water several times with a stick. He then threw something in it as if he were sowing, which he took from his hat. After he had left a mist began to rise from the spring, then formed into a great cloud, from which it hailed heavily. Dedier told many other people, with the result that no one dared to use the spring for more than a year, but afterwards he did not talk too much about what he had seen, since his wife was related to Claudin, who was '*un mauvais guarson*' ('a wicked man'). This was the classic style of hail-making associated with the sabbath, so Dedier evidently knew just what witches were supposed to do; the only odd thing about his account was that the witch had operated alone and by day.

One very damaging story came from the family of the first husband of Claudin's wife, although, since he was said to have been a regular visitor at the house of the victims (Jean Lietard's mother and stepfather), previous relations cannot have been bad. François Marchal gave a very full account of the incident that preceded the deaths of his sister Barbe and her second husband Morisot Gauthier six years earlier. Claudin had come to their house on Wednesday of Holy Week, asking to buy a *bichot* of barley,[22] which Morisot refused him, saying that he had already had two, but asked him to dine with them. Although Claudin said, at first, he would only do so if he had his barley, finally he sat at the table, near the water bucket. Morisot then asked for two drinks of water, after which he was suddenly taken with a fever and had to be put to bed. Barbe threw away the rest of the water, fearing that Claudin had poisoned it, and found a little rag with something white inside it, which she showed to François: when they put it on the fire it blazed up fiercely. Claudin had already left, after Barbe had given him his barley: Morisot died in eight days, and Barbe four days later. During Barbe's illness, Claudin came to the house, only for the sick woman to ask that he be driven out, since he was responsible for the state she was in – a comment that he pretended not to have heard. One of Barbe's daughters told a similar story, with the subtle difference that, according to her, Claudin had asked her later what her mother was saying; after she told him that nothing had been said, he made her a soup, in which she thought he had put something to cure her. At around the same time, Jeannon Deny reported hearing him swearing and blaspheming in the street because Mengin Badel had taken a field back from him, saying that 'the first time he went there he would not return in good health'. As Badel later told her, when he went to sow the field he met Claudin, who gave him an illness so serious that he had to crawl back home, subsequently being ill on and off for two years before he died. He had told another woman that Claudin had given him a '*loppin*' he carried in his body, of which he would die.[23] His widow Phelippa said that, on his deathbed, he told her that Claudin had offered to make him a drink to cure him, asking her to go and seek it. When she asked Claudin, he told her it was too late, because her husband was 'rotten inside'; although Claudin finally yielded to further persuasion and made Badel a drink, Badel soon died. The persuasion was presumably the occasion described by Mengin Gardeme, who explained that Badel had asked him to have supper with them when he invited Claudin. Gardeme had suggested that Badel should make sure Claudin had plenty to drink, in the hope of obtaining a cure; but, although they ate and drank heartily, the sick man died about a week later. Under interrogation Claudin systematically denied all the charges, saying that those who made them were liars. He made a number of scandalous assertions about his accusers, as when he claimed that Claude Utchin, wife of a village office-holder, who testified about Badel's suspicions, had been 'kept and debauched' by the local *curé*. He did agree that at the request of Mongin Padelt's wife he had placed some herbs against fevers which she had given him on Badel's arm, and that he had been to dine in his house, but insisted that he had not made him ill. His own explanation for the suspicious package was that he had been to tend a horse on the day mentioned, using some sulphur which he had then thrown away through the kitchen window. If this had fallen in the bucket it would have flared up when put on the fire, because sulphur did this even when wet.

None of this was likely to prevent Claudin being put to the torture; after enduring the rack for some time, he confessed to being seduced by Maître Persin five years earlier, when upset because of his poverty. He had killed the Gauthier couple with arsenic mixed with a little of the powder given him by Persin, which he had put in the bucket, then used more arsenic to kill Mengin Badel. The use of the natural poison arsenic as the main way of killing his victims stands out as the one unusual feature of this confession, but the real surprise is the end of the story. Three days after the torture session, the *prévôt* was irritably carrying out an enquiry into Claudin's escape from the castle – to effect which he had broken his chains, climbed out of a window and down the roof of a lean-to, then crossed the moat. The general view was evidently that he could not have done this on his own, particularly since he was still suffering from the after-effects of the torture, which indicated that he had probably been helped by his two guards, who were from la Neuveville, and one of whom was a close relative. Whether Claudin managed to get clean away it is impossible to tell, but a man with his adventurous past might have had a better chance than most of pulling this off. As with numerous other cases, it had apparently needed the charges from other suspects to bring out major suspicions that had been festering for several years: it might be that the reputation as a '*mauvais garçon*', which Claudin also shared with some other male suspects, was quite an effective deterrent to potential accusers. A tough character that had already obtained a pardon for homicide was not likely to be anyone's idea of a pushover. This case gives a very good idea of how a mixed bag of suspicions could accumulate over time, to be deployed when denunciations by other accused witches provided the trigger for a series of trials. Although there was a distinctly masculine character to Claudin's behaviour and his social world, the pattern underlying the charges was the very standard one of grievances followed by revenge, and the story included gestures that implied a desire to cure the sufferers.

A final case that combines thoroughly male behaviour with very typical witchcraft elements is that of the poor cobbler Jean Antoine, *alias* de Socourt [072], from the small town of Charmes. Although he had twice been named as an accomplice 11 years earlier, he only went on trial in the summer of 1607 when the porter of the Moselle gate, Nicolas Fouesse, became *partie formelle* against him.[24] Fouesse alleged that three years earlier, when he had asked Jean's sons to put down some fruits they were bringing in by his gate, they and their father had made to attack him, but he deterred them with a hatchet he was holding. Jean threatened that he would repent, since which time he had been coming to their lodge and demanding wood and other things, which Nicolas and his wife had been frightened to refuse him. Finally, in view of his general reputation, he had decided to ask for proceedings against him. Since Jean would later describe Fouesse as a drunkard full of malice there was evidently no love lost between them; one may still wonder whether such a relatively subordinate figure would have brought a charge without some wealthier and more powerful backers, on which the record is predictably silent. One of these might have been the draper Nicolas Thieriat, who had recently prevented Jean from renting a room in his house, then seen his teenage son sicken before a mysterious night-time visit from Jean brought him healing. Nicolas said that he had wanted to become *partie formelle* himself before his friends dissuaded him, so the idea of mounting a prosecution had been around for some months at least. There was a suggestion of professional jealousy in this case too, when the widow of another cobbler reported a dispute over payment and a threat to her husband, followed by his rapid death from an unknown sickness. At his request, she had fetched Jean to provide healing, which he attempted using some grease: this was presumably the horse grease he later admitted to supplying to other people, a by-product of his trade that was widely used as a remedy. There was a rather similar pattern in other charges concerning the deaths of another man, two younger unmarried men, and a boy and a girl, with disputes and threats usually mentioned as the background. The remaining allegations from the 16 witnesses included the illness of a girl, the deaths of a cow and a pig, and an occasion when a woman had been blown into the river by a sudden gust of wind.

Jean was evidently about 60 and had been married four times, his first three wives having died quite early, and then his fourth (who had been named as a witch along with him in 1596) very recently. The judges were suspicious about this and pressed him for details, originally getting a set of very plausible explanations in terms of natural causes: Jean was plainly upset when told there were widespread rumours that he had killed his wives. Once he confessed, however, he admitted that the Devil had persuaded him that he 'was very feeble to put up with so much' from his fourth wife, so he killed her with flowers (provided by the Devil) in her soup. Later, he put back the date of his seduction and incorporated the deaths of his second and third wives as well, in each case accompanied by that of a child he did not know how to care for on his own. Meanwhile, the court had requested enquiries in the surrounding villages to check on some of his confessions, from which the *prévôt* returned with the information that those he questioned:

> greatly feared him, as did several others in these villages, where he was often round and about, rarely being refused anything for which he asked, since he was so greatly feared and suspected of the crime of witchcraft.

So, here was a male witch who was poor and elderly, tried to heal at least some of his victims, attracted suspicions by aggressive begging, and disposed of his wives as some female witches were alleged to have done of their husbands. If all this might equally as well have been attributed to a female suspect, one unusual feature of Fouesse's original denunciation was the implication that Jean and his two sons (aged 22 and 20 at the time of the trial) were acting in concert: had he become more objectionable to his neighbours now that he was joined by two young men? Jean sounded concerned about the impact the trial would have on his sons, and by the next March a reference to them in another trial [074] reveals that they had left Charmes, probably a wise decision on their part. Some other references imply that they were not alone among individuals in their position; young men clearly had more opportunities when it came to migration – a factor that might have had some impact on the numbers of trials.

V

Whether one looks at the statistics or at the details of the trials, then, the majority of male defendants in Lorraine have to be seen as witches first and foremost, rather than as a special group fundamentally different to their female counterparts. Even at the level of the magical healers, it is hard to draw clear distinctions on a gendered basis. On this showing, the central concepts of witchcraft had such a powerful hold on the minds of both the people and the local elites that they could bridge the gender gap without any sign of strain. This did not, of course, mean that gender was ignored or suppressed within the stories that were told. The more detailed accounts of the Lorraine sabbath gave men a prominent role – often as the leaders who wanted to spoil the crops, while, in another form of fantasy, they were liable to be identified as werewolves. Their stories about the original seduction by the Devil were fairly drab and predictable, naturally lacking the sexual element that was standard in women's accounts: the diabolical visitor normally found it sufficient to offer them some money, accompanied by the promise of riches sufficient that they would never want again. Occasionally, he was more specific, offering to help with a legal case or make a troublesome wife behave better, while those men who were not miserable because of their poverty often explained their vulnerability by being angry at some injustice or misfortune. These were hardly major contrasts, and both sexes tended to offer rather feeble explanations for their strange gullibility. When it came to actual bewitchments male witches were naturally supposed to take action against those with whom they were in regular contact, so the really significant differences show up over the afflictions of women and children. One other respect in which a clear pattern emerges is the way men so often derived their reputation from a family history of previous accusations: in this sense, it can be argued that a very high proportion of all cases had their origin in the feminine sphere. Once men were sucked into the pool of suspects, however, the dynamics hardly differed at all. They quarrelled with other members of the local community, were alleged to have taken revenge by hidden diabolical means, often made gestures towards helping their supposed victims, and tried to defend their reputations. In short, the behaviour attributed to them reflected their status as witches much more than it did their gender.

Notes

1. R. Briggs, *The Witches of Lorraine* (Oxford, 2007; hereafter WL); ch. 11 (331–68) is specifically about male witches, but they feature prominently throughout the book. Abstracts of all the trials can be found on the website at http://www.history.ox.ac.uk/staff/robinbriggs/. Reference numbers to the site are given in square brackets in the text or notes; the archive references can be found on the site.
2. E. Labouvie, 'Men in Witchcraft Trials: Towards a Social Anthropology of Magic and Witchcraft', in U. C. Rublack (ed.), *Gender in Early Modern German History* (Cambridge, 2002), 49–68. The generalization about male suspects is on p. 60; it is, of course, only one among numerous suggestions made in this enterprising piece.
3. W. Monter, 'Toads and eucharists: The male witches of Normandy, 1564–1660', *French Historical Studies*, 20(4) (1997), 563–95.
4. WL, 332.
5. WL, 331, 335–8.
6. WL, 331, 336–7, 340–2.

7. Labouvie, 'Men in witchcraft trials', 57–8.
8. For Jean Gerardin (Dompierre, 1615), WL, 64 and [063]; for Jean Aulbry (Le Vivier d'Étival, 1604), WL, 350–3 and [231].
9. WL, 188–9 and AD Vosges G710 [342].
10. Jean Goeury (Saint-Léonard, 1600), WL, 269 and [196]; Anthoine Didier Valdexey (le Souche de Clefcy, 1615), [281].
11. Jean Parmentier (Champegnoult, 1618), [010]; George de Hault (Clingotte, 1596), WL, 356–9 and [156].
12. WL, 88 and [081A] (Rolbes, 1581).
13. For Jean Didier Finance (Mandray 1581), WL, 332–5.
14. WL, 88–90, 353–5.
15. WL, 88.
16. WL, 363–4.
17. Labouvie, 'Men in witchcraft trials', 55.
18. Ibid., 54.
19. WL, 296–330.
20. One problem is that many accusations referred to the losses of numerous animals, sometimes giving a monetary value, but otherwise not specifying numbers or types. All such claims have been given a notional value of five, and classified as animals; there were 45 against men and 40 against women.
21. The prévôt was the local legal and administrative agent for the Duke of Lorraine.
22. A bichot was a small local measure of grain.
23. Loppin means literally a 'morsel' and, by extension, a 'small piece' of anything. In this case, the afflicted man seemed to be imagining the alleged bewitchment by Claudin as a tangible 'morsel' he carried in his body.
24. Partie formelle was a legal term meaning the formal accuser in a legal case, who was personally responsible for initiating a prosecution against the accused.

3
Men as Accused Witches in the Holy Roman Empire

Rolf Schulte

On 11 February 1612, in Bergedorf, a village close to Hamburg, a court accused an aged man named Joachim Witte of witchcraft. Too many rumours had been circulating about him performing occult activities and, after hearing the testimony of several witnesses, the court decided to torture him. After the use of thumbscrews, the 70-year-old Witte quickly admitted to having bewitched animals at various local farms: his forced confession included 37 cows, 20 pigs, 24 horses and seven calves. He claimed that the Devil had ordered him to kill these 88 animals. With this statement, he admitted the two crimes necessary for conviction as a witch: *maleficium* (harmful magic) and a demonic pact. Three women, supposedly Witte's 'accomplices' from villages near Bergedorf, were also arrested and tortured but did not confess to having performed witchcraft.

At this point, the authorities in Hamburg and Lübeck (who held jurisdiction over the village) stepped in and criticized what they considered to have been the over-hasty use of torture against Witte. Witte had to remain in custody, but the accused women were released. When word about this decision spread in the locality, however, many peasants armed with pitchforks and spears gathered, stormed the court building and occupied it for two days and nights. They demanded the burning of the corpse of Joachim Witte, who had died in the meantime, and whom they regarded as a proven male witch. At the same time, they called for the repeated and more severe torture of the three suspected women. The Lübeck and Hamburg authorities refused to be intimidated by this act of rebellion, however. After the angry mob had retreated, they took action to resolve the matter in accordance with their original decision. The corpse of the deceased – but in their opinion innocent – aged Witte was given a Christian burial, while the three supposed female 'witches' were allowed to return to their respective villages. The rebellious peasants were sentenced to pay high fines for their insubordination.[1]

This witch-trial from 1612 was typical of the witch-hunts that occurred in the Holy Roman Empire in the early modern period in two crucial respects. First, this trial shows clearly that the desire for witch-hunts came 'from below', with accusations initiated by ordinary people who lacked formal legal and political power themselves.[2] In certain parts of the Empire, these people even organized themselves into *Hexenausschüsse* (witch-hunting committees) in order to gather evidence against alleged witches as rapidly and effectively as possible.[3] In the Witte case, however, the accusers' requests for more zealous official action against witchcraft did not receive the authorities' consent. Second, the Witte trial was typical in terms of the gender balance of those accused, with three women and one man prosecuted. This ratio reflects the significant proportion of men of all ages who fell victim to witch-hunts in the Holy Roman Empire as a whole.[4]

I

In the early modern period, the Holy Roman Empire was a patchwork of around 300 quasi-autonomous states of various sizes (including duchies, margraviates, imperial cities, and arch-bishoprics) and 1500 territories belonging to minor territorial lords, many of whom still held important rights of criminal jurisdiction over their subjects. United only very loosely by imperial political and legal institutions, the lack of unity in the Empire was further emphasized by the Peace of Augsburg of 1555, which allowed all rulers to determine the confessional allegiance of their territories. Although the Peace of Augsburg recognized only Catholicism and Lutheranism, Calvinism was subsequently introduced in some territories as well. The absence of strong central control over the exercise of criminal jurisdiction in the many different territorial units of the Empire, combined with the significant degree of judicial autonomy possessed by local rulers, help explain why witch-hunts were exceptionally severe in some territories, and why the overall number of trials and executions in the Holy Roman Empire is at least around half of the total for the whole of early modern Europe.[5]

Is it possible to quantify how many of those caught up in the witch-trials in the Holy Roman Empire were men? Comparative analysis for the early modern period is made difficult by the empirically problematic nature of the available data. Issues such as gaps in the records, the changing quality of historical source material, and the inaccuracy of figures in contemporary records (including several cases of exaggerations) from a time when the accurate keeping of statistics was unknown, are commonly acknowledged problems. Statistical discussion must thus be limited to what historical investigation has generally identified and accepted as plausible and to what is possible at this stage of ongoing research. Even then, it is not always possible to ascertain the exact numbers of trials and executions in any one area, and existing data have to be complemented by scholarly estimations based on a close analysis of the relevant sources. My approach to the question of quantification is based on an analysis of data from 82 monographs of regional witch-persecutions in the Holy Roman Empire published before 2007. All the monographs included in this analysis had to satisfy rigorous scholarly standards and be systematically structured; these criteria were imposed in order to avoid incorrect conclusions being drawn on the basis of inaccurate statistics. Even so, the results given in Table 3.1 can only be regarded as a provisional overview, as there are still many gaps in the research for many imperial territories in the early modern period; statistical analyses are even lacking (perhaps surprisingly) for some of the regions that experienced the most numerous and savage witch-hunts.

The term 'persecution victims' in Table 3.1 and throughout this chapter has been chosen deliberately to indicate that my analysis includes anyone taken to court for witchcraft, whatever the outcome of their trial. This is an important point, as often data on witch-persecution from the early modern period include only the number of executions that occurred. However, witch-trials did not always and inevitably end with a death sentence; depending on the respective ruler, territory, court or even type of trial, the accused had varying chances of escaping a capital punishment and being released from custody. A release from custody in the early modern period cannot be equated to an acquittal in the modern sense of the word, however, and by no means resulted in what we might now term the 'rehabilitation' of the alleged witch. The accused individuals who were not executed remained socially isolated after their trials, were stigmatized, and lived in constant fear that suspicions against them would be revived. The non-capital punishment of banishment was tantamount to a life of poverty on the road, which, in early modern society, frequently meant a life – and, consequently, death – in almost inconceivably wretched circumstances. Witch-trials thus had many victims in addition to those executed by the courts, and the following statistics therefore work with this broader interpretation of the term.

As Table 3.1 shows, the witch-persecution in the Empire was clearly directed mostly against women, who were called *Hexe* (witch) in

Table 3.1 Proportion of men accused in Witch-Trials in the Holy Roman Empire, by region (1480-1760)[6]

Region[7]	Persecution victims (total)	Persecution victims (male)	Percentage
West	c. 8200	c. 2200	c. 27
Southwest	c. 3700	c. 800	c. 22
Southeast	c. 3600	c. 1250	c. 35
East	c. 1800	c. 300	c. 17
Central	c. 5200	c. 1200	c. 23
Northwest	c. 1600	c. 200	c. 13
North and Northeast	c. 4200	c. 600	c. 14
Holy Roman Empire	c. 28300	c. 6550	c. 23.1[8]

German. The analysis of the numbers of male victims is not meant in any way to detract from this fact but, rather, to help fill a gap in the existing research on the gendering of witch-hunting. After all, the connection between female gender and suspicion of witchcraft was by no means automatic or straightforward, given that around one in four of all of those prosecuted were men. Moreover, Table 3.1 does not yet include the figures for the persecution hotspot of Luxembourg, with its comparatively high proportion of male victims,[9] since these are not yet available in full detail. Once these are included, the overall proportion of males will increase to nearly 24 per cent. The German language even had gender-specific terminology for male victims of witch-trials: they were known as *Hexenmeister* (witch-masters) or *Hexenmänner* (witch-men). Table 3.1 also shows that there were regional differences in the prosecution of men for witchcraft, differences that were the result of variations in the processes of denunciation, the charges brought in court, and the verdicts reached and carried out. Table 3.2 illustrates this variation in greater detail at the level of individual territories.

Table 3.2 shows that the proportion of men tried for witchcraft varied significantly throughout the Empire, from a meagre five per cent in the County of Schaumburg to 68 per cent in the Duchy of Carinthia. Why was this the case? The rest of this chapter will explore answers to this question by means of detailed analysis of the witch-hunts in three territories that experienced varied levels of male involvement in

Table 3.2 Proportion of men involved in Witch-Hunts in selected territories of the Holy Roman Empire[10]

Bishopric of Bamberg (1595–1680)	26%
Duchy of Brunswick (1577–1670)	9%
Franche-Comté (1434–1676)	33%
Duchy of Carinthia (1492–1765)	68%
County of Flanders (1495–1692)	27%
Duchy of Holstein (1544–1735)	12%
Duchy of Mecklenburg (1336–1777)	15%
Prince-bishopric of Salzburg (1531–1749)	59%
County of Schaumburg (1552–1659)	5%
Duchy of Styria (1546–1746)	34%
County of Vaduz (1648–1680 only)	40% (approx.)

witch-trials: the Duchy of Carinthia in Austria (68 per cent), the Prince-Bishopric of Bamberg in Franconia (26 per cent), and the Duchy of Holstein in north Germany (12 per cent).

II

In Catholic Carinthia, the main period of witch-persecution occurred relatively late in comparison with the rest of the Holy Roman Empire (in the seventeenth century); witch-hunts here also ended comparatively late (well into the eighteenth century). Men constituted the majority of all of those caught up in these hunts as alleged witches, making up 68 per cent of the total of 256 people accused of witchcraft between 1460 and 1772. Figures 3.1 and 3.2 show the chronological fluctuations in the rate of accusation und the gendering of prosecution in percentages in Carinthia.

These figures show that accusations of witchcraft in Carinthia were made mainly against women up until around 1630. At this point, however, the prevailing stereotype of the witch seems to have turned around: from 1630 onwards 70–100 per cent of the accused were men.[11] Statistical evidence on the gendering of prosecution for the years 1580–89 and also 1730–50 is inconclusive because of the low number of trials that occurred during these periods, but this does not alter the overall picture in any meaningful manner.

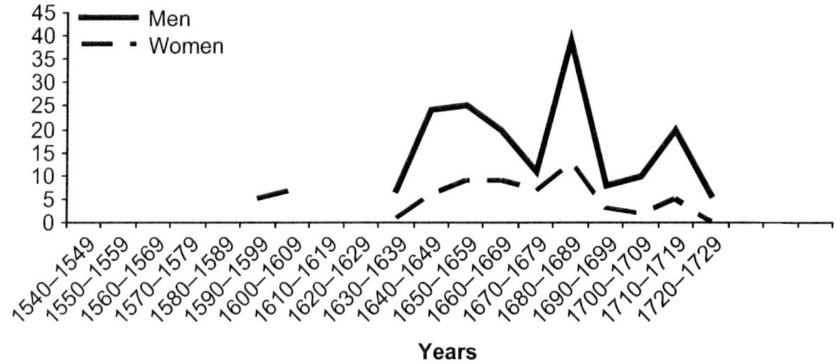

Figure 3.1 Duchy of Carinthia: Witchcraft persecutions by sex, 1540–1729 (numbers accused)

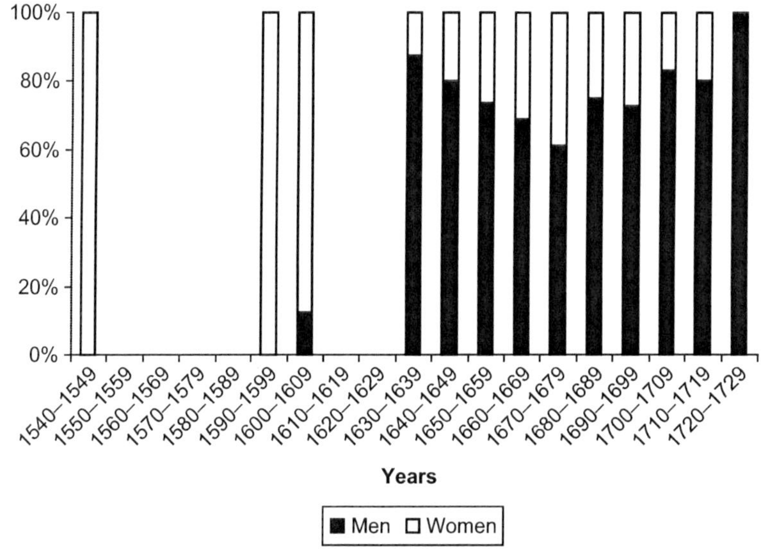

Figure 3.2 Duchy of Carinthia: Witchcraft persecutions by sex, 1540–1729 (percentage)

Typical for Carinthian witch-trials was the combination of confession to a demonic pact and to the working of weather magic. While women were also accused of the theft of milk by means of magic, men were hardly ever prosecuted for this crime. Between 1630 and 1720, so-called weather magic was the charge most often levelled against males accused of witchcraft: they were assumed to have used their compact with the

Devil in order to cause hail or torrential rain that damaged crops, usually out of a desire for revenge.[12] In almost 20 per cent of cases involving men, however, the type of harmful magic attributed to them departed from this pattern. Courts in Carinthia, for example, proceeded against male witchcraft suspects on the grounds that they were *Wolfbanner*, a German term meaning men who were responsible for magically orchestrating the attacks of dangerous wolves against the inhabitants of the region. In a smaller number of cases, men were charged with having transformed themselves into werewolves.[13] These types of maleficient activity were linked imaginatively with the demonic pact because it was believed that no one other than the Devil himself could exercise power over such wolves. There was, however, a crucial difference between the werewolf and the *Wolfbanner*. The werewolf changed his original human nature into something different, whereas the *Wolfbanner* remained human but, in this capacity, commanded a dangerous animal to attack his fellow humans. A combination of suspicions of weather magic and the magical command of an aggressive wolf cropped up in a significant number of cases and, although it was not a crime associated exclusively with men, it was particularly prominent in cases involving men of the lowest socio-economic class who worked seasonally as herdsmen. These men looked after livestock on the Alpine pastures during the summer months and, as a result, lived at a distance from the settled communities of the valleys, with which they had only irregular opportunities for contact. In the winter, however, such seasonal herdsmen survived by resorting to itinerant begging.[14]

The social profile of alleged witches in Carinthia was relatively homogenous overall, as half of them were members of the lowest and most marginal social class: that of beggars. This high proportion of beggars can be explained by the fact that accusations and denunciations made against members of the higher social classes were suppressed and not pursued at law. For example, the courts did not choose to pursue most of the allegations of witchcraft made against priests or members of the nobility, and even charges against peasants were sometimes dropped without an investigation.[15] Many physically-handicapped people were also found amongst the male vagrants tried for witchcraft in Carinthia, as well as individuals whose ability to work for a living in the early modern agrarian economy was lower than average for other reasons. Many of the male vagrants caught up in the witch-trials (both adolescents and adults) must have been mentally impaired in some way, as the judges often described them as simple-minded.[16]

How can this obvious focus of the Carinthian witch-trials on male vagabonds be explained? The long-term economic depression that was a dominant feature of the Holy Roman Empire in the seventeenth century reached its south-eastern parts late, but hit hard and led to the increased pauperization and marginalization of the lower classes in Austria. As the population doubled between 1527 and 1754 (from 1.5 to 2.7 million in Austria and from 150,000 to 250,000 in Carinthia), the proportion of unemployed marginal groups at the bottom of the social hierarchy rose to 20 per cent.[17] In this context, the Carinthian vagabonds' way of life changed and their chances of survival worsened. As the result of a combination of the general diminution of available resources and the erosion of the traditional norms of Christian charity, the beggars had to fight more aggressively for their subsistence. They began to use threats, which they supported with claims of being able to work magic. If their respective employers (usually peasants who were integrated into the social hierarchy) did not honour their agreements, the vagabonds had no means by which to enforce fulfilment. Aggressive threats were therefore part of a defensive strategy used by beggars in order to avoid being tricked out of the proper payment for the seasonal occupations that they increasingly took on to make ends meet.[18]

The fact that the Carinthian witch-hunts focused predominantly on men can be explained in terms of the structure of early modern vagrant groups. Poor relief officials generally regarded men as more mobile and better able to subsist by their own efforts than women. This prevented them from receiving organized charitable alms. Men constituted the largest proportion of mobile vagrant groups, while the majority of resident beggars were women:[19] this gendering of the patterns of vagrancy was also found in Carinthia. In times when charitable relief was hard to obtain, beggars often formed small groups in order to survive and to increase their powers of intimidation. Therefore, it is hardly surprising that, once arrested and tried for witchcraft, they denounced their fellow vagabonds to the courts, thereby ensuring that entire companies of beggars might be dragged into witch-trials as a result.

III

In the Franconian Prince-Bishopric of Bamberg, secular and ecclesiastical authority was united in the person of the territorial ruler, the Catholic Prince-Bishop. Surviving records show that a total of 780 people were accused of witchcraft between 1595 and 1680. The courts in Bamberg condemned to death 61 per cent of all alleged witches (and of all the men accused of witchcraft) and did not even spare the lives of some of the leading members of the male urban elite of Bamberg. The persecutions only subsided when the Emperor and the influential

Imperial Aulic Court intervened to question the severity of the legal procedures used to try alleged witches in Bamberg. The persecutions finally drew to an end when the town was occupied by Swedish troops in the wider context of the Thirty Years War. A significant proportion of all those caught up in witch-trials in Bamberg were men, although not as many as in Carinthia. As Figures 3.3 and 3.4 show, in Bamberg 26 per cent of all accused witches were male, and even during the peak period of persecution between 1620 and 1629 no more than one third of the victims were men.[20]

In the Bamberg witch-trials, only a small number of accusations were provoked by conflicts between neighbours followed by some sort of misfortune believed to have been caused by *maleficium*: this type of

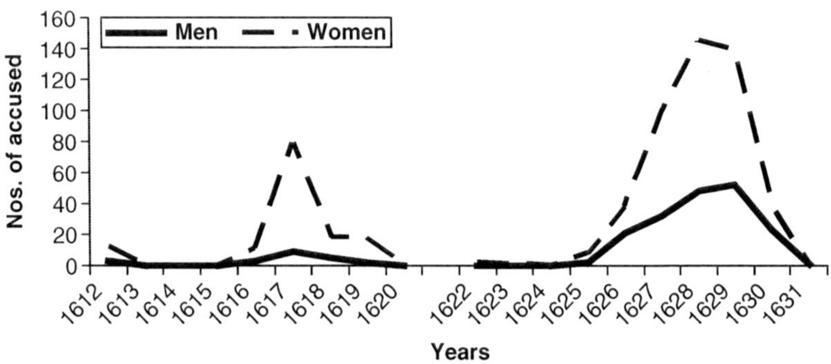

Figure 3.3 Bishopric of Bamberg: Witchcraft persecutions by sex, 1610–1635 (numbers accused)

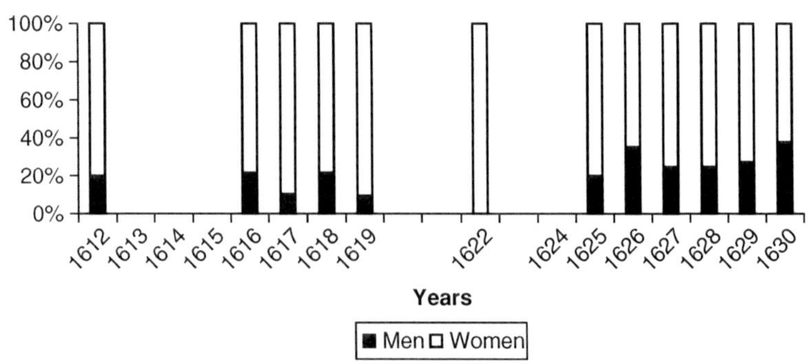

Figure 3.4 Bishopric of Bamberg: Witchcraft persecutions by sex, 1610–1635 (percentage)

trial featured mainly in the early phase of the prosecutions. Instead, the vast majority of the accused were arrested because women and men who had already been imprisoned and interrogated on charges of witchcraft had denounced them as accomplices whom they had allegedly seen at the witches' sabbath. This was the principal dynamic of the trials that occurred from 1616 onwards. The idea of the sabbath as a collective, nocturnal meeting of many witches, taken from the demonological witchcraft paradigm, thus played a central role in the witch-persecutions of this territory. One of the elite men caught up in the trials was the 55-year-old mayor, Johannes Junius, who was executed in 1628, shortly after his wife had been burned as a witch. Despite his high status, Junius had to endure the same physical torture and mental anguish during his interrogations that many other victims had to cope with, and wrote one of the most detailed accounts of it in a letter to his daughter:

> Many thousand times good night, my daughter Veronica so dear my heart. Innocent I came to jail, innocent I was tortured, innocent I must die. For whoever comes to the house either must become a witch or be tortured for so long that he claims something pulled from his imagination, and, God have mercy, figures out something to say...But be sure you do not make this letter public...Good night, for your father Johannes Junius will never see you again, 24 july anno 1628.[21]

One can best comprehend the scale and massive social impact of the Bamberg witch-persecution by thinking about the main street of the city, where most families of the social elite lived: about half of the house-owners and landowners from this street, and many of their wives and other family members, were charged with witchcraft, convicted, and executed. In addition to Junius, 18 of the city's mayors and town-councillors were prosecuted, as well as the secretary to the treasurer of the Prince-Bishop, the chancellor of the Prince-Bishopric (Dr Haan), the Superintendent of the Exchequer, the district tax collector, and many other officials. The level of witch-persecution was so severe in Bamberg for ten years that it led to the replacement of one entire group of leading men with another: one faction of the politically powerful men of the town, led by the Suffragan Bishop, fought against another faction of Bamberg's highest social class, using allegations of witchcraft as one of the weapons in their conflict.[22] This factionalism escalated during the early years of the seventeenth century, when the councillors and officials who had risen to prominence before Counter-Reformation efforts in the Prince-Bishopric intensified were attacked by the hardliners who had a more zealous approach to the Counter-Reformation in general, and to witch-hunting in particular.[23]

The impression that the men caught up in the Bamberg witch-trials came only from the rival groups of ruling elites and government officials is not, however, correct. The victims also included craftsmen such as bakers, butchers, smiths and shoemakers. The large number of innkeepers and coopers is especially noteworthy. This can be explained by the fact that brewing enjoyed great prominence in the city as a whole and, perhaps, also by the fact that these professions were linked imaginatively by the public to the alleged magical poisoning of food and drink. Members of the lowest social classes were denounced as sabbath-attenders as well, and servants, day-labourers, fishermen, musicians, and grave-diggers were also burned as witches.[24]

IV

For the Lutheran Duchy of Holstein (including, for statistical purposes, the small Duchy of Saxony-Lauenburg),[25] located in the very north of the Holy Roman Empire, records survive of 453 people tried for witchcraft between 1530 and 1735. As Figures 3.5 and 3.6 illustrate, most were women, with only 12 per cent of the total tried being men. It was only in the final phase of witch-trials in this region that the courts began to try an increasing number of men, although even this increase did not affect the relatively low proportion of men accused of witchcraft overall.[26]

The significant gendering of witch-persecution in this region is even clearer when we look not only at the numbers accused, but also at the ultimate fate of those tried for alleged witchcraft. Trials brought against women ended in execution in 74 per cent of cases, whereas trials against men ended in capital convictions in only 62 per cent of cases. Men also had a much better chance than women of being released without punishment: this happened to men in 25 per cent of cases and to women in only 10 per cent of cases. Women were, thus, not only accused of witchcraft in much higher numbers in this area, they were also treated much more severely by the courts as a result of such accusations than were men, who had a much better chance of being released or at least surviving a witch-trial without being sentenced to death. There were also significant gender differences in the types of harmful magic attributed to men and women. Allegations of causing illness or death in humans and of harming cattle were brought against women in 59 per cent and 47 per cent of cases respectively. Men were also charged with harming cattle (in 39 per cent of cases), but the next most numerically significant

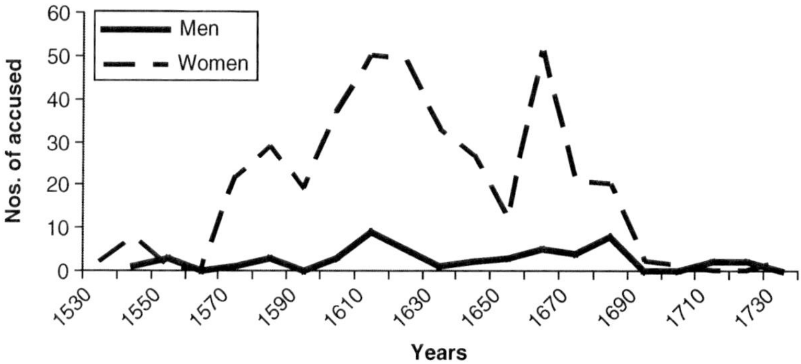

Figure 3.5 Duchy of Holstein and Saxony-Lauenberg: Witchcraft persecutions by sex, 1530–1730 (numbers accused)

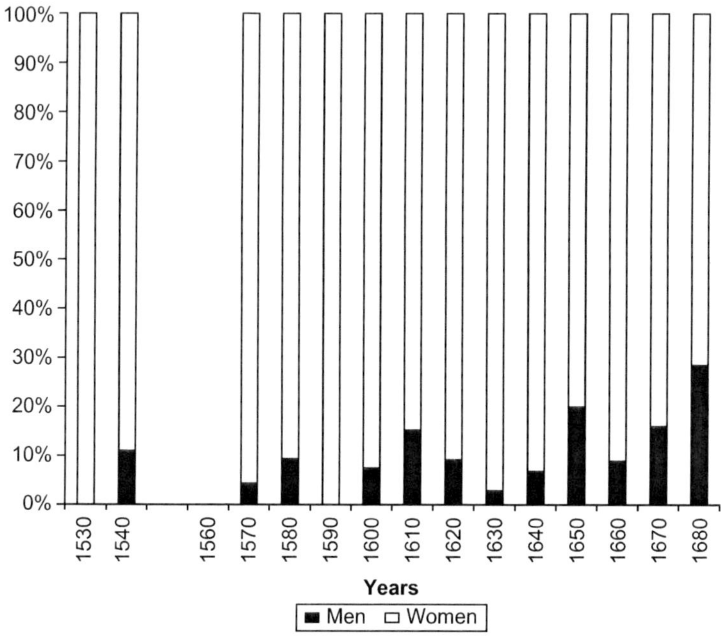

Figure 3.6 Duchy of Holstein and Saxony-Lauenberg: Witchcraft persecutions by sex, 1530–1730 (percentage)

charge was that of harming horses (33 per cent). Love magic was of hardly any significance in the witchcraft cases from this region, but one man was charged with having used it, thus demonstrating that it was not imagined as an exclusively female crime.[27]

For this region, there is one particularly discernible occupational group that became the target of witch-trials: that of herdsmen. Their constant contact with animals, and the fact that they spent most of their time out-of-doors, meant that they gained rich experience in healing animals and could forecast weather changes very precisely. As these abilities could seem to be unnatural in the eyes of the general public, herdsmen were regarded with ambivalence. On the one hand, they were considered to be social 'pariahs', because they belonged to a dishonourable profession but, on the other hand, they were respected by peasants as men with magical healing powers.[28] As the author of the first German dictionary, J. H. Zedler, put it in 1735, 'The shepherd is very good at veterinary problems'.[29] Thus, herdsmen were the typical equivalent of the English 'cunning men' outside of large urban centres in an agrarian society such as Holstein. If they were encountered in an interpersonal conflict, or if an attempt at healing by a herdsman went wrong, the situation could quickly escalate into a witch-trial. Herdsmen thus often constituted what I have categorized as 'primary' male witches in Holstein. This meant that they were tried as individuals in their own right, either in one-off trials or in trials that came at the start of a longer series of trials. I categorize 'secondary' male witches as those who were drawn into trials either as a result of denunciations made by other suspects, once a series of trials was already underway, or because they were related to women – often their wives – who had already been denounced as witches.[30] Blacksmiths were another occupational group targeted in Holstein, although in smaller numbers than the herdsmen. As with the herdsmen, blacksmiths also had well-founded veterinary knowledge. People also saw them in a similarly ambivalent light: on the one hand, they might be healers of horses but, on the other, diseases in horses might be the result of their magical aggression.[31]

What conclusions can be drawn from this brief examination of trials in Carinthia, Bamberg, and Holstein? The key point is that there was no single dominant pattern of conflict that resulted in men being tried for witchcraft and, as a result, there was no stereotypical male witch for the early modern Holy Roman Empire. In Bamberg, for example, men of the upper as well as lower social classes could be accused of witchcraft: the social status of male suspects was therefore heterogeneous. Homogeneity in the ages of male suspects was equally conspicuous by its absence, especially in Carinthia, where the witch beggars consisted of old as well as very young vagabonds. The ages of the male suspects in Bamberg and Holstein also varied, although the majority seem to have been of old age or middle-to-old age by early modern standards. As far as marital status was concerned, the majority of the male witches in Holstein and Bamberg were married, in contrast to the Austrian beggars, who tended to be single and to have no permanent relationships with women. Using the categories of 'primary' and 'secondary' male witches as defined above, we can see that, in Holstein, the numbers of men who fell into these categories stood in a ratio of 60 to 40 per cent, respectively, whereas in Carinthia it was precisely the opposite, with the ratio standing at 40 to 60 per cent, respectively. While such a categorization of male suspects is very difficult to arrive at for Bamberg, the figures for Holstein and Carinthia show that men were not just drawn into witch-trials as boy-witches, participants in the sabbath, or as the relatives of accused women, but also as primary suspects – in other words, as suspects accused of witchcraft on their own and in their own right.

V

The final context within which we can usefully consider and compare the gendering of witchcraft prosecution for the Holy Roman Empire is that of confessional difference. Were there significant differences in the patterns of witch-persecution in Catholic and Protestant territories, and to what extent might these be linked to theologically different ways of imagining witchcraft? Table 3.3 seeks to offer answers to the first part of this question.

While there were some notable exceptions (for example, in the Prince-Bishoprics of Eichstätt and Augsburg, and the Electorate of Saxony),[32] Table 3.3 suggests, overall, that the gendering of witch-persecution differed according to the confessional context. Lower proportions of male witches were mostly found in the Lutheran territories of the Empire, while the percentage of male witches in the Catholic territories was often much higher. This was particularly the case in the territories of the fanatical Counter-Reformation Prince-Bishops, where a significant proportion of men – in addition to a majority of women – became caught up in the especially savage persecutions that occurred in such areas. For example, in the so-called *Zauberer-Jackl* (Sorcerer-Jack) trials that took place in the Prince-Bishopric of Salzburg in the late seventeenth century, about 80 per cent of the victims were men;[33] by contrast, in the Protestant territory of Mecklenburg, which also experienced large-scale witch-hunts, men made up only 15 per cent of those prosecuted. We can, perhaps, begin to explain this difference in the proportion of male witches in Catholic and Protestant territories by looking at the different views about the gender of supposed witches in Lutheran and Catholic theology.

Table 3.3 Proportion of men accused of Witchcraft in selected Catholic and Protestant territories of the Holy Roman Empire (by percentage)[34]

Catholic territories		**Protestant territories**	
Upper Austria	69	County Ansbach	7
Lower Austria	34	Duchy Brunswick-Wolffenbüttel	10
County of Baden-Baden	31	County Büdingen	10
Bishopric Bamberg	25	County Hesse(n)-Kassel	13
Counties Blankenheim	20	County Hesse(n)-Darmstadt	2
Prince-abbey Ellwangen	20	Duchy Holstein	12
County Flanders	27	Duchy Mecklenburg	15
Duchy Carinthia	68	Bishopric Minden	10
Electorate Mainz	24	Earldom Montbéliard	18
County Vaduz/ Liechtenstein	40 (approx.)	County Nassau	12
Duchy Lorraine	28	Duchy Saxony-Lauenburg	12
Duchy Luxembourg	>25	'Thuringia' (protestant)	13 (approx.)
Bishopric Paderborn	30	County of Schaumburg	5
Bishopric Salzburg	59	Bishopric Ratzeburg	10
Duchy Styria	39	Bishopric Verden	6
County Tirol	48	Vorpommern	11
Vorarlberg	20	Duchy Württemberg	15
Duchy Westphalia	37		

In the Catholic Latin Vulgate version of the Bible, which had been compiled in the fourth century from a mixture of Hebraic, Aramaic and Greek original sources, a passage from the Old Testament often quoted in favour of witch-hunting was Exodus 22:18, which stated: '*Maleficos non patieris vivere*', meaning: 'Do not let the sorcerers live'. This particular use of language in the Catholic Vulgate clearly included men as possible demonic agents,[35] an idea that was taken up by Catholic writers of demonologies in the early modern period. For example, famous Catholic theologians such as the Suffragan Bishop of Trier, Peter Binsfeld, or the Professor of Theology at the Universities of Graz and Lüttich, Martin Del-Rio, spread their ideas about witchcraft as a non-gender-specific crime, by means of which both men and women could join forces with the Devil, in their widely-read demonologies in the sixteenth and seventeenth centuries.[36] Catholic jurists such as Jean Bodin and Nicolas Rémy supported these views in their theoretical and historical accounts of witch-trials.[37] Ruling elites in Catholic territories tended to regard these monographs as more trustworthy during the early modern period than the infamous late-fifteenth-century *Malleus Maleficarum* by the Dominican Institoris.

Catholic authors did not merely see witchcraft as fitting into a medieval tradition of heresy; they also regarded it as a new and deviant form of heretical activity – in fact, as a super-crime that had never existed before and that separated itself from all other forms of heresy through the destructive potential witches were supposed to possess as a result of their ability to work harmful magic. The fusing of witchcraft with heresy had become clear in a letter written by Pope Alexander VI in 1500, when the man who was the highest authority in the Catholic Church called the newly discovered deviants (that is, witches) '*haeretici malefici*' in Latin, an expression that can be translated either as 'heretical magicians/sorcerers' or 'magical heretics'.[38] The connection between heresy and sorcery was thereby theoretically confirmed, as both terms were synthesized linguistically to label this new form of deviance. As far as Catholic thinking was concerned, heretical activities and meetings were thus not exclusively associated with either gender in theory or reality. The Roman Catholic Inquisition had executed women as heretics, but linked the crime of heresy mainly with the male gender, and Catholic authorities never lost sight of this tradition of associating men with heresy during the period of the witch-hunts.

Lutherans in the Holy Roman Empire, on the other hand, had a different view of the gendering of witch-persecution, but one that was also linked in crucial ways to the linguistic construction of the witch in scriptural exegesis. Luther saw women as more likely to become witches, in the tradition of the Biblical figure of Eve. He could read Hebrew and his (in fact, more accurate) translation of Exodus 22:18 was: 'Do not let the female sorcerers live'.[39] Luther's version of this passage was not regarded by Protestant theologians merely as some sort of theoretical observation but, rather, as an explicit Biblical instruction for action. Therefore, Protestants, with their emphasis on the exact interpretation of the Bible, saw women as the source of witchcraft.[40] The confessional differences in the gendering of witch-persecution may also be linked tentatively with different ways of imagining the witches' sabbath. A more gender-neutral stance on who could be a witch was most commonly found amongst theologians and demonologists who integrated the idea of the witches' sabbath into their philosophies in an explicit and detailed way. Catholic authors were, on the whole, more likely to believe in the reality of such nocturnal gatherings, while Protestants followed Luther in adopting a much more sceptical attitude towards sabbaths (although, of course, the reality of witch-hunts in Protestant territories did not always reflect the theoretical scepticism of this viewpoint).[41] Men were thus especially likely to end up as the victims of witch-hunts in those territories where belief in the sabbath was firmly accepted by the relevant courts, and this was more likely to be the case in Catholic areas.

This brief discussion of witch-trials in the early modern Holy Roman Empire thus suggests that the comparative analysis of male involvement in early modern witch-trials can only be undertaken once we know enough about regional variations in the gendering of prosecution. At the same time, however, regional variation should not blind us to the fact that there might well have been more generally significant factors, operating particularly at the level of the ruling elites and based on confessional difference, and the possible influence of key demonologies that cut across geographical boundaries to influence witch-trials and ways of imagining witches. It is by considering the balance of such factors that answers to questions about the gendering of witch-persecution will best be found.

Notes

1. For the records of the trial involving Joachim Witte, see Staatsarchiv Hamburg: Nr. 415–1, Lübecker (Senats-)Akten betreffend Bergedorf I, vol.130, fasc.A.
2. Wolfgang Behringer argues that this desire to hunt witches from below came from popular concern about crop damage during a period of climate change known as the Little Ice Age, see W. Behringer, *Witches and Witch-Hunts. A Global History* (Cambridge, 2004), ch. 4, especially 83–9.
3. See, for example, R. Voltmer, 'Monopole, Ausschüsse, Formalparteien. Vorbereitung, Finanzierung und Manipulation von Hexenprozessen durch private Klagekonsortien', in H. Eiden and R. Voltmer (eds), *Hexenprozesse und Gerichtspraxis* (Trier, 2002), 5–67.
4. This conclusion about the gender ratio of witch-persecution in the Holy Roman Empire is taken from my own research, see R. Schulte, *Hexenmeister. Die Verfolgung von Männern im Rahmen der Hexenverfolgung von 1530–1730*

im Alten Reich, 2nd edn (Frankfurt am Main, 2001); the first edition was published in 2000. A revised English translation of this work, including new material, is available as *Man as Witch. Male Witches in Central Europe* (Basingstoke, 2009).

5. See Behringer, *Witches and Witch-Hunts*, 149–51 (although Behringer uses the boundaries of present-day Germany rather than the early modern Holy Roman Empire for his statistical analysis).
6. See Schulte, *Hexenmeister*, for the overall analysis. Since 2000, I have added statistical data from the following sources to my analysis: R. Decker, 'Paderborn, prince-bishopric of', in R. M. Golden (ed.), *Encyclopedia of Witchcraft. The Western Tradition* (hereafter *EOW*), vol. III (Santa Barbara CA, 2006), 869–70; J. Dillinger, *'Böse Leute'. Hexenverfolgungen in Schwäbisch-Österreich und Kurtrier im Vergleich* (Trier, 1999), 96–100; J. Durrant, 'Eichstätt, prince-bishopric of', in *EOW*, vol. II, 307–8; R.-P. Fuchs, *Hexenverfolgung an Ruhr und Lippe. Die Nutzung der Justiz durch Herren und Untertanen* (Münster, 2002), 145; R. Füssel, *Hexenverfolgungen in Thüringer Raum* (Hamburg, 2003), 200, 217; B. Gehm, *Die Hexenverfolgung im Hochstift Bamberg und das Eingreifen des Reichshofrates zu ihrer Beendigung* (Hildesheim, 2000), 69–70, 110; G. Gersmann, 'Münster, bishopric of', in *EOW*, vol. III, 794–5; P.A. Heuser, 'Die kurkölnischen Hexenprozesse des 16. und 17. Jahrhunderts in geschlechtergeschichtlicher Perspektive', in I. Ahrendt-Schulte *et al.* (eds), *Geschlecht und Hexenverfolgung* (Bielefeld, 2002), 133–74, see especially 138–40; E.M. Kern, 'Austria' in *EOW*, vol. I, 70–5; S. Kleinöder-Strobel, *Die Verfolgung von Zauberei und Hexerei in den fränkischen Markgraftümern im 16. Jahrhundert* (Tübingen, 2002), 197; M. Kosir, 'Slovenia' in *EOW*, vol. IV, 1052–4; K. Moeller, '"Es ist ein überaus gerechtes Gesetz, dass die Zauberinnen getötet werden". Hexeverfolgung im protestantischen Norddeutschland', in R. Beier-de Haan *et al.* (eds), *Hexenwahn. Angste der Neuzeit: Begleitband zur gleichnamigen Ausstellung* (Berlin, 2002), 96–107, see especially 105; K. Moeller, *Dass Willkür über Recht ginge. Hexenverfolgung in Mecklenburg im 16. und 17. Jahrhundert* (Bielefeld, 2007), 224–31; J. Monballyu, 'Die Hexenprozesse in der Grafschaft Flandern (1495–1692). Chronologie, Soziographie, Geographie und Verfahren', in H. Eiden and R. Voltmer (eds), *Hexenprozesse und Gerichtspraxis* (Trier, 2002), 279–314, see especially 287; H. Rabanser, *Hexenwahn. Schicksale und Hintergrund. Die Tiroler Hexenprozesse* (Innsbruck, 2006), 96–100, 194; R. Schulte, *Hexenverfolgung in Schleswig-Holstein vom 16.–18. Jahrhundert* (Heide, 2001); W. Rummel, 'Hexenverfolgungen Kurtrier', in G. Gersmann (ed.), http://www.historicum.net/themen/hexenforschung/lexikon/regionnundorte/ (2000); D. Vanysacker, 'Netherlands, southern', in *EOW*, vol. III, 813–18; M. Wilde, *Die Zauberei- und Hexenprozesse in Kursachsen* (Cologne, 2003), 308; M. Tschaikner, '"Der Teufel und die Hexen müssen aus dem Land". Frühneuzeitliche Hexenverfolgungen in Liechtenstein', *Jahrbuch des Historischen Vereins für das Fürstentum Liechtenstein*, XVI (1998), 106–7; M. Tschaikner, 'Hexenverfolgungen Vorarlberg', in G. Gersman (ed.), http://www.historicum.net/themen/hexenforschung/lexikon/regionen-und-orte/ (1999); M. Zeck, 'Reichsstadt Rottweil', in S. Lorenz and J.M.Schmidt (eds), *Wider alle Hexerei und Teufelswerk. Die europäische Hexenverfolgung und ihre Auswirkung auf Südwestdeutschland* (Ostfildern, 2004), 429.
NB: All statistics used are of those accused of witchcraft of known gender.

7. *West*: Franche-Comté, Montbéliard, Lorraine, Saar, Mainz, Trier (Electorates), Gerolstein-Blankenheim, Spanish Netherlands (Flanders, Luxembourg, Bouillon, Namur, Cambrai).
   Southwest: Baden-Baden, Ellwangen, Hohenberg, Hohenlohe, Hohenzollern, Mergentheim, Swabian-Austria, Vorderösterreich, Vorarlberg, Vaduz, Württemberg.
   Southeast: Bavaria, Salzburg, Austria (Upper and Lower Austria, Liechtenstein/ Vaduz, Styria, Carinthia, Tirol, Carniola).
   East: Saxony, Silesia.
   Central: Würzburg, Bamberg (Bishoprics), Hesse-Kassel, Büdingen, Thüringia, Cologne (Electorate), Paderborn, Ruhr-Lippe.
   Northwest: Lippe, Brunswick-Wolfenbüttel, Minden, Münster, Schaumburg, Osnabrück, Verden.
   Northeast: Holstein, Sachsen-Lauenburg, Mecklenburg, Vorpommern.
8. In 2001, I calculated that 24 per cent of all those involved in witch-trials in the Holy Roman Empire were men; see Schulte, *Hexenmeister*, 81. This overall average has gone down slightly since then to 23.1 per cent, because I have factored in new research into witch-trials in Mecklenburg, where comparatively few men were prosecuted for witchcraft.
9. See the essay by R. Voltmer in this volume, and also R. Voltmer, 'Luxembourg, duchy of', in *EOW*, vol. III, 677–80. The figures given by M.-S. Dupont-Bouchat, 'La répression de la sorcellerie dans le duché de Luxembourg aux XVIe et XVIIe siècles', in M.-S. Dupont-Bouchat *et al.* (eds), *Prophètes et sorciers dans les Pays-Bas, XVIe-XVIIe siècle* (Paris, 1978), 127–38, seem far too low. Voltmer's additional research results are to be published in 2010.
10. Gehm, *Hexenverfolgung im Hochstift Bamberg*, 268; Gerhard Schormann, 'Hexenverfolgung in Schaumburg', *Niedersächsisches Jahrbuch für Landesgeschichte*, 45 (1973), 145–69, see especially 163; Gerhard Schormann, *Hexenprozesse in Nordwestdeutschland* (Hildesheim, 1977), 86–7; B. Rochelandet, *Sorcières, Diables et Bûchers en Franche-Comté* (Besançon, 1997), 16–18; Schulte, *Hexenverfolgung in Schleswig-Holstein*, 69, 77; Monballyu, 'Hexenprozesse in der Grafschaft Flandern', 287; Schulte, *Hexenmeister*, 104, 246; Tschaikner, 'Frühneuzeitliche Hexenverfolgungen in Liechtenstein', 100–11; H. Pohl, *Hexenglaube und Hexenverfolgung im Kurfürstentum Mainz* (Stuttgart, 1988), 212; H. Gebhard, *Hexenprozesse im Kurfürstentum Mainz des 17. Jahrhunderts* (Mainz, 1989), 233–8; R. Briggs, 'Women as Victims? Witches, Judges and Community', *French History*, V (1991), 438–50, see especially 442; Moeller, *Hexenverfolgung in Mecklenburg*, 224–31; U. Schönleitner, *Zauberei- und Hexenprozesse in Österreich* (Geisteswissenschaftliche Diplomarbeit, University of Vienna, 1986/7), 33; H. Valentinitsch, 'Die Verfolgung von Hexen und Zauberern im Herzogtum Steiermark – eine Zwischenbilanz', in H. Valentinitsch (ed.), *Hexen und Zauberer. Die große Verfolgung – ein europäisches Phänomen in der Steiermark* (Graz/Vienna, 1987), 297–316.
11. These are my own calculations drawn from archival records from Carinthia and other sources; for a fuller discussion, see ch. 8 of Schulte, *Man as Witch*.
12. See *ibid.*; M. Wutte, 'Hexenprozesse in Kärnten', *Carinthia I. Geschichtliche und volkskundliche Beiträge zur Heimatkunde Kärnten/Mitteilungen des Geschichtsvereins für Kärnten*, CXVII (1927), 27–67, especially 43, 57; F. Byloff,

Hexenglaube und Hexenverfolgung in den österreichischen Alpenländern (Leipzig, 1934), 63, 90, 103; K. B. Hauser, 'Aus dem Archive', *Carinthia*, LXXI (1881), 118–90, see especially 153–6; Schönleitner, *Zauberei und Hexenprozesse*, 66, 158–60.
13. Kärntner Landesarchiv GV-SA Fasz. 35a. HA Porcia Fasz. XXIII a Nr. 98; see also ch. 8 of Schulte, *Man as Witch*.
14. M. Swatek, 'Die Wolfbanner. Der Wolfberger Hexenprozeß von 1705/06', *Carinthia*, CXCIII (2003), 315–43.
15. S. Gosler, *Hexenwahn und Hexenprozesse in Kärnten. Von dem Ende des 15. Jahrhunderts bis zum ersten Drittel des 18. Jahrhunderts* (Graz, 1955), 132; A. von Jaksch, 'Ein Hexenprocess in Paternion im Jahre 1662', *Carinthia*, LXXXIII (1893), 9–14.
16. Wutte, 'Hexenprozesse in Kärnten', 50–2, 55.
17. E. Bruckmüller, *Sozialgeschichte Österreichs* (Vienna, 1985), 215–64; R. Sandgruber, *Ökonomie und Politik. Österreichische Wirtschaftsgeschichte vom Mittelalter bis zur Gegenwart* (Vienna, 1995), 103–34.
18. N. Schindler, 'Die Entstehung der Unbarmherzigkeit. Zur Kultur und Lebensweise der Salzburger Bettler am Ende des 17. Jahrhunderts', in N. Schindler, *Widerspenstige Leute. Studien zur Volkskultur in der Frühen Neuzeit* (Frankfurt am Main, 1992), 258–314, see especially 269–71.
19. R. Jütte, *Poverty and Deviance in Early Modern Europe* (Cambridge, 1994), 41, 149–50; H.. Valentinitsch, 'Frauen unterwegs. Eine Fallstudie zur Mobilität von Frauen in der Steiermark um 1700', in H. Wunder and C. Vanja (eds), *Weiber, Menscher, Frauenzimmer. Frauen in der ländlichen Gesellschaft 1500–1800* (Göttingen, 1996), 223–36.
20. These calculations are based on the data given in Gehm, *Hexenverfolgung im Hochstift Bamberg*, 191–3, 292–362.
21. The case of Junius is discussed in L. Apps and A. Gow, *Male Witches in Early Modern Europe* (Manchester, 2003), 76–89; the letter by Junius is reproduced in full on 159–64. The house to which Junius referred was the prison built especially to hold those accused of witchcraft during the large-scale hunts in Bamberg.
22. Gehm, *Hexenverfolgung im Hochstift Bamberg*, 191–3, 268–70.
23. Behringer, *Witches and Witch-Hunts*, 110–13.
24. R. Walinski-Kiehl, *Prosecuting witches in early modern Germany, with special reference to the Bishopric of Bamberg, 1595–1680* (unpublished M.Phil. thesis, Portsmouth Polytechnic, 1981).
25. The analysis for the period 1530–1730 is restricted to the area of present-day Holstein, which consisted of the Duchy of Holstein, the Duchy of Saxony-Lauenburg, several other smaller territories, and the Imperial City of Lübeck. These territories belonged to the Lower Saxon Circle, in which imperial law ruled.
26. These calculations are based on research and data in Schulte, *Hexenmeister*, 210. Statistics on the gendering of persecution for the period 1690–1730 are inconclusive because of the low number of cases, but they do not alter the overall picture.
27. These statistics are based on my own research and calculations; see Schulte, *Hexenverfolgung in Schleswig-Holstein*, 84–97; Schulte, *Man as Witch*, ch. 7.
28. Schulte, *Hexenmeister*, 228–34.

29. J. Zedler (ed.), *Großes vollständiges Universal-Lexicon aller Wissenschaften und Künste, welche bishero durch menschlichen Verstand und Witz erfunden wurden* (Halle, 1732–49), vol. XIII, 3259.
30. See Schulte, *Hexenmeister*, 215, 234–5 for definitions of primary and secondary male witches.
31. See, for example, Schulte, *Hexenmeister*, 222.
32. See J. Durrant, 'Eichstätt, prince-bishopric of', in *EOW*, vol. II, 307–8; W. Behringer, 'Augsburg, prince-bishopric of', in *EOW*, vol. I, 67–8; Wilde, *Die Zauberei- und Hexenprozesse in Kursachsen*, 308.
33. Young male vagrants were the main target of these *Zauberer-Jackl* trials in late-seventeenth-century Salzburg. However, before 1680 most prosecutions for witchcraft in Salzburg were against women, so the overall percentage of men accused of witchcraft in Salzburg was 59 (see Table 3.3).
34. See footnotes 6, 7 and 10, and Schulte, *Hexenmeister*, 61–76; J. M. Débard, *Le pays de Montbéliard du Wurttemberg à la France* (Montbéliard, 1992), 25–6; Decker, 'Paderborn'; Füssel, *Hexenverfolgungen in Thüringer Raum*, 200, 217; Heuser, 'Die kurkölnischen Hexenprozesse', 137–40; M. Kepplinger, *Vorstellungswelten und Lebenswelten- Hexenprozesse in Oberösterreich* (Geisteswissenschaftliche Diplomarbeit, University of Vienna, 1988), 38–40; E. M. Kern, 'County of Tyrol', in *EOW*, vol. IV, 1137–8; J. Koppenhöfer, *Die mitleidlose Gesellschaft. Studien zu Verdachtsgenese, Ausgrenzungsverhalten und Prozessproblematik im frühneuzeitlichen Hexenprozess in der alten Grafschaft Nassau unter Johann VI. und der späteren Teilgrafschaft Nassau- Dillenburg (1559–1687)* (Frankfurt am Main, 1995), 90; T. Lange and J. R. Wolf, 'Hexenverfolgung zur Zeit Georg I', *Archiv für hessische Geschichte und Altertumskunde*, LII (1994), 139–98; W. Mährle, 'Fürstprobstei Ellwangen', in Lorenz and Schmidt (eds), *Wider alle Hexerei und Teufelswerk*, 377–86, see 383; Moeller, *Hexenverfolgung in Mecklenburg*, 224–31; H. C. E. Midelfort, *Witch Hunting in Southwestern Germany 1562–1684. The Social and Intellectual Foundations* (Stanford CA, 1972), 181; Moeller, 'Hexeverfolgung im protestantischen Norddeutschland', 105; W. Nieß, *Hexenprozesse in der Grafschaft Büdingen* (Büdingen, 1982), 44–5, 103–6, 126–8, 142, 169–70, 177–8, 183, 233–4, 265, 271, 277, 301; Monballyu, 'Die Hexenprozesse in der Grafschaft Flandern', 287; A. Raith, 'Herzogtum Württemberg', in Lorenz and Schmidt (eds), *Wider alle Hexerei und Teufelswerk*, 225–36, see 227; S. Schleichert, 'Hexenprozesse in der Landgrafschaft Hessen-Kassel', *Hessisches Jahrbuch für Landesgeschichte*, XLIII (1993), 39–76, see especially 65, 69; J. Scheffler, G. Schwerhoff and G. Wilbertz, 'Umrisse und Themen der Hexenforschung in der Region', in G. Wilbertz *et al.* (eds), *Hexenverfolgung und Regionalgeschichte. Die Grafschaft Lippe im Vergleich* (Bielefeld, 1994), 9–25, see 19; C. Schneider, 'Markgrafschaften Baden-Baden und Baden-Durlach', in Lorenz and Schmidt (eds), *Wider alle Hexerei und Teufelswerk*, 213–24, see 219; Schönleitner, *Zauberei- und Hexenprozesse*, 32; Schormann, 'Hexenverfolgung in Schaumburg', 163; Schulte, *Hexenmeister*, 76–7, 98; A. Vater, *Hexenverfolgung in den nassauischen Grafschaften im 16. und 17. Jahrhundert* (PhD thesis from the Phillips-Universität Marburg, Marburg, 1988), 111–15; the essay by Voltmer in this volume; K. Wohlschlegel, 'Deutschordenskommende Mergentheim', in Lorenz and Schmidt (eds), *Wider alle Hexerei und Teufelswerk*, 387–402, see 391; J. Wook, '"Ick Beke

Piepers von limbergen, Bekhenne…". Hexenverfolgung im Bistum Verden', *Praxis Geschichte*, IV (1991), 38–43, see 43.

35. P. Gasquet and H. Quentin (eds), *Biblia sacra iuxta Latinam vulgatam versionem* (Rome, reprinted edition from 1929), 193.
36. See Martin Del-Rio, *Disquisitionum magicarum libri sex* (Cologne, 1633), liber II, questio IV und XV, liber II, 159, liber V, 633, sect. I, 695, liber V, 775–8 ; and Peter Binsfeld, *Tractat von der Bekenntnuß der Zauberer und Hexen* (Munich, 1592), where female as well as male witches are mentioned regularly in the titles and descriptions of the different chapters. For detailed analysis of this point, see Schulte, *Hexenmeister*, 124–8, 143–7, and ch. 5 of *Man as Witch*.
37. See Jean Bodin, *De la Démonomanie Des Sorciers* (Paris, 1580), livre II/1, 52–9; II/4, 79–83; livre II/7, 104–7; livre II/8, 113–17; livre III, 133 v; livre III/5; livre VI/4, 190–3; livre V, 224–6, 230–241; and Nicolas Rémy, *Daemonolatriae libri tres Nicolai Remigii serenissimi ducis Lotharingi consiliis interioribus et in eius ditione Lotharingia cognitoris publici* (Frankfurt am Main, 1597), 1/6, 27; 1/19, 126; 2/1, 183; 2/9, 253; 3/12. For more detailed analysis, see Schulte, *Hexenmeister*, 124–8, 141–3, and *Man as Witch*, ch. 5.
38. This source is reprinted in J. Hansen (ed.), *Quellen zur Untersuchung des Hexenwahns und der Hexenverfolgung im Mittelalter* (Bonn, 1901), 30.
39. Martin Luther, *Die gantze Heilige Schrifft Deudsch* (Wittenberg, 1545), 163.
40. See for example Johann Georg Godelmann, *Von Zäuberern, Hexen und Unholden* (Frankfurt am Main, 1592), 1/ 83, 2/263, 3/434. For discussion of other Protestant authors, see Schulte, *Hexenmeister*, 107–79, and Schulte, *Man as Witch*, ch. 5.
41. On Protestant demonology, see S. Clark, *Thinking with Demons. The Idea of Witchcraft in Early Modern Europe* (Oxford, 1997), 139, 142, 529; S. Clark, 'Protestant Demonology: Sin, Superstition and Society (c. 1520–c.1630)', in B. Ankarloo and G. Henningsen (eds), *Early Modern Witchcraft. Centres and Peripheries* (Oxford, 1990), 45–81, see 58; W. Behringer, *Hexen- und Hexenprozesse* (Munich, 1995), 354–6.

4

Witch-Finders, Witch-Hunters or Kings of the Sabbath? The Prominent Role of Men in the Mass Persecutions of the Rhine-Meuse Area (Sixteenth–Seventeenth Centuries)*

Rita Voltmer

I

The early modern witch-hunts can, in one very clear sense, be labelled as a manifestation of legalized male violence against women, given that they were authorized by the writings and opinions of theologians and jurists and conducted by a legal system that was – literally – 'manned' by judges, court assessors, jurymen and informers, and supported by local clerics.[1] They also targeted women in greater numbers than men: the overall ratio for early modern Europe and New England is 75–80 per cent women to 20–25 per cent men. This point must be stressed before any analysis of male involvement as accused witches is attempted, although we need also to bear in mind that the early modern legal system was generally characterized by a significant level of embedded juridical violence that affected men and women accused of serious crimes other than witchcraft – such as theft, robbery, murder, infanticide, or adultery. Moreover, the proportion of women amongst the victims of witch-persecution ranged considerably both chronologically (from witch-hunt to witch-hunt), and geographically (from region to region), with men even outnumbering women in certain areas – such as Normandy, the Pays de Vaud, Finland, Estonia or Iceland.[2] When analysing the gendering of witch-persecution, we must also remember that the apparently simple question of why more women than men were suspected as witches overall still excites great debate amongst historians of witchcraft, who by no means agree on a simple explanatory model in response. Arguably, no such model exists, because witch-trials occurred in so many regionally varied formats (from single trials to mass panics) and in quite different legal systems in Europe and in the transatlantic colonies; because they were based upon regionally and socially different systems of witch-beliefs; and because they were linked to ideas about motherhood, the family, masculinity, and femininity that varied according to religious confession.[3] In this context of complexity, 'grand' explanatory theories about the gendering of witch-persecution are almost bound to prove inadequate on closer examination, especially if they are based on merely a few case studies or on assumptions made about one region and applied uncritically to another.[4]

Of course, the jurists and theologians who wrote demonological treatises both for and against witch-hunting tended to foreground the old, poor, widowed woman as particularly susceptible to witchcraft, portraying her either as the wilfully wicked concubine of the Devil (in the case of those who supported persecution) or as the innocent, melancholic victim of diabolic delusions (in the case of critics who wanted to end the hunts). In reality, however, this stereotype had limited purchase. In the mass witch-hunts that occurred in the western and southern parts of the Holy Roman Empire in the late sixteenth and seventeenth centuries, women of any age, fecundity and marital status were charged with witchcraft, as were children and adolescents, and men of all ages and backgrounds. In the Prince-Bishoprics of Bamberg and Würzburg, for example, members of all status groups – and even clerics and mayors – were executed as witches.[5] Moreover, we must also be careful not to imply some sort of 'national' generalization on the basis of regional research: two recent publications on gender and witch-hunts in the early modern Holy Roman Empire have 'Germany' in their titles but are, in fact, regional case studies.[6]

In 1972, Erik Midelfort suggested that the stereotype of the witch as an old poor woman 'broke down' at the end of phases of severe persecution in certain areas in the south-eastern part of the Empire. The idea was that once the supply of these easy targets ran out, men and those of higher social status were ever more likely to be accused. According to Midelfort, this widening of the persecutory net helped cause a 'crisis of confidence' in the judicial procedures for prosecuting witches, which encouraged local authorities to bring witch-trials to an end.[7] In the Rhine-Meuse area, however, as we shall see later, this was not the case at all: the stereotype did not break down towards the end of the severe hunts in Trier, St Maximin or Manderscheid-Gerolstein because it had had little or no impact to start with. Shortly after trials in these territories began, men of relatively high social status who had been personally involved in the judicial machinery of prosecution as witch-hunters were at risk of being prosecuted themselves. Once accused or denounced, these former witch-hunters were forced, by means of physical and psychological torture, to confess to witchcraft, and to admit to and describe in detail their supposed sexual intercourse with a demon in the shape of a woman or a man.[8] Some members of the juridical authorities believed that they could detect the most powerful *patroni sagarum* (literally 'patrons of the witches') behind the mask of the righteous, pious, zealous witch-hunter.

This stereotype of the 'witches' patron', or 'king of the sabbath' was created for the first time in the Catholic territories of the Rhine-Meuse region, where mass prosecutions occurred at the end of the sixteenth century in the Duchy of Luxembourg, the Electorate of Trier and the territory of the Imperial Abbey of St Maximin.[9] Here, the medieval idea of the heretical sect consisting of both male and female members and acting under the leadership of male Devil-worshippers was still alive and, with the added ingredients of the witches' specific 'crimes' (harmful magic, sex with the Devil), was easily re-awakened by learned jurists and theologians, with devastating consequences. As Johannes Reckschenkel, a high-ranking cleric from Cologne, wrote in 1598, describing the situation as he perceived it in and around the city of Trier:

> It seems as if Satan has established his domicile in Trier. In this area he is seducing entire villages, even men, some of them famous for literacy, some of them turned grey in age; his demonic art has infected people of both sexes and turned them into madness, so that they don't flinch from sacrificing their souls to the hellish demon himself.[10]

Reckschenkel was clearly deeply shocked by the news that even learned men might fall prey to the Devil, but other contemporary sources – such as travel reports, diaries, chronicles, and official and private letters – also commented in a similar, horrified vein about villages devastated by witch-hunts, where both female and male inhabitants had been executed in such high numbers that some travellers claimed to have noticed woods on the hillsides made of stakes. These written lamentations about the apparent presence in the area of a large yet secret sect of witches – which supposedly included many high-ranking, wealthy, once politically powerful men, and even clerics – helped to spread ideas about the possibility and range of male witches to a much wider audience, at the same time as they doubtless frightened their male authors to the core.[11]

II

The rest of this chapter falls into five parts. I will begin by presenting an overview of the mass witch-trials that occurred in the area between the Meuse, Rhine and Moselle rivers, and then discuss how the gendering of persecution changed there with the onset of large-scale trials. Then, I will focus on what Peter Binsfeld, Suffragan Bishop of Trier, author of a hugely influential demonology, and one of the most zealous clerical promoters of witch-hunts, thought about male witches. I will then present the six categories of male witch that I see as emerging as distinct types in the trials from this area, before finishing with a discussion of whether or not men accused of witchcraft had a better chance of defending themselves, or were better treated in the course of their trials than women.

The early modern witch-hunts that occurred in this area enjoy the dubious distinction of being the first mass persecutions in any Catholic territory in the Holy Roman Empire, in which more than 6000 people of both genders were executed as witches. Certain historians, particularly in the English-language historiography, name the persecution 'the Trier super-hunts',[12] but this is a geographic over-simplification. Trials actually occurred in various neighbouring yet judicially and politically autonomous territories (including the Electorate of Trier) situated in an area in the western part of the Empire bounded by the rivers Rhine, Meuse and Moselle. Hunts here were not endemic, but epidemic, with inter-related 'hotspots'. Detailed explanation of this massive witch-panic can be found elsewhere:[13] here, I want to mention three crucial factors that were also important for the gendering of the process of persecution. First, in most of the territories of this area witchcraft was classified as an 'exceptional crime', in the prosecution of which all the restrictions of normal legal procedure could be ignored. This meant that torture was used without restraint, even if local courts formally paid lip-service to the imperial code of criminal legal procedure (the *Carolina* of 1532) or to territorial ordinances.[14] It is often very hard to ascertain exactly how torture was used in any particular trial, as the formal legal records – unsurprisingly – tried to cover it up. This was true especially of the mass persecutions in the Imperial Abbey of St Maximin, the Duchy of Luxembourg and the counties of Manderscheid, where deliberate breaches of law, the use of leading questions, excessive cruelty and the inhumane conditions of custody were, as far as possible, concealed, while the apparently 'proper' conduct of trials was emphasized in the written record.[15] We are only able to catch a fleeting glimpse of the horrific reality of the interrogations under torture that were carried out in the prison cells from other sources: the appeals that victims and their families were sometimes able to send to higher courts, and the contemporary criticisms of witch-hunting written by Cornelius Loos, Friedrich Spee or Hermann Löher.

Second, witch-trials were so intensive in this area because the prosecuting courts saw it as essential to force suspects not only to confess to witchcraft themselves, but also to name their alleged accomplices. This was because the judges believed in what Christina Larner defined as 'sabbath witchcraft',[16] in which the essence of the crime lay in the witch's alleged pact with Satan, combined with repeated meetings with other witches. As Larner suggested, contemporaries had many different ways of imagining these witches' sabbaths: they might be mere feasts, or include sexual orgies between the witches and their demon lovers. Sometimes witches paid homage to the Devil in the shape of a black dog or male goat by kissing its backside and, in its most extreme shape, the sabbath was imagined as a black mass. Acts of harmful magic, such as the raising of hailstorms or spreading of plague, were supposedly planned and prepared at the sabbath. Witches were, thus, imagined to be acting as an organized group that threatened society – the early modern equivalent of modern-day terrorists. Forced denunciations regarding supposed participation in these imaginary sabbaths were crucial in spreading the hunts throughout the Rhine-Meuse area, as they had the tendency to cross territorial borders. Indeed, at the peak of persecution, the incriminating testimonies given by neighbours against alleged witches in their communities, which reflected specific local social conflicts, decreased greatly in importance, while a single denunciation about attending the sabbath forced from a condemned witch might constitute sufficient evidence with which to charge another person. Such denunciations were often manipulated by torture and bribery and, as Walinski-Kiehl has shown for the mass witch-hunts in seventeenth-century Bamberg,[17] in the late sixteenth century, men could already fall prey to witch-hunts simply as a result of being named as sabbath accomplices.

Third, the dynamic and gendering of the witch-hunts in the area under discussion can be explained by the fact that witch-hunts in

Luxembourg, the Electorate of Trier, and the territory of the Imperial Abbey of St Maximin were organized by communal pressure groups called *Hexenausschüsse* (witch-hunting committees) or *monopoles* (in the Duchies of Luxembourg and Lorraine).[18] These committees had the job of gathering the evidence necessary to bring a suspect to trial for witchcraft in the first place, and only men – including local lay jurymen or court assessors, clerks, landlords and clerics – were appointed by their respective communities to join such committees. Cunning men, witch-finders and local priests also helped the committees to identify and unmask reputed witches in their communities, while all villagers had to pay 'witch taxes' to fund the enterprise. The informers and witnesses against alleged witches were also predominantly male. These committees were banned formally in Luxembourg in 1591, although they continued to act secretly in witch-trials behind a figurehead, who would pretend to be an individual formal accuser according to proper legal procedure. Committees worked even more in the background of trials in the Duchy of Lorraine, while the Elector of Trier (following the example of Luxembourg) tried unsuccessfully to gain control over the activities of the local witch-hunting committees after 1591. The omnipresence of men at all procedural levels of the witch-hunts, from the selection of suspects to the preparation and conduct of trials, combined with an imaginative concept of the sabbath that was relatively gender-neutral, meant that the chances of men being accused as witches increased as the trials spread and escalated.

Between 1560 and 1683 approximately 3000 witchcraft trials took place in the Duchy of Luxembourg, one of the 17 provinces of the Habsburg Netherlands; at least 2000 ended with the execution of the accused, making the Luxembourg witch-hunts amongst the most savage in western Europe. Although many trial records are lost, we still have written evidence for about 1000 cases.[19] At least 25 per cent (and probably more) of the suspected witches were men. Some – such as local court assessors, village officials and clerics – came from the higher social ranks, while others – such as witch-finders, healers, herdsmen, or millers – came from lower down the social hierarchy. From Luxembourg, the witch-hunts spread into the Electorate of Trier, which was also influenced by the witch-persecutions in the Duchy of Lorraine.[20] Unfortunately, most of the Trier trial records were destroyed after 1652, so it is very difficult to say exactly how many people were tried for alleged demonic witchcraft between 1487 and 1660. There is only certain evidence for about 557 executions and, due to inadequate evidence in a third of all cases, we know neither the social status nor the gender of the victims.[21] An overall scholarly estimate of trials and their outcomes puts the total number of executions for the Electorate at approximately 1000, which was around 1.3 per cent of the total number of inhabitants of the territory.

From Lorraine, Luxembourg and the Electorate of Trier, witch-hunting infected the relatively small and compact territory of the Imperial Abbey of St Maximin. This was situated near to the city of Trier but was an entirely autonomous political and judicial entity: witch-trials were carried out here without any legal participation or formal intervention by the Electors of Trier. In St Maximin, the organization of witch-persecution attained a deadly level of perfection: at least 400 people were executed for witchcraft here between 1586 and 1596, from an overall total of executions for the territory of around 500. As the territory of St Maximin contained only around 2200 inhabitants, this meant that over 20 per cent of them died at the stake, thus ranking the St Maximin witch-hunts as probably the worst witch-panic in all of early modern Europe. The records of more than 280 trials have survived, as well as accounts detailing the costs of the persecution, and lists of denunciations and executions. Around a third of all witches tried by the St Maximin authorities were men, often from the wealthier and more influential ranks of their respective villages. The social status of executed women seemed to be similar: many accused women came from households whose heads held such positions in village government as stewards, local officials, or assessors of the local court, while poor widows were in a minority.

From here, witch-hunts spread rapidly to the territories of the Eifel region. The Catholic counties of Manderscheid-Kail, Manderscheid-Blankenheim, and Manderscheid-Gerolstein, which contained fewer than 5000 inhabitants in total, were particularly badly affected. Between 1580 and 1638 around 300 trials ended in executions. With the exception of some isolated trials around 1580 and 1590, the witch-hunts in these counties were initiated and promoted by the Counts themselves. About two thirds of the trial records and the records of the accounts of the trials have survived. The witch-persecutions in the Eifel territories produced fewer male victims – they constituted between 12 and 22 per cent of the total executed – but these included some local priests, healers and, again, some high-ranking local officials and court assessors.[22]

III

When we look at the gendering of witch-hunts across time, we can see that, in the individual trials that preceded the mass persecutions in the Rhine-Meuse-Moselle area, nearly all the accused were women. For example, 16 women, nearly all of lowly social status, were burned as witches in the city of Trier between 1459 and 1582, while most victims during this period in the Duchy of Luxembourg were also female. Men were occasionally tried for witchcraft, but the records from this phase of witch-hunting are too fragmentary to tell us anything certain about their social status. It seems as if the more traditional idea of the individual malevolent witch, which was not yet influenced by the concept of sabbath witchcraft, dominated the thinking of the lower orders and the elites until the mid-sixteenth century. Even though the concept of the witches' sabbath was known to some of the learned elite by this point, this knowledge did not seem to have influenced the legal procedure of trials in any significant or systematic way.[23] However, from around 1586 things began to change: the idea of the sabbath spread and became increasingly important; high-ranking, wealthy people of both genders became the targets of witchcraft slanders and witchcraft accusations much more frequently from this point onwards; and men were drawn into witch-trials as accused witches in larger numbers. By what mechanisms did the all-important sabbath concept gain such currency? An important role was played by the learned notary Peter Omsdorf, who was active in the St Maximin trials. We know that Omsdorf was familiar with the idea of the sabbath (which was already being discussed in contemporary demonological and juridical treatises), and that he introduced it in the first known St Maximin trial in 1572. In his capacity as clerk and notary, Omsdorf went on to conduct every witchcraft trial in St Maximin until 1596, and also almost every witch-trial in the surrounding administrative districts of Trier.[24]

Another key role in spreading ideas and heightening anxieties about witchcraft in the region was played by the Jesuits, who had been established in the city of Trier in 1560 and in the city of Luxembourg in 1594.[25] The Jesuits were zealous champions of the Counter-Reformation whose work was backed by Peter Binsfeld, the Suffragan Bishop of Trier. They fought on a broad front against every sort of heresy and deviation from orthodox Catholic belief. In their opinion, the Devil was responsible for spreading false religious ideas, as well as for improper religious practices and 'superstition'. The moral code propagated in Jesuit sermons, tracts, and missionary activities branded sexual sins and religious deviation in particular as mortal sins resulting from seduction by the Devil; their catalogue of moral and religious failings could be interpreted as evidence of witchcraft. As a result, the lower orders began to believe that adulterers, drunkards, thieves, rogues, and troublemakers had to be witches as well. Moreover, in the city of Trier, Jesuit preachers called for severe persecution of all witches without sparing the rich and influential. Significantly, Jesuits also diffused the sabbath concept of witchcraft with their sermons, tracts, and missionary travels.

The first man to be charged with sabbath witchcraft in the city of Trier was its wealthiest and most influential citizen, Dr Dietrich Flade, who was executed on September 18 1589.[26] Before this point Flade had – amongst several other official roles – acted as the bailiff of the high criminal court in Trier, in which capacity he had overseen witch-trials and sentenced eight women to death for witchcraft. He was brought to trial himself for many different reasons, although arguably the most crucial was the fact that he had acted as a moneylender in Trier and its environs, and was considered avaricious and ambitious. Denounced by male and female witches who had been executed in the nearby territory of St Maximin, Flade was named as the king of the sabbath, who – together with other high-ranking male citizens – led the witches' sect and destroyed crops with weather magic for the express purpose of making a profit during times of famine by selling their private stocks of grain. Flade's execution dramatically shattered any assumption that high social and political rank protected individuals from being tried as witches. In fact, it acted as a catalyst for subsequent trials against high-ranking men and women. Nearly half-a-dozen former lord mayors, councillors, and even some members of the high clergy, as well as parish priests were subsequently tried for witchcraft. Even some aristocratic members of the chapter of the Trier cathedral were named as witches, and the terrible news that the highest echelons of the Trier clergy were riddled with alleged witches ultimately reached the Pope. These denunciations and executions of rich and distinguished men brought about neither a general collapse of witch persecutions, nor the 'crisis of confidence' in witch-hunting postulated by Midelfort.[27] On the contrary, Flade's execution marked the starting point in a series of trials against other prominent males. The trial against him also aroused interest throughout the Holy Roman Empire. The hugely influential Catholic demonologist Martin Del Rio mentioned it in the witchcraft treatise he published between 1599 and 1600 as the most striking example of the idea that, behind the façade of a witch-hunting judge, the evil 'king' of the witches might be hidden. Del Rio even named Flade explicitly as a *patronus sagarum*, or patron of witches, who had misused his judicial power in order to fulfil this role. Del Rio's condemnation of Flade's supposedly corrupt character was so powerful that it has even led some historians to conclude – mistakenly – that Flade had, in fact, been an opponent of witch-trials before his own arrest, an interpretation for which there is no evidence whatsoever.[28]

At the local level, the Suffragan Bishop of Trier and Catholic demonologist Peter Binsfeld was the first to be influenced by the Flade trial: he also played a crucial role in spreading ideas about male witches in his demonology, *Tractatus de confessionibus maleficorum et sagarum*, which was first published in Trier in 1589.[29] Binsfeld never participated personally in any trials, but he was well acquainted with the officials of the criminal courts in the city and the Electorate of Trier and of St Maximin. He must have had knowledge of some of the St Maximin trial records, as he included extracts from the confessions of both male and female 'witches' from St Maximin in the second edition of his treatise, published in 1591. In his demonology, Binsfeld emphasized the threat posed by the evil sect of witches and called for more severe persecution of them, especially against the wealthy, high-ranking witches – by whom Binsfeld really meant suspected male witches. Binsfeld imagined the sabbath to include both men and women, and he was eager to declare that men were seduced by the Devil through the sins of greed, lust, and drunkenness. In the 1591 edition of his demonology, in what was clearly a reference to the Flade case, he again emphasized that the confessions of condemned witches must be truthful because they were made not only by old, weak-minded women but also strong-minded men, even scholars and clergymen. For Binsfeld, the presence of male witches who were not only participants in, but also kings of the sabbath demonstrated how very threatening this heretical sect was. Like van der Eerden, I would argue that in his demonology Binsfeld was clearly rebutting the ideas put forward by the witch-hunt critic and court physician to the Duke of Jülich-Cleves, Johann Weyer.[30] Weyer had published a treatise in 1563 in which he had branded the witch-hunts as a massacre of the innocents, because confessions of witchcraft were made only by weak-minded, insane, old women who had committed no crime at all.

IV

What sort of men – in terms of age, social, and occupational status – were drawn into witch-trials in the Rhine-Meuse region, and why? I would like to begin to offer an answer to these questions by outlining the six distinct categories of male witch that emerge from the trial records, although we must bear in mind that a man accused of witchcraft could belong to more than one of these categories.[31] Before discussing these categories, it is important to point out that most of the male witches from this region were accused in their own right, and not (as is often assumed more generally in the historiography) because they were related to a female witch.[32] Of course, any individual who belonged to a household in which women or men had already been identified as witches stood at greater risk of being suspected of witchcraft him- or herself. This acquisition of suspicion by association could affect even affinal relatives and servants within the household, because witchcraft was imagined less as heritable and more as something contagious and learnable, easily spread or taught to others.[33] Furthermore, there are numerous examples from this region of women being accused as alleged witches instead of their husbands, sons, or other male relatives, or because the women were related to an already executed male witch. Such cases show that the dynamic of 'accusation by association' could work the other way around, with women being dragged into trials because of their men-folk. Political, economic and social conflicts between men were more easily fought out by means of their legally much more vulnerable wives, mothers and daughters, and the most effective way to dishonour – and even financially ruin – an entire family was to accuse one of its female members of witchcraft.

The boy-witch was the first distinct category of male witch to emerge in the Rhine-Meuse region. Male youngsters played a prominent role in spurring on trials in the early stages of the great witch-hunts in the city and Electorate of Trier and in St Maximin.[34] Some of the youngsters were shepherd boys, while others came from wealthy peasant families. They claimed to have been kidnapped by female witches who had taken them to the Sabbath, where they had acted as pipers or drummers. It is hard to say with any certainty whether these boys were forced to make these supposedly 'voluntary' confessions, or whether they were mere pawns in the hands of the Jesuits. What we can say, however, is that their confessions reflected the sabbath concept of witchcraft with its male and female participants, and that their own supposed attendance at the sabbath as musicians marked an important imaginative step in integrating men more explicitly into the collective gatherings of witches. Moreover, most of the boy-witches were held in the Jesuit College in Trier, although the idea behind this policy was that, there, they would be best able to gain the pious instruction needed to bring them back into the Christian community. However, their main function in reality was to serve as witnesses for witch-prosecutions by naming all the alleged witches they had seen at the sabbath. In St Maximin and other surrounding districts, some of these boys were kept in custody for several years, during which time they served as witnesses against members of their own family as well as other suspects, amongst them high-ranking males: at least three of the boy-witches from the Electorate of Trier and St Maximin denounced Dietrich Flade as a witch. After gaining adulthood at the age of 14 most of them were executed, although the poor survival of sources means that we cannot say with certainty how many of them were beheaded or burned. A few young girls played a similar role, but in much smaller numbers than the boys: boy-witches again played significant roles in the witch-hunts in this region in the seventeenth century.

Peter Binsfeld encouraged the use of the boy-witches by the Jesuits, and wrote in support of this practice in his demonology. According to Binsfeld, there could be no better eyewitness than a child who had been introduced to the Devil by its parents. He pointed out that, without the evidence given by child-witches, no-one would be able to unmask the rich and influential leaders of the sabbath. Binsfeld also included the confessions made by one of the boy-witches who had been held in custody in St Maximin for a prolonged period in the 1591 edition of his demonology. Here, we can once again see the deadly interplay between demonological ideas and legal procedures as they were mediated through the writings of Binsfeld. His knowledge of, and support for, the handling of the boy-witches by the Trier Jesuits shaped what he wrote about child-witches in his treatise, and his writings, in turn, influenced procedures in the witch-trials in St Maximin. It is plausible to argue that, between them, the Jesuits of Trier and Binsfeld helped create this particular category of the boy-witch in the late sixteenth century. Binsfeld's demonology – which was well received across both Catholic and Protestant Europe, as well as in the transatlantic colonies (Salem) – spread his ideas about boy-witches, thereby significantly influencing the role that they played and the ways in which they were treated in subsequent witch-hunts in other regions.

The second group of males that came under suspicion of witchcraft in the Rhine-Meuse area was – paradoxically – that of the witch-hunters, who fell under suspicion of being witches themselves because of their close involvement in the processes of witch-prosecution. This was because of the way in which witch-hunting was organized in the region. As we saw in the earlier discussion of the witch-hunting committees, men of the urban and rural communities participated actively in the processes of prosecution by becoming members of the committees. Some of them often travelled long distances on committee business and, thus, played a decisive role in spreading rumours and accusations of witchcraft to a wider audience. As committee members, and also as court assessors, local men were omnipresent in witch-trials and, as a result, they were themselves increasingly at risk of being suspected, denounced and executed as witches. Some of these accused men tried to defend themselves by pointing out that they had been amongst the first to hunt witches. The argument used by those who now prosecuted them showed not only what a vicious circle such witch-hunters were unavoidably trapped in, but also how commonplace the hunting of male witches had become. Proponents of this counter-argument maintained that, because so many members of witch-hunting committees and so many court assessors had been identified as witches, it was clear that the most evil male witches hid behind the mask of the zealous witch-hunter! Even though some of those witch-hunters who were tried for witchcraft themselves had a female relative who had been executed as a witch, while some of them were notorious troublemakers, most of them seem not to have had reputations for witchcraft before they were denounced by one or two other alleged witches.

Ironically, some of the men involved formally in the legal machinery of witch-trials were also accused of witchcraft, not because they were too zealous in their pursuit of witches, but because they had become sceptical about the witch-burnings. Implicit or explicit criticism of the hunts was potentially fatal, as Hermann Löher, a former jurymen from Rheinbach (near Bonn, in the Electorate of Cologne), discovered.[35] Löher witnessed severe witch-hunts from inside the court-room and, on finally being suspected of witchcraft himself, was forced to flee for his life to Amsterdam in 1636. In 1676, he wrote and published his *Hochnötige Unterthanige Wemütige Klage der Frommen Unschültigen* (*Much Needed, Humble, and Woeful Complaint of the Pious Innocent*). This autobiographical tract sold hardly any copies, but is very valuable for historians, as it describes the dramatic events during the witch-hunts in Rheinbach in the 1630s that occurred under the *Hexenkommissar* (Witch Commissioner) Franz Buirmann, who tyrannized not only the accused witches, but also most of the court members. These Witch Commissioners were learned jurists, requested by local communities to conduct witch-trials, and sent by the Elector's council to advise the unlearned jury; in reality, however, they monopolized the whole lawsuit and conducted witch-trials openly in order to advance themselves financially and socially. In Rheinbach, most of the jurymen were opposed to the cruel procedures of Buirmann, who ordered the use of excessive torture against suspected witches, but Buirmann used brutal tactics to keep the court officials in line: he executed the wives of two rebellious jurors as witches. All members of the local court who had opposed Buirmann's methods were ultimately accused of witchcraft as well, apart from two men who were called 'yes-jurymen' by Löher because they had supported Buirmann in every way. Those who did not flee in time were executed. Another notorious Witch Commissioner, Dr Johann Möden, conducted trials in a similarly brutal and corrupt manner in the Eifel counties of Manderscheid-Gerolstein and Manderscheid-Blankenheim, and in the minor lordship of Bürresheim. Möden had every opportunity to manipulate the denunciations made by confessing witches about whom they had seen at the sabbath: one of his prime tactics was to encourage denunciation of members of the local court who were opposed to the massive witch-hunts. Similar patterns of manipulated denunciations used against mayors, jurors, and officials emerged in mass-trials in other parts of the Holy Roman Empire in the seventeenth century.[36] These seventeenth-century trials might well have been influenced by the discussion of the case of Dietrich Flade by Martin Del Rio in his demonological writings of 1599 and 1600. In his discussion of the Flade case, Del Rio had suggested that a hesitant attitude towards witch-trials on the part of a judge or court official was strong evidence of that individual being a witch himself.[37]

The third category of male witch that we find in the Rhine-Meuse region was that of the political or social adversary: feelings of enmity, jealousy, and rivalry, and wider political and social conflicts all played a part in influencing the denunciations of both male and female witches. Labouvie has also observed that most cases against male witches in the nearby Saar region were a result of conflict management within the male sphere of communal responsibility and activity, although this observation cannot be applied generally to other areas, as Briggs shows for the Lorraine witch-hunts.[38] In the Rhine-Meuse area, it was not only male peasants who used witchcraft slander and witchcraft denunciation in order to discredit a personal adversary and possibly bring about his or her execution. There are also numerous cases showing that witch-trials were used by some territorial lords, and also by certain lords who were the heads of high criminal courts, to get rid of political opponents, annoying creditors, and corrupt manorial or local officials.[39] The most notorious (but by no means the only) example of this process was the conspiracy planned by the Lord of Hamm, a small lordship near Luxembourg, with the Count of Manderscheid-Kail and two powerful officials from the Electorate of Trier, all of whom oversaw large-scale witch-hunts in their respective territories and districts. Their mutual target was Johann Schweistal, a wealthy and powerful court assessor in the small town of Bitburg, who was the creditor and deadly enemy of these four men. It was easy for them to encourage an increasing number of denunciations against Schweistal from those forced to confess to witchcraft, in which he was named as the king of the sabbath and leader of the witches' sect in Luxembourg.[40]

The trial of Dr Dietrich Flade must also be set in the context of the political and social conflicts that affected the city of Trier in the late sixteenth century. The city's rulers had failed in their attempt to gain autonomy within the Holy Roman Empire, and the ensuing humiliating capitulation to the power of the Elector of Trier in 1580 meant that their standing and legitimacy were seriously compromised. They – and, particularly, people connected in any way with the political and economic depression experienced in late-sixteenth-century Trier – were regarded by most citizens as corrupt traitors and opportunists, and were particularly vulnerable to suspicions of witchcraft, because it was believed that individuals first fell into sins such as ambition and greed through their seduction by the Devil. After 1585, the municipal authorities in Trier could no longer resist popular pressure in favour of witch-trials, which was accompanied by this time by riots and disturbances. The authorities' hesitant, indecisive action in the matter only succeeded in raising the suspicion that they, too, belonged to the witches' sect. The execution of Flade in 1589 pandered in part to this popular anger against witchcraft, and set in motion a train of events, in the course of which almost all of the men who had been involved in the humiliating political defeat of the city in 1580 were executed.

A fourth category of male witch, which emerged particularly in the Eifel regions of Luxembourg and the counties of Manderscheid, was that of the 'rogue'. In these areas, a significant number of men were tried as witches because their social conduct – and especially sexual misdemeanours, such as adultery, sodomy, bestiality, and incest – made them vulnerable to accusation. Here, we can see quite clearly the link between witch-trials and the effects of the Jesuits' missionary work in favour of the Counter-Reformation, which criminalized sexual misbehaviour, drunkenness, cursing, and other violations of the ideal of the pious male household head. Itinerant Jesuits preached these ideas even in the smallest villages of the region, thus encouraging the peasants to interpret social, religious and sexual misconduct as evidence of witchcraft, even in men. This process took slightly longer in the Eifel region than in Trier, as the Jesuit order was established in Luxembourg only in 1594.[41]

The two final categories of male witch that emerged in the Rhine-Meuse region can also be linked clearly to the missionary work of the

Jesuits and their campaign to establish a new moral code: the priest-witch and the cunning man. Numerous priests were tried for witchcraft in the area in the sixteenth and seventeenth centuries, although they fall into three distinct sub-groups.[42] In the first were the many priests who were accused of witchcraft because they were not living up to the newly emphasized standards of clerical celibacy and, instead, continued to share their lives and beds with concubines. Many of these female 'housekeepers', some of whom had been sexually violated by their clerical masters, were themselves tried for witchcraft and infanticide. In the process, they denounced their masters not only as accomplices, but also as plotters of the child's murder and as leaders of the witches' sect. In the Manderscheid counties of Gerolstein and Blankenheim, for example, a large-scale disciplinary crusade was started in the early-seventeenth century against parish priests who were manifestly not living according to the new Counter-Reformation ideal of the learned, disciplined, ascetic, and pious priest propagated by the Jesuits, but who were still co-habiting with their concubines and children and who, in some cases, acted as money-lenders, seduced female peasants, and were suspected of using illegal magical rituals of healing and blessing. However, other clerics, who had acted as the confessors to condemned witches, were tried for witchcraft, not because of any perceived moral failings, but because they (like the secular officials who opposed witch-hunts) were openly critical of witch-persecution. The third sub-group of priest-witches is best ranked with my sixth and final category of male witches: that of the cunning men.

As part of their campaign to propagate the new ideals of Counter-Reformation piety, the Jesuits and Peter Binsfeld fought against all kinds of popular 'superstition', including soothsaying, the use of religious objects and phrases in healing rituals, and the use of cunning folk to identify alleged harmful witches. Despite their attempts to teach people that such superstitious practices were wrong, the subculture of popular magic – with its use of the services of cunning folk – was resilient and widespread, socially.[43] However, over time a gradual change in attitude towards cunning women and men can be noticed for the Rhine-Meuse area. In the first mass witch-panic in the sixteenth century, male and female healers and witch-finders did not become a prime target for accusations in either Luxembourg or Trier. However, the seeds of the new disciplinary codes planted by the Jesuits and other agents of the Counter-Reformation began to yield fruit during the first third of the seventeenth century. During this period, in some of the Eifel regions of Luxembourg and Manderscheid, villagers and townspeople who had begun to absorb the Counter-Reformation message no longer shielded their healers and witch-finders, but denounced them to the authorities. Clergymen, hangmen, or millers who had acted as witch-doctors – magical experts who used their skills to identify harmful witches, and to counteract and protect against the effects of harmful magic – were now tried for witchcraft themselves. A famous case occurred in the later seventeenth century in Echternach, where the municipal executioner, who was also a witch-finder, prominent cunning man, healer, rogue, drunkard, and troublemaker, was accused of having used black magic with the help of a powerful book of magic.[44] Before the accusation, the executioner had, in fact, been heavily involved in the process of witch-persecution himself: in his official capacity as executioner and torturer, he had tortured suspects and pricked them for the Devil's mark, and burned the condemned. He was the first man ever to be tried for witchcraft in Echternach, and was released from custody after refusing to confess under moderate torture. The court was apparently still confident in his abilities as a witch-finder, however, as the six women he had named under interrogation as witches were all subsequently tried and executed.

For the purposes of comparison with other regions, it is also interesting to note the types of men who were not vulnerable to accusations of witchcraft in the Rhine-Meuse region. For example, apart from a few exceptions, male vagrants, beggars, or treasure-seekers were not accused of witchcraft in this area, although such men became one of the main targets of witch-hunts in other parts of the Holy Roman Empire (such as Carinthia, Salzburg, and the Tirol) during the seventeenth century. In the *Zauberer-Jackl* (Sorcerer-Jack) witch-hunts that occurred in Salzburg in the late 1670s, for instance, young vagrant men and boys made up the majority of those executed as witches and Devil-worshippers.[45] There was one final group of men who participated in the witch-hunts in the Rhine-Meuse-Moselle region to their great personal financial and social benefit, and yet (with only a few rare exceptions) managed to escape denunciation as witches: the clerks and notaries who participated in and guided the questioning of suspects, and who drew up the trial records. Their privileged position enabled them to keep their own names out of the lists of witchcraft suspects, and to manage the keeping of trial records generally to their own advantage. This position brought its own risks, however. Many complaints about the unfair manipulation of trial records by clerks and notaries – sometimes in favour of the witch-hunting committees – were brought by accused witches and their families before the imperial appeal courts, and some notaries in

Luxembourg and the Electorate of Trier were accused and punished (one was even executed), not as witches, but for the corrupt management of witch-trial records.[46]

V

Wealthy and influential men who did come under suspicion of witchcraft in the Rhine-Meuse area did, of course, have more options than poor women and men for defending themselves and their female relatives against such charges. Such men and their families usually found it easier than the unlearned, poorer suspects to make formal complaints about abuses in witch-trials at courts of appeal in Germany and, especially, in Luxembourg. These complaints helped to uncover legal scandals and highlight the excessive use of torture in witch-hunts in the region. As a result, some territorial lords tried to bring the persecution of witches by lower courts within their jurisdiction more firmly under their control. In the long term, these attempts restrained and – eventually – brought about the cessation of witch-hunts. Suspected male witches also had a range of strategies of defence that they might use before the pre-trial investigation against them even started. For example, they tried to discourage potential witnesses from giving incriminating testimony against them by means of threats of violence, blackmail, or bribery. If all these strategies failed and they were arrested, men found it easier than women to escape from custody.

Once in prison, men might have been confident – at least, initially – that their superior physical strength would enable them to endure the torture without confessing. Even the jurors and court assessors, who before their own arrests had seen torture inflicted on suspects at firsthand, seem to have underestimated hugely the physical and psychological impact that the agonies of torture would have on them. In reality, some were already demoralized by the humiliating procedures of being stripped of their own clothes (and thus the outward signs of their former social status) and of having their beards (a prominent sign of masculine honour) forcibly shaved, before the torture even started. To lose one's honour by being touched by the dishonourable executioner (who was also the torturer), and to be forced into confessing horrible sins must have been especially shameful for men who had enjoyed relatively high social status before their arrests. Some did revoke their confessions after regaining some strength in their prison cells, but, in the long-term, even these men were broken by the raw violence of torture. Once condemned, it seems that convicted men particularly feared death at the stake, probably because burning was thought to be a more dishonourable form of execution than beheading. A court assessor in Manderscheid-Blankenheim, for example, whose resistance broke after revoking his confession of witchcraft three times, finally made the witchcraft confession his interrogators wanted to hear, but added that he had also planned to murder the Count of Manderscheid-Blankenheim. He pleaded desperately to be beheaded rather than burned, claiming this alleged crime of high treason as justification!

It thus seems that men accused of witchcraft – and, especially, the former witch-hunters amongst them – endured not only physical, but also intense psychological pressure in custody, as they were forcibly deprived of the outward signs of their former status and honour. In the course of interrogation and torture, they were also forced to relinquish their sense of themselves as ideal patriarchs that headed households with honesty, integrity and self-control, as they were confronted with allegations of acts such as adultery, sodomy, and incest. As a result, it seems that more men than women who were tried for witchcraft in this region chose the ultimate option of suicide in gaol rather than to see the trial through to its bitter end.

Other male defendants, however, tried to regain some psychological sense of control over proceedings by means of a very different strategy: they presented themselves to the court as compliant instruments in the legal process of witch-hunting, giving detailed confessions with long lists of alleged accomplices. Finally, at the stake, such men took on the role of the repentant sinner, smitten with remorse over his sins and supportive of the authorities by calling for even more severe witch-hunts. The trial records of former judges and jurors do not contain any hints of remorse on their part that they had once been personally involved in the hunting of witches, although this is perhaps unsurprising. In fact, by detecting alleged 'kings of the sabbath' behind the masks of former witch-hunters, and then by executing them publicly, the persecuting authorities gained even greater justification to pursue witch-hunts with increased severity, and without any 'crisis of confidence' in their own ability to do so. On the whole, then, men accused of witchcraft had no better chance of escaping execution than women once they were put to torture; indeed, the differences of gender and social status tended even to be erased visibly by the physical and psychological effects of torture and incarceration, leaving victims – shaven and dressed in hair-shirts – whose gender was hard to ascertain. If any differences existed at all, then perhaps they worked in favour of female defendants who – perhaps because they were more accustomed to suffering humiliation, violence, and pain in everyday life – were thus better able to withstand torture and despair than men. This was, at least, a point made and bitterly lamented by contemporary demonologists.

VI

During the massive witch-hunts in the territories of Luxembourg, Trier, St Maximin and in the Manderscheid counties, men played prominent roles as both witch-hunters and as targets of accusation and denunciation, although this fact must always be set against the much higher number of female victims of the trials. In the context of their battle against all manner of heresy, the Jesuits seem to have been responsible for introducing the idea of a 'dual-gendered' sabbath into the legal proceedings of witch-trials, in the first instance by means of the music-playing boy-witch, who denounced people of both sexes as participants in the sabbath. The cases of Dietrich Flade and other men of similar status functioned to confirm everyone's worst fears about the witches' sect; that the Devil had seduced not only poor, weak-minded, old women, but also powerful men of high status, including officials and clerics. This fact reminds us that we should not simply count the percentage of men accused and executed as witches, but also think about their social status – and, in this case, their prominent role as former witch-hunters – when assessing the impact that their trials had on contemporaries. For the Jesuits – and, especially, for Binsfeld – the high-ranking male witches refuted all of the arguments of critics and sceptics against witch-persecution, as they demonstrated how large and dangerous the witches' sect had become: as a result, Binsfeld had added justification for pushing secular courts and officials to hunt witches more zealously. Any member of the authorities who was less-than-enthusiastic in hunting witches risked giving evidence of his own supposed 'infection' with witchcraft. Moreover, in order to show that the judicial system fought the malevolent sect of witches without making any distinctions of rank, at least some of the men who had acted as eager witch-hunters had – at some point – to be unmasked as witches themselves. This logic reached its apogee in the ostentatious executions of the so-called 'sabbath kings'. Here, we can see that the inclusion of men at the sabbath did not lead to greater gender equality, as, even in this imagined anti-world, social and gender hierarchy stayed in place: wealthy officials became kings of the sabbath and women remained subjected.

The key ideas that emerged in the course of the severe witch-hunts in the Rhine-Meuse area in the late sixteenth century – about the dual-gendered sabbath, the presence of boy-witches, and the possibility that men (even of the highest rank) might be witches – were then spread to a wider audience in the rest of the Holy Roman Empire by the writings of two influential demonologists, Peter Binsfeld and Martin Del Rio. Binsfeld seems to have emphasized the concept of the male witch in order to strengthen his arguments against the witch-hunt critic, Johann Weyer, while Del Rio used Binsfeld's tracts in the writing of his own, later demonology in favour of witch-hunt.[47] Del Rio's writings helped underpin the mass persecutions that occurred in the seventeenth century in Catholic (and even some Protestant) territories of the Empire, and which saw an increasing number of male witches and child-witches. Through Binsfeld and Del Rio, then, the events of the Rhine-Meuse witch-hunts, which included their particular gender profile, came to shape and influence subsequent episodes of persecution.

Notes

*This chapter presents some of the findings from the research for my Thesis of Habilitation on the witch-hunts in the smaller territories of the Rhine-Meuse region: *Hexenverfolgungen in kleinen Herrschaften – Grundlagen, Strukturen, Vergleiche, Deutungen* (forthcoming 2010). I have otherwise researched and published extensively on the witch-trials in this area. My notes will therefore refer to my publications, which give full references and quotations, rather than directly to primary sources.

1. For discussion of the term 'witch-hunt', which is used currently for all kinds of legal prosecutions as well as for lynchings of witches, see C. Larner, 'Witchcraft past and present', in C. Larner, *Witchcraft and Religion. The Politics of Popular Belief*, A. Macfarlane (ed.) (Oxford, 1984) 79–91, at 90–1; B. P. Levack, *The Witch-Hunt in Early Modern Europe*, 3rd edn, (Harlow, 2006), 2.
2. See R. Briggs, 'Women as victims? Witches, judges and the community, *French History*, 5 (1991), 438–50, at 442.
3. For some recent historiographical overviews on the question of why most witches were women, see C. Opitz-Belakhal, 'Frauen- und geschlechtergeschichtliche Perspektiven der Hexenforschung', in G. Gersmann, K. Moeller, J. M. Schmidt (eds), *Lexikon zur Geschichte der Hexenverfolgung*, historicum.net, URL: http://www.historicum.net/no-cache/persistent/artikel/5654 (accessed 24 January 2008); K. Hodgkin, 'Gender, mind and body: Feminism and psychoanalysis', in J. Barry and O. Davies (eds), *Palgrave Advances in Witchcraft Historiography* (Basingstoke, 2007), 182–202; R. M. Toivo, 'Women at Stake: Interpretations of Women's Roles in Witchcraft and Witch Hunts from the Early 20th Century to the Present', *ARV Nordic Yearbook of Folklore*, 62 (2006), 187–205; M. Wiesner-Hanks, 'Gender', in R. M. Golden (ed.), *Encyclopedia of Witchcraft. The Western Tradition*, vol. II, (Santa Barbara, CA, 2006) 407–11 (hereafter *EOW*); U. Bender-Wittmann, 'Gender in der Hexenforschung: Ansätze und Perspektiven', in D. R. Bauer, S. Lorenz and J. M. Schmidt (eds), *Geschlecht, Magie und Hexenverfolgung* (Bielefeld, 2002), 13–37.

4. Briggs, 'Women as victims?', 450; W. de Blécourt, 'The making of the female witch. Reflections on witchcraft and gender in the early modern period', *Gender & History*, 12 (2000), 287–309, at 288.
5. See A. Rowlands, 'Würzburg, prince-bischopric of', in *EOW*, vol. IV, 1230–2; R. Walinski-Kiehl, 'Bamberg, prince-bishopric of', in *EOW*, vol. I, 87–9.
6. Perhaps for commercial reasons, the titles of some recent publications imply that the author is dealing with Germany, but they are, in fact, regional case studies: see L. Roper, *Witch Craze. Terror and Fantasy in Baroque Germany* (New Haven CT, 2004), who deals with case studies from Augsburg, Marchtal and Würzburg; and J. B. Durrant, *Witchcraft, Gender and Society in Early Modern Germany* (Leiden, 2007), who examines the Prince-Bishopric of Eichstätt, where the mass persecution focused on women belonging to the urban political and craft elite.
7. See H. C. E. Midelfort, *Witch Hunting in Southwestern Germany 1562–1684* (Stanford, CA, 1972), ch. 6, especially 150, 158, 162–3; ch. 7, especially 178–90.
8. On this point, Wiesner-Hanks ('Gender', 407) is completely wrong to suggest that men were never asked about sexual contact with demons.
9. See R. Voltmer, 'Einleitung', in R. Voltmer and K. Weisenstein (eds), *Das Hexenregister des Claudius Musiel. Ein Verzeichnis von hingerichteten und besagten Personen aus dem Trierer Land (1586–1594)* (Trier, 1996) 9*–104*; R. Voltmer, 'Hexenverfolgungen im Maas-Rhein-Mosel-Raum – Ergebnisse und Perspektiven', in F. Irsigler (ed.), *Zwischen Maas und Rhein – Beziehungen, Begegnungen und Konflikte in einem europäischen Kernraum von der Spätantike bis zum 19. Jahrhundert* (Trier, 2006), 153–87; R. Voltmer, '"... ce tant exécrable et détestable crime de sortilège". Der "Bürgerkrieg" gegen Hexen und Hexenmeister im Herzogtum Luxemburg (16. und 17. Jahrhundert)', *Hémecht. Revue d'Histoire Luxembourgeoise. Zeitschrift für Luxemburger Geschichte*, 56 (2004), 57–92; R. Voltmer, 'Germany, West and Northwest', in *EOW*, vol. II, 429–37; R. Voltmer, 'Luxembourg, Duchy of', in *EOW*, vol. III, 677–80; R. Voltmer, 'St Maximin, prince-abbey of', in *EOW*, vol. IV, 1082–3; W. Rummel, *Bauern, Herren und Hexen. Studien zur Sozialgeschichte sponheimischer und kurtrierischer Hexenprozesse 1574–1664* (Göttingen, 1991); J. Dillinger, *'Böse Leute'. Hexenverfolgungen in Schwäbisch-Österreich und Kurtrier im Vergleich* (Trier, 1999).
10. See A. Heinz, '"Bei den Trierern scheint der Böse Geist seinen Sitz aufgeschlagen zu haben". Ein bisher unbekannter Bericht des Kölner Kartäuserpriors Johannes Reckschenkel (1526–1611) über Hexenverfolgungen im Trierer Land', in G. Franz and F. Irsigler (eds), *Hexenglaube und Hexenprozesse im Raum Rhein-Mosel-Saar*, 2nd edn (Trier, 1996) 449–57, at 451.
11. See my publications cited in note 9, and also: R. Voltmer, 'Zwischen Herrschaftskrise, Wirtschaftsdepression und Jesuitenpropaganda. Hexenverfolgungen in der Stadt Trier (15.–17. Jahrhundert)', *Jahrbuch für westdeutsche Landesgeschichte*, 27 (2001), 37–107; R. Voltmer, '"Germany's first superhunt"? – Rezeption und Konstruktion der sogenannten Trierer Verfolgungen (16.–21. Jahrhundert)', in K. Moeller and B. Schmidt (eds), *Realität und Mythos. Hexenverfolgung und Rezeptionsgeschichte* (Hamburg, 2003), 225–58.
12. This phrase is, for example, used by W. Monter, 'Witch Trials in Continental Europe, 1560–1660', in B. Ankarloo, S. Clark and W. Monter, *The Athlone*

History of Witchcraft and Magic in Europe. The Period of Witch Trials (London, 2002), 1–52, at 23. I have reconstructed the process by which this imprecise term entered and influenced the historiography of witchcraft in Voltmer, '"Germany's first superhunt"?'

13. See Voltmer, 'Hexenverfolgungen im Maas-Rhein-Mosel-Raum', 170–86; W. Rummel and R. Voltmer, *Hexen und Hexenverfolgungen in der Frühen Neuzeit* (Darmstadt, 2008), 86.
14. See R. Voltmer and H. Eiden, 'Rechtsnormen, Gerichts- und Herrschaftspraxis bei Hexereiverfahren in Lothringen, Luxemburg, Kurtrier und St. Maximin während des 16. und 17. Jahrhunderts', in R. Beier-de Haan, R. Voltmer and F. Irsigler (eds), *Hexenwahn. Ängste der Neuzeit* (Berlin, 2002), 60–71.
15. See R. Voltmer, 'Hexenjagd im Territorium der Reichsabtei St. Maximin (16.–17. Jahrhundert): Zwei Untertanen-Supplikationen (1595/um 1630)', in W. Reichert, G. Minn and R. Voltmer (eds), *Quellen zur Geschichte des Rhein-Maas-Raumes: ein Lehr- und Lernbuch* (Trier, 2006), 226–71; K. Stegmann, *'Die gefangene leugknet alles'. Untersuchungen zu Entstehungsbedingungen und Ausprägungen frühneuzeitlicher Hexenverhörprotokolle* (MA dissertation, University of Münster, 2006); published at http://www.historicum.net/themen/hexenforschung/thementexte/magisterarbeiten/; E. Topalović, *Sprachwahl – Textsorte – Dialogstruktur. Zu Verhörprotokollen aus Hexenprozessen im 17. Jahrhundert* (Trier, 2003).
16. Larner, 'Witchcraft past and present', 80–1.
17. See R. Walinski-Kiehl, 'Males, "masculine honour" and witch hunting in seventeenth-century Germany', *Men and Masculinities*, 6 (2004), 254–71, at 267.
18. See W. Rummel, 'Communal persecution', in *EOW*, vol. I, 201–3; R. Voltmer, 'Monopole, Ausschüsse, Formalparteien: Vorbereitung, Finanzierung und Manipulation von Hexenprozessen durch private Klagekonsortien', in H. Eiden and R. Voltmer (eds), *Hexenprozesse und Gerichtspraxis* (Trier, 2002), 5–67. There is much ongoing debate about the status and significance of these witch-hunting committees. Johannes Dillinger, who based his study of the witch-hunts in the Electorate of Trier on very sparse surviving primary source material, suggested that the committees were established by local communities as instruments for regaining political and juridical autonomy (see Dillinger, *'Böse Leute'*). However, even if the committees were rooted in a strong tradition of village autonomy, I would argue that Dillinger takes the idea of 'communalism' and its expression through witch-hunting committees too far. During the more than hundred years of witch-hunting in the Rhine-Meuse-Moselle area, the composition of the committees changed from decade to decade and from territory to territory, depending on the scope given to them by the territorial government, the local lordships, or by the bailiffs and district magistrates. Moreover, the local officials can in no way be characterized as 'agents' of the sovereign government, as Dillinger suggests. For further discussion, see W. Rummel, 'Das "ungestüme Umherlaufen" der Untertanen. Zum Verhältnis von religiöser Ideologie, sozialem Interesse und Staatsräson in den Hexenverfolgungen im Rheinland', *Rheinische Vierteljahrsblätter*, 67 (2003), 121–61; and R. Voltmer, 'Konspiration gegen Herrschaft und Staat? Überlegungen zur Rolle gemeindlicher Klagekonsortien in den Hexenverfolgungen des Rhein-Maas-Raumes',

in J. Dillinger and J. M. Schmidt (eds), *Staatsbildung und Hexenprozess* (Bielefeld, 2008), 213–44.

19. For discussion of the primary sources, see Voltmer, 'Hexenverfolgungen im Maas-Rhein-Mosel-Raum', 160–70; and R. Voltmer, 'Ein Amerikaner in Trier. George Lincoln Burr (1857–1938) und sein Beitrag zu den Sammelschwerpunkten "Hexerei und Hexenverfolgungen" an der Cornell University (Ithaca/New York) sowie an der Stadtbibliothelk Trier. Mit einem Inventar', *Kurtrierisches Jahrbuch*, 47 (2007), 447–89.
20. In Lorraine, about 28 per cent of all accused were male, see R. Briggs, *The Witches of Lorraine* (Oxford, 2007), 331–68. For more on the witch-hunts in Lorraine, see W. Monter, *A Bewitched Duchy. Lorraine and its Dukes 1477–1736* (Geneva, 2007); J. Rœhrig, *À mort, la sorcière! Sorcellerie et répression en Lorraine XVIe–XVIIe siècles* (Strasbourg, 2007); E. Biesel, *Hexenjustiz, Volksmagie und soziale Konflikte im lothringischen Raum* (Trier, 1998).
21. See Dillinger, *'Böse Leute'*, 97–105; including the very uncertain numbers given by chronicles and the Jesuit *Litterae Annuae*, Dillinger counts 788 trials with 699 executions.
22. See the somewhat dated works by H. Breiden, *Die Hexenprozesse der Grafschaft Blankenheim von 1589 bis 1643* (PhD thesis, University of Bonn, 1954); A. Kettel, *Von Hexen und Unholden. Hexenprozesse in der West- und Zentraleifel* (Prüm, 1988), as well as the very helpful first overview by W. Rummel, 'Hexenverfolgungen in den Manderscheider Territorien (1528–1641)', in *Die Manderscheider. Eine Eifler Adelsfamilie. Herrschaft–Wirtschaft–Kultur*, exhibition catalogue (Koblenz, 1991), 37–48; R. Voltmer, 'Hexenprozesse in der Herrschaft Kail unter Dietrich II. von Manderscheid-Kail (1591–1613)', in E. Gerten, J. Kreutz and C. Rech (eds), *Oberkail. Geschichte eines Dorfes in der südlichen Eifel* (Neuerburg, 2001), 47–52, 402–3; R. Voltmer, 'Hexereiverfahren und herrschaftspolitische Interessen: Die Prozesse Eisenschmitt (1592, 1595 und 1600)', in E. Gerten (ed.), *Eisenschmitt. Von der mittelalterlichen Eisenhütte zum Eifeler Wohn- und Erholungsort* (Wittlich, 2006), 327–36, 442–3.
23. We must, however, beware of sweeping generalizations. In the 1570s in the city of Trier, for example, a defamation suit took place involving allegations of harmful magic that made no mention of the sabbath, whereas an exceptional trial was held in the territory of St Maximin at around the same time in which four women and one man were tried for sabbath witchcraft; see Voltmer, 'Herrschaftskrise', 56–9.
24. See R. Voltmer, 'Claudius Musiel oder die Karriere eines Hexenrichters. Auch ein Beitrag zur Trierer Sozialgeschichte des späten 16. Jahrhunderts', in G. Franz and F. Irsigler (eds), *Methoden und Konzepte historischer Hexenforschung* (Trier, 1998), 211–54, at 250–1.
25. See Voltmer, 'Herrschaftskrise'; R. Voltmer, 'Jesuits (Society of Jesus)', in *EOW*, vol. III, 586–9.
26. See George Lincoln Burr, 'The Fate of Dietrich Flade', *Papers of the American Historical Association*, 5 (1891), 189–243; R. Voltmer, 'Flade, Dietrich', in *EOW*, vol. II, 378–9; R. Voltmer, 'Der Fall des Trier Stadtschultheißen Dr. Dietrich Flade: Vom Hexenrichter zum Hexenmeister', *Damals. Das Magazin für Geschichte und Kultur*, 6 (2002), 14–19; J. Dillinger, 'Richter als Angeklagte. Hexenprozesse gegen herrschaftliche Amtsträger in Kurtrier und Schwäbisch-Österreich', in H. Schnabel-Schüle (ed.), *Vergleichende*

Perspektiven – Perspektiven des Vergleichs. Studien zur europäischen Geschichte von der Spätantike bis ins 20. Jahrhundert (Mainz, 1998), 124–69.

27. See note 7.
28. Voltmer, 'Germany's first superhunt?', 251–7.
29. For biographical notes on Binsfeld, see J. Dillinger, 'Binsfeld, Peter', in *EOW*, vol. I, 122–5; for Binsfeld's involvement in the Maximin and Trier witch-hunts, see Voltmer, 'Herrschaftskrise'; on Binsfeld's demonology, see also R. Schulte, *Hexenmeister. Die Verfolgung von Männern im Rahmen der Hexenverfolgung von 1530–1730 im Alten Reich*, 2nd edn (Frankfurt am Main, 2001), 138–9.
30. See P. C. van der Eerden, 'Der Teufelspakt bei Petrus Binsfeld und Cornelius Loos', in G. Franz and F. Irsigler (eds), *Hexenglaube und Hexenprozesse im Raum Rhein-Mosel-Saar*, 2nd edn (Trier, 1996), 51–71, at 53.
31. Alison Rowlands suggests five ways in which men became involved in witch trials in the German Imperial Free City of Rothenburg ob der Tauber, although no men were ever executed for witchcraft there: as alleged sabbath-attenders; as self-confessed boy-witches; as secondary witches who were related to a female witch; as cunning men; and in their own right. See A. Rowlands, *Witchcraft Narratives in Germany: Rothenburg, 1561–1652* (Manchester, 2003), 160–8. Rolf Schulte divides the male witches of the northern German territories of Holstein, Sachsen-Lauenburg and Lübeck into the two categories of 'primary' and 'secondary' male witches: the latter were related to a female witch. See Schulte, *Hexenmeister*, 215–43.
32. Robin Briggs also casts doubt on this assumption in his detailed study of the Lorraine witch-hunts; see R. Briggs, *The Witches of Lorraine*, 335–40. For examples of men who were accused because they were related to reputed female witches from Rothenburg, see Rowlands, *Witchcraft Narratives*, 161.
33. See R. Voltmer and K. Weisenstein (eds), *Das Hexenregister des Claudius Musiel. Ein Verzeichnis von hingerichteten und besagten Personen aus dem Trierer Land (1586–1594)* (Trier, 1996), 401–11, for genealogical tables giving details of the households of 17 'witch-families'; and Briggs, *The Witches of Lorraine*, 359–62.
34. Voltmer, 'Herrschaftskrise', 67–102. For examples of boy-witches from Rothenburg, see Rowlands, *Witchcraft Narratives*, 160–1.
35. For biographical details on Löher, see H. de Waardt, 'Löher, Herman (1595–1678)', in *EOW*, vol. III, 665–6. For Löher's tract, see Herrmann Löher, *Hochnötige Unterthanige Wehmütige Klage Der Frommen Unschültigen*, T. P. Becker and T. Becker (eds) with commentaries by T. Becker, R. Decker and H. de Waardt (internet publication, historicum.net, 2001): http://extern.historicum.net/loeher/
36. As Robert Walinski-Kiehl has demonstrated for Bamberg in 'Males, "masculine honour" and witch hunting', 266.
37. Voltmer, '"Germany's first superhunt"?', 254.
38. E. Labouvie, 'Men in Witchcraft Trials: Towards a Social Anthropology of 'Male' Understandings of Magic and Witchcraft', in U. Rublack (ed.), *Gender in Early Modern German History* (Cambridge, 2002), 49–68; Briggs, *The Witches of Lorraine*, 366–7. Briggs also has an example of a conspiracy conducted as a witch-trial against an elderly village notable; see *The Witches of Lorraine*, 353–5.

39. See R. Voltmer and W. Rummel, 'Die Verfolgung eigener Interessen durch Untertanen, Funktionäre und Herrschaften bei den Hexenjagden im Rhein-Maas-Mosel-Raum', in H.-G. Borck (ed.), *Unrecht und Recht. Kriminalität und Gesellschaft im Wandel, 1500–2000* (Koblenz, 2002), 297–339, at 327–8.
40. For discussion of the Schweistal case, see B. Fuge, '"Le roi des sorciers": Ein luxemburgischer Hexereiprozess vor dem Grand Conseil de Malines, ca. 1590–1609', in H. Eiden and R. Voltmer (eds), *Hexenprozesse und Gerichtspraxis* (Trier, 2002), 69–121.
41. See R. Voltmer, 'Gegen die Unzucht. Nachtridentinische Sittenreform, Kriminalisierung und Verfolgung devianter Sexualität im Erzbistum Trier (16. und 17. Jahrhundert)', in H.-G. Borck (ed.), *Unrecht und Recht. Kriminalität und Gesellschaft im Wandel, 1500–2000* (Koblenz, 2002), 481–511; R. Voltmer, 'Konflikt, Streit, Gewalt: Geschlechterverhältnis und Sexualität in den Dörfern des Luxemburger, Eifeler und Trierer Landes zur Zeit der Hexenverfolgungen', in R. Voltmer and G. Gehl (eds), *Alltagsleben und Magie in Hexenprozessen* (Weimar, 2003), 33–46. Robin Briggs presents comparable categories in his discussion of male witches in Lorraine in sections entitled 'Rash Talk and Suspicious Conduct' and 'Sexual Misconduct and Witchcraft'; see Briggs, *The Witches of Lorraine*, 342–53.
42. See A. Kettel, 'Kleriker im Hexenprozeß. Beispiele aus den Manderscheider Territorien und dem Trierer Land', in G. Franz and F. Irsigler (eds), *Methoden und Konzepte der historischen Hexenforschung* (Trier, 1998), 169–91.
43. For examples from Rothenburg, see Rowlands, *Witchcraft Narratives*, 162–4.
44. See R. Voltmer, 'Henker, Heiler, Hexenbanner – Hexenmeister? Der Fall des Echternacher Scharfrichters und Wasenmeisters Caspar Back (17. Jahrhundert)', in F. Irsigler and G. Minn (eds), *Porträt einer europäischen Region. Der Rhein-Maas-Raum in historischen Lebensbildern* (Trier, 2005), 156–77. On herdsmen and animal healers as witches, see also Briggs, *The Witches of Lorraine*, 340–2.
45. See Schulte, *Hexenmeister*, 243–64; G. Mülleder, 'Salzburg, prince-archbishopric of', in *EOW*, vol. IV, 1000–1.
46. See Voltmer, 'Der "Bürgerkrieg" gegen Hexen und Hexenmeister', and Rummel, *Bauern, Herren und Hexen*, 255–8.
47. See Schulte, *Hexenmeister*, 143–7.

5

Why Some Men and Not Others? The Male Witches of Eichstätt

Jonathan Durrant

I

Eichstätt, a small, fractured prince-bishopric on the fringes of the Bavarian Duchy, experienced a relatively intense series of witch-persecutions between 1590 and 1631. Of those arrested for witchcraft in the territory over this period, only about 12 per cent (or, up to 35 suspects) were men.[1] These figures are low, even when compared with gender ratios among witch-suspects in other German and western European witchcraft episodes, and one might be tempted to ignore them as an insignificant aberration.[2] Yet, the presence of these men in the Eichstätt data is perhaps the most troubling aspect of this particular series of witch-hunts. Whilst it is a relatively simple exercise to explain why well over 200 women were arrested in the principality over the same period, the arrests of men such as Enders and Georg Gutmann, Valtin Lanng, Hans Baur and Michael Hochenschildt can seem arbitrary. The prosecutions of the female witch-suspects were undertaken in a systematic fashion as the local judges and, later, ecclesiastical witch-commissioners worked their way through the names of accomplices supplied by witch-defendants faced with the threat of torture. As the first witches arrested were mainly women, their alleged accomplices tended to be drawn from their everyday networks of female kin, neighbours, and friends. The interrogators therefore soon possessed a very long list of female accomplices, a list that could have sustained persecution well beyond 1631 had circumstances not forced an end to it then. The interrogators also chose to ignore the very many denunciations of male witch-accomplices made by both the female witches and some of the men they did arrest.[3] But why did they choose these men in the first place when so many of the other alleged but unmolested male accomplices were of a similar age and status?

There are, of course, an increasing number of potential explanations for the presence of male suspects in the witchcraft data as historians attempt to account for them in plausible ways, but none seems entirely adequate for the Eichstätt cases. Perceived magical skill, deep-rooted factionalism, religious tension, and personality, for example, seem to have had very little impact on why the male witches of Eichstätt were denounced as accomplices and, later, cited before the witch-commissioners.[4] Reflecting on the data from these cases, it appears that the answer to the 'Why men?' question lies less in personal skills, beliefs, and characteristics than in a combination of other factors: the naming process in which accomplices were identified, the positions the suspected men were able to maintain within their communities, and the progress of the local witch-persecution. These factors are particular to the Eichstätt experience of witch-hunting, and it is difficult to use them to develop a general Continent-wide theory about the prosecution of male suspects. I will also argue that this particularity indicates that gender was not significant in popular conceptions of the 'witch', either in Eichstätt, or much of the rest of Europe.

In analysing the Eichstätt cases, it is important to know the identities of the men, and how they came to be arrested by the witch-commission. With this data, I will evaluate, as far as possible, the circumstances that might have led the interrogators to these individuals. The question 'Why not other men?' is trickier and, to a degree, any answer will be impressionistic and speculative, but it is a necessary question that many historians of the witch's gender elide. Too often, their studies focus narrowly on the men or women accused – overlooking the obvious complication that the characters of these suspects and the circumstances that made them vulnerable to witchcraft accusations were shared by many other Europeans. There were some exceptions – such as Chonrad Stoeckhlin, or the 'Ladies from Outside' – but, broadly-speaking, for every 'exemplary' Margery Stanton or Ursula Grön, there must have been thousands of curmudgeonly, very poor, old women who suffered difficult relations with their neighbours without being suspected – much less accused – of witchcraft.[5] The period of intense witch-persecution was, perhaps not coincidentally, also a period in which many individuals found themselves pushed to the margins of societies unable to cope adequately with rising numbers of indigent persons.[6] As this situation worsened throughout the first decades of the seventeenth century, the number of potential witches must have increased, but the geographical, chronological, and statistical patchiness of witch-persecution, even within principalities such as Eichstätt or counties such as Essex, suggests that this potential was not often realized. The failure to recognize the ubiquity of these marginalized characters is where too many studies that attempt to analyze the 'women question' are flawed, especially where they propose a theory that seeks to demonstrate that witch-persecution was a phenomenon driven, in part, 'from below'.

Given that burdensome poverty and old age were common to many women at this time, they and gender can only have been relatively insignificant factors in turning the potential for accusation into reality. Rather than seeking narrow generalizations with which to answer the 'gender question', and for which many exceptions can be found, we should be striving, instead, for a comprehensive range of reasons why individuals could become vulnerable to indictment as a witch. This was the challenge implicitly set by Robin Briggs more than a decade ago, when he defended the 'wide range of analyses and explanations offered in [*Witches and Neighbours* (1996)]', but it has rarely been taken up.[7] Asking why some men were arrested and others avoided suspicion or prosecution helps define the limits of this range in ways that a focus on female witches cannot. The statistics about these female witches have been handled poorly. A tendency to seek lowest common denominators (female, old, poor, and marginalized), which can be forced into a shocking stereotype, blurs and demeans the harrowing experiences of large numbers of individual suspects, such as those in the Eichstätt case, who were mostly married mothers, highly integrated into dense networks of association. The wide geographical and chronological distribution of the many fewer cases of male witches means that the men involved shared fewer personal or social characteristics, and the data resist rigid typification. The differences between cases remain, and have to be incorporated into the analysis rather than glossed over in favour of a misleading stereotype.

II

The maximum possible number of male witches arrested over the four decades of intense witch-persecution in the Prince-Bishopric of Eichstätt is 35. The actual figure, taking into account errors in the collation of data by the Nazi *Hexensonderkommando* (Witchcraft Special Research Unit) and earlier historians, is more likely to have been 29. All of these men were arrested during the third, longest, and most intense phase of persecution (1617–31) – the majority in its final six years.[8] Apart from one or two exceptions such as the priest Father Johann Reichard, they tended to be married, middle-class, and mostly middle-aged, and bound to their village or town communities by profession, politics, and family. The youngest men arrested by the witch-commissioners – the brothers Enders and Georg Gutmann – were also the first. The brothers were both in their twenties when they were arrested in December 1617.[9] Whilst the occupations of these two men are not known, their father had been the *Richter* (judge) of the village of Pietenfeld; he was also a tavern-keeper, a respectable occupation in the principality.[10] Later male witches were older, ranging from Valtin Lanng who was in his thirties to men such as Paulus Danner, who had adult grandchildren. Lanng was a cobbler, Danner a brewer. Other men, mostly in their forties and fifties, included several members of families that made up the secular elite of the town, such as Lorenz Bonschab, Christoph Lauterer, Jacob Rabel, Michael Rottinger, and Hans Stigeliz. Bonschab's family was very well connected. His sister Maria married the chancellor of the principality, Bartholomäus Richel.[11] Lauterer and a male member of the Rehel family were *Bürgermeister* (town mayors) when they were arrested;[12] Stigeliz was the *Spitalmeister* (Master of the Hospital).[13] Of the other men, Lorenz Brandt was a tailor, Michael Hochenschildt a tavern-keeper, and another, probably one Hans Wagner, a carter.[14] The lowest status male witch was probably Michael Ghayer, a horse-herd of about the same age as his friends the Gutmann brothers.[15] No witches, male or female, came from other lesser social groups such as the numerous, yet poor cloth-workers who did not sit on the local secular councils.[16] All of the witches, as far as one can tell, were Catholic, and resisted the temptation to migrate to one of the many Protestant states within or on the borders of the principality. With one exception (Anna Harding), no witch of either sex was associated with magical practices.[17]

The restricted social milieux from which the Eichstätt witches were drawn meant that almost all of the male witches were also related by consanguinial or affinal ties to suspected or convicted female witches. As well as Lorenz Bonschab's sister, they included several other members of the extended Bonschab family (Anna, Barbara, Kunigunda and Ursula), Anna Schiller (mother of the Gutmann brothers), Anna Spät (Georg Gutmann's mother-in-law), Barbara Khager (Ghayer's mother), the wives of Lanng and Rottinger, Danner's daughter, and Rabel's wife Barbara and her sister-in-law by a previous marriage, Barbara Apotheker. The marital ties and the corresponding relationships recognized through witnessing marriages and standing as godparents to children would have cemented political alliances formed through participation on the councils, and through less formal friendships.[18]

This profile for the male witches mirrors that for the much larger body of female suspects in Eichstätt; they, too, were married, mostly middle-class, and mostly middle-aged. These women – as with the sisters-in-law Barbara Rabel and Barbara Apotheker, or the gossips Anna Schiller, Anna Spät, and Barbara Khager – were bound by various formal and informal relationships that found expression in the interrogation transcripts, in the same way as their menfolk.[19] Such profiles and relationships allow one to discount several factors by virtue of which, it has been argued, some men found themselves before witch-hunters. Neither the male nor the female witches of Eichstätt can be said to have been marginalized economically, or by their age: nor was there an attack on men or women who overtly or otherwise laid claim to another religious belief or to magical practices. To understand why anyone was arrested as a witch in the principality, regardless of their sex, one must look to other explanations.

III

Apart from its gender emphasis, the social profile of the typical Eichstätt witch was exclusively the by-product of the processes of interrogation. The final phase of persecution, during which all the male suspects were arrested, began among respectable men and women in the outlying villages of the district of Eichstätt. It is not possible to ascertain why this should have been the case, because the extant interrogation documentation begins after the first suspects were arrested in late 1617. The persecution then rapidly spread the few kilometres to the town of Eichstätt itself, to which it was then confined with only a handful of exceptions. The processes by which the persecution escalated were typical of a chain-reaction hunt. By the time the suspect was asked about her accomplices, she had already confessed to being a witch, sealing the pact with the Devil, performing all the acts of sacrilege one associates with heresy, and harming various of her neighbours. To facilitate her confession, the suspect would have been tortured, psychologically abused, and sometimes harassed physically or sexually in the town hall where she would have been held during her trial.[20] When she began naming her accomplices, the suspect would have been a broken woman, eager to please her tormentors and avoid further pain. It is not surprising that most suspects at this point readily reeled off a list of names for the witch-commissioners. Generally, the interrogators did not need to resort to anything harsher than reminding the suspect not to denounce individuals who had already been executed, and verbally prompting the flow of names. The suspect was not physically or mentally in a position to develop and sustain complex strategies to protect her friends and closer neighbours, and the lists of accomplices therefore reflect the deeply intimate relationships of small-town life. Many of these relationships can be traced through the baptismal and marriage registers, and confirmed in other parts of the suspects' confessions.

As the persecution began among respectable middling-sort men and women, it was inevitable that it should escalate among this social class to the exclusion of almost all other groups. As I have noted, artisans such as the cloth-workers, numerous as they were, did not feature in the persecution, either as witch-suspects, accusers, or witnesses. Similarly, only one servant was brought before the commissioners as a witch, and her testimony did not lead to a further escalation among that group, or the villagers in Berching where she was resident at the time of her arrest.[21] Only a handful of other witches were not attached to the families of the local secular elite by birth or marriage. They included the priest Reichard, and the healer and prostitute Anna Harding. Their professions did, however, bring them into close proximity with these families.[22]

Accounting for the general social profile of the Eichstätt witch is a relatively straightforward task. Accounting for her femininity is more complex. The earlier phases of persecution in 1590–2 and 1603 focused exclusively on women, and significantly more women than men were arrested at the very beginning of the third phase of persecution. The networks of association to which these women belonged and which helped fuel the witch-hunts also tended to be highly gendered, and their existence goes some way to providing a broad explanation of the gender ratio in the data. They do not, however, help explain why such a high proportion (about 88 per cent) of the witches arrested in Eichstätt were female. This figure masks another, more intriguing set of statistics. The proportion of men denounced as accomplices by individual witch-suspects did not always correspond to the proportion among those arrested by the witch-commissioners. Twelve of the 30 accomplices named by Margretha Bittelmayr, for example, were men.[23] The lists of accomplices provided by two male witches, Peter Porzin and Hans Stigeliz, offer an even starker contrast with the execution data; they were dominated by their male associates (over 70 per cent in each case).[24] If the interrogators had been following their own procedures rigorously, the naming process would have led to a greater proportion of male suspects at a much earlier date than the final six years of the persecution; it also had the potential to transform the hunt into a male-dominated one. This did not happen and, therefore, another dynamic must have influenced the focus on female witches.

IV

The process of selecting suspects for arrest adopted by the witch-commissioners almost certainly accounts for the significant discrepancy between the proportion of men denounced as accomplices and the proportion finally indicted as witches. This process had its foundation in both the interrogators' demonological outlook and their learned misogyny. I agree with Lara Apps and Andrew Gow that judges such as the Eichstätt commissioners took what one might call a flexible approach to the binary opposition that seems to have dominated their thinking about who could, and who could not be a witch.[25] This flexible approach allowed them to cast men, regardless of age and social status, in the role of witch as the examples described above demonstrate. For the Eichstätt commissioners, therefore, the notional dual classification system, if they could have articulated it at all, was at best a guiding principle. For them, as for the author of the *Malleus maleficarum* (c.1486) and other demonologies, witches were more likely to be women, because they were more likely to be weak-minded.[26] For the same reason, these female witches were also likely to lie. On this basis, it would have been possible for the witch-commissioners to dismiss the denunciations of alleged male accomplices as mere delusions or malicious attacks. Classic demonology would have allowed both of these options. The ninth-century *Canon episcopi* articulated the belief that witches, as the followers of Diana, were deluded into believing that they had flown to Sabbaths, and performed various heretical rites there; by implication, not one of the people they claimed to have seen at these gatherings could really have been there, even if they, too, were followers of pagan cults.[27] The *Malleus*, on the other hand, warns of the vengeful acts that female witches might perpetrate against their neighbours and, given the opportunity, their judges and warders.[28] It was probably this combination of beliefs that led to the concentration on the alleged female accomplices in Eichstätt. Whilst their male counterparts were left to one side, however, they were not necessarily dismissed or ignored.

A significant practical problem for the Eichstätt interrogators was that they were unable to prosecute more than a handful of witchcraft cases simultaneously. The town hall could only accommodate a few prisoners at any one time, and they were tried by two teams of commissioners and one executioner and his assistant, working in a limited amount of space. Whilst this meant that progress on the witch-hunt was slow, it also forced the interrogators to keep their records in good order, because they knew that they would have to refer to them much later. These records included lists of denunciations against named individuals abstracted from ongoing cases. The most striking of these lists is that compiled for Paul Gabler. There are three versions of this list of the 22 denunciations laid against him between 1622 and the end of the persecutions in 1631.[29] Clearly, the commissioners were taking careful note of these denunciations, even though Gabler was never arrested.

Understanding the prejudices of the witch-commissioners, and the processes by which they chose to arrest women, helps explain why there was a higher proportion of men among alleged accomplices than arrested suspects, and why the commissioners did not evince any trouble prosecuting a succession of male witches. It does not, however, help one understand why only certain men found themselves before the commissioners. There are three possible explanations that need to be examined in this regard: that these men were denounced more often than others by witch-suspects under interrogation; that they maintained closer ties to female witch-suspects than the unmolested men; and that their relationships with other men of a similar status were fractious, perhaps to the extent of creating factions within the polity.

V

Once the final phase of persecution was well under way in Eichstätt, suspects tended to be arrested after they had been denounced as accomplices by a series of other witches. As with Margretha Bittelmayr, Christoph Lauterer, for example, was denounced by 21 witch-suspects, one fewer than Paul Gabler; Peter Porzin was denounced by 15.[30] In contrast, the interrogation transcripts reveal that the men who avoided prosecution seem to have been named very few times in the extant lists of alleged witch-accomplices. The clergyman Christoff Otto von Muckenthal, for example, was denounced by five suspects, and Hans Danner (a baker) and Georg Schwarz (a servant) by two each.[31] At first glance, it would appear that men such as Lauterer and Porzin were arrested simply because they had been 'seen' at the witches' sabbaths by many more suspects. If this were the case, the interrogators would have been following a clearly defined procedure, arresting suspects not merely on the basis of gender, but also on that of greater *indicia*.

Such an impression is, however, false. One knows how many suspects named Bittelmayr, Lauterer, and Porzin because the witch-commissioners recorded that information on their files. Had they not been arrested, the existing documentation would show (incorrectly) that Porzin had only been denounced as an accomplice by two suspects, and Bittelmayr by just one.[32] This is because the survival of the interrogation transcripts and related material is patchy. A great deal of information can be gleaned from the documents that do survive, but not all of it is available for each individual. If other interrogation transcripts and the abstracted lists of denunciations laid against Muckenthal, Danner, and Schwarz were available, one might find that they, as Gabler, had also been seen by many of the witch-suspects at their gatherings. It seems, therefore, that the number of times a man was denounced as an accomplice did not increase the likelihood that he would eventually be arrested as a witch.

VI

If the witch-suspects did not denounce one group of men any more frequently than another, did the male suspects perhaps maintain closer ties to female witch-suspects than their neighbours? One of the more dismissive interpretations of the presence of men in the witch-trial data is that they tended to be related to female witches under investigation. Apps and Gow have neatly pointed out the inconsistencies in this argument, but the issue bears further brief discussion.[33] I noted above several examples that show that the male witches of Eichstätt were closely related to their female counterparts, either by birth or marriage. One could also observe that nearly all of the women in this list were tried and executed before their male kin. It is not possible, however, to rehearse the relationship argument from this data. Most of the female witches were married, or only recently widowed and, because the majority had spent their entire lives in the wider bishopric or principality, if not the town and its surrounding district, they all had numerous male kin in the area. If a close relationship with a female suspect was a significant factor in identifying a male suspect, these dense and intricate kinship networks would have nurtured many more male witches than were actually prosecuted.

A second problem with this interpretation is that there were men, such as Georg Mayr, who retained contact with and, in Mayr's case, tried to help free their suspected wives and other female kin. Mayr gained access to Maria, his imprisoned wife, in a failed attempt to get her pregnant and, by this means, seek clemency from the interrogators.[34] To gain access to the town hall, he had bribed Maria's bed-watcher and the wife of the caretaker. He then had sex with a woman who was eventually executed as a witch. In doing so, he imperilled his person and his soul; according to early modern demonology, Maria might well have harmed him by her touch, or seduced him into the witch sect. And yet, neither Georg Mayr, nor his brother who had helped him, nor the two town hall employees were arrested as witches. As early in the final phase of persecution as 1618, the interrogators were not making the presumption that close contact with a witch, even where it involved criminality and intimacy, cast suspicion on her relative.

It is also the case that the female kin of male witches did not necessarily find themselves accused of witchcraft. Enders and Georg Gutmann were forced to name their younger siblings, Jacob, Richella, Catharina and Lorenz.[35] Although their ages ranged from seven to 15 years, which might have protected them from prosecution in the early years of this hunt, the interrogators did not return to them after they reached adulthood. Neither did the interrogators pursue Enders's wife, who was still alive when he was arrested; in fact, she does not seem to have been named by any of her in-laws or their friends who were tried as witches. It cannot, therefore, be said that a relationship with a witch of either gender made an individual more vulnerable to denunciation by a witch-suspect, or to arrest by the witch-commissioners.

VII

A further possible explanation for the presence of particular men among the Eichstätt witches is that their characters made them vulnerable to arrest. After completing his account of his activities as a witch, Georg Gutmann was asked how he had sinned further. He answered by describing fornication with a maid (which left her pregnant), the theft of some grain from his family, and bestial acts committed in his youth.[36] Several witches, male or female, also confessed to fornication; in Margretha Bittelmayr's case with another woman, usually as a prelude to sex with the Devil.[37] Michael Hochenschildt remembered a disagreement with Valtin Lanng's wife over a pair of shoes, and confessed to harming the livestock of men with whom he had quarrelled (one of whom he claimed to have hit).[38] In her description of Michael Girtenstihl as one of her accomplices, Bittelmayr characterized him as vexatious.[39] In the absence of a witch-persecution, most of these criminal or anti-social acts could have got these men into trouble, especially at a time when the reformists were driving the political and spiritual agenda in the Prince-Bishopric. If they had not been arrested, the men might, at the very least, have disturbed the peace, and found themselves marginalized by their neighbours.

Gutmann's activities aside, however, these confessions of wrongdoing are really very minor. Neighbours tended to rub along with vexatious individuals who were integrated into the community, as Girtenstihl seems to have been; and fornication was commonplace. Hochenschildt's disagreements revolved around isolated incidents that had happened many years before his arrest – he could not recall any recent episode– and, as he observed to his interrogators, the problem of the shoes caused 'no mortal enmity'.[40] Even if Girtenstihl and Hochenschildt were vulnerable to arrest because they tended to be argumentative, they were not representative of the male witches in the territory. None of the others confessed to, or was accused of similar acts.

If one compares this slight evidence of anti-social behaviour among male witch-suspects with the descriptions of Paul Gabler's behaviour at the witches' sabbaths, one can place it in clearer perspective. From the 22 denunciations laid against Gabler, one gains the impression that he was a charismatic individual. In six of these denunciations, he is described as kissing the confessing suspect or one of her accomplices, and sometimes dancing, making merry, or fornicating with them.[41] No other male accomplice is described as having the same irresistible pull for the wives of his colleagues. The suspects might, of course, have taken the opportunity to express fantasies that they or their gossips had entertained about Gabler. Nonetheless, the descriptions must have been troubling for the witch-commissioners. As secretary to the court council, Gabler was responsible with them for imposing the bishop's reformation agenda on his subjects. One key element of this agenda was to regularize marriages. Many couples of the secular elite had not bothered to get married properly and were, from a Catholic Reformation perspective, fornicating.[42] Laying aside the witchcraft, Gabler's apparent behaviour at the sabbaths seemingly undermined the agenda he should have been implementing. As with Georg Mayr's illicit attempt to get his wife pregnant, it must have been considerably more worrying to the commissioners than the odd quarrelsome individual. And yet, neither Gabler nor Mayr was arrested as a witch. Character might have played some role in individual witchcraft cases, but it was neither a factor that linked male witches, nor one that the interrogators resorted to systematically as they worked their way through the many names they had been given.

VIII

A more promising interpretation of the men arrested as witches lies in the possibility that the secular elite was divided in some way, although probably not to the extent that it was split by factionalism. As far as one can tell, any friction within this elite was not deep-rooted, as it was in Rye where the witch-trials gave it dramatic expression;[43] it was, instead, imposed – one might say, artificially – on the political structure by the activities of the witch-commissioners. The families of almost all the men who sat on councils in Eichstätt were affected by the persecution, but to differing degrees. For those families that only saw their womenfolk go to the stake, it is not at all clear why the men who were also denounced frequently as accomplices were spared. I think it is possible, however, to explain why Paul Gabler was not indicted.

Gabler occupied a unique position in Eichstätt politics. Unlike many of his colleagues on the court and other councils, he was not well integrated into the social and political fabric of the town. He had not migrated far – his home district was Berching, about forty kilometres from Eichstätt – but the distance was significant. His choice of godmother for his three daughters is revealing. Gabler appointed Susanna, abbess of the cloister in nearby Mariastein. Her representative at the baptismal ceremonies was Regina Thiermayr, a relation of the vice-chancellor. This choice contrasts markedly with those made by old Eichstätt families, who routinely honoured friends with godparentage.[44] Gabler's motive seems to have been to establish himself better in the political hierarchy and, perhaps, ingratiate himself with the bishop who would have known Susanna well. In the end, however, the Thiermayr family offered little protection from the activities of the witch-commission, as women from it were also executed as witches.[45] Having secured the position of secretary to the bishop's court council, Gabler found himself sitting on the committees that heard and approved the indictments of witch-suspects before the investigations withdrew behind the closed doors of the interrogation chamber.[46] His relative isolation from the established political elite of Eichstätt – evinced not only by his choice of godmother, but also by the fact that none of his colleagues asked him or his wife to stand as godparents to their children – meant that it was in his interests to cultivate good relations with other men such as the commissioners.[47] To most of the other councillors in Eichstätt, the commissioners were relative outsiders whose only substantial contact with any of the inhabitants of the town would have been with the town hall staff, the executioner, and the few citizens, such as Gabler, who worked with them. It is quite probable, therefore, that these commissioners knew Gabler well enough to doubt the denunciations laid against him.

Such familiarity might well have protected Frau Baumgartner, whose husband had also heard the indictments of a number of witch-suspects, Georg Mayr, and most of the clergymen and their servants who were denounced as accomplices.[48] Mayr had been the court scribe when his wife was arrested. He would have worked in the town hall and, as the conspiracy to get his wife pregnant shows, knew many of the people who were also employed there. It is likely therefore that he was better known to the interrogators than Lorenz Bonschab or Michael Hochenschildt, for example. These same interrogators would also have maintained close relations with the clergymen who had been denounced. As Eichstätt was a cathedral town at the forefront of regional Counter-Reformation initiatives, it attracted a considerable number of religious inhabitants. They formed a small community apart from the secular networks of the town, and their different lifestyles and reforming vision no doubt created strong bonds. As some of the denounced priests also worked for the commissioners – Herr Welcker, for example, spied on the suspects in custody, reporting their conversations to the interrogators[49] – it was, perhaps, difficult for the commissioners to cast their religious colleagues in the role of witch.

One can therefore argue plausibly, if not definitively, that some men, even among those related to witch-defendants, benefited from their professional proximity to the witch-commissioners. If the interrogators knew a man well enough, they could easily doubt that he or, occasionally, his wife or servants were witches. Unfortunately, whilst we do have an idea why some men might have been above suspicion, and why men generally could be arrested without much intellectual difficulty, we are still no nearer understanding why particular men such as Bonschab or Hochenschildt were indicted. All one can say for certain is that they were denounced by a number of witch-suspects with whom they were intimate as kin, friends, colleagues, or neighbours, and that the interrogators were convinced that those denunciations constituted sufficient evidence to try them. The commissioners seem, however, to have been more willing to pursue these men towards the end of the witch-hunt, which might suggest that potential female suspects were decreasing in number (which was not the case) or that, having observed the progress of the persecution, they were increasingly likely to believe that the sect had penetrated deep into the political and social networks of Eichstätt men. We will probably never know the real reason why they were convinced in these cases.

IX

It does not matter greatly that one cannot use the Eichstätt data to construct an explanatory model for the existence of male witches. Unsatisfactory interpretations reflect the complexities and untidiness of witchcraft cases, and the fear and uncertainty of those who watched their friends and neighbours die, only to wonder if they might be next. Although I have eschewed an explanatory model, and highlighted in its place tentative conclusions about the presence of male witches, I want to conclude this chapter with a brief, and perhaps more cogent discussion of the gender of the witch.

A great deal of scholarly time has been spent on defining and explaining away the stereotypical female witch. One of the problems with this approach is that historians tend to ignore the very many exceptions to it, including both male witches and the typical female suspect one finds in the Eichstätt example (married, middle-class, and middle-aged). When they have attempted to address these exceptions, they frequently develop sophisticated theories that are difficult to apply to the actual cases. Apps and Gow, building on a foundation laid by Fritz Graf, argue that male witches were possible because demonologists and judges understood them – perhaps subconsciously – to be feminized by acting in ways incongruent with ideal masculine behaviour or possessing features that diminished their masculinity.[50] The question that naturally follows is: Did the male witches discussed in this chapter exhibit behaviour or physical characteristics that might be interpreted as womanish? The answer is categorically 'No'. None of the male suspects was possessed of the characteristics that Apps and Gow suggest were indicative of feminization. None, for example, was blind or unnaturally malodorous, neither can any of them be said to have been intellectually or emotionally weak; none of them had been seduced by heretic Protestants, for example, or resorted to magic. Prior to their arrests, their lives were almost exemplary in terms of masculine attributes and life-stories. They established households integrated into various local networks, they were economically productive and politically active, they participated in Catholic ritual, and they enjoyed procreative sex. In this, they were no different from other men of their social milieux that managed to avoid arrest. It was only after they had been forced to confess to witchcraft that they began to exhibit womanish qualities – notably the weak-mindedness that facilitated seduction by the Devil, and the use of secretive, underhand means to harm their neighbours. But the conventional confession narrative demanded the inclusion of these things; they could not be avoided by a suspect facing torture. The men were not arrested because they were weak-minded in the first place, neither were they deliberately feminized by the witch-commissioners so that they could reconcile their presence with a misogynistic demonological outlook.

Whilst I find the feminization argument weak, I do agree with the implication of Apps and Gow's discussion that demonologists and judges were partially responsible for the presence of men in the witchcraft data; this is also the implication of Rolf Schulte's survey of demonological literature as it concerned the gender of the witch.[51] If the witch-hunters had been unable to conceive of male witches, they would not have pursued them at all. The question one should really be asking, therefore, is not 'Why did they prosecute some men?', but 'Why did they not prosecute more men?' The problem that judges such as the Eichstätt witch-commissioners had was that they were men themselves, and they were educated. They probably understood the attraction of the intellectual challenges presented by Lutheranism and Calvinism, because these heresies, however flawed, were based not on emotional reflexes but, rather, on rigorous biblical exegesis conducted by educated men. They might well have understood the attraction of demonic ritual magic, too, because it also demanded a high degree of intellectual endeavour. Alongside the scholarship required of demonology, these clerical witch-commissioners had spent their lives resisting the temptation to enjoy worldly pleasures, such as sex and financial gain. They had been helped in their abstinence by their relative seclusion from secular life, and by the financial and spiritual assistance afforded by the Church. The men with whom they spent much of their time nurtured the manly virtues of scholarship and asceticism. The opposites of these scholars for the commissioners would not have been laymen, who were more susceptible to sin; they would have been the women who did not have access to the learning they had enjoyed, and who were, to a large degree, denigrated in that scholarship. Without that learning, these women could not be fortified against the wiles of the Devil. They were, therefore, weak-minded and vulnerable to his enticements and, consequently, more likely to become witches. Female witches were more plausible than male ones, which is perhaps why witch-hunters were reluctant to prosecute so many suspected men.

If witch-hunters found female witches more plausible, the Eichstätt suspects seem not to have had any trouble imagining either sex in the role of witch. At one level, the stereotypical female figure of the witch circulated widely in early modern German culture. The etchings of female witches executed by Baldung Grien, Dürer and Deutsch are familiar to students of witch-persecution, and reflect the dominance of these figures in contemporary pamphlet literature and plays elsewhere, especially in England.[52] The vast majority of early modern English pamphleteers who recounted witchcraft episodes, for example, concerned themselves with the more sensational trials of poor female witches. The first four extant pamphlets, telling of assize trials between 1566 and 1579, are concerned with only three episodes of witchcraft, two of which focus on the same woman (Elizabeth Frauncis).[53] Against the background of the new English witchcraft legislation of 1563, any witchcraft story must have been potentially newsworthy, but very few made it into print. What is striking about the cases reported in these pamphlets is the detail of the relationships with the familiars, the characters of the women (single, marginalized, and possibly Catholic) and the acts of malevolence that they perpetrated; they conform to the stereotype in ways that less detailed cases (the majority of English ones) do not. These cases continue to generate discussion, albeit in a less sensational, more scholarly fashion.

At the popular level, in Germany, the stereotypical image of the witch might not have carried much weight. It is reasonable to assume that the inhabitants of the principality were acquainted with the image. They were almost certainly aware of the Catholic demonological view drawn from the *Malleus maleficarum*, because that was the subject of much preaching in Eichstätt.[54] No doubt middling-sort women, until the extent of the persecutions became obvious, chose to assume that the weak women of the *Malleus* were not themselves but, rather, the same weak, poor and sometimes dishonourable women who resided at the edges of the community, selling sex and abortions to supplement whatever alms and other relief they might also receive; in other words, they recreated the misogynistic image along the class prejudices that grounded the stereotype. This image of the crone was probably reinforced, in part, by the physical appearance of the convicted witches who were led through the town to the stake. Many months, sometimes years, incarcerated in the town hall in unhygienic conditions, isolated from the world, insufficiently fed, and subject to torture and psychological torment would have taken their toll on middling-sort women; they might well have left their prison transformed from the soberly dressed housewife into the wild old hag. And yet, the Eichstätt witch-suspects, when forced to name accomplices, did not do what we might expect them to have done, and adopt the image to deflect the persecution away from their friends and neighbours. They did not make the connection between traditional witch images and witch accomplices, and name poor, old, marginalized women with whom they had little to do on a daily basis.

One reason for this must have been the desire to avoid the torture used to keep testimony flowing. The failure of every single witch to make the connection also suggests, however, that the stereotype was not ingrained sufficiently in their minds. At least in the longest, most intense phase of persecution from 1617, a degree of familiarity with events elsewhere in the region might have stripped the stereotypical image of its utility. Although we do not know whether pamphlets dealing with witchcraft circulated in the principality, one that was likely to have attracted the attention of its inhabitants was published in the *Zwo Hexen Zeitung* (1616). It related the trials that had recently happened in another of the Franconian prince-bishoprics, Würzburg, and began by stating that in this territory 'men and women, young and old, poor and rich who practised witchcraft and magic were executed and burned'.[55] Whilst female suspects dominate the remainder of the pamphlet, the author tells of their acts of magic and sacrilege, rather than deviating into descriptions of physical appearance and character. The reader is therefore left with the impression that anyone, regardless of gender or status, could fall prey to the Devil's temptations. This impression would have been confirmed by news that individual Eichstätt inhabitants would have received from friends, family, and other contacts who had witnessed the trials and executions in Würzburg. When the witch-persecutions did begin in earnest in Eichstätt the following year, it is possible that these reports created a widespread fear that the witch sect had penetrated as deeply there as it had among other Catholic Franconians not so far away. The stereotypical witch simply had no function in this context.

Despite all the preaching and pamphleteering, it is also the case that witchcraft was not the only topic of local conversation. More immediate concerns must have included the poor harvests, which would have impacted deeply on small towns and their rural hinterlands, and the very real threat of soldiers laying waste to what supplies were left. Eichstätt was, after all, stuck between Bavaria and the Upper Palatinate, and its neighbours included prominent Lutheran princes. The threat of military devastation was realized in 1634, when the Swedes razed four fifths of the town to the ground. Until the final phase of witch-hunting was well underway, the witch-trials in the territory, and the news of similar cases from elsewhere were perhaps short-lived diversions from the increasing hardships of everyday life for many inhabitants of the principality, regardless of their social status.

The gender of the witch was, therefore, a significant factor in the escalation of witch-hunting in Eichstätt, but not in the ways in which historians have usually interpreted it. Showing how male suspects might have found themselves before the witch-commissioners, and why there were not more of them, casts doubt on interpretations that seek explanations for the high number of witches, in part, in the needs and beliefs of ordinary people who sometimes colluded in witch-trials. If witch-hunting reflected changes in attitudes towards social obligations, for example, or attacks on women (especially elderly crones), one would expect marginalized, perhaps older women to be dominant among the witch-suspects. They were not. The gender of the witch, as much as her class, was the by-product of the interrogation process, which forced suspects to name their neighbour: it was highlighted further by witch-hunters, whose prejudices against women were reinforced by their relationships with other men. Given that most witches seem to have been executed not in isolated witchcraft episodes, but in the major witch-persecutions, one can plausibly argue that the gender of the witch was imposed 'from above'.

Notes

1. The figures are discussed in J. B. Durrant, *Witchcraft, Gender and Society in Early Modern Germany* (Leiden, 2007), xiii–xiv and 3–7.
2. On occasion, historians discussing the 'women question' even omit reference to the presence of significant numbers of men in the data. Ingrid Ahrendt-Schulte, for example, notes in her popular account of female witches that 80,000 women were tried as witches in central European courts, but she does not inform her readers that as many as 20,000 men might also have been put on trial in this area, *Weise Frauen – böse Weiber. Die Geschichte der Hexen in der Frühen Neuzeit* (Freiburg im Breisgau, 1994), 16. This approach clearly misrepresents the gender issue for a readership that might not be familiar with scholarly debates about witchcraft.
3. This naming process, and its consequences for the profile of the typical Eichstätt witch, are discussed in Durrant, *Witchcraft, Gender and Society*, 61–84.
4. John Samond was one such witch who possessed magical skill; his case is discussed in L. Apps and A. Gow, *Male Witches in Early Modern Europe* (Manchester, 2003), 47–52; The Haan family might be seen implicitly as victims of factionalism, B. Gehm, *Die Hexenverfolgung im Hochstift Bamberg und das Eingreifen des Reichshofrates zu ihrer Beendigung* (Hildesheim, 2000), 149–61.
5. On the exceptions, see W. Behringer, *Chonrad Stoeckhlin und die Nachtschar. Eine Geschichte aus der frühen Neuzeit* (Munich, 1994), and G. Henningsen, '"The Ladies from Outside": An Archaic Pattern of the Witches' Sabbath', in B. Ankarloo and G. Henningsen (eds), *Early Modern European Witchcraft: Centres and Peripheries* (Oxford, 1990), 191–215; Keith Thomas uses Stanton's case as an 'exemplary' one, *Religion and the Decline of Magic* (1971; reprinted London, 1991), 662–3; Grön is the startling example of an old crone used by Lyndal Roper in *Witch Craze: Terror and Fantasy in Baroque Germany* (New Haven, CT, 2004), 170–2.

6. On the relationship between witch persecution and contemporary crises, see W. Behringer 'Weather, hunger and fear: Origins of the European witch hunts in climate, society and mentality', *German History*, 13 (1995), 1–27.
7. R. Briggs, *Witches and Neighbours: The Social and Cultural Context of European Witchcraft* (London, 1996), 397.
8. J. B. Durrant, 'Witchcraft, Gender and Society in the Early Modern Prince-Bishopric of Eichstätt' (PhD thesis, University of London, 2002), appendix 1, Distribution of witch trials in Eichstätt: Gender, 298–300, gives an annual breakdown of the gender data.
9. Staatsarchiv Nürnberg (hereafter StAN), Hexenakten 48 (E. Gutmann), 14 December 1617 (a.m.), and (G. Gutmann), 13 December 1617 (p.m.).
10. A large number of Eichstätt councillors were also tavern-keepers, Durrant, *Witchcraft, Gender and Society*, 137.
11. Bundesarchiv Aussenstelle Frankfurt, FSg.2/1-F 13 669 (Eichstätt L–Z), frames 92–3.
12. StAN, Hexenakten 49 (C. Lauterer); Rehel is described thus in the testimonies of others, for example Hexenakten 45 (H. Stigeliz), 23 May 1628.
13. StAN, Hexenakten 45 (H. Stigeliz).
14. In Hochenschildt's trial, the interrogators referred to Brandt as the *Langschneider* (tall tailor), StAN, Hexenakten 45 (M. Hochenschildt), 14 March 1628; in his manuscript compilation of data about the inhabitants of Eichstätt, Franz Xaver Buchner twice noted that Hochenschildt was a tavern-keeper, *Eichstätter Familienbuch 1589–1618* (Diözesanarchiv Eichstätt, compiled 1930s–1950s), 176 and 374. For the carter, see StAN, Hexenakten 48 (H. Wagner?).
15. There is no file on Ghayer, but his profession is given in StAN, Hexenakten 48 (B. Haubner), 25 January 1618 (p.m.).
16. The data on occupations in Eichstätt are tabulated in appendix 2, Occupations of suspected witches or their households, in Durrant, *Witchcraft, Gender and Society*, 253–4.
17. Her case is discussed in detail in *ibid.*, 174–5 and 182–8.
18. These bonds were complex, and it is difficult to summarize examples for each here. I have, however, discussed the last of these in 'Friendship in Catholic Reformation Eichstätt', in L. Gowing, M. Hunter and M. Rubin (eds.), *Love, Friendship and Faith in Europe, 1300–1800* (Basingstoke, 2005), 66–87.
19. See, for example, Durrant, *Witchcraft, Gender and Society*, 89–127.
20. On the abuse of suspects in custody, see *ibid.*, 199.
21. StAN, Hexenakten 48 (K. Pronner).
22. Harding was, for example, bribed by two of her female clients – one of whom was Jacob Rabel's wife, Barbara – not to name them as accomplices, StAN, Hexenakten 48 (A. Harding), 18 June 1618 (a.m.).
23. StAN, Hexenakten 45 (M. Bittelmayr), 29–31 October, 2 November, and 5–7 November 1626.
24. StAN, Hexenakten 45 (P. Porzin), 20 and 22–25 September 1627, and (H. Stigeliz), 23–26 May 1628.
25. Apps and Gow, *Male Witches*, 135–7.
26. See the summary of this viewpoint in *ibid.*, 131–2.
27. E. Peters, *The Magician, the Witch and the Law* (Brighton, 1978), 71–8.

28. Part III, Question 15, for example, advises judges on how to protect themselves against the acts of harmful magic of the witch-suspects; see Heinrich Institoris, *Malleus Maleficarum*, translated and annotated by P. G. Maxwell-Stuart (Manchester, 2007), 230–3.
29. StAN, Hexenakten 43 (P. Gabler – denunciations), 48 (P. Gabler – denunciations) and (P. Gabler – table of denunciations).
30. StAN, Hexenakten 45 (M. Bittelmayr), 15 October 1626 (a.m.), Hexenakten 49 (C. Lauterer – denunciations), and Hexenakten 45 (P. Porzin – denunciations).
31. Details of these denunciations can be found in Durrant, *Witchcraft, Gender and Society*, 64 and 66.
32. The two suspects who denounced Porzin would have been Margretha Hözler and Bittelmayr, StAN, Hexenakten 45 (P. Porzin – denunciations), nos. 6 and 8. The only extant denunciation of Bittelmayr was made by Kunigunda Bonschab, Hexenakten 48 (K. Bonschab), 31 January 1618 (a.m.).
33. Apps and Gow, *Male Witches*, 47–52.
34. The interrogators put this motive to Maria on the afternoon of 23 November 1618, StAN, Hexenakten 48 (M. Mayr – investigation); the case is discussed in detail in Durrant, *Witchcraft, Gender and Society*, 199–236.
35. StAN, Hexenakten 48 (E. Gutmann), 13 January 1618 (a.m.), and (G. Gutmann), 1 February 1618 (a.m.).
36. *Ibid.* (G. Gutmann), 31 January 1618 (a.m.).
37. StAN, Hexenakten 45 (M. Bittelmayr), 16 October 1626.
38. *Ibid.* (M. Hochenschildt), 14 March 1628, and 16 March 1628 (a.m.).
39. *Ibid.* (M. Bittelmayr), 6 November 1626.
40. *Ibid.* (M. Hochenschildt), 14 March 1628.
41. StAN, Hexenakten 43 (P. Gabler – denunciations), Denunciations 11–13, 16, 18 and 20.
42. For example, Georg Mittner and Barbara Koller had three children together before their marriage in 1597, twins shortly after it, and another three children who must have been conceived legitimately, Buchner, *Eichstätter Familienbuch*, 237–8.
43. A. Gregory, 'Witchcraft, politics and "good neighbourhood" in early modern Rye', *Past and Present*, 133 (1991), 31–66.
44. Buchner, *Eichstätter Familienbuch*, 127.
45. Anna Thiermayr, wife of the vice-chancellor, was one of the suspects who denounced Hochenschildt, StAN, Hexenakten 45 (M. Hochenschildt), 14 March 1628.
46. See, for example, *ibid.* (P. Porzin), 10 September 1627 (a.m.).
47. Only a cook and a tanner chose Paul and Anna Maria Gabler as godparents to their children, Buchner, *Eichstätter Familienbuch*, 343 and 404.
48. Dr Baumgartner sat with Gabler on StAN, Hexenakten 45 (P. Porzin), 10 September 1627 (a.m.).
49. For example, in the case of Valtin Lanng, *ibid.* (V. Lanng), 13 July 1618 (p.m.).
50. Apps and Gow, *Male Witches*, 127–37.
51. R. Schulte, *Hexenmeister. Die Verfolgung von Männern im Rahmen der Hexenverfolgung von 1530–1730 im Alten Reich* (Frankfurt am Main, 2000), 107–78.

52. These German images are usefully contextualized in Roper's chapters on 'Fertility' and 'Crones', in *Witch Craze*, 127–78 *passim*.
53. These have been reprinted with commentaries in M. Gibson (ed.), *Early Modern Witches: Witchcraft Cases in Contemporary Writing* (London, 2000), 10–24 and 33–71.
54. W. Behringer, *Hexenverfolgung in Bayern. Volksmagie, Glaubenseifer und Staatsräson in der Frühen Neuzeit* 3rd edn, (Munich, 1987), 204, note 284.
55. 'Manns vnd Weibspersonen jung vnd alte / arm vnd reiche / so der Hexernkunst vnd Zauberey erfahren / hinrichten vnd verbrennen', Anon, *Zwo Hexen Zeitung* (Tübingen: n.p., 1616), unfoliated.

6

Giandomenico Fei, the Only Male Witch. A Tuscan or an Italian Anomaly?

Oscar Di Simplicio

In 1599, a blacksmith called Giandomenico Fei was tried on charges of witchcraft by the Sienese Inquisition in the Tuscan town of Montepulciano. This case was unusual, not only because it involved a man, but because Giandomenico holds the dubious honour of being the only man to be tried on such charges in the region of Tuscany subject to the tribunal of the Roman Inquisition in Siena. Was his case a local anomaly that can be dismissed as irrelevant to the overall pattern of witchcraft beliefs and witch-trials in this region? Or does closer examination of the case of even one male witch give the historian important insights into broader questions about the gendering of witch-persecution? The aim of this chapter is to explore answers to these questions. However, before beginning, I would like to sound a note of caution about the interest in gender that has come to dominate the field of witchcraft studies in the late twentieth century. My work on witchcraft in early modern Italy has persuaded me that witchcraft beliefs, and the cognitive processes in which such beliefs were rooted, were not, first and foremost, 'about' gender; they were, rather, about the fear of evil powers and how to counteract them. We must, thus, be careful not to focus too exclusively on the question of gender in relation to witchcraft, as this might be misleading, both in terms of the questions posed and the conclusions reached.

I

It is hard to establish whether or not the case of Giandomenico Fei was merely a local anomaly in the Italian context, because of the current patchy state of Italian witchcraft studies. As recently as 1999, Marijke

Gijswijt-Hofstra wrote, in an overview of witchcraft in the Mediterranean countries, that 'It is also noticeable that the middle of Italy is still a blank spot',[1] an assessment that can, at best, be described as a polite euphemism. Nearly a decade later, an overview of Italian witchcraft is hampered by a shortage of reliable, up-to-date, regional studies. And, from the point of view of witchcraft and masculinity, we know far too little to sketch out anything except some broad temporal and geographical references on a map that is otherwise replete with the kind of blank spaces upon which ancient cartographers wrote *hic sunt leones*. Why is this? The question is puzzling, considering the fact that one of the pioneering works in the field of witchcraft studies came from Italy, and dealt primarily with male witches. In *I benandanti*, published in 1966, Carlo Ginzburg analyzed the trial records of men from the Friuli region who practised rites of an ecstatic agrarian cult to ensure the fertility of fields, and who were eventually tried by Inquisitors as witches. Published in English in 1983 as *The Night Battles*, *I benandanti* is now regarded as one of the seminal texts (along with those published in England in the early 1970s by Keith Thomas and Alan Macfarlane) that gave impetus to the late-twentieth-century rejuvenation of the study of witchcraft. Ginzburg's book was not, however, an anticipation of the interpretative paradigm for witchcraft accusations suggested by Thomas and Macfarlane, and which was influenced by their interest in social anthropology.[2] Subsequent Italian witchcraft studies have also kept largely aloof from broader trends in European witchcraft research. Moreover, they have tended to be based on a random exploitation of trial records that has made a systematic delineation of beliefs and the sociological context of accusations impossible. They have also been mainly interested, not in witchcraft in particular, but in the policies of the Inquisition towards magic in general.[3] Important opportunities for new research, based on a thorough analysis of all cases of witchcraft and magic reported to the tribunals of the Inquisition, have emerged since the opening of the former Roman Inquisition archives in 1998, however. This research has, thus far, produced a regional monograph, in which I have proposed a sociological analysis of witchcraft and witch-trials in Siena that can be placed in the comparative framework provided by the wider historiography of European witchcraft.[4] Whether the conclusions of this chapter are valid beyond Siena will, of course, depend on future research into other regions of early modern Italy.

II

The trial of Giandomenico Fei fell under the jurisdiction of the tribunal of the Roman Inquisition in Siena. Established in the 1560s, this tribunal had jurisdiction over the old Sienese Republic, which had been absorbed after 1559 into the Medicean Duchy (later Grand-Duchy) of Tuscany. By the early-seventeenth century, the tribunal exercised its rule through a dense network of vicariates. The population of the 'New State' of Siena remained stationary between 1580 and 1720 at slightly over 100,000 people: that of its capital, Siena, fluctuated between 15,000 and 17,000. Most of the inhabitants of the region were clustered in some 132 nucleated villages. Religious matters were administered by the Archbishopric of Siena and its six small suffragan bishoprics. Local General Inquisitor Fathers, who were Franciscan friars in Tuscany, also had great influence on matters of religion in the region, however. In the short term, these Inquisitors also took over cases of *maleficia*, or harmful magic, despite the fact that these were technically considered crimes of 'mixed jurisdiction' (*mixto foro*), subject to both secular and episcopal courts. Their power in such matters was subordinate only to the Roman cardinals of the Inquisition.[5] Throughout this chapter, I define witchcraft strictly as *maleficium*, or harmful magic. In deeply Catholic Siena, as in Protestant England, 'it was the popular fear of *maleficium* which provided the normal driving force behind witch prosecution'.[6] The role of the Devil and his relationship with alleged witches rarely worried villagers. The type of demonic witchcraft found in Church teachings was marginal at the popular level: for example, of the 176 women accused of harmful magic in the region, only ten admitted having taken part in a witches' sabbath, seven after being severely tortured and three after being threatened with torture.[7]

A close reading of Sienese Inquisitorial trials uncovers a system of village witchcraft beliefs that functioned to explain misfortune and to resolve conflicts. Crucial to this system was the existence of the 'anti-witch' specialist: the cunning man or woman (called *indovino* and *indovina*, respectively, in Italian) who offered a wide range of services to his or her clients. As soon as villagers interpreted some misfortune as an act of harmful magic, they adopted the age-old strategy of having their suspicions confirmed, and the individual deemed responsible for the harm identified by the *indovino* or *indovina*. Then, they could attempt to persuade or compel the witch to withdraw the spell. Such a 'natural control' of witchcraft operated within a dynamic power network in which opposing forces (represented by the anti-witch specialist and the witch) confronted each other in order to gain victory, and in which health, life, and death were at stake,[8] as the following example shows:

> In 1692, from the hamlet of Cuna a messenger was sent by Domenica di Paolo, supposedly bewitched by Frasia, in order to contact Giacomo, a cunning man of some reputation in the treatment of *putti guasti*

> [literally 'rotten' children], and to ask for his mediation on the matter. The messenger reported that Giacomo contacted Frasia but that she denied any guilt, maintaining that she could not cast spells because her father had deliberately cut a finger off her right hand; but Giacomo replied he knew she could cast spells anyway; nevertheless Frasia stood firm, and in the end Giacomo threatened Frasia, saying 'If you don't heal her [the child] I'll make you walk'.[9]

The interrogations of witnesses and defendants have left abundant evidence of such a system operating independently from the official persecution of witches, and from the judicial mechanisms and demonological beliefs that underpinned persecution at the elite level. We might even suggest that the opportunities for informal conflict resolution offered by cunning men and women helped account for the relatively low number of reported cases of *maleficium* in Siena, as people preferred to use anti-witch specialists rather than the courts in the fight against witches. Certainly, witch-trials in Central Italy, as those in England, remained an endemic rather than an epidemic phenomenon. However, the informal system in Italy was weakened from the late sixteenth century onwards, as the enforcement of general papal anti-magic policies targeted the activities of the anti-witch specialists as well as those of allegedly malevolent witches. Evidence for a blurring of the boundaries between the categories of 'good' and 'bad' magic as a result of these new papal policies can be seen in an important linguistic shift: archival records show that the words *strega* (meaning a female harmful witch) and *stregone* (meaning a harmful male witch) could be used to denote female and male anti-witch specialists, competing with the older terms *indovina* or *indovino*.

As can be seen from Figure 6.1, harmful, anti-social witchcraft (*maleficia*) was one element within a larger set of magical practices that can be identified from cases brought before the tribunal of the Inquisition in Siena. Mastery of these practices was believed to be essential in order to achieve specific goals – such as predicting the future, finding lost or stolen objects, discovering treasure, healing illness, or securing the devotion of an unwilling lover. Figure 6.1 shows the proportional distribution of these various practices: interestingly, weather magic was absent from the picture.[10]

Is it possible to identify a clearly defined male or female form of magic from this data? In Tuscany, did 'special gender-specific orientations and assessments emerge, which may be viewed as the results in part of a traditional understanding of magic, and in part of functional societal role assignments', as Eva Labouvie has suggested for the Saar region of early modern Germany?[11] The 1544 people under investigation for

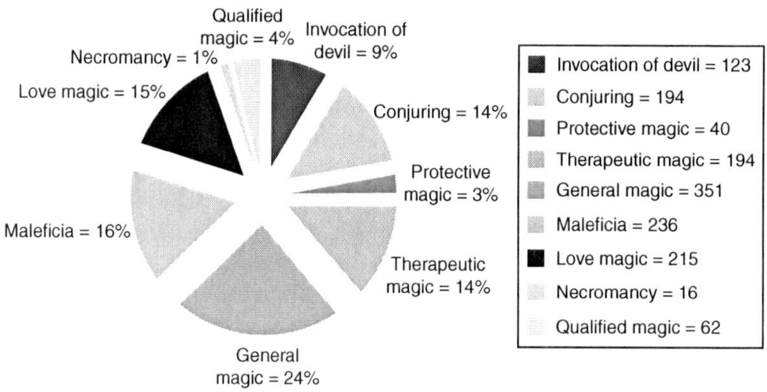

Figure 6.1 Number of cases of *Maleficia* and magic tried before the Inquisitorial Tribunal in Siena, 1580–1721[12]

magical crimes (including harmful magic) by the Sienese Inquisition from 1580 to 1721 were divided reasonably equally between men and women, albeit with a slight imbalance: 675 were men (44 per cent of the total, including 161 clerics), and 869 were women (56 per cent of the total, including 13 nuns). What happens, however, if we focus on specific magical crimes? Does the gender ratio remain fairly even, or does it become skewed towards men or women? The results of this analysis are shown in Tables 6.1 to 6.4, which focus on the crimes of love magic, conjuring, invocation of the Devil, and therapeutic magic, respectively.

Tables 6.1 to 6.4 suggest that overall women's involvement in these magical practices decreased from the second half of the seventeenth century. There are also some gender differences. Men came to dominate the practice of conjuration in the second half of the early modern period (Table 6.2): these were mainly cases of treasure seeking. A similar male predominance for the period 1651–1721 can be found in the cases of invocation of the Devil displayed in Table 6.3: these were mostly episodes involving the making of Faustian-type pacts. Conversely, therapeutic magic (Table 6.4) remained a field of predominantly female activity throughout the early modern period. Similarly, love magic (Table 6.1), perhaps unsurprisingly, was also more strongly associated with women, mostly prostitutes, especially in the first half of our period.[13] Overall, however, and despite these changes over time, the statistics do not support the idea that there was a radically gender-differentiated view of these magical practices in early modern Tuscany. We cannot therefore conclude that an absolutely clear male understanding of non-malevolent magic existed.

On the other hand, 'the "black" side of magic, to which, according to popular belief, witchcraft belonged',[14] was a matter of almost exclusively female concern. Statistical analysis of the Tuscan data on harmful magic shows that, of the 178 people accused of witchcraft, 176 (or 99.14 per cent) were women. How can we explain such a striking gendering of this element of the magical belief system?[15] To help answer this question, Tables 6.5 to 6.7 provide a sociological profile of the accused witches, while Table 6.8 shows the targets of the acts of *maleficia* they were alleged to have committed.

Table 6.1 Numbers of men and women investigated by the Inquisitorial Tribunal in Siena for love magic, 1580–1721

Years	Men	Clerics	Women
1580–1650	47	(20)	124 (71%)
1651–1721	58	(16)	71 (45%)

Table 6.2 Numbers of men and women investigated by the Inquisitorial Tribunal in Siena for conjuration, 1580–1721

Years	Men	Clerics	Women
1580–1650	35	(11)	52 (59%)
1651–1721	74	(12)	21 (22%)

Table 6.3 Numbers of men and women investigated by the Inquisitorial Tribunal in Siena for invocation of the Devil, 1580–1721

Years	Men	Clerics	Women	Nuns	Totals
1580–1650	5	(4)	8 (61%)	(4)	13
1651–1721	73	(14)	34 (31%)	(13)	107

Table 6.4 Numbers of men and women investigated by the Inquisitorial Tribunal in Siena for therapeutic magic, 1580–1721

Years	Men	Clerics	Women	Totals
1580–1650	18	(8)	51 (74%)	69
1651–1721	50	(2)	75 (60%)	125

Most Tuscan witchcraft cases emerged from small villages containing a few hundred people. Witchcraft in this region was a neighbourhood crime, with accuser and accused usually living in close proximity to one another. Almost all the accused witches lived in a close-knit network of human relationships. Many were married (see Table 6.6) and, even if they were widows, this did not mean that they led a socially marginal life: there is little or no evidence from Central Italy of the isolated witch free of social control. Table 6.5 shows that 41 of the accused were older women aged 50 and over, while 38 were younger pre-menopausal women aged 49 and under. Demographic analysis does not, however, suggest that there was a distinct pattern of post-menopausal witches targeting young victims with their harmful magic.

A feature common to all witches, according to the prevailing belief system, was the power to lift the spells that they had cast in the first place: those who could harm were, thus, believed capable of healing,

Table 6.5 Ages of women investigated on charges of Witchcraft by the Inquisitorial Tribunal in Siena, 1580–1721[16]

Cohort	Number of accused witches
15 to 19	2
20 to 29	9
30 to 39	8
40 to 49	19
50 to 59	12
60 to 69	16
70 to 79	12
80	1

Table 6.6 Marital status of women investigated on charges of Witchcraft by the Inquisitorial Tribunal in Siena, 1580–1721

Marital status	Number of accused witches
Single	5
Married	53
Widows	65

Table 6.7 Occupations of women investigated on charges of Witchcraft by the Inquisitorial Tribunal in Siena, 1580–1721

Occupations	**Number of accused witches**
Wet-nurses	2
Shopkeepers	1
Bakers	2
Servants	6
Midwives	7
Whores	20
Sharecroppers	7

Table 6.8 Targets of the *Maleficia* of women investigated on charges of Witchcraft by the Inquisitorial Tribunal in Siena, 1580–1721

Targets of *maleficia*	**Number of accused witches**
Adults	56
Beasts	17
Infants	145
Infants and adults	10
Storms	1
Uncertain	15

at least in the limited sense of negating their own acts of aggressive bewitchment against others. However, the records of witch-trials point to the existence of two subtly different categories of harmful witches who performed their evil deeds differently. Into the first category fell witches whom we might describe as 'social' or 'healer' witches: these were people who occupied some sort of role within society that was associated with the more general practice of healing. These might be wise women, wet-nurses, or midwives, and (at least, hypothetically) men such as blacksmiths, who also provided villagers with medical advice. The second type of harmful witches were those who had no pre-existing healing role within the community and who cast their spells by supernatural means based purely on some internal and personal force of malevolence.

The strong gendering of the practice of harmful witchcraft shown in the Sienese data can be linked to the fact that contemporaries understood it as a neighbourhood crime. Trial records show that almost all of the Sienese witches 'were women because the accusations were rooted in neighbourhood conflicts which developed in the female sphere of private and community life',[17] around issues such as health-care, motherhood, childcare, and feeding the household. In this context, it is no surprise that infants were the most common target of reported acts of *maleficia*, at 68 per cent of the total (see Table 6.8).

III

To what extent can this analysis of magic and witchcraft help us understand the making of the malevolent male witch Giandomenico Fei? His case occurred in 1599, at the point when the 80-year-cycle of witchcraft trials overseen by the Inquisition in Siena was at its peak, and in Montepulciano, a town with fewer than 4000 inhabitants.[18] In the same year, Roberto Bellarmino, a hugely influential figure in the Italian Counter-Reformation, who had been born in Montepulciano, was made a cardinal: one of his servants was summoned as a witness in the Fei trial. The pre-trial investigation into the allegations made against Fei was started by the Episcopal court of Pienza. However, the Inquisition quickly asserted its jurisdiction over the case: it had already established control over all matters of faith in the region by the end of the sixteenth century, and witchcraft, as a crime of heresy, thus came under its purview. Between May and October 1599, the Sienese General Inquisitor, the Conventual Franciscan Father Zaccaria Orceoli, received detailed instructions on how to repeat the interrogation of witnesses, and on the manner and frequency with which to torture the defendant. Orceoli was also ordered to travel from Siena to oversee proceedings in Montepulciano in person, an exceptional occurrence that indicates clearly that the Fei trial was a local *cause célèbre*.

Giandomenico Fei was accused of having bewitched several infants (three and, perhaps, as many as four) and eventually causing their deaths. In 1599, he was in his early fifties, at the peak of his personal power, according to early modern ways of imagining the lifecycle. Interestingly, there is a significant amount of Sienese evidence pointing to mid-life as the time of maximum vulnerability to charges of witchcraft for women: Table 6.5 shows that the ages of 31 of the 79 accused witches for whom age is known fell between 40 and 59, perhaps suggesting that local anxiety about their supposed power was heightened during this stage of their life-course. The trial records also show that Fei had a strong and rather abrasive personality. Once, arguing with a fellow villager, he could not restrain himself from cursing loudly. Semidea, mother of one of the dead infants, testified that:

> While I was in bed about to deliver he went to my husband and told him: 'You did not leave me in peace, and I'll make you repent'... And within two weeks the baby fell sick and after death three holes were discovered in his corpse.[19]

Fei was a blacksmith. In Italy – as was also the case in many other countries – the fact that blacksmiths worked with fire had, over the centuries, fostered the belief that this occupational group possessed mysterious, magical powers, and general Sienese Inquisitorial sources show that blacksmiths provided people with medical advice, possibly in relation to animals as well.[20] The question as to whether or not Fei was considered to be a healer locally is one of the most crucial points of his case. I would argue, however, that he was NOT considered in this manner. Fei was accused of curing a baby of worms, and he half-admitted the charge – but this was the only piece of evidence of any sort of healing activity from his entire trial. More dangerously, Father Orceoli accused him of having healed (*risanato*) some infants. Fei repudiated strenuously this clear allusion to the idea that he possessed the power to both harm and heal – in other words, that he was a witch.

Fei was a man of some substance economically. He owned a house that he had already bequeathed to his 21-year-old niece, Antonia of Agapito Fei. Fei lived with her, having kept the life tenancy of the house for himself. He had been married twice, the second time in his late forties to a younger woman of questionable reputation. This second marriage had been contested by his relatives; an action that resulted in a lawsuit for which we unfortunately lack the details. Under interrogation, Fei remarked that 'I have several enemies because I did several jobs and [they] did not want to pay me'[21] These financial conflicts, together with the criticized second marriage, might have encouraged local inhabitants to want to fabricate some of the evidence in the case against Fei, as there are clear hints of false testimonies in the trial. For example, 21-year-old Arcangelo, who owed Giandomenico some 20 ecus, accused the blacksmith of 'having visited his baby, who later died and the doctor discovered four fingerprints on one side' (of the baby's corpse). Other deponents also had a vested interest in getting rid of Fei, because they owed him money for work he had done for them, even though they were not victims of his alleged acts of witchcraft.

Malice as a motivation for witchcraft accusations can be proven unequivocally in several other Sienese witchcraft trials.[22] In some cases, accusations seem to have been motivated purely by malice; in others, the situation was more ambiguous, with deponents using accusations in the context of ongoing local feuds with alleged witches at the same time as they clearly believed that such witches were capable of acts of harmful magic. Was the latter the case in Montepulciano? We cannot know for sure, as at a certain point all witch-trials become frustratingly opaque to the historian searching for clear-cut explanations of motive. On the one hand, we know that the individual who denounced Fei formally to the Episcopal court in the first place was a straw-man, and that Fei's sudden imprisonment and formal prosecution for witchcraft looked like a foregone conclusion. Moreover, while trying to defend himself against the charges, Fei said of his bad reputation that 'My fame is not born by my works but by their [my enemies'] tongues'.[23] Finally, there was some suggestion that evidence might have been planted in Fei's house in order to prejudice the case against him. It was searched after his arrest, and many apparently incriminating items were found in a trunk he owned: a cruet filled with human oil, a book in Hebrew; another one written in red ink and illustrated with painted devils, supposedly used to find lost objects and to affect women's will; some other books and manuscripts; and some bones, which had been put there deliberately, according to one witness.[24]

On the other hand, however, there is overwhelming evidence from the trial records that Fei was a reputed *stregone* (harmful male witch) who wielded a menacing power amongst his neighbours. Once he was jailed, many witnesses gave vent to suspicions and grudges they had been accumulating against him for ten years. Father Orceoli summoned 13 men and 11 women as witnesses in the case, a roughly balanced distribution by gender that can be found in all other Sienese witchcraft trials.[25] With just two or three exceptions, all the witnesses declared that Fei was publicly considered a *stregone*, and that his reputation predated his imprisonment. For example, Fulvio of Cristofano, one of the main accusers, told the Inquisitor that 'If he is released from prison we can't bring up our children ... He is considered a *stregone* and it might be some 8 years that he has [had] such [a] reputation'.[26] In two of the cases of bewitched infants, the parents reported that, since their babies had been consumed by illness, they had blamed Fei, with the usual assumption that it must have been him because he had such a bad reputation locally. Underlying neighbourhood conflicts that might have induced an accusation of *maleficium* were absent from the picture. For example, some years before the trial, the baby of well-off butcher Domenico of Leonardo had fallen sick. Convinced that her baby was bewitched, Domenico's wife Clementia had fried the heart of a buck.

The belief was that the first person to come over the threshold after the completion of this ritual would be the witch – it was Giandomenico Fei. When a second baby fell sick, the suspicion and anger of the butcher and his wife were so strong that Domenico went in person to the smithy to threaten Fei. The baby recovered soon after this encounter 'without any medicine' – in other words, without Fei going to see the baby. The father remained uncertain about the cause of the child's recovery, testifying about Fei that 'I cannot judge that his fame is created by his enemies, but not even by *certa scientia* [by direct experience; direct eye-witness] can I say that he caused my baby and other babies to rot'.[27]

This convergence of harming and healing was, however, a crucial, incriminating circumstance in Fei's trial. Loaded with demonological meaning, it pointed to the binary power of the witch to heal that which he or she had previously harmed. It was not an isolated occurrence. Fulvio of Cristofano also testified against Fei that:

> I think he bewitched my seven-month-old infant; I believe it because he has such fame, and I add that I called on the said Fei and he healed the baby. How he healed him I don't know.[28]

Even Fei's own niece, Antonia, laid a charge of infanticide against him, albeit in a rather contradictory deposition. She told the tribunal that:

> I don't think he is a *stregone*, and I don't know by whom he got such fame. Four years ago he took my baby in his arms...The baby began to cry, and he gave him back to me. The baby suddenly stopped taking the tit [refused to breast-feed] and died the day after. With neighbours I complained he had wasted away my baby. He scolded me and threatened to beat my husband.[29]

Apart from a few lucky exceptions, the documentation from most Sienese witch-trials does not allow the historian to reconstruct the slow process by which an individual acquired a reputation for witchcraft. The Fei case is no exception in this regard, although witness testimonies do point to the fact that problematic social exchanges between Fei and his neighbours, which the latter had interpreted according to witchcraft beliefs, had been accumulating over a time span of 10 years. What finally encouraged neighbours to bring the matter to court in 1599, when local witchcraft beliefs were translated into formal judicial action, and Fei was finally accused, jailed, and tried? Again, we cannot answer this question precisely, although witness testimony suggests that there were four episodes that were regarded as particularly damning evidence against the blacksmith by the Roman Cardinals who ultimately oversaw the trial. In the first, a notary named Giuseppe Franchi claimed to have caught a glimpse of Fei in the dead of night, lurking bare-footed near a church, holding a candle, a skull and a book in his hands. In the second, a plaintiff named Lucretia accused Fei of having used love magic against her sister, Agnes, saying that:

> He [Fei] gave her the egg-yolk of a black hen to eat. And since then Agnes has proved unable to leave her lover and kept saying: 'If he lived in Hell and I in Paradise, I would feel compelled to leave Paradise to join him in the Hell'.[30]

The third key episode was the evidence given by Clementia, the wife of the well-off butcher Domenico, in relation to the frying of the buck's heart, which was discussed earlier. Finally, the fourth episode was one of alleged magical healing, in which a woman named Dorotea reported that Fei had cured her baby of worms by reciting a prayer and anointing the infant's forehead.

Whatever triggered the trial, the outcome was very clear. Luckily for the blacksmith, by the last decade of the sixteenth century the 'burning times' were over, as far as the Inquisition was concerned. On 25 September 1599, Father Orceoli received a letter from Cardinal Giulio Antonio Santoro with the following instructions on how to resolve the Fei case:

> Reverend father, regarding the trial, my most illustrious colleagues have decided that you give him the strappado... And if after the torture or a *territio* nothing else comes out you have to forbid him to practise healing, and release and sentence him to 5 years of exile from his home town.[31]

IV

The confrontation between Giandomenico Fei and his accusers revealed in the trial records shows not only that his neighbours, convinced that his ominous power was a real threat to the community, turned to the law for revenge, but also that they were motivated to win a feud that was driven by vested interests. This is the *what* of the story. But *who* was Giandomenico Fei? What kind of witch was he? Due to our limited information on the Montepulciano case, it is impossible to say more about his personality. One way forward, however, is to try to gain further insights about him by focusing on the women accused of witchcraft in Siena, and checking their personalities against what we know of Fei's elusive profile. This might help us to understand how this particular male witch was made, and also how broader gendered stereotypes of witchcraft operated in the region. A useful starting point for this endeavour is an important passage from the *Malleus Maleficarum*, in which Heinrich Kramer, drawing on his experience as an Inquisitor in the late fifteenth century, outlined witchcraft as a system, and described witches and their power as follows:

> Sorceresses appear in three kinds (those who harm but are unable to heal, those who cure and do not harm ... and those who harm and heal) as was discussed in Part One of the treatise.[32]

The language of the fanatical witch-hunter needs further decoding, but what is important to note here is the fact that the witchcraft beliefs of the villagers of Central Italy were very similar to those expressed by Kramer, with the three types of witches neatly represented in the reality of village life. Let us have a closer look at them.

The third type of witch referred to by Kramer, that both healed and harmed, was the type most often found in the Sienese State. These were the 'social' or 'healer' witches touched on earlier: wet-nurses, midwives, and wise-women. Their power consisted in healing the harm that they were believed to have caused, and which they also believed they had caused. Typical examples of these harming/healing witches were Angelica from Radicondoli (who was tried in 1594), Maria from Roccastrada (tried in 1589), and Antonia from Monticiano (tried in 1609).

Angelica was married and in her seventies in 1594, and lived in Radicondoli, a village with around 500 inhabitants. She was reputed to have 'a good hand' with which to treat bewitched babies, as a fellow villager testified to the Inquisition:

> *Inquisitor*: Do you know that some people have taken persons to Angelica to be cured?
>
> *Villager*: In this land it is universally known that as soon as rotten infants are discovered they must be taken to Angelica because she has a good hand with infants (*putti*).[33]

We should not assume that Angelica was an ordinary folk-healer: she was a specialist whom we may anachronistically label a paediatrician, as her trial offers no evidence of her treating adults. People turned to her when infants fell ill and witchcraft was suspected as the cause. On such occasions, as the depositions demonstrate, a scene was staged, in which both the victim's parents and the supposed witch deliberately avoided saying anything explicit about bewitchment. In 1594, the little daughter of a woman named Alessandra was being consumed by illness; neighbours thought the child had been bewitched, and suggested to Alessandra that she resort to Angelica for help, because of the latter's 'good hand' with infants. As Alessandra testified:

> Only I was warned to say that the baby had another sickness... I took the baby to her... Angelica beforehand reassured me she was not bewitched... But it was all a fake, because she knew she was rotten ... Angelica unswaddled my baby and after handling her for a while stretching her legs and arms, then gave her back to me saying she wouldn't die of that sickness.[34]

Why did both parties to this exchange go to such lengths to deny bewitchment as the cause of the child's condition? The crucial point was that, if Angelica had diagnosed a spell as the cause, and then treated and cured the child, this would have been very dangerous for her, as it would have helped to confirm her identity as a harming/healing witch. Many narratives, reporting similar scenes played out in the drama of village witchcraft, survive in the Inquisitorial court records and follow much the same pattern. The insistence by parents to have their sick babies treated shows a general belief in the ambivalent power of the witch, a belief that enhanced the self-confidence of the witch, and eventually increased her agency. For example, Angelica was not afraid to boast about her powers publicly. In a possession case, she once shouted at her fellow villagers: 'Have you seen: I scared her, and more devils will be discovered in her!' Her anger and aggression did not spare even a cleric locally responsible for exorcisms, who noted in a letter to the Inquisitor in which he urged her capture that:

> This land is full of rotten children ... Everybody is blaming big Angelica (*Angelicona*). She threatens to stab whoever is willing to testify... even me; and she keeps repeating that I am more *stregone* than she.[35]

Maria was a 45-year-old midwife from Roccastrada. She was also an herbalist, a knowledge that might have increased her medical skill. Her medical experience was certainly wide, extending even to the nobility. The Sienese noble Alberto Luti told the Inquisitor that:

> I maintain for sure the said Maria bewitched me because she was the only one able to cure me…I think that those who are being consumed because of strange sicknesses are caused to waste away by her and she heals them.[36]

Another witness reported that 'Maria superstitiously practised healing, so that whenever the infants (*putti*) fell sick everybody put the blame on her, but came to her to have them healed'.[37] Maria and Angelica were both women of some financial substance, for whom money was important, and they were also well integrated into the networks of village sociability. Both were bold and aggressive in character, prone to cursing. Under interrogation, Maria confronted the Inquisitor, slapping the bench and shouting 'I'm not a witch'. Later, she switched to irony, saying to the Inquisitor 'Watch me, I'm not crying, therefore I'm a witch' – a dangerous reference to the belief that witches were unable to shed tears. 'And that with much audacity', remarked the Inquisitor on her behaviour in custody.[38] After a mild verdict, Maria was released. She returned to Roccastrada and walked down the main street shouting threats of retaliation: 'Those who witnessed against me will repent…There will be no more births in this village…'.[39]

The power and personality of Antonia from Monticiano were more complex. In her late sixties, she was a well-off widow who gave alms to others, but she was also assertive, and had a tendency to try to teach moral lessons to other inhabitants of Monticiano. The testimony of witnesses at her trial suggests that this moralizing took the form of a low-level culture of 'prediction': all villagers attributed to Antonia the puzzling power to prophesy events and misfortunes. For example, she was reported to have said that:

> This woman will have a boy on Monday; [or] this other one won't carry on successfully any pregnancy; [or] death is approaching us, older women, but a young man will die sooner than us…[40]

Antonia also had a domineering character, and was quick to threaten retaliation against others. As she was well off, quite a few villagers owed her money, and at least one of her debtors seems to have been motivated to accuse Antonia of witchcraft maliciously. At her trial, one witness admitted having been advised to provide false testimony by her main accuser. The latter was a local social climber who owed Antonia money, and who accused her of having bewitched him with a glass of wine. Clearly, this accusation was triggered by a long and bitter feud.

However, several other allegations came from villagers who had not been loaned money by Antonia. Their testimony before the Inquisition was thus probably fairly reliable, and motivated mainly by their genuine fear of Antonia's art and power. It is important to note that the trial provides only flimsy evidence about Antonia's healing activities: clearly, she did not have a reputation as a healer. She was, however, thought to possess a harmful touch, as the statement by local sharecropper Lorenzo indicated:

> I remember years ago we had an argument about some cherries, and she patted my shoulder. Suddenly my flesh shivered, the day after I fell sick and since then I have been consumed with illness throughout winter. Feeling hopeless I went then to a healer, some Barbara, and found Antonia in her house. Antonia asked me about my health, told me not to worry, and had me eat some pears... I felt immediately healed and had the strength to run home... And this is the truth.[41]

On one occasion, Antonia was summoned by the parish priest to the church, where she found the supposedly bewitched young Maddalena with her mother. Maddalena was crippled and unable to swallow any food. The mother threatened retaliation against Antonia, and the priest admonished Antonia loudly to stop doing harm, saying 'Antonia, enough, you have done too much of it. Enough, Antonia!' Antonia left the church grumbling. A public showdown took place the next day. Antonia went to the bakery where she met the bewitched girl, gave her some biscuits and touched the girl's shoulders. After eating the biscuits, Maddalena immediately recovered. Antonia had thereby consciously and publicly healed the harm she was believed to have inflicted.

The first type of witch referred to by Kramer in the *Malleus Maleficarum* was the witch who harmed, but was unable to heal. In other words, these were NOT harming/healing witches of the 'social' type but, rather, those for whom we have no evidence of positive restorative communal activities. One such witch was Manfilia from Cotone, a married woman who was probably in her sixties when she was tried in 1594. She was well integrated into the social networks of her village, and was probably no worse off economically than those who accused her of witchcraft. Amongst the score of witness depositions given to the court, there were no hints of any healing activity; we even lack evidence of episodes of counter-magic in which she was compelled to withdraw the spells she had supposedly inflicted. Villagers expressed a clear fear of her long-standing and destructive supernatural powers, although the latter appear to have been purely psychic. For example, her stare was believed to have caused whole families to waste away, as one witness informed the Inquisitor:

> Thirty years ago in the dead of night big Tommy saw Manfilia together with two other women lurking around the graveyard... He caught a glance of her and felt his hair bristle... The day after at the Mass she stared at him... In the short run big Tommy died and so did all his descendants, and nobody was left of them.[42]

Another witness, called Antea, also recalled what had happened to her 15 years earlier:

> Being a young girl I was sent by my mother to collect chestnuts... I saw a bunch of eight or nine women dancing under the chestnut-tree and I recognized Manfilia who told me to keep quiet and not to talk with anybody about it. I lost my voice, all my hair fell and I almost died.[43]

A similar power of harmful fascination was believed to emanate from the look of Antonia la Palandrana from Grosseto, who was tried for witchcraft in 1604. Antonia was a 40-year-old whore who terrorized to death Bartolomeo, one of her customers. Once, in the dead of night, he had run into Antonia and had tried to follow her. She had disappeared suddenly 'and from this very fact he was so terrified that he fell sick and died within five or six days'. Antonia had been plaguing the inhabitants of Grosseto for years before the local official responsible for criminal acts denounced her to the Inquisition in 1604, thereby ending the power that she had wielded by means of her bewitchments.[44] The – literally– spell-binding power of some witches' eyes was well summarized in a denunciation made by Francesco of Giovanni from Ricomagno in 1673, when he complained to the Inquisition about a confrontation he had had with a woman called Agia, whom he accused of having bewitched his child:

> *Agia*: To your *citto* (little boy) I didn't do either good or harm because I didn't touch him.
>
> *Francesco*: It is true that you did not touch him, but you saw him with your own eyes. ... Now, take this *citto* and heal him if you want the salt you asked me for yesterday.[45]

The second type of witch defined by Kramer was the witch who healed, but did no harm – a reference to the anti-witch specialists, or cunning folk, in which rural Central Italy (and Europe as a whole) abounded. They formed a specific occupational group that has recently received much attention from historians of witchcraft and magic. For Central Italy, even a rough calculation of their number and gender is impossible, as most are referred to only fleetingly and anonymously in the sources: deponents often commented just that 'I went to the cunning man/woman'. Some, such as the cunning man named Giacomo whom we have already met in a case from 1692, probably had only a local reputation; they surfaced occasionally in denunciations or trials. Others operated on a more business-like, regional scale. On the basis of evidence given in trials for therapeutic magic, we can tentatively postulate the existence of a gender-differentiated hierarchy of anti-witch specialists, with cunning men possibly ranking higher than cunning women.[46] There were not many of these higher status anti-witches in total, however. The evidence suggests that not every one of the 22 administrative districts of the Sienese State had one of them, which suggests that, instead, there was middle- and even long-range mobility amongst the people who went to them for help. Cunning folk tended to stay in one place, and were often referred to by their place of residence, such as the most reputed Tuscan cunning man, the Galatrona, who was thus named after the tiny hamlet in which he lived. The regional fame of the Galatrona went back to the time of Lorenzo de Medici and, although we find traces of his medical activity throughout the seventeenth century, we have no idea about the 'real' identity of the individuals disguised behind the place name.

As the restoration of health was their main concern, we can consider cunning men and women as service providers within the pluralistic medical marketplace of the early modern period. They were more than that, however, because they also fulfilled a pivotal role in the contemporary system of witchcraft. People turned to them to receive specific help against bewitchment and, in cases of harmful magic affecting infants, their expertise was often performed by means of rituals, using the clothes of the victims. Claims about the source of their power were never made explicit in the court records, although some cunning women were reported to have inborn gifts. Allegedly born on Ascension Day, they had received an egg and some ears of wheat in their hands and, as a result, were believed to possess a special gift of grace that enabled them to identify and heal illnesses resulting from witchcraft. There is strong evidence that cunning men had a tendency to form dynasties. There is also evidence of a smattering of literacy amongst the cunning men of Central Italy; some could read, and at least one could write as well. Four out of the 118 cunning men we can identify from the records had noteworthy occupations: two were sword-makers, one was a gunsmith, and one a blacksmith. On closer scrutiny, however, none of the four could be classified as a real anti-witch specialist: they operated, rather, on the margins of anti-witch activity. They might function as healers and were, in fact, asked to provide some medicine. However, there is no evidence that people turned to them for help in cases of unnatural sickness, or to have bewitchments hidden in clothes discovered, or witches detected. Sometimes, they were only requested for help in matters of protective magic, when they were asked to provide magical belts and rings.

No cunning folk were ever reported to have committed crimes of harmful magic, a crucial point in our understanding of the witchcraft belief system of Central Italy. It has recently been suggested that 'the correlation [between witchcraft cases and cunning folk] is sufficiently strong to suggest that those who practiced "cunning" ran a definite risk' of being accused of witchcraft.[47] This was not the case in the Sienese State, however. The cunning folk caught up in the judicial machinery of the Inquisition were denounced for practising healing, not for performing harmful witchcraft. It is true that the system of differentiating between healing and harming always contained ambiguities, and that these ambiguities increased as local Tuscan communities were slowly integrated into higher systems of political and judicial control, such as those of the regional state and the post-Tridentine Catholic Church, whose crucial 1586 papal Bull, *Coeli et terrae*, criminalized any form of popular healing activity. The trial against Lisa di Gallena, a cunning woman of higher status, provides an explicit example of the effect of this Bull on people's perception of healing rituals. In 1588, in the hamlet of Pari, the young Sienese nobleman Aspremio Borghesi had a nightmare in his country house. His brother, having been awakened by the noise, rushed into the bedroom and saw Aspremio standing on his bed waving a sword. Aspremio explained his nightmare to the Inquisitor in the following manner:

> We were eleven or twelve people and were having a vigil. We were talking about this Lisa...I said how do you know she is a witch; I was answered...'Can't you see all her bewitchments: she keeps healing around with prayers all the day long'...And this reasoning happened because an Edict had come, forbidding to heal with the use of prayers...That very night I went to bed with this fantasy and Lisa appeared to me.[48]

However, despite the increased blurring of imaginative and linguistic categories in relation to healing and harming magic that occurred as a result of the papal legislation from the late sixteenth century onwards, the testimony of many witnesses before the Inquisition demonstrated their continued ability and desire to distinguish between healing and harming magic. Witnesses at the trial of Lisa di Gallena, for instance, stood firm in denying that she was a harmful witch, repeating that 'She drives out witches'. In testimony from the trial of another high-status *indovina* (cunning woman), Caterina from Ricomagno, in 1612, the perception that she was on the side of the victims in the fight against harmful magic was even clearer, despite a blurring of linguistic categories that resulted in the use of the term *strega* (harmful female witch) in relation to her:

> I know her since I know the good and the evil...She is a *strega* by public voice and fame. I had a rotten little boy and the said Caterina came over. She then told me it was necessary to have two masses said for him, and said an oration over the child and took a piece of cloth and gauged it thrice, and I didn't hear because without secrecy the medicine in worthless.[49]

What kind of witch was Giandomenico Fei, then, in relation to the three types listed by Kramer? Despite the increasing linguistic ambiguity of the term *stregone*, Fei was not one of Kramer's second type of witches, the cunning man. There is not a single reference in his trial records to the usual comings and goings of clients needing the services of an anti-witch specialist. The terminological puzzle is therefore solved: by labelling the blacksmith a *stregone* people meant that he was a harmful male witch. Was he then a witch of the third type, who could harm and heal – in other words, was he one of the 'social' or healer witches of Central Italy? It is tempting to surmise that blacksmiths might fulfil this role, and this is what the verdict delivered by Cardinal Giulio Antonio Santoro on his case, in which he ordered Fei to stop the practice of healing, seems to imply. However, on closer scrutiny the trial evidence does not support this conclusion. In Montepulciano there was no evidence of mothers going to Fei to have their sick infants manipulated, and he does not even seem to have forged magic belts or rings, like the afore-mentioned sword-makers and gunsmiths, who routinely gave out medical advice without ever being accused of witchcraft.[50] Fei's *maleficia* were also believed to have vanished after he was seriously challenged about them, as his confrontation by the butcher Domenico shows: this was another example of the 'natural control' of harmful witchcraft – discussed earlier – in practice.

Should we then conclude that Giandomenico Fei was a witch of Kramer's first type, who could harm but not cure? I am inclined to think so, and to believe that Fei was thought to posses and emanate some psychic strength that was similar to the special power of fascination possessed by other harmful female witches in Siena, like Manfilia of Cotone, or Antonia la Palandrana of Grosseto, or Agia, who was thought capable of staring people to death. There is plenty of evidence in the trial records from Central Italy of such 'involuntary witchcraft', of a widespread belief 'in the existence of persons whose eyes had a special power of fascination'.[51] Fei's malevolent power was probably reinforced by the shadowy atmosphere surrounding his job and by the deeper power he was believed able to draw from books, although we do not know the extent to which he actually practiced magical rituals. As a male witch, however, the key point is that his power and personality are much the same as those possessed by the harmful female witches: all the episodes of harmful magic recounted in Montepulciano could just as easily have been committed by the harmful female witches I have discussed. On the basis of this conclusion and in theory at least, the inhabitants of Central Italy were clearly capable of thinking about witches and the harm that they caused in ways that were undifferentiated by gender. Overall, their testimonies about Manfilia, Antonia and Giandomenico Fei, as well as their statements about Angelica and Maria, were first and foremost about witchcraft: the lived experience they had of witchcraft and of social interaction with reputed witches, with all its complexities, uncertainties and anxieties. In the end, the inhabitants of Central Italy spoke an ambiguous language when they spoke about witchcraft, and one that included ideas of agency, activity and authority. Witches were believed to wield a complex power in their communities and the key characteristics of their cases show that what was important for their neighbours was not so much their gender as the fear they generated, based on the belief in their evil powers and the ways in which these could affect village life.

V

To suggest that people in Central Italy could imagine men as harmful witches in theory is all very well, but in practice we cannot ignore the hard fact of the statistics, which demonstrated that 176 out of the 178 people accused of harmful magic in the region were women. This overwhelming predominance of female witches transformed witchcraft in the Sienese State from a 'sex-related' to an almost 'sex-specific' crime. In order to help explain this local variant in the gendering of witch-persecution we might usefully turn to an analysis of the crimes of harmful magic such witches were thought to have committed.[52] The prevalence of infanticide amongst these crimes accounts in part for the overwhelming feminization of witchcraft in this region. Acts of infanticide took place within a female sphere of social action that involved the bearing, feeding, raising and healing of children – activities of huge importance that demarcated women's lives in profound ways but which could also easily go wrong. A useful line of enquiry for future research would be to verify for Central Italy whether or not 'mothers who killed their children were tried simply for infanticide' when trials for witchcraft stopped in the second half of the 17th century.[53]

It is hard for historians to say much about the long-term processes by means of which the primal fears of pre-historic communities became personified as 'demons' or 'witches'. We can, however, say that 'The [...] demonic ancestors of the human witch' were eventually embodied in the daunting, mythical creatures of classical mythology, such as Circe, Medea, Dipsias and Canidia.[54] Ideas of night witches merged with the negative Christian stereotype of woman, which was rooted in the biblical representation of Eve as the origin of all carnal sin. However, the key texts of late-medieval demonology maintained a gender-undifferentiated image of the witch, at least until the late fifteenth century. The publication of the *Malleus Maleficarum* in 1486 marked a crucial turning point in ways of imagining witches, as it emphasized the existence of female witches linked to various areas of women's social activity (as wet-nurses; wise-women; midwives; whores). This new way of imagining the witch proved – literally – fatal for women in the witch-hunts of the early modern period, especially as it tended to be strengthened by the campaigns of social disciplining that were attempted as a result of the Reformation and Counter-Reformation and which tended to emphasize the moral principles of a revitalized patriarchy.

We are unfortunately unable to provide more detail on the possible impact of the new ideas contained in the *Malleus* on central Italian witch-beliefs during the fifteenth century because of a lack of specific fifteenth-century criminal sources for the region. We can, however, suggest speculatively that there existed some strong local bias in favour of imagining harmful witches as female that stemmed from the late-medieval period and that continued to shape the ways in which people in the Sienese State imagined witches in the sixteenth and seventeenth centuries. In this context, the violent anti-witchcraft preaching of Saint Bernardino in Siena in 1427 might well have been significant, given his dramatic call for witches to be sent 'to the fire, to the fire, to the fire'. Bernardino's campaign against witchcraft was essentially undifferentiated in its gender terminology, but his very strategy of preaching in this manner helped to put women, and their supposedly sinful sexuality, at the centre of the phenomenon.[55] Of course, there is a gap of 150 years between Bernardino's preaching campaign and the (almost) 'gender-specific' witch-hunts undertaken by the early modern Inquisition, so it is very hard to prove a definitive link between the two. However, between 1540 and 1570 there is, for instance, evidence of a lay tribunal sentencing eight witches to the stake, one of whom was a man. We can perhaps speculate, then, that a still non-gendered demonological witch-stereotype was undergoing a final fusion with much more ancient ideas about women as evil witches. The fusion of the two might have had an influence upon – and, in turn, been strengthened by – the moral campaigns of the post-Tridentine Catholic Church. Recent statistics from the Sienese criminal church court records show that an unrelenting imposition of Counter-Reformation moral codes overlapped with the late-sixteenth-century peak in the Inquisition's policing of what it deemed to be criminal magical activity. Moral disciplining of the faithful began in earnest after an apostolic visitation of the Sienese diocese in 1575, and aimed to implement the Tridentine marriage decrees, and to morally cleanse Siena by banning concubines and physically confining prostitutes to certain parts of the city. As a result of this drive, fornication became the main moral offence in Siena.

In the light of this wider moral campaign, it is no coincidence that the available data on the occupational activity of Sienese witches show that seven women out of 20 were young whores who were still active. When, in 1639, Friar Simon, a parish priest, was asked by the Inquisitor about the lives of three village women accused of witchcraft, his response is no surprise: it is probably a blend of traditional ideas from Saint Bernadino with a new Counter-Reformation emphasis on the immorality of fornication:

> *Inquisitor*: De vita dictarum mulierum
>
> *Friar Simon*: You figure out they all have been whores or daughter of whores; because the art of witchcraft is connected with the practice of whoredom.[56]

That these ideas were shared lower down the social scale is shown in a deposition given by a 50-year-old Sienese woman called Agnesa Pasqui, who explained in 1650 that:

> If women when young commit carnal sins, later in their life they act as pimps to find lovers for younger women; and when they are too old they become witches and make sex with the devil.[57]

Testimony such as this reminds us that the female gendering of witchcraft needs to remain a key focus of historical inquiry. This point is made with the following caveats, however: the emphasis on gender should not distract historians of witchcraft from the fact that fear, and the question of how to fight, it were primal preoccupations of human beings. Neither should historians let themselves be distracted from the fact that witchcraft accusations and persecutions cannot be separated from the waxing and waning of people's preoccupations with fear over the centuries. Fear was, and still is, an ancestral and overarching reality in human lives.

Notes

1. M. Gijswijt-Hofstra, 'Witchcraft after the Witch-trials', in B. Ankarloo and S. Clark (eds), *The Athlone History of Witchcraft and Magic in Europe. Volume 5: The Eighteenth and Nineteenth Centuries* (London, 1999), 95–188, at 136.
2. C. Ginzburg, *Il benandanti. Stregoneria e culti agrari tra Cinquecento e Seicento* (Turin, 1966). This was first published in English as *The Night Battles* by Routledge and Kegan Paul in 1983. Norman Cohn has suggested that the book was of limited relevance beyond Italy, commenting that: 'I can't see that the book throws any light at all on the nature of European witchcraft', *New Republic*, 192 (25 February 1985), 39.
3. See, for example, G. Romeo, *Inquisitori, esorcisti e streghe nell'Italia della Controriforma* (Florence, 1990). However, Ruth Martin's *Witchcraft and Inquisition in Venice, 1550–1650* (Oxford, 1989) is an anticipatory attempt to make use of a whole Inquisitorial archive.
4. O. Di Simplicio, *Inquisizione, stregoneria, medicina. Siena e il suo stato 1580–1721* (Siena, 2000); O. Di Simplicio, *Autunno della stregoneria, Maleficio e magia nell'Italia moderna* (Bologna, 2005).
5. See O. Di Simplicio, *Le lettere della Congregazione del Sant'Ufficio all'Inquisizione di Siena (1581–1721)* (Trieste, 2008). The Inquisition, or Holy Office, was a college of cardinals, based in Rome.
6. Keith Thomas, *Religion and the Decline of Magic. Studies in Popular Beliefs in Sixteenth- and Seventeenth-Century England*, 2nd edn (Harmondsworth, 1973), 548.
7. Di Simplicio, *Autunno*, 302–3.
8. This definition of a 'natural control of witchcraft' is taken from the work of the late Christina Larner, *Witchcraft and Religion: The Politics of Popular Belief* (Oxford, 1984), 127–9.
9. Di Simplicio, *Autunno*, 194. In making this threat, Giacomo is boasting that he can compel Frasia to go over ('walk') to Domenica's house to withdraw the spell, thus claiming that his power is greater than Frasia's.
10. There is only one marginal reference to storms in all of the Sienese source material: one female witch was denounced for having boasted that she had performed several acts of harmful magic, amongst which was the causing of a storm (see Table 6.8).

11. E. Labouvie, 'Men in witchcraft trials: Towards a social anthropology of 'male' understandings of magic and witchcraft', in U. Rublack (ed.), *Gender in Early Modern German History* (Cambridge, 2002), 49–68, at 52.
12. 'Qualified' magic includes the use of sacramentals. 'Therapeutic' or 'healing' magic refers to a wide range of options used by patients within the context of a pluralistic (and predominantly illicit) medical system. 'General' magic covers several minor superstitions that cannot otherwise be categorized under the more specific headings.
13. The breakdown of love magic by occupations was as follows:
    Men: clerics, 36; nobles, 5; soldiers, 3; uncertain, 61.
    Women: midwives, 2; whores, 51.
14. Labouvie, 'Men in witchcraft trials', 63.
15. I have not included 7 cases of ligature love magic in this total of witchcraft crimes. Love magic in general was an ambiguous art, often affecting male sexual performance only in a selective way (it might, for example, prevent a man from performing sexually with his wife but not with his mistress). Three cases of ligature (the magical/symbolic tying of knots) to prevent the consummation of marriage were performed by men, some mavericks. None of them had the reputation of a sorcerer comparable to the sort of reputation of the female specialists, who were mostly whores. Francis Bacon had quite correctly remarked that 'Anybody may do it [the knots]' (cited in Thomas, *Religion and the Decline of Magic*, 552).
16. These age cohorts are based on the 79 cases where this information is given. The two male witches are not included in this table.
17. É. Pócs, 'Why witches are women', in *Acta Ethnographica Hungarica*, 48(3–4) (2003), 367–83, at 375.
18. Archivio della Congregazione della Dottrina della Fede, Rome, Vatican City (hereafter ACDF), *Siena, Trials*, 10, mixed-up pagination. Other than the Fei case, the Sienese sources contain only one other trial for *maleficium* involving a man. It is a rather atypical case from 1594, concerning the uncertain death of a young boy supposedly poisoned by his love rival (ACDF, *Trials*, 12, 662–717) Cesare Alberti. There is also a very brief report about an infanticide case from the village of Radicondoli from 1672, in which the main suspects were Domenico Cinci, 'publicly reputed a *stregone*', and his wife, Caterina, a wet-nurse. Due to its brevity, the denunciation is of little use, however.
19. ACDF, *Siena, Trials*, 10.
20. In Normandy, 'blacksmiths were frequently involved in illicit forms of veterinary medicine', see W. Monter, 'Toads and the eucharists: The male witches of Normandy, 1564–1660', *French Historical Studies*, 20 (1997), 563–95, at 584.
21. ACDF, *Siena, Trials*, 10.
22. On this thorny point, see the discussion by Jonathan Barry of the issue of malicious accusation, 'Introduction: Keith Thomas and the Problem of Witchcraft', in J. Barry, M. Hester and G. Roberts (eds), *Witchcraft in Early Modern Europe. Studies in Culture and Belief* (Cambridge, 1996), 1–45, at 13–14.
23. ACDF, *Siena, Trials*, 10.

24. We do not know whether or not Giandomecio was literate. He did not sign his interrogation, although this does not necessarily mean that he could not read.
25. There is an exception. At the Montisi trial, in 1621, an overwhelming majority of witnesses (39 out of 52) were women. They testified against five witches of dubious moral reputation in what was a sort of ethnological competition on the marriage market, with the aim of seizing the locally available sexually adult males. See Di Simplicio, *Autunno*, 240–62.
26. ACDF, *Siena, Trials*, 10.
27. ACDF, *Siena, Trials*, 10. The sick baby had recovered after Domenico's showdown with Fei, but 'without any medicine' (in other words, without Fei going to see the baby), so Domenico only assumes that his confrontation with Fei made the blacksmith withdraw his spell.
28. ACDF, *Siena, Trials*, 10.
29. ACDF, *Siena, Trials*, 10.
30. ACDF, *Siena, Trials*, 10.
31. See Di Simplicio, *Le lettere*, for further discussion. *Territio* meant literally a 'scare' or fake torture, suggested by the Inquisition for use against a defendant deemed physically incapable of being subjected to real torture. In the *territio*, the defendant was stripped of his clothes, laid on the rack, and tied as if undergoing real torture. Unfortunately, in Fei's case we do not know whether he was subjected to real torture or the *territio*; we are also not informed whether his banishment was enforced or not.
32. Henricus Institoris, O.P. and Jacobus Sprenger, O.P., *Malleus Maleficarum*, edited and translated by C. S. Mackay, Vol. II, *The English Translation* (Cambridge, 2006), II, ch. 2, 233. See also Part One: 'For sorceresses come in three varieties. Some heal and harm, some harm but are unable to heal, some only seem to heal, that is, to remove injuries, as will be explained below' (Ivi, I, Q. 9, 151).
33. Di Simplicio, *Autunno*, 145.
34. Di Simplicio, *Autunno*, 145, and *Inquisizione*, 204.
35. Di Simplicio, *Inquisizione*, 182.
36. Di Simplicio, *Autunno*, 147.
37. Di Simplicio, *Autnnno*, 147.
38. Di Simplicio, *Autunno*, 148.
39. Di Simplicio, *Autunno*, 148.
40. Di Simplicio, *Autunno*, 224.
41. Di Simplicio, *Autunno*, 233.
42. Di Simplicio, *Autunno*, 140–1.
43. Di Simplicio, *Autunno*, 140–1.
44. Di Simplico, *Autunno*, 295–9.
45. Di Simplicio, *Autunno*, 136.
46. On cunning folk, see Di Simplicio, *Autunno*, 193–222.
47. S. Clark, 'Witchcraft and Magic in Early Modern Culture', in B. Ankarloo, S. Clark and W. Monter (eds), *The Athlone History of Witchcraft and Magic in Europe. Volume 4: The Period of the Witch Trials* (London, 2002), 97–169, at 113.
48. Di Simplicio, *Autunno*, 31.

49. On Lisa and Caterina, see Di Simplicio, *Autunno*, 210–4.
50. Di Simplicio, *Autunno*, 197.
51. Thomas, *Religion and the Decline of Magic*, 520, 553. Generally speaking, to consider magical healing and maleficient harming as 'equivalent' might oversimplify our understanding of a witchcraft system (see Clark, 'Witchcraft and Magic', 112, for further discussion). In fact, the healing/harming dichotomy went hand-in-hand with a second, common early modern belief that spells could be withdrawn only by the malevolent person who had cast them.
52. This is, of course, a weak point of witchcraft studies, since we are still unable to explain many regional and national variations of *maleficia*. Why, for instance, were there so many storm-making witches in Central Europe and almost none in seventeenth-century Essex or Central Italy? Why were there so few instances of *maleficia* involving animals in Central Italy, and so few examples of ligature cases in England? 'It is worth asking whether regional variations are structured [in] "systems of differences"', as Peter Burke notes in 'The Comparative Approach to European Witchcraft', in B. Ankarloo and G. Henningsen (eds), *Early Modern European Witchcraft. Centres and Peripheries* (Oxford, 1990), 435–41, at 438–9.
53. B. P. Levack, 'The Decline and End of Witchcraft Prosecutions', in B. Ankarloo and S. Clark (eds), *The Athlone History of Witchcraft and Magic in Europe. Volume 5: The Eighteenth and Nineteenth Centuries* (London, 1999), 1–93, at 81.
54. E. Pócs, *Between the Living and the Dead. A Perspective on Witches and Seers in the Early Modern Age* (Budapest, 1999), 16.
55. Valerie A. Kivelson insists on the point that sins of the flesh preoccupied Orthodox Christianity far less than the Christian one, a fact that 'rendered the logic of Western association between women and witchcraft meaningless in Muscovy'; see V. A. Kivelson, 'Male witches and gendered categories in seventeenth-century Russia', *Comparative Studies in Society and History*, 45 (2003), 606–31, at 616–7.
56. Di Simplicio, *Autunno*, 295.
57. Di Simplicio, *Autunno*, 101.

7

Men and the Witch-Hunt in Scotland

Julian Goodare

The Scottish witch-hunt was one of the more severe in Protestant Europe. Out of a population of approximately 1 million, about 4000 witches were formally accused, and perhaps 2500 were executed. Scotland, with something over two executions per thousand of population, thus had four times the European average of 0.5 executions per thousand.[1] Of course, the European average conceals wide variations, but it should be borne in mind that Scotland's witch-hunt was not merely more severe than its neighbour England's; it was severe in absolute terms. Witch-hunting involved a web of power, and Scotland is an important place in which to study the various roles that men played in it – as witchcraft victims, as witchcraft prosecutors and, sometimes (though not often), as witches themselves.

The records of Scottish witchcraft are good in some respects, disappointing in others. Witchcraft was a secular crime between 1563 and 1736, and almost all trials occurred in this period. Most trials were authorized centrally, and a record of this authorization usually survives, at least after 1608. So, we can obtain a good statistical sense of the pattern of *accusations*. The trial record itself is much less likely to survive, unless the trial was held in the central justiciary court, as it was in about ten per cent of cases. The remaining trials were held in temporary local courts that rarely preserved archives. Thus, estimating numbers of *executions* depends on extrapolating an execution rate from fragmentary evidence.

The present chapter will take a largely qualitative, rather than quantitative, approach. For the thematic questions that it raises, statistics are not usually available; not only do we lack reliable statistics for executions, we also lack them (to take one example) for the proportion of witches who were folk-healers. In the tradition established by

Christina Larner, the brilliant pioneer of the subject, the chapter will instead draw conclusions from readings of individual cases and other qualitative evidence. Rather than telling individual stories in detail, it will range widely over the surviving material in order to present a picture of what is likely to have been typical.[2]

Some more statistics may nevertheless be mentioned at this point. These, as the previous ones, come from the online 'Survey of Scottish Witchcraft'. The Survey identified 468 men and 2702 women formally accused of witchcraft. The proportion of men accused was thus 15 per cent.[3] The figures of 20 or 25 per cent commonly quoted as typical for Europe indicate that the Scottish witch-hunt was relatively misogynist. This intensified somewhat during Scotland's five great witchcraft panics of 1590–91, 1597, 1628–30, 1649–50 and 1661–62; the proportions of men and women remained constant, but the likelihood of a woman being executed increased.[4] The relatively high proportion of women among Scotland's witches probably reflects the severity of its witch-hunt overall.

I

Witch-hunting in Scotland was a governmental operation. Many cases were initiated – or, at least, supported – by neighbours' complaints, and it is hard to see how witch-hunting could have occurred without such complaints. However, no Scottish study has identified the kind of *organized* popular pressure for executions that fuelled some witchcraft panics in Germany.[5] On the contrary, Stuart Macdonald has argued that 'the populace did not initiate witch-hunts'. Scotland's powerful system of presbyterian church courts took the initiative; they heard a rumour of witchcraft, or received a complaint by someone who had been slandered by being called a witch, and called for witnesses to come forward. The witnesses were sometimes willing, sometimes reluctant.[6] Moreover, the authorities did not restrict prosecutions to those witches identified by neighbours; they broadened the hunt further. Especially during the five great panics, many localities saw chain-reaction hunts in which large numbers of people were named as witches by other confessing witches, and convicted on the basis of their own confessions with little or no neighbours' testimony against them.[7]

Recent surveys of the role of the state in Scottish witch-hunting have emphasized the coordinating role of central government, and the pivotal role of local elites. Local elites initiated prosecutions but, because local courts lacked jurisdiction to execute witches, they had to seek central permission. They would assemble documentation – a process often coordinated by the kirk session or presbytery – and apply to the Privy Council. The Privy Council examined the prosecution's documentation, and conducted a dry run of the trial; only if this were likely to lead to a conviction did the Privy Council grant a commission of justiciary allowing the trial to be held in the locality.[8]

Governmental authority was also related to more general issues of patriarchal power. With the expansion of bureaucracy, the power of the propertied elite was less dependent on direct military force, and more on office-holding and patronage. Bloodfeud, the traditional means whereby elite men asserted their power and settled their disputes, was gradually eliminated by governmental action in the period c. 1598–1625.[9]

Scotland was notable for the intensity of the moral discipline that the Protestant church wielded after the Reformation.[10] In the Lowlands, at least, there came to be a kirk session in every parish, backed up by a regional presbytery and higher courts. The kirk session, consisting of the minister and a dozen lay elders, sought out and punished a variety of moral offences, notably fornication and adultery, but also sabbath-breaking, 'scolding' (women's quarrelling), and slander. Punishing slander could mean punishing someone for having called someone else a witch. Eradicating 'superstition' could mean punishing pilgrimages to holy wells (a remnant of Catholic ritual) or magical practices. The eradication of witchcraft was a small, if dramatic, part of the remit of the presbyterian system; and the church courts – actually, or potentially, in close touch with the community – were in a good position to identify people with reputations for witchcraft.

The stage between reputation and prosecution was important, since reputations were often constructed among women, while prosecutions, obviously, were controlled by men. Robin Briggs has noted a 'crucial gap' between female rumours and male trials.[11] Similarly, Carol Karlsen writes of New England that 'The records do not allow us fully to see a woman becoming a witch'.[12] Scotland, with its church courts conducting sometimes extensive pre-trial investigations, might well be a good place to study this further.[13] What one can say is that ordinary Scotswomen were willing to complain directly to the minister, without a male intermediary. Agnes Aitken, testifying against her mistress Katherine Black in Alloa in 1658, said that after one suspicious incident she 'sweare shoe should goe and tell the minister, but they [that is, Black and her husband] disswaded hir from goeing'.[14]

Once the kirk session or presbytery had identified a witchcraft suspect, it would usually bring in a small group of local lairds (landed proprietors) who would later be able to apply for a commission of justiciary. The minister, elders and lairds would interrogate the suspect to take down their confession – this was where torture, usually in the form of sleep deprivation, could occur – and would record depositions from aggrieved neighbours. In a town, the role of the lairds would be taken by the bailies, the leaders of the burgh council.

One alternative or supplementary type of evidence, increasingly used in seventeenth-century Scotland, was the Devil's mark: this was sought by an expert male 'pricker', of whom at least eight are known to have been active. It was important for prickers to be men, in contrast to practice in England and elsewhere where intimate body searches of women were carried out by women.[15] Two of the Scottish prickers actually turned out to be women dressed as men: 'John Dickson' was really Christian Caldwell, while the other woman is known only by her alias, 'Mr Paterson'.[16] The pricker's quasi-professional skills contrast with the innate witch-finding powers claimed by a few witches, all apparently female. The most notorious was Margaret Aitken, the so-called great witch of Balwearie, who claimed during the 1597 panic to detect witches by a mark in their eyes.[17]

Once a dossier of evidence had been compiled, it would be time to apply to the Privy Council for a commission of justiciary. After 1597, at least three commissioners were normally needed, of sufficient social standing to negotiate directly with the leaders of the government, and to be accepted as criminal judges. Commissions of justiciary were usually granted to lairds, often to those who were already judges in local courts. If the Privy Council agreed to grant the commission, the newly appointed commissioners would return to the locality; appoint a court officer, clerk and dempster; summon an assize of 15 local, propertied men; and hold the trial. The dempster, a traditional official who proclaimed the verdict, could double as the executioner. Instead of granting a commission, the Privy Council could send the case for trial in the central court of justiciary, where professional defence advocates sometimes participated. All these roles were filled exclusively by men.[18] It was a patriarchal world, and this was relevant to witch-hunting.

II

One of the most important questions in Scottish witchcraft research concerns the role of witch-hunters – men who did not merely carry out their duty in trials, but who went out of their way to orchestrate and promote them. It is intuitively plausible that some people were more keen on witch-hunting than others. Given their near-monopoly of the public sphere, the role of active witch-hunter fell, in practice, to men. The fact that most witches were women was relevant, but we need to focus on the men's motivation. Can 'witch-hunters' in this active sense be identified and distinguished from those who took part in prosecutions dutifully? And if so, can anything meaningful be said about the witch-hunters' motives? This chapter cannot answer these questions in full, but it will outline the issues and make some suggestions.

The concept of the 'witch-hunter' as a distinct individual who went out of his way to prosecute witches receives powerful qualitative support from the detailed research of Louise Yeoman. She studied five prosecutions of rich women for witchcraft, and found that each was actively driven forward by a man with an identifiable motive. Thus, the prosecution of Euphemia MacCalzean – one of the North Berwick witches of 1590–91 – was pressed by David Seton, bailie of Tranent; Yeoman showed that Seton's wife was the sister of MacCalzean's husband, and that he felt aggrieved over an inheritance that had gone to MacCalzean and not him. Although such motives could not apply to the prosecutions of ordinary, non-propertied witches, there were further common factors in the prosecutions. Yeoman's witch-hunters were all quarrelsome, in a perhaps characteristically masculine way; Seton also tried to work up a witchcraft charge against his rival John Cockburn and, when this failed, he killed him. They were also troubled by debt, ill fame or other inadequacy. Witch-hunting seemed to offer such men a chance to vindicate themselves to their communities, though they often failed.[19]

Elite men in the localities might thus have been spurred into witch-hunting by perceiving themselves and their property as under threat from witchcraft. In a number of cases, the threat was to lairds' sons. Of course, peasants too could see their children as witchcraft victims, but the attacks on lairds' sons – and it was almost always their sons, those who would inherit their landed property – seem numerous enough to be treated as a distinct group. To take one example from 1662, Isobel Goudie is best known for her elaborate confessions about flying and covens, but she also mentioned that she and her associates had made a clay image with which to destroy the sons of John Hay of Park. One of the associates was Janet Braidhead, who also mentioned an attack on the sons of John Hay of Lochloy.[20]

One way of looking at these questions would be to hypothesize that some men among these local elites would develop an obsession with witchcraft prosecution, and would take part in one case after another, in order to save society from the satanic threat represented by witchcraft conspiracy. Matthew Hopkins was like this in England. Scotland generally offered better prospects for the serial witch-hunter because its legal concept of the witch – focused on the demonic pact – allowed the prosecution of suspects with no prior reputation in the community. Serial witch-hunters need not have had Hopkins's high profile, especially with Scotland's paucity of witchcraft pamphlets; they might simply have been parish activists.[21]

Identifying such men, and researching the nature of their involvement with witchcraft, would be a major project. Preliminary identification of serial witch-hunters could be done using the 'Survey of Scottish Witchcraft', which identifies various types of people involved in witchcraft prosecutions: pre-trial investigators, trial commissioners, prickers. Several hundred men were involved in five or more cases, and a few in up to 30. However, detailed research would be needed to establish which of them were merely diligent local officials, and which were committed activists.

In the meantime, we should make the best we can of impressionistic evidence. The attitudes of a male witch-hunter can be sampled in a letter from a man better known for his opposition to witch-hunting. Sir George Mackenzie of Rosehaugh, as a legal writer and as Lord Advocate from 1677 to 1686, played a key role in discouraging prosecutions;[22] but, in 1661–63, he was a justice depute (a judge in the court of justiciary), and presided over numerous trials in the great witchcraft panic of that period. In seeking his arrears of pay for this, he wrote:

> If souldiers who killd on[e] man at most in two years wer weel payd, should not I who killd hundreths and more justly and without any self defence, as they did, expect som acknowledgement. I ordourd and establisht the reeling forces and brought the lousnesse of that court to som method.[23]

This, with its military analogy, was a distinctly masculine self-presentation of the witch-hunter. James VI, in his book *Daemonologie* (1597), had made a similar analogy.[24] James was important to Scottish witch-hunting, injecting a political dimension into it that gave it significance at all levels of society.[25]

III

One of the earliest recorded mentions of Scottish 'witches' concerned men. The so-called 'Statutes of King William', probably dating from the fourteenth century, contained a statute 'Of infamous men' that included 'witches' among a long list of offenders.[26] There has been discussion of how witches came, in the late Middle Ages, to be seen as generally female;[27] the transition clearly occurred in Scotland, though it might not be traceable in detail. The transition from male to female witches is an example of a broader issue: the nature of witchcraft stereotypes and their relationship with real witches.

It has generally been agreed that there was a stereotype of a witch. Early modern folk could conceptualize witches and discuss the idea of them separately from discussing concrete individual witches. Clearly, no stereotype witch could be 85 per cent female. Some scholars have assumed that there could be only one stereotype witch, and have thus assumed that when people thought of the abstract idea of a witch, they always envisaged a woman. However, Willem de Blécourt has recently made the breakthrough of conceptualizing plural witchcraft stereotypes:

> Within a gendered society the idea of an ungendered witch was unimaginable. A witch was either male or female and a male witch stereotype will by its contrast have strengthened rather than weakened the female one. To comprehend this fully, we have to realise that men could be classified under the female stereotype and women under the male one.[28]

He adds: 'Apparently there was no male witch stereotype current in Scotland'.[29] I made a similar point in greater detail in my own paper on women:

> The male witch, from the Devil's point of view, was the poor relation of his female counterpart. Rather than a distinctive set of masculine characteristics, what he had were the same as the female witches but fewer and weaker. He made the demonic pact, as the women did; he angered his neighbours, as they did. He just did it less dramatically.[30]

Most Scottish male witches generally resembled female ones, with the differences being that their malefices were few, their demonic pact was undramatic, and they almost never had sex with the Devil.[31] Given the importance attached to sex between female witches and the Devil, this last was a crucial omission. The male witch in Scotland, from this point of view, was a watered-down female one.

Nevertheless, some of Scotland's male witches were distinctive. In my paper I went on to identify 'faint signs of a distinctive male relationship with the Devil'. Several male witches could summon up the Devil, whereas female ones almost always had to wait until the Devil chose to appear to them. A few male witches had batons or wands, probably symbols of authority (on which more in a moment). A few were also physically punished by the Devil, whereas the Devil did not usually beat women.[32] Further research might show whether Scotsmen accused of witchcraft displayed a distinctively masculine concern for their honour.[33]

Were male witches in Scotland assimilated to the female witchcraft stereotype? Before attempting to answer this question, it would be worth pointing out the breadth of the female stereotype in Scotland. Alison Rowlands sums up much recent European historiography as suggesting that 'witches were predominantly imagined by contemporaries as the evil inverse of the good wife and mother; as women who poisoned and harmed others rather than nurturing and caring for them'.[34] For Lyndal Roper, the issue seems even simpler: 'the answer' to the question of why so many witches were women is that witches were believed to 'attack fertility'.[35] In Scotland, however, things were not so simple. Lauren Martin has studied female witchcraft suspects who were involved in quarrels. She finds that 'the quarrels tended to be about aspects of female labour such as cloth production, dairying and healing', and only 'occasionally' involved the 'work of motherhood'. There was often a distinction between the topic of the quarrel and the object of alleged magical harm, so that a quarrel over cloth production could be followed by an attack on the victim's children. In other cases, the witch could be accused of attacking the victim's business prosperity, as when, in 1629, Isobel Young was alleged to have caused Cuthbert Simpson 'to misthryve and go bak in his estait' after a dispute about cloth purchase.[36] This cannot be comprehended under the blanket term 'fertility'. Scottish female witchcraft stereotypes included an assumption that women would be involved in a wide range of economic activity, and their quarrels and curses reflected this.

Lara Apps and Andrew Gow argue that 'male witches were implicitly feminised', because witches were weak-minded, and weak-mindedness was associated with women; male witches were 'womanly "fools"'.[37] This, if qualified by the observation that there were different kinds of male witches, is congruent with de Blécourt's argument that some male witches had a female stereotype applied to them. A Scottish example is Thomas Leys, in Aberdeen in 1597. He was caught up in the prosecution of his mother, Janet Wishart, a classically quarrelsome female witch with a long reputation. Wishart was convicted through neighbours' testimony alone, but immediately after her execution, her son was interrogated and made a lurid confession of having attended a witches' sabbath with a number of other people, mainly women. The interrogators could not extract much information from him about malefice, and were reduced to accusing him of guilt by association in his mother's maleficent activities, showing that they were willing to accept a man as guilty of them. This might also indicate that they saw Leys as 'weak-minded', in Apps and Gow's terms, since, although an adult, he had followed his mother's lead. The leaders of the witch-hunt also prosecuted Leys' father and sisters, but the assize acquitted them. Thomas Leys, however, was convicted, and his confession sparked a major witchcraft panic.[38]

Another aspect of the female stereotype was that it was women who would normally initiate other witches. Quite a few male witches, in Scotland as elsewhere, were accused as husbands of female witches, and it is here that we find the concept – perhaps over-stressed, in the past – of men as secondary targets of witchcraft accusation.[39] Usually, when a married couple were both accused, it was assumed that the wife had prior responsibility.[40] One possible exception, Janet Braidhead in 1662, confessed that her husband, John Taylor, 'entysed' her to become a witch.[41] However, although Braidhead was interrogated and presumably tried, there is no record that Taylor was. The case of Patrick Lowrie in 1605 might represent a different kind of exception; his powers seem to have been acquired in an unusual and, perhaps, distinctively masculine way when his father cursed him.[42]

This is a good point at which to mention that quarrelling and cursing were integral to the female witchcraft stereotype; yet, cursing hardly ever features in male witches' trial records.[43] Perhaps early modern Scotsmen did little cursing, or perhaps little significance was attached to such curses as they might have uttered. Cursing, like scolding, seems to have been perceived as virtually a female monopoly.[44] This can be illustrated from the trial of John Burgh, a charmer, in 1643. Five of the 22 charges against him alleged harm done; for instance, he had attempted unsuccessfully to cure John Kidd of a disease and Kidd had paid him 40 shillings, whereupon Burgh, 'being discontent with the money being over litle', caused Kidd's business prosperity to 'evanische and goe frome him'. In this charge, and two others, there is the hint of a quarrel, but no more than a hint. Burgh might well have quarrelled with these people, but the point is the reticence of the legal record on the subject.[45] For a woman, the courts were interested in the details of the quarrel, the nature of the misfortune that followed, and the connection between these; but not for a man. Men were perhaps assumed to assault their opponents physically, or to sue them in the courts, rather than cursing them. An assumption that men did not normally curse their antagonists may have been one of the most powerful mechanisms for limiting the number of witchcraft accusations made against them.

The question of male or female stereotypes might be sidestepped by following an argument of Malcolm Gaskill. He sees some witchcraft accusations as being made against 'members of an unpopular household', rather than against individuals.[46] Alison Rowlands also discusses 'witch-households', though she sees the women in them as having been in the front line of accusation.[47] For a Scottish example, we could take Andrew, Katherine and Elizabeth Ratter, in Shetland in 1708: a brother and sisters, occasional folk-healers, with a bad reputation for begging, quarrelling, and inflicting malefice. It seems that they had a collective reputation in which Andrew was fully participant; more malefices were attributed to him than to his sisters.[48] But such cases are uncommon. Scotland clearly had at least one female witchcraft stereotype of the kind outlined by de Blécourt; did it also have one or more male stereotypes?

When seeking distinctive male witches, one place to look would be to those known as warlocks or wizards, all of whom were men. Most male witches were called 'witches', but the term 'warlock' was quite common. Patrick Lowrie, in 1605, was described in his dittay (indictment) as a 'cowmone and notorious sorcerer, warlok and abuser of the peopill'. He was a folk-healer, and a number of his alleged malefices were connected with cures or attempted cures. He was popularly known as 'Pait the Witch'.[49] A 'warlock' was not necessarily perceived as maleficent; William Ford, who had to do penance in 1597 for 'consulting with a warlow [that is, warlock] in Newcastell in England', had presumably been seeking what he saw as a *bona fide* magical service.[50] James Hutchison, preaching on witchcraft in 1697, mentioned 'a warlock, that is a he-witch in our Scots language'.[51] 'Wizard' was rare, perhaps eclipsed by 'warlock'.[52] Further research might reveal why some people needed a separate word for a male witch.

Cunning folk in Scotland, as elsewhere in Europe, were not generally targeted by witch-hunting, but could find themselves accused if they were perceived to have used their powers for evil, instead of good. Gender ratios among Scottish cunning folk require further study. Joyce Miller's pioneering study of 'charmers' (the usual, generic Scottish term) found two thirds women, one third men.[53] Owen Davies has argued that this group should be broken down into amateur healers (the category for which the term 'charmer' was used in England) and professional cunning folk proper, and that the latter might well have been two thirds men (as in England and elsewhere).[54] Because of the prominence for women of quarrels followed by misfortune, charmers or cunning folk formed only a small proportion of the women accused of witchcraft; for men, it was a large proportion. Since male witchcraft suspects were often asked about healing, this probably helped to form one stereotype of a male witch. Perhaps they were part of a stereotype that was neither gender-specific nor gender-neutral but, rather, was applied separately to women and men, with awareness of their slightly different roles in healing.

Some male witches were also criminals for reasons unconnected with witchcraft. David Roy, in 1601, tried to use witchcraft and potions to seduce his employer's daughter 'by the dobbing on ane apple and infusing of ane portioun of his awn natur [that is, semen] in it'. He then laced her drink with 'Spaniyie fleis' (cantharides), and then consulted a witch. When all this failed to work, he raped her.[55] Such behaviour, however, seems too distant from witchcraft, and perhaps too rare, to have constituted a stereotype.

One male witchcraft stereotype emerges when we consider questions of authority. Since at least the time of Aquinas, theologians had debated the question of the Devil's authority-structure:[56] the confessions of several Scottish witches allow us to glimpse something of how this was conceptualized by their interrogators. The witches themselves largely imagined a folk Devil with limited powers.[57] However, some witches spoke of having a recognized place in the Devil's authority-structure, and this was evidently felt to be sufficiently meaningful for their interrogators to record it. The authority-bearing witches, it turns out, were virtually all men.

We may begin with the North Berwick witches of 1590–91. Geillis Duncan, whose confessions launched the panic, said that John Fian 'was their register'. Fian himself, a schoolmaster, confessed 'that at the general meetings of those witches he was always present; that he was clerk to all those that were in subjection to the devil's service bearing the name of witches; that alway he did take their oaths for their true service to the devil, and that he wrote for them such matters as the devil still pleased to command him'.[58] The Devil once appeared to Fian 'with a white wand in his hand', and Fian attempted to renounce his service. The Devil answered 'that once [that is, eventually] ere thou die thou shalt be mine', and 'brake the white wand'.[59] Scottish officials carried wands and, when they were deforced (resisted) in the course of their duties, they would formally break the wand. The Devil's use of written records and an official wand made him a symbolic bureaucrat, telling us something of the forms of regular authority that were respected in early modern Scotland.

Further authority-bearing witches were found in the seventeenth century. Robert Grieve from Lauder in 1649 confessed that he was 'the *Devils Officer* in that Country for warning all Satans Vassals to come to the Meetings, where, and whensoever the Devil required, for the space of eighteen years and more'.[60] John McWilliam Sclater, accused in 1656, had been appointed 'cloak-bearer' to the Devil.[61] John Young in Mebestown was the 'officer' for Isobel Goudie's coven in 1662.[62]

The idea of a male leader as an 'officer' seems to have come up whenever there was any suggestion of an organized group. The North Berwick witches, supposedly led by the Earl of Bothwell, and Isobel Goudie, who mentioned her 'coven', are prominent cases; both were deployed extensively by Margaret Murray to prove her theory of a surviving pagan witchcraft cult. Coinneach (Kenneth) Odhar, who passed into later Gaelic folklore as the 'Brahan Seer', was originally a 'principal or leader of the art of magic' whose arrest was ordered in 1578 as the alleged leader of a group of witches in Easter Ross.[63] There was a panic over a second treasonable witchcraft conspiracy against James VI, in 1597 – 'another North Berwick' – also led by a man, Malcolm Anderson.[64]

The concept of authority-bearing male witches prompts a further comparison with female witches. Larner argued that the demonic pact was seen as a 'standard feudal relationship';[65] but this idea has been challenged by Martin, who argues that it was more akin to a marriage. Specifically, it was like 'irregular marriage', which in Scots law meant that the consent of both parties, followed by sex, constituted a valid and binding marriage, even without church formalities. The advantages of this argument are clear: it fits the Scottish elite's emphasis on sex with the Devil, normally an integral part of any confession to the demonic pact. It also moves the demonic pact from the public sphere of 'feudal' relationships to the domestic sphere of sexual intimacy. But, of course, as Martin points out, this understanding of the demonic pact worked only for female witches. Male witches were 'aberrations from the norm of the heterosexual structure of the demonic pact'. For a few, the problem was solved by having them confess to having had sex with the queen of the fairies (whom the interrogators construed as a demon). Martin argues that John Neill, in 1631, had a 'master–pupil relationship with the Devil', and that this was typical of male healers.[66] The Devil forbade John Fian to marry, perhaps seeing a wife as a rival for his allegiance, though Fian had a good deal of extra-marital sex of a characteristically masculine type.[67] Scottish elites' understanding of the demonic pact as being akin to marriage might have encouraged the large female majority of prosecutions.

The idea that male witches could have quasi-political roles in the Devil's organization probably constitutes the Scottish elites' single most distinctive interpretative model for them. For such male witches, it moves the demonic pact back into the public sphere – and even, perhaps, back to Larner's idea of a 'feudal relationship'. However, like Martin, I would prefer an alternative model for public relationships: that of the covenant. Larner, too, pointed out the importance for seventeenth-century Scots of covenanting theology, in which salvation was achieved through a covenant (that is, a contract) between God and the individual believer. This kind of covenant was private, but there was also the concept of a covenanted nation, through which Scotland as a whole promised allegiance to the cause of God.[68] Witchcraft trial documents often called the demonic pact a 'covenant'. This idea should not be pressed too far, as the word was used in both men's and women's trials; but there are indications that men had more of a public, political relationship with the Devil than women.

IV

Men, witchcraft and authority came together in another, related way. Scotland had several political witch-hunts, in which witches were either employed by a political faction, or were believed to have been so employed. The witches themselves might be male or female, but their clients were male. Some of the political conflicts were national, while others operated at the level of an individual landed kindred. Some of the witchcraft conspiracies were real, while others were imaginary – but they were all about the exercise of power in a masculine world.

The first recorded case was in the fifteenth century. An apparent conspiracy against James III by his brother the Earl of Mar, in 1479, led to Mar's execution and to that of 'mony weches and warlois', apparently of both sexes.[69] The North Berwick conspiracy against James VI seemed genuinely frightening in 1590–91, as did its successor in 1597.

Turning to cases within landed families, in the 1570s Hector Munro apparently conspired with his stepmother, Katherine Ross, Lady Foulis, to kill his brother, Robert Munro of Foulis, in order to gain his inheritance.[70] In a power struggle within Clan Campbell in the early 1590s, John Campbell of Ardkinglass was suspected of the assassination of his rival John Campbell of Calder and approached a group of witches in the hope of magically regaining the favour of his chief, the Earl of Argyll.[71] John Stewart, younger brother of the Earl of Orkney, was accused of having conspired with a witch, Alison Balfour, to make away with the Earl. The Earl had Balfour tortured and executed in 1594, but Stewart was acquitted in 1596.[72] Some of the magical attacks on lairds' sons could also be considered as part of this category of political witch-hunt. There were also elite parallels to the case of David Roy, where elite men used witchcraft to achieve straightforwardly criminal ends.[73]

The power of witchcraft was not the same as political power. Magic was a technical skill, while political power – at least when legitimate – carried status. A witch could hex a king, or an assassin could stab him; but neither the witch nor the assassin wielded the same kind of power as the king. The person who did that – or, who sought to do it – was the king's political rival who ordered the assassination; and that person was bound to be male. Political men were hardly ever accused of witchcraft themselves, they were accused of procuring the services of others. Even with the main exception to this rule, the Earl of Bothwell in the North Berwick panic, the accusations against him were essentially that other witches practised magic against the King 'at your command'.[74] The fact that Bothwell was acquitted might even indicate a closing of ranks to prevent accusations of witchcraft spiralling up into the political class – something that occasionally happened in political panics on the Continent. In political witchcraft, therefore, Scotsmen feared that lower-class witches, who were usually female, might have their technical skills orchestrated by high-status men seeking political power. They did not fear that high-status men might be witches, and certainly not that lower-class witches might seize power for themselves.[75]

The idea that some elite men were 'consulters' of witches, exploiting the witches' power for political ends, could nevertheless be related to the idea that they were themselves witches or, more specifically, necromancers. Necromancy (the summoning of evil spirits for magical purposes) was part of a learned magical tradition, not used by folk-healers.[76] Richard Graham, one of the North Berwick witches, probably had not conspired against the King but was undoubtedly a necromancer, and there seem to have been several others.[77] Here, it might be worth focusing on the way in which a spurious reputation for necromancy could be acquired. The leading Scottish Reformer, John Knox, was dogged throughout his career by hostile accusations of necromancy.[78]

A Catholic polemicist alleged that Knox's colleague John Willock, superintendent of Glasgow, had a son who had 'raised the deuil zour doctor, in Arthuris Seate'.[79] John Napier of Merchiston, the renowned inventor of logarithms, had interests in alchemy and astrology; he was popularly rumoured to have made a pact with the Devil and to have a black cock as a familiar.[80] Ministers who had been dismissed from their parishes for some offence seem to have been particularly likely to be named as witches or necromancers, though the accusations against John Kello (1570), George Sempill (1630), and Gideon Penman (1678) did not progress beyond a preliminary investigation.[81] One renegade minister, the highlander Patrick MacQueen, really practised magic in the 1590s, providing his services to Campbell of Ardkinglass, who believed that he could make up and build a castle between sundown and sunrise.[82]

Elite men who consulted witches were the subjects of a distinct group of stories. These stories hinged on the man's belief in the 'response' that he received from the witch. Such 'witches', who were basically diviners, seem to have had little in common with the witches appearing in the courts. The central feature of these stories was an unusual kind of prophecy: what Stith Thompson has called an 'enigmatical prophecy'.[83] Most of the prophecies in Thompson's catalogue were direct rather than 'enigmatical'. Some were favourable, more were unfavourable; but the story usually concerned the inexorability of fate, and the impossibility of avoiding one's known fate. Numerous folk-tales involved outwitting by equivocation, but rarely of a prophetic type. More often, the equivocations were deceptive bargains or promises, or simply strategies for success. As for the Devil in folk literature, he was rarely a deceiver; usually, he was himself deceived.[84] There were many 'enigmatical prophecies' in classical literature, notably those of the Delphic oracle, but the tradition seems to have dwindled in the Middle Ages.

The most celebrated case of 'enigmatical prophecy' was, however, Scottish: the story of Macbeth and the witches. Macbeth was a real Scottish king (1040–57) who featured prominently in histories. The most influential history of Scotland in its day was that of Hector Boece, published in 1527.[85] The prophecy opening his Macbeth story was a direct prediction that Macbeth would become king, encouraging him to kill King Duncan. The 'enigmatical prophecy' came later, when Boece introduced a clearly identified witch:

> Ane wiche, in quhom he [that is, Macbeth] had gret confidence, said, to put him out of all feir, That he suld nevir be slane with man that wes borne of wife; nor vincust, quhill [that is, until] the wod

> of Birnane wer cum to the castell of Dunsinnane. Macbeth, havand gret confidence in thir wourdis, set aside all feir of deith...for be the ta prophecy, he belevit it wes unpossible to vincus him; and be the tothir, unpossible to sla him.[86]

The story continued as in Shakespeare's later version: Macbeth believed himself secure until, too late, the truths concealed behind the prophecy were revealed.

Several other Scottish stories turned on such prophecies.[87] One from the narrative of Sir John Scott of Scotstarvet, written c.1655–70, illustrates the concept of the 'response'. Captain James Stewart, Earl of Arran, briefly dominated Scottish politics in the mid-1580s. He and his Countess, Elizabeth Stewart, were flamboyant and much-resented figures.[88] Scott told the following story of them:

> His lady got a response from the witches, that she should be the greatest woman in Scotland, and that her husband should have the highest head in the kingdom; both which fell out; for she died, being all swelled in an extraordinary manner; and he, riding to the south, was pursued by the Lord Torthorald...and was killed, and his head carried on the point of a spear.[89]

Such 'enigmatical prophecies' seem to form a distinctive Scottish narrative tradition that might repay further research. It complemented, rather than superseded, the conventional type of inexorable witches' prophecy.[90] All these stories were told in, and about, the public sphere of political witchcraft activity. The interest in them focused not on the female witch, but on the male political figure.

V

Witch-hunting in Scotland was about power: state power over the common folk, religious power over deviant belief, and the whole community's power over the uncanny magical threats that lurked in an uncertain world. It was also about masculinity, and about male power over women. Witchcraft might have been 'sex-related', but witch-hunting was certainly 'sex-specific'.[91] Growing fears of witchcraft helped the male authorities to assert their control over a wide range of domestic behaviour that had not hitherto concerned them. The remarkable effectiveness of the presbyterian discipline system tended in turn to sharpen fears of witchcraft, first by uncovering more of it, and then by launching serial witch-hunts. Fears of witchcraft also allowed some men – how many, we do not yet know – to launch themselves into active careers as witch-hunters, presenting themselves as saviours of the community.

When men were accused of witchcraft themselves, this sometimes feminized them by associating them with patterns of female behaviour. However, there was more than one stereotype available to be applied to male witches. Some male witches were, or were assumed to be, cunning folk. Some – probably a minority, but a distinctive and prominent minority – were thought of as wielding characteristically masculine types of power. They were either part of the Devil's authority-structure and thus implicitly superior to female witches, or they were learned necromancers, or they were using magic to engage in masculine political struggles. With this latter category, though, the political men were seen mainly as *employing* lower-class witches, not as being witches themselves, which might indicate that the men who wielded political power found it particularly difficult to imagine one of their own number as a witch. Stories about witchcraft, too, operated in this masculine political world. It has been argued that one significant stage in the decline of Scottish witch-hunting came with the so-called Glorious Revolution of 1689, after which the state reluctantly accepted religious pluralism and ceased to claim godly legitimacy.[92] This meant a reduction in the ideological power wielded both by the government and by its opponents, and a concomitant increase in political stability. Men could breathe a sigh of relief. The end of witch-hunting gave women even stronger reasons to celebrate.

Notes

1. For the European average see R. M. Golden, 'Satan in Europe: The Geography of Witch Hunts', in M. Wolfe (ed.), *Changing Identities in Early Modern France* (Durham, NC, 1997).
2. Christina Larner's classic work is *Enemies of God: The Witch-Hunt in Scotland* (London, 1981), complemented by her collected essays, published posthumously as *Witchcraft and Religion: The Politics of Popular Belief* (Oxford, 1984); A recent revival of Scottish witchcraft studies has produced several works, including L. Normand and G. Roberts (eds), *Witchcraft in Early Modern Scotland: James VI's* Demonology *and the North Berwick Witches* (Exeter, 2000); S. Macdonald, *The Witches of Fife: Witch-Hunting in a Scottish Shire, 1560–1710* (East Linton, 2002); J. Goodare (ed.), *The Scottish Witch-Hunt in Context* (Manchester, 2002); J. Goodare, L. Martin and J. Miller (eds), *Witchcraft and Belief in Early Modern Scotland* (Basingstoke, 2008); and B. P. Levack, *Witch-Hunting in Scotland: Law, Politics and Religion* (London, 2008). Publications

from 1992 to 2002 are reviewed by Stuart Macdonald in '*Enemies of God* revisited: Recent publications on Scottish witch-hunting', *Scottish Economic and Social History*, 23 (2003), 65–84. In the context of the present chapter, particular mention should be made of J. Goodare, 'Women and the witch-hunt in Scotland', *Social History*, 23 (1998), 288–308.

3. J. Goodare, L. Martin, J. Miller and L. Yeoman, 'The Survey of Scottish Witchcraft, 1563–1736', www.shc.ed.ac.uk/witches/ (archived January 2003, updated October 2003, accessed April 2006; hereafter SSW). There were a further 42 for whom the name is not sufficiently complete to determine their sex, and a further 625 unnamed people or groups of unknown size. The total of known individuals was thus 3837, but the existence of groups, plus the likelihood that further records have been lost or remain undiscovered, means that the number formally accused is likely to have exceeded 4000.
4. I am grateful to Dr Liv Helene Willumsen for sharing with me these points from her ongoing analysis of SSW. This revises the pre-Survey conclusions reached by Goodare, 'Women and the witch-hunt', 291.
5. Particularly that in Trier: see W. Behringer, *Witches and Witch-Hunts: A Global History* (Cambridge, 2004), 93–7.
6. Macdonald, *Witches of Fife*, 175–8.
7. 'Just under 49 per cent of accused witches were accused in a group of 6 or more people from one parish per year, 21 per cent of witchcraft suspects were accused in a group of 3–5 other people and 35 per cent were accused either alone or with only one other person': L. Martin, 'Scottish Witchcraft Panics Re-examined', in Goodare *et al.* (eds), *Witchcraft and Belief*, 132.
8. J. Goodare, 'Witch-Hunting and the Scottish state', in Goodare (ed.), *The Scottish Witch-Hunt in Context*; B. P. Levack, 'Absolutism, state-building, and witchcraft', in his *Witch-hunting in Scotland*. A focus on the 'witch-accusing community' is recommended by Martin, 'Scottish Witchcraft Panics Re-examined', 133–8.
9. K. M. Brown, *Bloodfeud in Scotland, 1573–1625* (Edinburgh, 1986); J. Goodare, *The Government of Scotland, 1560–1625* (Oxford, 2004), ch. 12.
10. See, in general, M. F. Graham, *The Uses of Reform: 'Godly Discipline' and Popular Behavior in Scotland and Beyond, 1560–1610* (Leiden, 1996); M. Todd, *The Culture of Protestantism in Early Modern Scotland* (New Haven, CT, 2002).
11. R. Briggs, *Witches and Neighbours*, 2nd edn (Oxford, 2002), 237–8.
12. C. F. Karlsen, *The Devil in the Shape of a Woman: Witchcraft in Colonial New England* (New York, 1987), 150.
13. The subject is discussed by Macdonald, *Witches of Fife*, and by A. L. Cordey, 'Witch-Hunting in the Presbytery of Dalkeith, 1649–1662' (University of Edinburgh MSc thesis, 2003).
14. British Library, Egerton MS 2879, fo. 7v.
15. C. Holmes, 'Women: Witnesses and witches', *Past and Present*, 140 (August 1993), 45–78, at 71–5.
16. Larner, *Enemies of God*, 110–12; W. N. Neill, 'The professional pricker and his test for witchcraft', *Scottish Historical Review*, 19 (1922), 205–13.
17. J. Goodare, 'The Scottish Witchcraft Panic of 1597', in Goodare (ed.), *The Scottish Witch-Hunt in Context*, 58–60, 68–9.

18. There was one female executioner – the wife of the executioner who died on the day that he was due to execute William Barton: George Sinclair, *Satan's Invisible World Discovered*, Thomas G. Stevenson (ed.) (Edinburgh, 1871), relation 25.
19. L. A. Yeoman, 'Hunting the Rich Witch in Scotland: High-Status Witchcraft Suspects and their Persecutors, 1590-1650', in Goodare (ed.), *The Scottish Witch-Hunt in Context.*
20. Pitcairn (ed.), *Trials*, iii, II, 605, 609–10, 612–3, 617.
21. Cf. the men who orchestrated women witnesses in England: Holmes, 'Women: Witnesses and witches', 52–8.
22. B. P. Levack, 'The Decline and End of Scottish Witch-Hunting', in Goodare (ed.), *The Scottish Witch-Hunt in Context*, 168–79.
23. Mackenzie to [Earl of Lauderdale], 5 Nov. [1667?], quoted in Andrew Lang, *Sir George Mackenzie* (London, 1909), 46.
24. Goodare, 'Women and the witch-hunt', 308.
25. B. P. Levack, 'King James VI and Witchcraft', in his *Witch-Hunting in Scotland*, makes this point, and draws together much earlier research on James. One additional work is D. Willis, *Malevolent Nurture: Witch-Hunting and Maternal Power in Early Modern England* (Ithaca, NY, 1995), ch. 2, offering a perhaps over-ambitious psychological interpretation that also emphasizes James's masculine approach.
26. 'Statuts of King William', in John Skene (ed.), *Regiam Majestatem* (Edinburgh, 1609), 4 (separately paginated), c. 11. King William 'the Lion' reigned from 1165 to 1214, but these laws in their current form are unlikely to antedate the fourteenth century. The statute barred 'infamous men' from ecclesiastical office, and from acting as accusers or witnesses in court.
27. W. Stephens, *Demon Lovers: Witchcraft, Sex, and the Crisis of Belief* (Chicago, IL, 2002).
28. W. de Blécourt, 'The making of the female witch: Reflections on witchcraft and gender in the early modern period', *Gender and History*, 12 (2000), 287–309, at 298.
29. De Blécourt, 'The making of the female witch', 307.
30. Goodare, 'Women and the witch-hunt', 304.
31. The case of William Barton might be unique. He confessed to having had sex with the Devil in the form of a 'young Gentlewoman... beautiful and comely': Sinclair, *Satan's Invisible World Discovered*, 160–1. Sinclair, writing in 1685, dated this to 'about thirty years ago'. As we shall see, a few men confessed to sex with the queen of the fairies, construed by interrogators as a demonic figure.
32. Goodare, 'Women and the witch-hunt', 305.
33. Cf. R. Walinski-Kiehl, 'Males, "masculine honour," and witch hunting in seventeenth-century Germany', *Men and Masculinities*, 6 (2003–4), 254–71.
34. A. Rowlands, *Witchcraft Narratives in Germany: Rothenburg, 1561–1652* (Manchester, 2003), 135.
35. L. Roper, *Witch Craze: Terror and Fantasy in Baroque Germany* (New Haven, CT, 2004), 32.
36. L. Martin, 'The Devil and the Domestic: Witchcraft, Quarrels and Women's Work in Scotland', in Goodare (ed.), *The Scottish Witch-Hunt in Context*, 84–9 (quotations from p. 86).

37. L. Apps and A. Gow, *Male Witches in Early Modern Europe* (Manchester, 2003), 7, 13.
38. J. Goodare, 'The Aberdeenshire witchcraft panic of 1597', *Northern Scotland*, 21 (2001), 17–37, at 23–4, 27–8, 32.
39. Information on the marital status of Scottish witches is inadequate. The SSW has information on 468 male witches, of whom 78 (17 per cent) were stated to be married and five (one per cent) to be single: of these, none was stated to be widowed, and there was no information on the remaining 385 (82 per cent). Marital status was not recorded systematically, and a living spouse was more likely to be mentioned than a dead or non-existent one, but we do not know how much more likely. These figures, as with the equivalent ones for female witches, are thus largely meaningless.
40. Goodare, 'Women and the witch-hunt', 304–5.
41. Pitcairn (ed.), *Trials*, iii, II, 616.
42. Pitcairn (ed.), *Trials*, ii, I, 477–9.
43. Martin, 'The Devil and the Domestic', 85.
44. For female witches' curses, see Larner, *Enemies of God*, 142–4. For scolding, see J. G. Harrison, 'Women and the Branks in Stirling from 1600 to 1730', *Scottish Economic and Social History*, 18 (1998), 114–31.
45. *Selected Justiciary Cases, 1624–1650*, 3 vols, S. I. Gillon and J. I. Smith (eds) (Stair Society, 1954–74), iii, 597–603.
46. M. Gaskill, 'Witchcraft in Early Modern Kent: Stereotypes and the Background to Accusations', in J. Barry, M. Hester and G. Roberts (eds), *Witchcraft in Early Modern Europe* (Cambridge, 1996), 273.
47. Rowlands, *Witchcraft Narratives*, 158–9.
48. SSW.
49. Pitcairn (ed.), *Trials*, ii, I, 477–9. The phrase 'abuser of the peopill' derived from the 1563 witchcraft act: J. Goodare, 'The Scottish witchcraft act', *Church History*, 74 (2005), 39–67, at 52–3.
50. Quoted in Goodare, 'The Scottish Witchcraft Panic of 1597', 56.
51. James Hutchison, 'A sermon on witchcraft in 1697', George Neilson (ed.), *Scottish Historical Review*, 7 (1910), 390–9, at 392. I am grateful to Professor Brian P. Levack for this reference.
52. Sinclair mentioned a man 'who was the Devils Piper, a wizzard', and in his index called Alexander Hamilton ('Hattaraik') a 'wizzard', though in the text Hamilton was a 'warlock': Sinclair, *Satan's Invisible World Discovered*, 219, 125, and index. The term occurred in the title (though not the text) of the pamphlet *A Relation of the Diabolical Practices of above Twenty Wizards and Witches of the Sheriffdom of Renfrew in the Kingdom of Scotland* (London, 1697; Wing catalogue R823). Here, it may be an English term. I am grateful to Professor Brian P. Levack for this reference.
53. J. Miller, 'Cantrips and Carlins: Magic, Medicine and Society in the Presbyteries of Haddington and Stirling, 1603–1688' (University of Stirling PhD thesis, 1999), 212.
54. O. Davies, 'A Comparative Perspective on Scottish Cunning Folk and Charmers', in Goodare *et al.* (eds), *Witchcraft and Belief*, 186–7.
55. SSW.
56. H. P. Broedel, *The* Malleus Maleficarum *and the Construction of Witchcraft: Theology and Popular Belief* (Manchester, 2003), ch. 3.

57. Larner, *Enemies of God*, 145–56.
58. Normand and Roberts (eds), *Witchcraft*, 318.
59. Normand and Roberts (eds), *Witchcraft*, 321. The editors, unaware of Scottish official practices, interpret the gesture as 'the Devil's resignation of his authority'.
60. Sinclair, *Satan's Invisible World Discovered*, 46. Emphasis in original.
61. *Spottiswoode Miscellany*, ii, ed. James Maidment (1845), 67.
62. Pitcairn (ed.), *Trials*, iii, II, 603.
63. W. Matheson, 'The historical Coinneach Odhar and some prophecies attributed to him', *Transactions of the Gaelic Society of Inverness*, 46 (1969–70), 66–88.
64. Goodare, 'The Scottish Witchcraft Panic of 1597', 62.
65. Larner, *Enemies of God*, 148.
66. Martin, 'The Devil and the Domestic', 77–84.
67. Normand and Roberts (eds), *Witchcraft*, 226. I am grateful to Victoria Carr for this point.
68. Larner, *Enemies of God*, 172; Martin, 'The Devil and the Domestic', 79–80.
69. N. Macdougall, *James III* (Edinburgh, 1982), 130–2.
70. P. G. Maxwell-Stuart, *Satan's Conspiracy: Magic and Witchcraft in Sixteenth-Century Scotland* (East Linton, 2001), 135–41.
71. L. Henderson, 'Witch-Hunting and Witch Belief in the *Gáidhealtachd*', in Goodare *et al.* (eds), *Witchcraft and Belief*, 102–4.
72. P. D. Anderson, *Black Patie: The Life and Times of Patrick Stewart, Earl of Orkney, Lord of Shetland* (Edinburgh, 1992), 49–53, 156–7.
73. Such as Sir John Colquhoun of Luss, who, in 1631, seduced Katherine Graham, his wife's sister, using love philtres and a magical jewel provided by a German necromancer, Thomas Carlipis: E. J. Cowan, *Montrose: For Covenant and King* (London, 1977), 19–21.
74. Normand and Roberts (eds), *Witchcraft*, 284.
75. I owe this point to discussions with Victoria Carr, whose undergraduate dissertation at University of Wales, Swansea on the male witches of early modern Scotland is thought provoking.
76. J. Goodare, 'Scottish witchcraft in its European context', in Goodare *et al.* (eds), *Witchcraft and Belief*, 41–2. Cf. the 'bookish' male witches identified by E. J. Kent, 'Masculinity and male witches in old and New England, 1593–1680', *History Workshop Journal*, 60 (2005), 69–92, at 72–3.
77. J. Goodare and J. Miller, 'Introduction', in Goodare *et al.* (eds), *Witchcraft and Belief*, 5.
78. J. Goodare, 'John Knox on demonology and witchcraft', *Archiv für Reformationsgeschichte*, 96 (2005), 221–45, at 235–6.
79. J. H. Burns, 'Nicol Burne: "plane disputation bayth at libertie, and in presone"', *Innes Review*, 50 (1999), 102–26, at 117.
80. A. H. Williamson, 'Number and National Consciousness: The Edinburgh Mathematicians and Scottish Political Culture at the Union of the Crowns', in R. A. Mason (ed.), *Scots and Britons: Scottish Political Thought and the Union of 1603* (Cambridge, 1994), 197–200.
81. Goodare and Miller, 'Introduction', 5; *Register of the Privy Council of Scotland*, 38 vols, John Hill Burton *et al.* (eds.) (Edinburgh, 1877–), 2nd ser., iv, pp. xl-xli, 24, 50, 92–3; Sir John Lauder of Fountainhall, *Historical Notices of Scotish Affairs*, 2 vols, David Laing (ed.) (Bannatyne Club, 1868), i, 197–8.

82. Henderson, 'Witch-Hunting and Witch Belief in the *Gáidhealtachd*', 103.
83. S. Thompson (ed.), *Motif-Index of Folk Literature*, 6 vols, 2nd edn (Copenhagen, 1955–58), no. M305.
84. Thompson (ed.), *Motif-Index*, section K *passim*.
85. Hector Boece, *History and Chronicles of Scotland*, translated by John Bellenden, 2 vols, T. Maitland (ed.) (Edinburgh, 1821). The Macbeth story can be traced back to the chronicle of Andrew of Wyntoun, written in about 1400.
86. Boece, *History*, translated by Bellenden, ii, 269. In Shakespeare, these prophecies were delivered by apparitions conjured up by the same three witches who opened the story, but in Boece the 'wiche' was someone different from the 'weird sisteris'.
87. For one told by no less a figure than John Knox, see Goodare, 'John Knox', 242–3.
88. They have been proposed (plausibly, if not entirely convincingly) as real-life prototypes of Shakespeare's Macbeth and Lady Macbeth: Sir James Fergusson, 'The Man behind Macbeth', in his *The Man Behind Macbeth and Other Studies* (London, 1969).
89. Sir John Scot of Scotstarvet, *The Staggering State of Scottish Statesmen*, Charles Rogers (ed.) (Grampian Club, 1872), 43. For contemporary references to Lady Arran and witchcraft, see R. Grant, 'Politicking Jacobean women: Lady Ferniehirst, the countess of Arran and the countess of Huntly, *c.*1580–1603', in E. Ewan and M. M. Meikle (eds), *Women in Scotland,* c.*1100*–c.*1750* (East Linton, 1999), 97–100.
90. Another account of Arran's death focused on the 'response' he received (evidently from a witch) to beware of the valley in which his enemy would kill him – a straightforward story of inexorable fate: John Spottiswoode, *History of the Church of Scotland*, 3 vols, Mark Russell and Mark Napier (eds) (Spottiswoode Society, 1847–51), iii, 40.
91. Cf. Larner, *Witchcraft and Religion*, 87. The one woman symbolically involved in witch-hunting was the queen in whose reign the witchcraft act had been passed. Trial documents often mentioned that witches were transgressing 'the 73 act of Queen Mary': Goodare, 'The Scottish witchcraft act', 39.
92. Goodare, 'Witch-Hunting and the Scottish state', 144–5.

8

Masculinity and Witchcraft in Seventeenth-Century England

Malcolm Gaskill

I

Twenty years ago, in a now celebrated article, Joan Scott established gender as a 'useful category of historical analysis'. This, she argued, required an understanding, not merely of men's attitudes towards women, but of the reciprocal nature of the sexes. After all, as Natalie Davis had noted a decade earlier, historians of class are interested in patricians as well as plebs. In fact, it was the political aspect of gender that seized Scott's attention – specifically patriarchy, and the role of masculinity in its formulation. For patriarchy did not exude naturally from all men, as had been assumed, but was constantly regenerated through a range of symbols and rituals deployed in different contexts. In turn, masculinity itself was a social construction.[1] The idea that manhood is 'the key to unlock the strongbox of patriarchy' has been taken up by social historians of early modern England.[2] Alex Shepard has criticized the misrepresentation of patriarchy as a crude binary opposition invariably manifested as male domination when, in reality, male gender identities covered a spectrum of feelings and deeds, shot through with masculine ideals against which men, too, found it hard to measure up.[3] 'Like women', Shepard maintains, 'men also experienced antagonistic imperatives, and many adopted quite different codes of behaviour when asserting their manhood'.[4] Gender did not mean deterministic ideology; rather, a varied landscape of rich and deeply embedded experience.[5]

Ground-level assessments of gender, therefore, tend to tone down radical feminist interpretations;[6] the history of witch-trials, however, is different. Its exceptionally gendered nature makes it peculiarly resistant to revision; put simply, most accusers were men, while the accused tended to be women. It is true that women played key roles as accusers and witnesses, and that neighbourhood took precedence over sisterhood – assuming the latter had any contemporary meaning at all.[7] Yet, even this does not quite turn things around because, as feminist historians have insisted, patriarchy divides women.[8] A more constructive qualification, therefore, might be that a significant proportion of the accused were male. In certain parts of Europe, notably Finland and Estonia, an equal number of men and women were accused; in Iceland, most witches were male.[9] Even in places where female suspects predominated, as in some German states in the 1620s, outbursts of intense witch-hunting sucked increasing numbers of men – sometimes high-status men – into the conflagration.[10] Variation over time and territory was so marked that aggregation might conceal as much as it reveals; but, it would be fair to say that, on average, between 10 and 30 per cent of all witches were male, including 6000 who were actually executed – far more than were burned for heresy during the Reformation.[11]

Even this adjustment raises questions of definition. When we are talking about 'witches', can we rely on any consistency of meaning? Some regions had traditions of belief where certain social groups and trades, such as blacksmiths, were associated with occult arts; in Muscovy male vagrants were vulnerable to accusation; in Normandy, it was shepherds.[12] Furthermore, many suspects were wizards and sorcerers, male roles in most early modern cultures.[13] When men were accused of causing harm or *maleficium*, it was usually as the husbands and sons of female witches.[14] Guilty by association, it is possible that these men were 'implicitly feminized', adding anti-social emphasis to their spiritual inversion. To early modern minds, if patriarchy had the beneficial effect of making women behave as men, demonism conferred upon men the most despicable female characteristics – weakness, spite, envy, wantonness, and inconstancy.[15] Arguably, when a man was placed in a female category, this category remained essentially female; if so, the idea that witchcraft was sex-related rather than sex-specific might need modification. Perhaps, after all, we might see witchcraft as a uniquely female crime, regardless of the sex of the offender.[16]

Some men, however, were accused of *maleficium* without any connection to a suspected female or obvious marginality. Take three, apparently unrelated, characters named Godfrey. In 1616, John Godfrey, a glover from Lambourne in Essex, was tried at the assizes for bewitching a man to death. The following year in Kent, William Godfrey, a socially integrated yeoman farmer, was accused of a range of *maleficia*, from infesting a house with ghosts to causing the deaths of children. In Massachusetts, John Godfrey, an unmarried but settled man, was prosecuted several times in the 1660s for using a familiar spirit to injure his neighbours.[17] It is conceivable that these were exceptions that prove the female rule. In her study of Rothenburg ob der Tauber in southern Germany, Alison Rowlands found just one man accused as a maleficent witch in his own right.[18] But these cases remind us that, however strong the link between women and witchcraft – or, more correctly, between witchcraft and women – in the end, witchcraft constituted its own historical category.[19] This invokes Christina Larner's idea that witches were accused, not because they were women – or, for that matter, despite being men – but because they were witches. Possessed of gender as with anyone else, witches were entire unto themselves in demonic malevolence.[20]

There was no reason in Scripture, law or classical precept why a witch should not be a man; in fact, Protestant clergymen writing about witchcraft between the 1590s and 1640s insisted that men were far from immune.[21] This transformative half-century enhanced awareness of both patriarchy and demonology in English political and religious culture, with households galvanized to promote godly order, and dissidents forcibly aligned with Antichrist.[22] In this grand ideological scheme, the rule of fathers and misrule of demons were diametrically opposed; in practice, however, they were intertwined. Experience of the Devil consisted in human weakness getting the better of good intentions, ideals undermined by life's haphazardness, and by selfishness and greed. Belief in witchcraft is rooted in religion, but thrives on conflict – of which there was plenty in the first half of the seventeenth century, due to social and economic rifts between neighbours.[23] The idea of a 'gender crisis' is well known[24] but, if we also consider men, struggling to be good Christians and patriarchs in a competitive environment, it is obvious how they, too, fitted the bill as witches. For the pre-Civil War generation, manhood disregarded and abused could be as threatening as malevolent widowhood.

The subject of gender and witchcraft is therefore resistant to revision, not simply because it follows strong male–female adversarial lines, but because it is hard to see it as contemporaries did – putting their concerns before ours, replacing a modern epistemology with an early modern one.[25] This chapter explores patriarchy in terms of the construction of masculinity, and witchcraft as a power that caused suspects to be identified primarily as witches. Also, following the trajectory of women's history and the history of homosexuality, it considers male witches not as the passive victims of a super-ordinate culture, mere objects of persecution. They were conscious beings whose mentalities were bound up with those of their accusers and interrogators, and who dropped hints in the historical record about their world and their place within it.[26] Confessions are the richest source, but in England – where accusatorial justice obviated the use of torture – confessions were rare. Our best sample comes from the East Anglian witch-finding campaign of 1645–47, by far England's worst witch-panic and in marked contrast to the low level of prosecution in the first four decades of the seventeenth century. Some 250 people were examined during this episode, eliciting detailed accounts of diabolic treachery situated in mundane contexts. A sizable proportion of the suspects were men, whose confessions represent not only their social and religious failure, but a failing of masculinity.[27]

II

In the spring of 1645, an unstable compound of grievance, fear, misfortune, and opportunity exploded in the Essex port of Manningtree, triggering a chain-reaction of denunciations across the north-eastern part of the county. The pro-active stance of Puritan magistrates excited the witch-hating sentiments of two gentlemen, John Stearne and Matthew Hopkins, who took it upon themselves to tour England's eastern counties for over two years, conducting investigations to procure vivid evidence of diabolism. As many as one hundred people were executed. The witch-finders were paid for their services, but not enough to make them rich; neither is there any special reason to doubt the sincerity of their actions, which they carried out despite opposition from gentry, magistracy, and clergy. If their campaign was inspired only by an urge to fight Satan, then they were kindred spirits to the iconoclasts, godly soldiers and, in due course, regicides of the age. Moreover, Hopkins and Stearne did not invent the crimes for which suspects were tried: they were informed by villagers they met on their travels and, on many occasions, by the accused themselves.[28]

The witch-finders' *modus operandi* was uncompromising and, occasionally, savage. It was common for suspects to be confined, typically in their own homes, and watched closely for several days without sleep or sustenance. The intention, in theory at least, was to catch familiar spirits coming to feed, or to isolate the witch to the extent that the Devil and his demons abandoned him or her, leading to despair and penitence.[29] In practice, of course, the effect was to inflict terror, numbed only by delirium. Hallucinations and other distortions of perception followed, accompanied by a state of extreme suggestibility. From a modern perspective, a sleeping brain in a wakeful body dreamt out loud; but, to onlookers, it seemed as if God's providence had forced the guilty to betray the Devil.[30]

The mixed gender profile of these claustrophobic dramas is revealing. Many victims were women claiming that they, or their children, had been bewitched. The suspicions they shared with the witch-finders were generally backed by male relatives or neighbours. Then, there were the search-women. A confession was valuable evidence; but, even without one, Hopkins and Stearne might still be able to prove the diabolic covenant if a suspect was found to bear marks where, it was said, diabolic imps had suckled. Accused men were physically examined by the witch-finders themselves; female suspects, by midwives and other respectable women. Given that the majority of suspects were female, the search-women were linchpins of pre-trial procedure in most cases. A few, such as Mary Phillips of Manningtree, boasted of their expertise in diagnosis, and were required to travel considerable distances (and were well rewarded), as were Hopkins and Stearne themselves.[31] Searchers also took shifts as watchers – who, in any case, were typically both women and men, some of whom had a personal interest in seeing a witch brought to justice.

The final strand in the skein was the sex of the accused. In Essex, all 34 suspects in prison at Colchester in the summer of 1645 (29 of whom were tried) were women; but, for reasons obscure, once the witch-finders crossed into Suffolk, men entered the picture. Of 133 accused witches in that county whose sex is known, 21 were men, or 16 per cent. We might compare this not only to Essex in 1645, but also to the whole Home Circuit assizes between the accession of Elizabeth I and the outbreak of the Civil War. Here, 26 of the 354 people prosecuted for malefic witchcraft were male, or just over 7 per cent – less than half the proportion of men found in Suffolk.[32] The specific crimes alleged against men on the Home Circuit show a broad similarity with those against women – killing children, livestock, and so on – and the same was true of most of the male accused in Suffolk in 1645. John Chambers of Bramford, for example, confessed that he had sent his imps to perform various *maleficia*; he even claimed to have ordered a pair of toad-imps to murder his own child.[33] By far the most bizarre tale, though, was that of John Lowes, octogenarian vicar of Brandeston.

Lowes had been accused of barratry, invoking demons, *maleficium*, and harbouring witches, charges dating back over 30 years. He had also raised hackles over religion. As a young man, he seems to have inclined towards Puritanism, although his later sympathies may have been Laudian. Either way, he was enmeshed in a factional struggle of the sort where, when witchcraft was in the air, men might be at least as vulnerable to accusation as women. Disputes had been played out in the courts – quarter sessions, assizes, Star Chamber and Exchequer – but Lowes always bounced back. In 1645, however, he was interrogated under Matthew Hopkins's supervision, convicted at Bury St Edmunds, and executed. The fact that Lowes was a man was significant only in that ministers happened to be men; it was his clerical status, dubious opinions, and heavy-handed use of authority that caused a fatal collision with his parishioners.[34] In some ways, he resembles Dr John Lambe, wizard to the Duke of Buckingham until both were murdered in 1628. Here, the unpopularity of one became bound up with the other to the point that state policy seemed to be guided by the Devil. Suspicions of Catholicism, conjuration, and sexual deviance fuelled rumours, thereby undermining the masculinity of both figures. A real man, it was felt, had no need of magical power to make his way in the world.[35]

Karin Amundsen, who has studied Lambe from the gender angle, challenges the idea that the accusation of men as witches derived from the female concept, observing that 'male witches were often specific, rather than accidental, players in the witch-hunts'.[36] In a similar vein, Elizabeth Kent objects to the passivity that the 'feminized man' idea attributes to male witches. John Lowes, as Dr Lambe, was regarded as a real witch, not a lampoon of one. Witchcraft accusations could be malicious, but most were shaped and energized by genuine fear. In Lowes's case, furthermore, anxiety about the agency of the Devil fused with what Kent calls the 'acute fear of the masculine capacity to foster antisocial forces'.[37] Ultimately, though, men and women displayed a similar propensity for aggression, and perhaps this mattered more than the means by which it was expressed.[38]

Complexity of context is everything, then, and we should remember that causal factors clinically isolated by historians were once wrapped up in emotion.[39] The feelings of the accused are also worth considering. Confessing witches did not just mouth lines from the witch-finders' script, but worked in their life-stories to produce unique narratives steeped in shame, loss, and despair. However horrendous these diabolic liaisons sounded to the God-fearing majority, they may well have been experienced by the witch as moments of unprecedented triumph, emancipation, and joy – the fantasy of a superhuman male guardian and saviour intervening to cancel out the injuries of the past and safeguard a better future.[40] At the very least, these wretched people were going through what, today, might be called 'cognitive dissonance': conflicting emotions arising from incompatible beliefs and actions, eased by soothing, self-justifying simplification – a story one tells to oneself.[41] A parallel might be drawn with victims of possession, whose demonically inspired outbursts constituted what has been termed 'an abrogation of individual sovereignty', generating a blameless neutrality for those who found the ideological expectations of early modern households impossible to meet. In this way, demoniacs might receive sympathy, even admiration for their insights and prophecies.[42]

Neither were dreams of prosperity and salvation the special preserve of women: poor men with little 'individual sovereignty' to abrogate fell prey to the same delusion. After three days of watching, a man known only as Payne – in the same way as John Chambers, also from the Suffolk parish of Bramford – confessed that the Devil had appeared to him as a dog while he was struggling to plough a field. Conscious of the damning implications, Payne was seduced by Satan's offer of liberation from hardship. His despair can also be gauged by the fact that, on the eighth day of his confinement, he admitted to John Stearne that the Devil had also tempted him to suicide, after which, Payne recalled, 'I resined my soule frely from god & I give it freely to the divell'.[43] Similarly, John Chambers confessed that 'the devill told him in the shape of a boy that if he wold follow his directio[n] and make a covenant w[i]th him he shold want no thing'.[44]

The imps with which the Suffolk witches tormented their neighbours were powerful alter egos; some of the accused even named them after themselves: one of John Chambers's imps was called John. Scores settled by familiars were mostly economic in origin: debts unpaid, work unrewarded, promises broken, boundaries infringed. But there was also a sexual dimension. Lyndal Roper has described male confessions to diabolic sexual intercourse as 'unorthodox and convoluted', with the Devil transmuting into a female neighbour, sometimes several women, hinting at guilt over infidelity and promiscuity; other confessions bordered on bestiality.[45] English testimony of male covenants with Satan, especially involving blood, suggest solemn and intimate unions, which perhaps stopped short of homosexual acts only because this was not a private fantasy of the accused. The feeding of familiars, however, certainly hints at dubious sexuality. John Bysack of Great Waldingfield confessed that Satan's claw penetrated his doublet to get at his heart's blood to 'free him of hell-torments'. His imps arrived in the form of six snails, which fed from his body. According to John Stearne, Bysack managed this by leaving his bed at night (pretending to his wife that he was unable to get comfortable), then settling himself by the fire like a nursing mother.[46] Stearne also reported how John Scarfe of Rattlesden kept a rat in a box – an innocent enough pastime, until 'he tooke it out, and laid it downe on his belly, and put it to the place where the markes were found, where he said it sucked halfe an houre'.[47] Doubtless, the sheer physicality of such behaviour was shocking. A man held on remand at St Albans in the 1640s was said to have an entire female breast hanging from his side.[48]

The definitional axis, therefore, was not just male–female but human–beast, suggested throughout the early modern period by the intimacy between English witches and their animal familiars.[49] The two cut across each other in a physiological context. Humoral medicine taught that the female constitution was cooler than that of the male, causing women to age faster: menopause – and with it old age and social impotence – was commonly believed to begin at 50. James I's physician, Helkiah Crooke, explained that fertility commenced in the second seven-year sequence in a woman's life and ended in the seventh.[50] The effects of this difference were both mental and moral. 'That Females are more wanton and petulant then Males', explained Crooke, 'wee thinke hapneth because of the impotencie of their minds; for the imaginations of lustfull women are like the imaginations of brute beasts which have no repugnancie or contradiction of reason to restraine them'. And yet, he continued, wanton men – and male witches were nothing if not wanton – were so, not because they were feminine, but because they imitated the lives of animals.[51] It is hard to say how much of this uneducated folk understood; but, for all Crooke's learning, the symbolism and correspondences were crude enough to fit plebeian knowledge. Interpretative linkages were made instinctively, drawing on deep-seated cultural attitudes. Descriptions of the Devil by confessing witches point in this direction. Stearne recalled how a woman at Creeting St Mary in Suffolk revealed that Satan had 'the use of her body, but was heavier and colder [than a man]'.[52]

In an explicit sense, these men had failed as members of a divinely ordained natural world and Christian community, but, implicitly, they had also failed the test of manhood – and not once, but twice. First, they were poor and unable to cope as householders; second, they confessed to performing acts no decent man would contemplate. John Winnick was a poor servant in husbandry at Molesworth in Huntingdonshire, where the witch-finders ventured in 1646. The little money Winnick had managed to put aside he hid in the hay-barn, until one day it went missing. In rage and despair, he decided to consult a cunning man but, as he confessed, the very thought caused a bear-like spirit (in fact, no bigger than a rabbit) to appear, with whom he swapped his soul for his savings. Winnick protested that he never caused any harm, although he had sent an imp to induce a maidservant to steal food from her master. This pathetic admission speaks eloquently to the fantasies of marginal people in an age of hardship.[53] At a place near Molesworth, Thrapston in Northamptonshire, 'a very aged man' named Cherrie also confessed to compacting with Satan. A cowherd dependent on parish charity, he had been shown great kindness by a local landowner, Sir John Washington, whom he repaid by bewitching his cattle. 'The more he gave him', Cherrie admitted, 'the more power he had over him to do him mischief'. Here, then, we see the imagined reconfiguration of male prestige, a shake-up of the conventional calculus of wealth and power in a polarized community.[54]

Cherrie's crimes were heinous; but given his status they were, at least, comprehensible. How much worse, then, were the crimes of Rev. John Lowes of Brandeston, a privileged figure motivated not by want but by sheer wickedness. Under duress, he confessed that he had sunk a ship, drowning 14 men, and that his imps fed on teats beneath his tongue. Lowes, too, had failed as a man, and – unlike Bysack, Scarfe, Winnick, and Cherrie – a man of whom much had been expected by society. While in thrall to the Devil, he was reported to have preached as many as 60 sermons, cynically beguiling his parishioners and leading them into a spiritual wilderness. After the Reformation, the office of minister had been elevated to that of a responsible governor, a patriarchal representative of God and the king; for Lowes to become a witch was the most depraved dereliction of male duty imaginable.[55] Greater moral integrity might also have been expected of Henry Carre of Rattlesden, described by Stearne as 'a Scholler fit for Cambridge, (if not a Cambridge Scholler)' fallen on hard times. However poignant the witch-finder's account of how Carre forsook, first, God and then his own life, to contemporary ears this would have sounded like feeble, almost infantile, burbling. It was unmanly in the extreme.[56]

There are signs that some suspects resisted interrogation. Modern studies of torture indicate that many people hold out as long as possible, not only to prevent self-incrimination, but also to preserve dignity.[57] A number of women interrogated by Hopkins and Stearne retained their composure, while others broke and confessed defiantly but without penitence. In Manningtree, the first to confess, Elizabeth Clarke, admitted to Hopkins that she had slept with the Devil, 'a tall, proper, black haired gentleman' – 'a properer man than your selfe'. When Stearne asked with whom she would rather sleep, Hopkins or the Devil, she chose the Devil.[58] Men, too, put up a fight. In 1647, Stearne deposed to a magistrate at Ely that he had examined Robert Ellis of Stretham and had found '4 teats upon the entrance of his fundement' which he believed 'were drawen & suckt by evell spirits'. Ellis subsequently explained that these marks, almost certainly hernias or haemorrhoids, were the result of physical exertion, adding that 'he would not confess hime selfe to be a witch though thay puld hime a peeces w[i]th wild horses'.[59] As with the famous case of Johannes Junius, *Bürgermeister* (mayor) of Bamberg (1628), we see in such protestations not merely the desire to prove innocence, but also the need to restore honour lost through public accusation, and the literally degrading effects of imprisonment and interrogation.[60]

III

In 1995, Elspeth Whitney concluded a self-righteous historiographical review with the declaration that 'the witch hunts are so egregious an example of Western misogyny that many historians have repressed the importance of gender', insinuating that modern male commentators cannot help but add insult to the injuries inflicted by their forefathers.[61] In the last decade, historians of witchcraft have moved some way from this crude analysis; in fact, most were further ahead quite a long time ago. And yet, failure to make gender his central focus still renders a male historian vulnerable to the accusation of indifference. According to Joan Scott, 'gender is a primary way of signifying relationships of power'; this is almost certainly true – or, at least, certainly almost true: it is the attribution of primary status that is most likely to cause concern.[62] If gender were, indeed, at the heart of witchcraft accusations, then it was entirely dependent on the structures and movements of its physical setting. To make it the chief factor seems otiose, especially if the nagging subtext must remain the male domination of women. The study of masculinity, with all its varieties and the mixed fortunes of men in attaining it, adds shades of grey to the black-and-white contrariety of old-fashioned gender studies. And where witchcraft prosecutions are concerned, it suggests a more fluid model, and encourages us to treat male witches not as a pale and passive aberration, but as witches in their own right.

Insight depends on empathy and our imaginative bridges to a lost ordering of reality. The inversion of masculine control implied by the trial of East Anglian men as witches was doubtless real but, of course, it was never vocalized in those terms. Denunciations came hot and furious from the gut, not from the calmly reasoned mind. This helps to explain why the social profiles of the accused were more diverse than if accusers and witch-finders had cynically applied some standardized template of persecution. Contemporary observers were fully conscious of this heterogeneity. As John Stearne noted in his memoir, 'if I should goe to pen all of these sorts [of witches], then I should have no end, or at least too big a volume'.[63] And yet, all those accused in the 1640s shared something important. The careworn men cowering before the witch-finders might already have flunked the test of patriarchy, but their real offence was worse and plain to see: the service of Satan and a ghastly taste for destruction. In these terms, the accusation of men becomes entirely comprehensible. The difficult question remaining is this: Why during England's only major witch-hunt might the proportion of male accused have increased from the comparatively low levels prevalent in the south-east during the previous eighty years?

Emphasis on the diabolic pact after 1600 might be partly to blame. In Finland, the influence of European demonology from the 1640s increased the proportion of women accused; but this was a relative change given that, up to that point, witchcraft usually meant male-dominated sorcery.[64] In England, where the crime had mostly been malefic, raised awareness of the pact (emphasized in an Act of 1604) extended witchcraft from the domestic environment – spoiling butter and beer, poisoning food, hurting infants, and so on – into one that was more public, and therefore more male. The crime was politicized as apostasy and rebellion. At the same time, this transition might have made the witch seem less like Satan's master and more his servant – a reversal of roles which, it has been suggested, signified a reassertion of patriarchal hierarchy through demonology and the law.[65] Furthermore, the literal demonization of witchcraft was carried to its logical conclusion after the start of the Civil War, with its apocalyptic overtones and godly claims to spiritual warfare on the Parliamentarian side. The searing rhetoric was full of covenants sealed and sanctified, broken and betrayed, from the royal court to the humblest neighbourhood and, in specifically religious terms, between mortals and Christ or Satan.[66] 'There is not a Witch that hath the Devil at her beck', preached Cornelius Burges to Parliament in 1640, 'but she must seale a Covenant to him, sometimes with her blood, sometimes by other rites and devices, and perhaps he must suck her too'.[67]

Of 17 felons arraigned at Ely in 1647, 13 were accused of witchcraft, of whom five were men.[68] As in the case of John Lowes, one suspects that factional conflict lay at the roots of their accusation. Antipathy against these men can be linked to protests about fen drainage and breaches of custom dating back twenty years or more; after 1642, old alliances and animosities hardened into military allegiances.[69] The war effort also blurred boundaries between civilians and combatants in a broader sense, and so between male and female roles. One Parliamentarian newspaper reported in 1645 that the witches executed in Norfolk had prophesied that the King was doomed and that Prince Rupert's protective magic was wearing off.[70] The fashioning of a female royalist spy into a witch had similar resonances: a pamphlet of 1643 included her dying prediction that the Earl of Essex would be victorious.[71] The diabolic familiar was also marshalled for propagandist purposes. At the unconscious as well as the conscious level, imps were vehicles for fantasies of magical military participation, especially where women and children were concerned. The Everard family of Suffolk – Thomas, his wife, brother-in-law, and daughter – illustrate the point. Murderous, demon-worshipping witches all, they confessed to supporting the Royalist cause, including sending imps to fight for Prince Rupert.[72] In this way, one failed patriarch, a poor cooper from Halesworth, was ideologically connected to another: the King.

Contested masculinity, witchcraft prosecution, and the conflicts of the Civil War had converged in English society by the 1640s, with the law as their focus. Parliamentarian propagandists claimed that Charles I had broken the covenant with his people: rule without Parliament was rule without law. At the same time, the Tudor and early Stuart state had been built on the increased competency of statute, advancement of the office of magistrate, conflict-resolution in the courts, and promotion of a legal culture. Witches were executed because of the Witchcraft Act and the will of plaintiffs, justices, jurors, and judges to use it.[73] Here, we might turn to Susan Amussen's two models of early modern manhood: a 'traditional' one, where masculine self-assertion and preservation of honour were achieved through violence; and a 'reformed' version, where self-restraint and recourse to law were elevated as the highest ideals across the social order. The more wealth, property, and authority a man had, the easier the transition to reform; destructive witches, like all aggressors, marked out their meagre domains in blood, and thus symbolized the most dysfunctional elements of the state.[74] It is easy to see how enclosure, rural capitalism, declining custom, and the ruthless dictates of the market slotted into this picture. In the ranks of the able-bodied poor, from which so many witches were drawn, laboured a generation of men scarcely able to set up their own households, or feed their families without parish assistance. Immiseration brought emasculation.[75]

So, what of Matthew Hopkins and John Stearne? What can we learn about the East Anglian witch-hunt through their masculinity? It is easy to get lost up a blind alley. Sexuality was a source of anxiety in the period, but to leap from there to suggest, as Elspeth Whitney does, that early modern witch-hunts 'were a more or less direct projection of sexual anxiety' is unwarranted.[76] More sensitively, Diane Purkiss has argued that the Civil War exposed and exacerbated a sublimated crisis of masculinity particular to the 1640s; Hopkins's fantasies, as those of soldiers who abused defenceless women, 'seem motivated by similar anxieties about the fragility of masculine identity'.[77] Contrary to their alleged special hatred of women, however, the witch-finders were, as most men of their age, neither misogynists nor philogynists. Their enemy was the witch, and in the same way as William Dowsing, the iconoclast who purged Suffolk and Cambridgeshire of superstitious images, they applied their destructive energies wherever they detected evil.[78] Women might have given in to diabolic temptation with less fight, but they were no more wicked than men who succumbed. Indeed, female recourse to witchcraft was perhaps more understandable, especially among the poorest. When male witches were encountered, they were taken at face value as maleficent diabolists. Even opponents during the East Anglian witch-hunts concurred, Stearne observing that 'one may fall into this sinne as well as into any other ... and therefore whether men or women', while his critic, Rev. John Gaule, warned that, although most witches were female, 'let not the male bee boasting, or secure of their Sexes Exemption or lesse disposition'.[79]

The critical point here is the polarity of gender in early modern thinking; not the anathematization of women by men, but the interconnectedness of the sexes – and, as we have seen, even of different species – within the same frames of reference and contexts of experience. Witches were female in the abstract because, as Stuart Clark has demonstrated, 'the representational system governing them required for its coherence a general correlation between such primary oppositions as good/evil ... and male/female'.[80] And yet, this was a tendency in people's minds not a golden rule, and gender norms were determined by infinitely varied and ever-changing political and cultural circumstances. From day to day, social hierarchies were not governed by theoretical dichotomies, but by 'the delicate balance of mutual obligations and reciprocity'. This was something our subjects would have understood well.[81]

If Hopkins and Stearne were driven by prurience or perversion, it cannot be known, and should not be assumed. Perhaps sexual consciousness is less relevant to their campaign, or even to their masculinity, than we might think. Susan Amussen argues that a more important component of constructed manhood was a sense of independence. The extravagant political and legal liberties taken by the witch-finders at a time of administrative chaos certainly brought them a heady sense of self-determination. But their swagger was short-lived: as with the Devil's pact, the power they had seized proved illusory once order was restored after the war.[82] Ironically, the demise of the witch-finders' careers can be understood similarly to the way we understand the demonization of men as witches. The more they asserted the masculine ideal of independent status, the more it led them to break the law. By using torture, Hopkins and Stearne, in the same way as witches and murderers, reverted to the violence of the traditional model, and so were dishonoured. They found out the hard way that Amussen's reformed model 'further restricted access to manliness, and was thus central to the cultural conflicts of the early seventeenth century'.[83] The physician Helkiah Crooke taught that, compared with men, women were 'more churlish and fierce, but not stouter or stronger hearted'. In the end, the witch-finders proved that they could be passionate and assertive – 'churlish and fierce' – but these were not masculine qualities to be admired in any constant, reasoned, and obedient man.[84]

What Elspeth Whitney saw as male historians' indifference to gender – even, their latent misogyny – should instead be regarded as a refusal to reduce and trivialize it. Anything else, Robin Briggs argued soon after the appearance of her review, is anachronistic. Witchcraft he describes as 'a phenomenon which was permeated by gender, yet in much more subtle ways than any simple argument can convey'. Explanations need to be 'firmly bedded in the surrounding social realities' because witchcraft was 'a bundle of shared assumptions' that disintegrates once we start pulling out pieces that take our fancy.[85] The ties were complex, but, as Lara Apps and Andrew Gow propose, it seems likely that studying the male witch opens up a route to 'more nuanced understandings of the relationship between masculinity, femininity and witchcraft'.[86] Male witches were wicked because they gave themselves to the Devil and attacked their neighbours. But gender was relevant to their public censure less because they aped female values than because they failed to measure up to male ones. As Elizabeth Kent has argued, 'male witches were masculine others, whose poor practice of patriarchy cut across paradigmatic idealization of masculine virtue'.[87] Ultimately, though, male witches were witches – a historical category that, when we are striving to understand witchcraft on its own terms, deserves to be taken at least as seriously as gender.

Notes

1. J.W. Scott, 'Gender: A useful category of historical analysis', *American Historical Review*, 91 (1986), 1053–75; N. Z. Davis, 'Women's history in transition: The European case', *Feminist Studies*, 3 (1975–6), 90.
2. Quotation from L. Roper, *Oedipus and the Devil: Witchcraft, Sexuality and Religion in Early Modern Europe* (London, 1994), 107.
3. A. Shepard, *Meanings of Manhood in Early Modern England* (Oxford, 2003). See also S. D. Amussen, '"The Part of a Christian Man": The Cultural Politics of Manhood in Early Modern England', in S. D. Amussen and M. A. Kishlansky (eds), *Political Culture and Cultural Politics in Early Modern England* (Manchester, 1995), 213–33; E. Foyster, *Manhood in Early Modern England: Honour, Sex and Marriage* (London, 1999), especially ch. 1; A. Fletcher, *Gender, Sex and Subordination in England, 1500–1800* (New Haven, 1999), chs. 5, 16, 20; A. Bryson, *From Courtesy to Civility: Changing Codes of Conduct in Early Modern England* (Oxford, 1998), *passim*.
4. A. Shepard, 'Manhood, credit and patriarchy in early modern England, c.1580–1640', *Past and Present*, 167 (2000), 79.
5. On the relational nature of masculinity (and femininity), see M. Roper and J. Tosh, 'Introduction: Historians and the Politics of Masculinity', in *idem* (eds), *Manful Assertions: Masculinities in Britain since 1800* (London, 1991), 1–24.
6. See, for example, M. Daly, *Gyn/Ecology: The Metaethics of Radical Feminism* (Boston, MA, 1978); A. Dworkin, *Woman Hating* (New York, 1974).
7. C. Holmes, 'Women: Witnesses and witches', *Past and Present*, 140 (1993), 45–78; J. A. Sharpe, 'Witchcraft and women in seventeenth-century England: Some northern evidence', *Continuity and Change*, 6 (1991), 179–99. See also J. Sharpe, *Instruments of Darkness: Witchcraft in England, 1550–1750* (London, 1995), ch. 7.
8. E. Whitney, 'International trends: The witch "she"/the historian "he": Gender and the historiography of the European witch-hunts', *Journal of Women's History*, 7 (1995), 88; In general, see M. Hester, *Lewd Women and Wicked Witches: A Study of the Dynamics of Male Domination* (London, 1992); A. Llewellyn Barstow, *Witchcraze: A New History of the European Witch Hunts* (London, 1995). For an overview and critique, see D. Purkiss, *The Witch in History: Early Modern and Twentieth-Century Representations* (London, 1996), ch. 1.
9. B. Ankarloo and G. Henningsen (eds), *Early Modern European Witchcraft: Centres and Peripheries* (Oxford, 1990), chs 10, 12, 15.
10. H. C. E. Midelfort, *Witch-Hunting in South-Western Germany, 1562–1684: The Social and Intellectual Foundations* (Stanford, CA, 1972), 179–82; W.Behringer, *Witchcraft Persecutions in Bavaria: Popular Magic, Religious Zealotry and Reason of State in Early Modern Europe* (Cambridge, 1997), 224–9.
11. B. P. Levack, *The Witch-Hunt in Early Modern Europe*, 2nd edn (Harlow, 1995), 134; W. Monter, 'Male Witches', in R. M. Golden (ed.), *Encyclopedia of Witchcraft: The Western Tradition*, 4 vols (Santa Barbara, CA, 2006), iii, 712.
12. V. A. Kivelson, 'Male witches and gendered categories in seventeenth-century Russia', *Comparative Studies in Society and History*, 45 (2003), 606–7, 621; W. Monter, 'Toads and eucharists: The male witches of Normandy,

1564– 1660', *French Historical Studies*, 20 (1997), 563–95. See also W. Behringer, *Shaman of Oberstdorf: Chonrad Stoeckhlin and the Phantoms of the Night*, translated by H. C. E. Midelfort (Charlottesville, VA, 1998).

13. See O. Davies, *Cunning-Folk: Popular Magic in English History* (London, 2003), *passim*; P. G. Maxwell-Stuart, *Wizards: A History* (Stroud, 2004), especially chs 3–6.
14. Barstow, *Witchcraze*, 24–5. Almost half the male accused during the Salem witch-hunt of 1692 fall into this category: C. F. Karlsen, *The Devil in the Shape of a Woman: Witchcraft in Colonial New England* (New York, 1987), 40.
15. Quotation from L. Apps and A. Gow, *Male Witches in Early Modern Europe* (Manchester, 2003), 7. See also E. Labouvie, 'Men and witchcraft trials: Towards a Social Anthropology of "Male" Understandings of Magic and Witchcraft', in U. Rublack (ed.), *Gender in Early Modern German History* (Cambridge, 2002), 49–50.
16. W. de Blécourt, 'The making of the female witch: Reflections on witchcraft and gender in the early modern period', *Gender and History*, 12 (2000), 287–309. For a discussion of recent work on male and female witches that supports de Blécourt's views, see K. Hodgkin, 'Gender, Mind and Body: Feminism and Psychoanalysis', in J. Barry and O. Davies (eds), *Witchcraft Historiography* (Basingstoke, 2007), 196–8.
17. C. L'Estrange Ewen, *Witch Hunting and Witch Trials* (London, 1929), 208; M. Gaskill, 'The devil in the shape of a man: Witchcraft, conflict and belief in Jacobean England', *Historical Research*, 71 (1998), 142–71; J. Demos, 'John Godfrey and his neighbors: Witchcraft and the social web in colonial Massachusetts', *William and Mary Quarterly*, 33 (1976), 242–65. Lara Apps and Andrew Gow make the same point about John Samond, an Essex man tried in 1560–1, although in this case vital qualitative detail is lacking: *Male Witches*, 59–60.
18. This was the case of Michael Würth, 1662–3: A. Rowlands, *Witchcraft Narratives in Germany: Rothenburg, 1561–1652* (Manchester, 2003), 165–6. For a Russian trial from 1663, where five men confessed to compacting with Satan, and to bewitching women and children, see R. Zguta, 'Witchcraft trials in seventeenth-century Russia', *American Historical Review*, 82 (1987), 1204.
19. S. Clark, *Thinking with Demons: The Idea of Witchcraft in Early Modern Europe* (Oxford, 1997), ch. 8; Apps and Gow, *Male Witches*, 1–2, 10–4.
20. C. Larner, *Enemies of God: The Witch-Hunt in Scotland* (London, 1981), 102; Kivelson, 'Male witches', 622–3. Broadly, this is the argument of E. J. Kent, 'Masculinity and male witches in old and New England, 1593–1680', *History Workshop Journal*, 60 (2005), 69–92.
21. See, for example, William Perkins, *A Discourse of the Damned Art of Witchcraft* (Cambridge, 1608), 168. For a survey of contemporary opinion, see M. Gaskill, *Crime and Mentalities in Early Modern England* (Cambridge, 2000), 42–3. On demonologists' views in general, see Apps and Gow, *Male Witches*, ch. 4.
22. Foyster, *Manhood in Early Modern England*, 3–4; N. Johnstone, *The Devil and Demonism in Early Modern England* (Cambridge, 2006).
23. A. Macfarlane, *Witchcraft in Tudor and Stuart England: A Regional and Comparative Study*, 2nd edn (London, 1999). This interpretation is supported

by K. Thomas, *Religion and the Decline of Magic* (London, 1971), especially chs 16–7.

24. D. Underdown, 'The taming of the scold: The enforcement of patriarchal authority in early modern England', in A. Fletcher and J. Stevenson (eds), *Order and Disorder in Early Modern England* (Cambridge, 1985), 116–36; M. Ingram, '"Scolding women cucked and washed": A crisis in gender relations in early modern England?', in J. Kermode and G. Walker (eds), *Women, Crime and the Courts in Early Modern England* (London, 1994), 48–80.
25. D. Harley, 'Explaining Salem: Calvinist psychology and the diagnosis of possession', *American Historical Review*, 101 (1996), 310. See also Purkiss, *Witch in History*, 79.
26. For an illuminating discussion, see R. Briggs, *Witches and Neighbours: The Social and Cultural Context of Witchcraft* (London, 1996), ch. 7, especially 282–6.
27. The main sources are: *A True and Exact Relation Of the Several Informations, Examinations, and Confessions of the late Witches, arraigned and executed in the County of Essex* (London, 1645); John Davenport, *The Witches of Huntingdon* (London, 1646); John Stearne, *A Confirmation And Discovery of Witch-Craft* (London, 1648); a manuscript copy of testimony from the Bury St Edmunds assizes in 1645, British Library (hereafter BL), Add. MS. 27402, ff. 104–21; and the depositions taken in 1646–47 in the Isle of Ely, Cambridge University Library (hereafter CUL), Ely Diocesan Records (hereafter EDR), E12 Assizes 1647. For editions of much of this material, see C. L'Estrange Ewen, *Witchcraft and Demonianism* (London, 1933), 281–303; M. Gaskill (ed.), *The Matthew Hopkins Trials*, in J. Sharpe and R. M. Golden (eds), *Writings on English Witchcraft, 1560–1736*, 6 vols (London, 2003), iii.
28. M. Gaskill, *Witchfinders: A Seventeenth-Century English Tragedy* (London, 2005); J. A. Sharpe, 'The devil in East Anglia: The Matthew Hopkins trials reconsidered', in J. Barry, M. Hester and G. Roberts (eds), *Witchcraft in Early Modern Europe: Studies in Culture and Belief* (Cambridge, 1996), 237–54.
29. See the descriptions in John Gaule, *Select Cases of Conscience Touching Witches and Witchcrafts* (London, 1646), 78–80; Francis Hutchinson, *An Historical Essay Concerning Witchcraft* (London, 1718), 63.
30. D. Forrest, 'The methods of torture and its effects', in *idem* (ed.), *A Glimpse of Hell: Reports on Torture Worldwide* (London, 1996), 106, 108–9, 117–8.
31. See, for example, Widow Phillips's visit to Aldeburgh, for which she was paid a fee of £1: Suffolk Record Office, Ipswich, EE1/12/2, f. 249v.
32. These statistics are drawn from Ewen, *Witch Hunting*, 99, 218–21.
33. BL, Add. MS. 27402, f. 108v.
34. C. L'Estrange Ewen, *The Trials of John Lowes, Clerk* (n.p., 1937). See also Gaskill, *Witchfinders*, 138–44, 160–1, 272.
35. See M. Gaskill, 'Witchcraft, politics and memory in seventeenth-century England', *Historical Journal*, 50 (2007), 289–308.
36. K. Amundsen, 'The duke's devil and Doctor Lambe's darling: A case study of the male witch in early modern England', *Psi Sigma Historical Journal*, 2 (2004), 41.
37. Kent, 'Masculinity and male witches', 69–70, 75–8, quotation at 78.
38. E. Bever, 'Witchcraft, female aggression, and popular belief in the early modern community', *Journal of Social History*, 35 (2002), 967–8.

39. See G. Kern Paster *et al.* (eds), *Reading the Early Modern Passions: Essays in the Cultural History of Emotion* (Philadelphia, 2004), especially the introduction, 1–20.
40. For work that adopts this approach to the East Anglian confessions, see L. Jackson, 'Witches, wives and mothers: Witchcraft persecution and women's confessions in seventeenth-century England', *Women's History Review*, 4 (1995), 63–84; M. Gaskill, 'Witchcraft and power in early modern England: The case of Margaret Moore', in Kermode and Walker (eds), *Women, Crime and the Courts*, 125–45.
41. The classic work is L. Festinger, *A Theory of Cognitive Dissonance* (Evanston, IL, 1957). I am grateful to Dr Alan Findlay for alerting me to this.
42. D. Purkiss, 'Invasions: Prophecy and bewitchment in the case of Margaret Muschamp', *Tulsa Studies in Women's Literature*, 17 (1998), 235–53, quotation at 241; J. A. Sharpe, 'Disruption in the well-ordered household: Age, authority and possessed young people', in P. Griffiths, A. Fox and S. Hindle (eds), *The Experience of Authority in Early Modern England* (Basingstoke, 1996), 187–212.
43. BL, Add. MS. 27402, f. 108v.
44. *Ibid.*
45. L. Roper, *Witch-Craze: Terror and Fantasy in Baroque Germany* (New Haven, 2004), 90–2, quotation at 90.
46. Stearne, *Confirmation And Discovery*, 41–2.
47. *Ibid.*, 33.
48. [William Drage], *Daimonomageia. A Small Treatise of Sicknesses and Diseases From Witchcraft* (London, 1665), 40.
49. E. Wilby, *Cunning Folk and Familiar Spirits: Shamanistic Visionary Traditions in Early Modern British Witchcraft and Magic* (Eastbourne, 2005); J. Sharpe, 'The witch's familiar in Elizabethan England', in G. W. Bernard and S. J. Gunn (eds), *Authority and Consent in Tudor England* (Aldershot, 2002), 226–9. Elderly suspects who kept pets might be especially vulnerable: E. Fudge, *Perceiving Animals: Humans and Beasts in Early Modern English Culture* (Basingstoke, 2000), 134.
50. Helkiah Crooke, *Microcosmographia*, 2nd edn (London, 1631), 261; L. Botelho, 'Old Age and Menopause in Rural Women of Early Modern Suffolk', in L.Botelho and P. Thane (eds), *Women and Ageing in British Society since 1500* (London, 2000), 43–65. For links between age, fertility and witchcraft, see E. Bever, 'Old Age and Witchcraft Fears in Early Modern Europe', in P. N. Stearns (ed.), *Old Age in Pre-Industrial Europe* (London, 1983), 150–90; A. Rowlands, 'Witchcraft and old women in early modern Germany', *Past and Present*, 173 (2001), 50–89; Roper, *Witch-Craze*, chs 6–7.
51. Crooke, *Microcosmographia*, 276.
52. Stearne, *Confirmation and Discovery*, 31–2.
53. Davenport, *Witches of Huntingdon*, 3–4; Stearne, *Confirmation and Discovery*, 20–1.
54. Stearne, *Confirmation and Discovery*, 34–5.
55. *A True Relation Of the Araignment Of Eighteene Witches. That were tried, convicted, and condemned, at…St. Edmunds-bury in Suffolke* (London, 1645), 3; Stearne, *Confirmation and Discovery*, 23–4; BL, Add. MS. 27402, f. 114v.
56. Stearne, *Confirmation and Discovery*, 25.

57. See, for example, Apps and Gow, *Male Witches*, 72–3, 76.
58. Quotation at Stearne, *Confirmation and Discovery*, 15. See also *A True and Exact Relation*, 2–4.
59. CUL, EDR, E12 1647/18.
60. R. Walinski-Kiehl, 'Males, "masculine honour", and witch hunting in seventeenth-century Germany', *Men and Masculinities*, 6 (2004), 254–71.
61. Whitney, 'International trends: The witch "she"/the historian "he"', 93.
62. Scott, 'Gender: A useful category', 1067. Cf. Carol Karlsen's remark that 'the story of witchcraft is primarily the story of women': *Devil in the Shape of a Woman*, xii.
63. Stearne, *Confirmation and Discovery*, 32.
64. A. Heikkinen and T. Kervinen, 'Finland: The Male Domination', in Ankarloo and Henningsen (eds), *Early Modern European Witchcraft*, 321–2, 326–7.
65. D. Willis, *Malevolent Nurture: Witch-Hunting and Maternal Power in Early Modern England* (Ithaca, NY, 1995), 122–4, 147, 157–8.
66. Johnstone, *Devil and Demonism*, chs 6–8; F. Valletta, *Witchcraft, Magic and Superstition in England, 1640–70* (Aldershot, 2000), especially ch. 3.
67. Cornelius Burges, *The First Sermon Preached to the Honourable House of Commons…at their Publique Fast* (London, 1641), 64.
68. CUL, EDR, E12 1647/23. At the 1642 assizes, there had been nine prisoners (none of them witches), and in 1646 eight (three of them witches): EDR, E12 inquisitions 1644–5 (wrapper of bundle); E12 assizes 1647/5.
69. Gaskill, *Witchfinders*, 244. See also K. Lindley, *Fenland Riots and the English Revolution* (London, 1982), *passim*, and especially the case described on p. 92.
70. *A Perfect Diurnall of Some Passages in Parliament* (21–28 July 1645), 830.
71. *A Most Certain, Strange, and True Discovery of a Witch* (London, 1643).
72. *True Relation…Of Eighteene Witches*, 3–4; Ewen, *Witch Hunting*, 309–11.
73. J. Sharpe, 'The People and the Law', in B. Reay (ed.), *Popular Culture in Seventeenth-Century England* (London, 1985), 244–70; S. Hindle, *The State and Social Change in Early Modern England, c. 1550–1640* (Basingstoke, 2000), chs 3–5.
74. Amussen, '"The Part of a Christian Man"', 227.
75. On the connection between fear of economic failure and sexual impotence, see L. Roper, 'Stealing Manhood: Capitalism and Magic in Early Modern Germany', in *Oedipus and the Devil*, 125–44.
76. Whitney, 'International trends: The witch "she"/the historian "he"', 87.
77. D. Purkiss, 'Desire and its deformities: Fantasies of witchcraft in the English Civil War', *Journal of Medieval and Early Modern Studies*, 27 (1997), 103–32, quotation at 115.
78. See T. Cooper (ed.), *The Journal of William Dowsing: Iconoclasm in East Anglia during the English Civil War* (Woodbridge, 2001).
79. Stearne, *Confirmation and Discovery*, 12; Gaule, *Select Cases of Conscience*, 53. Hopkins did not express a view but, clearly, he regarded the cross-gender identity of witches as axiomatic: Matthew Hopkins, *The Discovery of Witches* (London, 1647).
80. Clark, *Thinking with Demons*, 129–33, quotation at 133.
81. H. Wunder, 'Gender Norms and Their Enforcement in Early Modern Germany', in L. Abrams and E. Harvey (eds), *Gender Relations in German*

History: Power, Agency and Experience from the Sixteenth to the Twentieth Century (London, 1996), 39–56, quotation at 43. See also Rowlands, 'Witchcraft and old women', 69–78; Bever, 'Witchcraft, female aggression, and popular belief', 956–7.

82. R. B. Shoemaker, *Gender in English Society, 1650–1850: The Emergence of Separate Spheres?* (London, 1998), ch. 3; Foyster, *Manhood in Early Modern England*, chs 2–4; Amussen, '"The Part of a Christian Man"', 214.
83. Amussen, '"The Part of a Christian Man"', 227.
84. Crooke, *Microcosmographia*, 276.
85. Briggs, *Witches and Neighbours*, 286.
86. Apps and Gow, *Male Witches*, 38. Discussing witchcraft, Heide Wunder has urged the active historicization of gender relations, so as to resist 'the ceaseless mythologizing that seeks to pin women down': *He is the Sun, She is the Moon: Women in Early Modern Germany* (Cambridge MA, 1998), ch. 8, quotation at 151–2.
87. Kent, 'Masculinity and male witches', 86.

9

The Werewolf, the Witch, and the Warlock: Aspects of Gender in the Early Modern Period

Willem de Blécourt

It has been suggested that the figure of the malevolent witch developed historically not merely in opposition to, but 'in part, from' that of the male sorcerer, or the practitioner of ritual magic.[1] This idea should be questioned, however, or at least qualified. In the context of the early witch-trials, witches were obviously closely related to heretics; in terms of imagery, they seem to have possessed traits in common with fairies.[2] In the context of medieval Europe, sorcerers have to be situated vis-à-vis clergymen, physicians, prophets, and mystics, although these were all categories of masculine power and expertise that frequently overlapped, even during this period. Moreover, the figure of the sorcerer himself was complex and in need of differentiation: it might denote a court astrologer, a necromancer, an occult philosopher, a fortune-teller, a local cunning man, or merely an occasional dabbler in the hidden arts, to name just a few possibilities. Did the figure of the sorcerer slip 'in and out of various categories in disconcerting fashion, making it difficult to pin down exactly what makes him different from any other kind of magical practitioner'?[3] Was a magician, to use another term, always necessarily male? The oppositions inherent within, and the constellations of, particular figures – their so-called 'person fields' – have to be carefully considered in terms of their historical viability, which is always situated in a particular historical context, and in terms of their usefulness for the present-day historian's task of elucidating past practices.

In this chapter, I will introduce another masculine figure, that of the werewolf, and ask in what kind of relationship he stood to both male and female witches (the term 'warlock' is an archaic old-English expression for sorcerer or magician, chosen in my title for its alliteration),[4] or indeed other categories of actual or alleged practitioners of magic. In his hybrid capacity, the werewolf seems, at least, to be related to the shifty sorcerer, but it has yet to be established to what extent. A discussion of werewolf concepts can profit from being framed in terms of questions about early modern masculinity, as well as about notions of sexuality and gender in general. At the same time, this adds even more complexity to an already complicated issue. In the context of the relationship between werewolf and warlock, the following question also arises: Since werewolves were subject to metamorphosis and also operated at the level of metaphor, how far was this also the case when it comes to magicians? At this point, these concerns can merely be raised for future consideration, as they are beyond the scope of this chapter.

Several short introductory remarks on masculinity are nevertheless imperative: it is, as yet, far from being a universal tool of historical analysis, and the results of its study are hardly building up to a possible 'profile' of all early-modern masculinities, as they are predominantly linked to the concepts of honour and violence.[5] For reasons explained below, masculinity will be seen here primarily as a normative concept: as an instruction, blueprint, and measuring rod of how to behave. Gender theory, in its turn, has still to be confronted with the prospect of proceeding beyond male and female (or combinations thereof), and moving into the third gender of the animal realm, if only from a human perspective. As will be argued in this chapter, a cultural approach to body and gender has to be genuinely cultural and not secretly materialistic, while at the same time, recognizing that for early modern people biological differences – such as those between male and female, and between human and animal – formed an integral part of their mental outlook.

I

In contrast to witchcraft historiography, recent reliable academic treatises on werewolves are extremely scanty. This is due both to a lack of interest in them, and a dearth of source material.[6] New presentations on the subject also have to position themselves against the many existing interpretations, which are inversely proportional to the research.[7] Within the boundaries of Europe, werewolves were not omnipresent and readily available for persecution as (alleged) witches were. In other words, the dispersion of the werewolf concept was fragmentary, or at least limited on a temporal and geographical scale.[8] Most werewolf historiography, nevertheless, neglects this point. One encyclopaedia entry simply summarizes him as 'a murderous cannibal wolf'. Another states that, in some trials, 'it is clearly shown that murder and cannibalism took place'.[9] The American literary scholar Charlotte Otten, in her turn, puts sexual aggression first, noting that 'trial records of cases of lycanthropy contain detailed accounts of rape, incest, murder, savage attacks, and cannibalism'.[10] Such observations are not based on thorough research, however, but merely on the published accounts of only seven werewolf trials – four from Franche-Comté, two from elsewhere in France, and one Germany. The list of French cases starts with the werewolves of Poligny, on trial in Besançon in 1521, and continues with Gilles Garnier in 1573 (also in the neighbourhood of Besançon), Jacques Roulet of Angers and the 'cannibal' tailor of Châlons (Nicolas Damont) in 1598, and the Gandillon family in St Claude (Franche-Comté) in the same year. It ends with Jean Grenier, who was banished to a monastery by the *Parlement* (High Court) of Bordeaux in 1603. This last trial, as Adam Douglas notes, 'marked the end of the werewolf fever in the French judicial system'.[11] The German case concerned Peter Stubbe from Bedburg, near Cologne, in 1589.[12]

The image of the murderous and cannibalistic werewolf already existed when Sabine Baring-Gould published his *Book of Were-Wolves* in 1865, in which he referred to all six of the Francophone trials. It was confirmed in 1933, when the self-proclaimed 'Reverend' Montague Summers presented his learned tome *The Werewolf* to the public. He had found a few trials in the literature that Baring-Gould had neglected. But, apart from the English version of the Stubbe pamphlet, which Summers published in full, he did not reveal much about these new cases and, in subsequent werewolf publications, they were again ignored. Among them was the 1598 trial concerning the 'warlock' Jacques Bocquet, executed with several witches who 'had shifted their shape to wolves and haunted the wood of Froidecombe' in the Terre de St Claude.[13]

The published details about these trials do, indeed, convey a cannibalistic image. In the translation by Summers, the Poligny werewolves 'Pierre and Michel attacked and tore to pieces a boy of seven years old. An outcry was raised and they fled. On another occasion they killed a woman who was gathering peas. They also seized a little girl of four years old and ate the palpitating flesh, all save one arm'. Giles Garnier slew a young girl and dragged her to a wood where 'he stripped her naked and not content with eating heartily of the flesh of her thighs and arms, he carried some of the flesh to Apolline his wife'. Other victims of Garnier included a girl, a ten-year-old boy and another boy of about 12 years. The tailor of Châlons used 'to decoy children of both sexes into his shop, and having abused them he would slice their throats and then powder and dress their bodies, jointing them as a butcher cuts up meat'.

Roulet's victim was a boy, who was found 'shockingly mutilated and torn. The limbs, drenched in blood, were yet warm and palpitating'.[14] Summers had a preference for the last word, whereas Baring-Gould paid more attention to feasting and described the children's flesh as 'delicious', 'eaten with great relish'. The element of shape-shifting was hardly present here, especially in the accounts of Baring-Gould. 'On this occasion,' he wrote of Pierre Burgot of Poligny, 'he does not seem to have been in his wolf's shape.' The men who prevented Garnier from devouring his final victim said that he had 'appeared as a man and not as a wolf'. Of the Châlons tailor, Summers states only that he was convicted 'for lycanthropy' and adds that 'under the shape of a wolf, he roamed the woods to leap out on stray passers-by and tear their throats to shreds'.[15] Finally, in Baring-Gould's version of the interrogation of Roulet, the man stated that he had killed and eaten a child when he was a wolf but, when questioned about the way he was dressed and about his head, answered that everything was the same as his interrogators could observe.[16] In other words, his humanity – and human responsibility – was emphasized, rather than his beastly traits.

Although the sources allow for these differences in presentation of the figure of the werewolf, they primarily reflect the divergent interpretation of the two authors. Both were connected to the Church, but Summers – as a defrocked Anglican and a pretend Roman Catholic priest[17] – placed most emphasis on the influence of the Devil, while the Devonshire parson Baring-Gould emphasized the human aspects of his werewolves. Only by quoting the early-sixteenth-century wolf sermon of the German preacher Johann Geiler von Kaisersberg at the very end of his book did Baring-Gould indicate that 'man must turn to God when He brings wild beasts to do him mischief'. Baring-Gould pointed out that Geiler, 'puts aside altogether the view that [werewolves] are men in a state of metamorphosis'. *The Book of Were-Wolves* bears this out. It might contain summaries and editions of most of the then available werewolf texts, but there are also chapters that only discuss murderers who were never described as 'werewolves', thus making it clear that its author regarded lycanthropy mainly as an extreme form of man's 'love of destroying life'. Werewolves were insane: 'the naturally cruel man, if least affected in his brain, will suppose himself to be transformed into the most cruel and bloodthirsty animal with which he is acquainted'.[18]

Summers thought that Baring-Gould wrote 'graphically and with vigour' and did not shy away from the 'terrible truth' of the subject, but that he had also inserted 'a great deal of extraneous matter'.[19] Against the popularizer Baring-Gould, Summers could easily claim the weight of authority: *The Werewolf* is littered with (untranslated) quotations in French and Latin. Summers, however, accepted the reality of the Devil and did not see any ground for questioning the statements of tortured people – in his view they were already 'wicked' and 'horrible'. Discussing the opinions of the French lawyer Jean Bodin, who had included material on werewolves in his hugely influential demonology, *De la démonomanie des sorciers* in 1580,[20] Summers noted: 'it is very certain by the common consent of all antiquity and all history, by the testimony of learned men, by experience and first-hand witness, that werewolfism which involves some change from man to animal is a very real and a very terrible thing'. In his bombastic style, Summers wrote as if taking part himself in the werewolf debate that raged around 1600. Bodin's theory was based on sound Christian doctrine, Summers found, whatever his enemies might have read into it. One of Bodin's critics, Jean de Nynauld, was a 'heretic' who contradicted 'the sense of the Scripture'.[21] This makes it difficult to consider Summers' book as anything more than a jumble of werewolf materials; his account of early modern debates is too biased to be of much historiographical use. He fell into the trap of anachronism and, as a psychiatrist observed in the late-twentieth century, he 'would have made a superb exterminator of hundreds of fellow humans if he had just been born a few centuries earlier'.[22] But Summers would have had difficulty in holding his ground in early modern times. Certainly, in his position on the werewolf, he outdid the Roman Catholic demonologists, as his assessment tried to combine irreconcilable views: 'By the force of his diabolic pact he [the witch] was enabled, owing to a ritual of horrid ointments and impious spells, to assume so cunningly the swift shagge brute that save by his demoniac ferocity and superhuman strength none could distinguish him from the natural wolf'.[23] With this conclusion, Summers reduced a complex historical debate to a personal concoction.

Baring-Gould, who rarely names his sources, seems to have made ample use of French and, to a lesser extent, German publications.[24] His account of a recent case of desecration of graves in Paris was taken straight from a French report.[25] The descriptions of the early modern cases ultimately derive from demonological publications, such as *De prestigiis daemonum* by the Rhineland physician Johann Wier, *Discours exécrable des sorciers* by the Franc-comtois judge Henry Boguet, and *Incrédulité et mescréance du sortilège* by Pierre de Lancre, a jurist and a member of the *Parlement* of Bordeaux from 1582 to 1616. Pamphlets provided additional data, such as the one about Gilles Garnier that was 'circulated through all the cantons of France, Germany and Flanders', as a contemporary remarked.[26]

Or *A True Discourse Declaring the Damnable Life and Death of One Stubbe Peter,* which appeared in London in 1590. The contents of these newssheets had also found their way into the early modern demonologies.[27] Summers, who translated several, consulted the latter directly. But since demonologists had their own agenda, the use of their works did not necessarily ensure accuracy. Accounts of witch-trials that started to appear in the course of the nineteenth century could have provided a counter-balance, as they sometimes incorporated records of werewolf persecution. But they were mainly in German (which Summers shied away from) and, as the compiler of witchcraft texts Henry Charles Lea remarked on the basis of the eighteenth-century *Bibliotheca sive acta et scripta magica*: 'wer-wolves are rarely found in the witch-processes. Of a hundred men, only three or four are accused of or confess to it'.[28] Witch-trials primarily involved women.

Modern popular accounts reduce the seven werewolf cases to one or two. For instance, Gordon Stein discusses Grenier and Roulet, and then remarks: 'There are several other cases similar to these, but they need not be mentioned, except in passing later'. Keith Roberts thought that 'the history of Stubbe Peter is typical for the reports about werewolves at that time'.[29] These conclusions are premature. Werewolf trials might have been relatively few and far between, but research into witch-trials has (especially in Germany) provided enough werewolf cases to develop a different image next to the one of the cannibal. In fact, a precise reading of the Peter Stubbe case (or Stump, to revert to his German name) already supplies an alternative.

II

In Germany, werewolf trials were introduced with the Stump case of 1589, situated in the area between Aachen and Cologne. Writing his demonology *De prestigiis daemonum* a few decades earlier, Johann Wier had not reported any regional werewolves, and had to suffice with referring to the Poligny case from Franche-Comté and to Livonian werewolves.[30] The accounts of the werewolf Peter Stump were constructed out of a mixture of legal concerns and stories that had spread from eastern France, particularly Franche-Comté.[31] Peter Stump was executed on 31 October 1589 in Bedburg (near Cologne). Pamphlets about his case were printed in Augsburg and Nuremberg, and in Denmark, Antwerp, and London.[32] It was the London edition of 1590 that single-handedly created the image of the Renaissance murderous and cannibalistic German werewolf, and the case was subsequently branded as 'the most celebrated European werewolf trial',[33] merely because the pamphlet was the main English text available. The Stump case, nevertheless, calls for caution. A German historian has even expressed serious doubts about whether the pamphlets actually referred to an historical event, one reason being that there are no surviving trial sources.[34] Only two other contemporary reports have been found so far, one by the Cologne pastor Hermann Weinsberg. In his diary entry for 1589, Weinsberg wrote that rumours had been circulating about the case during the entire summer, and then he started citing from a pamphlet: a peasant had lain with a female devil for 25 years and, in between, with his own daughter, denoting incest. He had a belt, and when he put it on he became a werewolf, but he kept his own mental faculties. In wolf's shape he had devoured 13 children, among them his own son. To punish him, hot irons were pressed into his body, his arms and legs were broken, and he was finally decapitated and burned. Weinsberg based this part of his account on a German text, possibly the pamphlet from Augsburg or a similar one. In his opinion, the murders and incest perpetrated by Stump fully justified the punishment, but Weinsberg was not so sure about the 'witcheries' (meaning the shape-changing), as he could not believe everything that was told and retold about them. Who could say whether it was fraud or fantasy, or not?[35]

Two elements in this account support the existence of an actual trial: people had been talking about it, as far as can be ascertained, before any pamphlet had been published. And there is the neat legal point, derived from Bodin, that Stump's 'mind and reason had remained intact',[36] which is not mentioned in any of the other surviving pamphlets, but betrays the presence of lawyers. It was the first German werewolf case,[37] and the French paradigms of murder, cannibalism, and deviant sexuality it echoed would not be repeated in the subsequent German werewolf cases in this combination. On the other hand, there is no mention of ointment; instead, a belt is featured, which does not occur in the reports from Franche-Comté (if the werewolves there used anything similar, it was a whole skin). Another distinctive German detail is that of a pole with a wooden wolf on top erected at the place of execution.

The other contemporary report was by the Dutch chronicler Arnoud van Buchell. On one of his journeys to Germany, he met a member of one of the ruling families of Cologne, who had witnessed Stump's execution and told him that the werewolf had once been his servant.[38] But the possibility that these pamphlets reveal a genuine event does not make them less sensational and fantastic. The news-sheet from Nuremberg added the (French) story about Stump being recognized by his missing hand after the wolf's paw had been cut off. This latter incident was absent from the London version, which otherwise seems to have included every known rumour conveyed to the printer by several letters from Germany. In the London account, the werewolf is said also to have copulated with his own sister, and deflowered several girls before murdering them. When humans were no longer available 'then like a cruell and tirannous beast he would woorke his cruelty on brut beasts in most sauadge [savage] sort, and did act more mischeefe and cruelty then would be credible'.[39] This could be read as cannibalism, although it can also suggest 'consumption' in the sexual sense. And, if Stump committed sexual acts, his 'working on brute beasts' points to no less than bestiality. One fragment even reads like a forerunner of the wolf from Red Riding Hood:

> he was straight transformed into the likeness of a greedy deuouring woolf, strong and mighty, with eyes great and large, a mouth great and wide, with most sharpe and cruell teeth, A huge body, and mightye pawes.

The story about Stump's arrest provides another narrative element in the London pamphlet. While hunters were chasing a wolf, they suddenly found a man, walking with a stick, where they had just seen the wolf. In 1573, a similar story was reported from Dole by a German student.[40] In its totality, the *Life of Peter Stubbe* represents an inversion of Christian family values and, more specifically, a subversion of the preservation of progeny. It opens with the admonition that those who forsake the Lord and despise 'his proffered grace' enter the 'path to perdicion and destruction of body and soul for euer'. A decapitated Stump is shown tied to the stake between his daughter and concubine, as a mockery of the crucifixion scene.

It seems, nevertheless, strange that Stump's werewolfery could have remained undetected for so long, the more so since his name was a nickname which literally meant 'stump', and translated into English as 'stub' or 'truncated' (as a regional dialect term for 'werewolf', it was still current four centuries later). If his nickname referred to his deviant sexuality, then it ironically stood for his short penis (some of the French werewolves had short 'tails' too).[41] But according to the stories, the belt provided him with a disguise 'wherby he might liue without dread or danger of life, and vnknown to be the executor of any bloody enterprise'. Thus, he could walk around in the streets of Cologne, in Bedburg, and in his hometown Erprath 'very ciuilly as one well known to all the inhabitants thereabout' without arousing suspicion. Almost a quarter of a century later, the notion of the werewolf's invisibility reappeared in Cologne;[42] it had obviously been kept in circulation since 1589. It is, nevertheless, debatable whether or not it constituted a more or less traditional local trait; it could also have been taken from Bodin's demonology.[43] The contrast between the werewolf's name and the peasant Stump's appearance in nearby towns indicates that his sexual deviance was more or less tolerated on his home-ground, and that at his trial his crimes were probably aggravated and augmented. They acquired narrative properties as they were grafted onto French concepts – the 1573 Garnier case, with its cannibalism, had also been distributed in Germany. Only in this way does it become possible to reconcile the traces of a legal event with the multitude of stories.

In the eyes of his judges, Stump was not a man, and they underlined this by having his body taken apart by the ritual of execution. This does not imply that they considered him feminine, such as witchcraft theory deemed about sorcerers;[44] it is far more likely that they saw him as a werewolf, the animal they were so keen to redefine. This was moreover shown by the erection of a kind of wolf statue on top of a wooden pole at the place of execution. Masculinity was not just displayed by the judges in their somatization of legal violence and their brutal exercise of power. The event was public – it was a stage on which, next to the criminal, the local aristocracy and other male authority figures paraded.

III

Understanding the Stump case in terms of masculinity involves a slightly different approach from that adopted in most other histories of manhood. Studying past masculinities amounts for the most part to juggling with constructs. As a cultural entity, encompassing notions of proper male behaviour, masculinity was fluctuating, with the speed and amount of change depending on the particular times. It was also defined within specific groups, regions, and denominations. It was related to age, in the sense that there were clear delineations between young boys, adolescents, married men, and widowers (even though it is debatable whether the concept of masculinity should be applied to formative phases). It was, presumably, also a matter of class, or whatever social hierarchy was current at the time. Approaching masculinity from a normative perspective, or as 'the approved way of being an adult male in any given society',[45] implies distancing ourselves from seeing it as everything that men did. For the latter, essentially biological, point of view can lead to peculiar observations, such as the idea that particular forms of masculinity would be 'disruptive' of 'patriarchal order', thereby creating an artificial 'paradox of masculinity'.[46] No society has ever been without the antagonism between prescribed and actual (or merely imagined) behaviour; what makes 'masculinity' worthwhile as a tool of historical analysis is precisely how people positioned themselves, or were positioned, within this field of tension. If actual expressions of what a man should be were different between one group, or even individual, and another, then it would make more historical sense to treat them as different masculinities, possibly in hegemonic order,[47] rather than as conflicting aspects of one overarching, non-historical 'masculinity'. Stump, although clearly a man, was not portrayed as a paradigm of masculinity; instead, he represented everything a man should not be. However, his case also showed the importance of family values and the male responsibility towards the next generation.

While, for the historical actor, masculinity would have been a matter of learning, and of acquiring a sense of what was expected at particular times and places – not only of men, but of women too – for the historian it amounts to painstakingly reconstructing its parameters, details, and variation. Early modern Europe possessed written systems of law that were meant to indicate boundaries of acceptable conduct, and to curb excessive behaviour. These were regionally different but also possessed common denominators, derived as they were from Roman codices, Saxon legislation, and Canon law.[48] On a practical level, sanctioned masculinity showed itself in the pursuit of war, commerce, politics, and learning. These are certainly the subjects of male history predating the gender turn, but they can also be studied as acts in which masculinity was asserted and tested. Research, however, has concentrated on unearthing unwritten rules of gendered behaviour, focusing on the relatively 'soft' themes of family, sexuality, and 'magical' communication.[49] In both cases, there is a severe danger of, yet again, overlooking women.[50] It is even more important, however, to recognize potential masculinity in women's discourses and femininity in men's, so as to untie the concept of gender from biological sex. Yet it is difficult to distinguish femininity in werewolf cases.

IV

In 1595 the provincial Court of Utrecht in the Dutch Republic conducted witch-trials against a number of inhabitants of Amersfoort, and introduced the werewolf accusation. The notion of conducting a criminal trial against a werewolf could have reached Utrecht in several ways.

It might have come through the pamphlet about the Stump case: the local University library there still has a copy. Another possible route was through the chronicler Arnoud van Buchell, who lived in Utrecht and who travelled along the Rhine and discussed werewolves with the Count of Nassau.[51] Or it might have come directly through the Count, who was closely related to the Dutch *stadholders*. Whatever route the information had taken, in the Dutch context, the addition of the werewolf accusation to the witch-image was an audacious move by the Utrecht Court, since the High Council in The Hague had just moved in the other direction by declaring the water ordeal in witch-trials illegal and freeing an accused witch (a point ignored in Utrecht as well). Since it is possible to compare the earlier witnesses' testimonies from the municipal court of Amersfoort (where the accused had been tried before) with the testimonies and confessions made before the Court in Utrecht, the absence of werewolves in Amersfoort can be established. In Amersfoort, a man called Volkert Dirksz had been accused of bewitching horses, and had been compelled to bless them to lift the bewitchment. Although having married into a family of witches, defined in the female line, Volkert's witchcraft was situated in the male sphere of influence.[52] When his daughter was interrogated, she confessed to dancing on the bleaching ground just outside Amersfoort with her female relatives, all in the shape of cats. In Utrecht, Volkert's sons were drawn into the proceedings and wolves were mentioned for the first time. Elbert, aged 13, told the councillors that:

> barely half a year ago, he, his father and Hessel his brother in the presence of his father's lord and master, of whom he did not know how he was dressed, had all been changed into wolves, on a field near Bunschoten at the Haar, in a dark night, and that he and his brother rounded the cattle up, without doing anything else, to have them bitten in the throat by his father, but that he and his brother had not bitten [the cattle].

Elbert's brother related a confusing story of how he had been with his godmother when the Devil had visited them in the shape of a naked black man, who had given him a piece of black leather and a piece of black woollen cloth with pins. The Devil had flown up the chimney with him into another room and had also fetched the red cat [a woman]:

> and in that room they danced together; after the dance the evil one said to the woman, you dirty beast, now you will come with me, and he bound a hairy belt around her body and when that was done

> the red cat changed into a wolf, and the evil one flew with him and the red cat out of the chimney to Eemland in the field, where he rounded up the animals, which were then bitten by the evil one and the red cat, both in the shape of wolves

The court also found witnesses who asserted that the brothers had admitted to them that they were the wolves that had killed their cattle.[53] These accounts – related by children, and somewhat vague and confused – indicate the peripheral position of the Dutch werewolves in relation to the developing German centre. In the Northern Netherlands, the new werewolf concept was added to the existing image of the male witch, whether it concerned the bewitching of animals within the male domain, or the acquisition of wealth and power.

These last two characteristics defined male witchcraft in large areas of Western Europe to a significant extent, although the picture was confused in the seventeenth-century political trials, when men were forced to confess to attendance at the Sabbath, or to having made a pact with the Devil without having been previously reputed as a male witch. When Briggs writes, however, 'that there is little or no sign that the male witches had been anything but masculine in their behaviour', he is referring to a different masculinity than I favour here.[54] When they had adhered to norms of manliness, male witches would not have been prosecuted; they found themselves in a witch-trial precisely because they had somehow crossed masculine boundaries. Male cunning folk could also end up in criminal trials, which also signals that they overstepped certain norms, and that their witch-finding or recovery of stolen goods was not seen as particularly manly – at least, not by the authorities.[55] This did not necessarily make them male witches, however, unless some of their professional identifications of (mostly female) witches had backfired and they themselves had been accused of bewitchments.[56] On an everyday level, the bewitching or enriching male witch was almost as current as his female counterpart, a point supported by the as yet sparsely researched slander trials.[57] During the process of turning a local suspicion into a persecution, however, most of the male witches, together with their specific brand of witchcraft, were filtered out.

V

If the Stump pamphlet was meant to sensitize people to werewolves, it generally succeeded; if it was meant to encourage them to hunt the beasts, it failed. No werewolf trials were initiated in southern Germany,

England, or Denmark, despite the publication of Stump pamphlets in these places. The late-sixteenth-century werewolf trials conducted in Protestant Nassau, within a hundred kilometres of Cologne, were only partially influenced by the narrative from Catholic Bedburg, since the Protestants had to reinvent the werewolf yet again.[58] Only to the west, in the Catholic Southern Netherlands, do we find both a version of the pamphlet text and corresponding werewolf trials. Although it is not known what the first werewolf in 1592 in Mechelen was accused of precisely, in 1598 another one was indicted for biting little children 'behind their ears, in their side, under their armpits and finally in the throat'.[59]

The Stump case might have acted as a paradigm and catalyst for a number of subsequent werewolf trials in the region, although its constructed werewolf was regularly adjusted to fit both local considerations and imagery. In the Netherlands, the same combination of male witch and werewolf as had been tried out in Utrecht surfaced a few months later in Arnhem, at the trial of Hans Poeck (officially known as Johan Martensen van Steenhuijsen). This man was not tortured and confessed voluntarily after staying afloat during the water ordeal he himself had demanded. It is, nevertheless, clear that he did answer questions, some of them leading. He claimed that, about three years earlier, after his leg had been injured by a horse, he had met a man walking on the dyke. When asked for food, the man had said: 'I will give you plenty if you will do my will'. Hans had hesitated but when the exchange was repeated several times – in the meantime, two women had passed by – he finally consented to renounce God. At that moment, he had felt something like hot or warm water on his face, the sign that his chrism was being removed. The Evil One – for Hans had encountered no other but him – had then given him a piece of cloth, saying: 'As long as you have this, you will succeed in everything'. Next, Hans confessed that he had been 'walking as a wolf' for three years. After turning into a wolf, he was still capable of human judgement, but could not speak.

This last element of his confession points again to Bodin's theory about the preservation of human intelligence and responsibility. The rest contains a combination of his bewitchments and his experience as a werewolf. Poeck had bewitched a woman innkeeper and several horses by hitting them with the piece of cloth given to him by the Devil. When he put it on his own head, he became a wolf. He claimed to have a belt (although this was probably in answer to a question), but he had hidden it in some house, in a hole behind a bed. Often eight or ten wolves had crowded round him, among them the Devil, likewise in wolf's shape. Once the Devil, still as a wolf, had thrown him into a ditch because

Hans did not want to bewitch animals for him. Another time the Devil had frightened his horses to such an extent that he had had to continue walking with him, again in the form of a wolf. They had gone to a certain place and, afterwards, he had returned to the horses, and there he was freed by two men who happened to pass by.[60] Once more, the nickname is the clue to the meaning of 'werewolf': *poe(c)k* derives from the Dutch verb *poekelen*, to carry (something or someone) on one's back (*pukkel* denotes a kind of rucksack). Hans Poeck was thus a man whom other people carried on their back. This indicates a homosexual act, as in all probability do his encounters with the Devil. His was the last werewolf trial in the Northern Netherlands, but slander trials show that the combination of werewolf and male witch was an insult in the eastern provinces throughout the entire seventeenth century. In a number of cases, this included the werewolf's connotation with sexual deviance.

In the course of a witch-trial in 1609, in Horst (near Gladbeck), a whole family was subjected to the water ordeal. When the father stayed afloat, he ascribed it to the incest he had committed, not to witchcraft. But when he heard that his children had confessed to being witches, he admitted to being a werewolf. The Devil, whose name was Federbusch (crest of feathers), had persuaded him to denounce the Holy Trinity and had fornicated with him (in other trials against men, the Devil is described as a woman, first). The Devil had also been with him at a dance, and had given him a belt. After this, he confessed to having 'bitten' several cows and foals. As before in Bedburg, a pole with a wooden wolf on top of it was erected at the place where he was strangled and burned.[61] The trial of Peter Kleikamp from Ahlen (south east of Münster) even started with an indictment for sodomy. Because the prosecutor could not uphold this, he switched to a witch-trial, for which less stringent rules of evidence applied. In this way, Kleikamp was made to confess, among other things, that in the form of a wolf he had 'bitten' a calf and 'shamed' a young ox. He had only six hours in which he could 'walk' as a wolf. More witch-like was the part of his confession where he admitted that he and some others had anointed themselves and then flown in the form of ravens, a detail that his interrogators might have borrowed from a description of a witch-trial in Liège.[62] In a case from Strasbourg in 1633, concerning a 16-year old boy from Molzheim, we find similar elements. The boy was accused of having:

> killed many cattle. Among others he had sat on the back of a cow in the shape of a raven and had pecked at it and eaten of it till it died, and as a fox he had hung on the tail of another [cow], till it had

> jumped to its death. He had made several maidens pregnant and had committed sodomy with a sheep while he was in the shape of a dog and with a pig while he was in the shape of a wolf.[63]

In the commentary on her compilation, Otten based her notion of sexuality on the Stump case, which she edited and reprinted; she emphasized that 'Stubbe' 'confessed to committing incest with his daughter and sister'. In his earlier book on 'the occult', Wilson, referring to the Garnier and Stubbe cases, stated that 'sexually frustrated peasants identified with werewolves'.[64] Although both authors present little further evidence, the role of sexuality was explicit from the start when the Poligny werewolves told their judges in 1521 that, when they were wolves, they copulated with female wolves, which gave them as much pleasure as with women (it is unclear whether here, as in Latin, the same word was used for bitches and whores). In the Châlons case from 1598, the tailor 'abused' the children – in all likelihood, sexually – before killing them, and, in 1599, the werewolf Verjuz in Franche-Comté was said to have committed incest with his mother.[65] A girl who acted as a witness in the trial against the teenager Jean Grenier in 1603 stated that she had been attacked by a wild animal 'which was fatter, but shorter than a wolf and which had a short tail'. Later, Grenier boasted that he was that animal, 'and that if he had managed to get her on the ground he would have given her a good bite'.[66] A historian has called this a 'sexual phantasm', and I am inclined to agree with him.[67] The 'short tail' will have referred to the boy's penis and the 'bite' to sexual intercourse.

VI

Some pamphlets display a troubled relation with historical events. Two years after the Stump story, an even more sensational report appeared in Augsburg, supposedly describing events in Jülich, only a few kilometres from Erprath, where Stump had committed his crimes. It related the story of more than 300 women who had, supposedly, changed into wolves and killed many men, boys, and cattle. Of them, 24 were discovered because a boy had found his mother's belt, tried it on and become a werewolf himself. When this frightened the other children, the neighbours gathered to get rid of the wolf. But the boy implored them not to harm him; he had only put on the belt by accident, and his mother had done it every day. She was subsequently imprisoned and tortured, and confessed to having accomplices. In those days the execution of two dozen women for witchcraft was quite plausible and, when all the convictions from the area from Osnabrück to Trier are added up, the figure of 300 does not appear excessive either.[68] The episode about the boy, however, was clearly a legend that survived into the twentieth century,[69] and the idea of such an extraordinary number of female werewolves was pure fantasy. The Augsburg printer who published the pamphlet was known for his sensationalism, and he probably wanted to match the success of his colleague who had printed the Stump pamphlet. Only very occasionally was a woman accused of being a werewolf. Moreover, the pamphlet about Jülich is extremely sexist: it ascribes a male trait to a group of women, thus rendering them less female, and describes how these manly women attacked and devoured men, and 'sucked up their blood and ate their brains'.

The existence of some of the female German 'werewolves' might only have been due to the fact that, during a witch-trial, a woman was forced to admit to having changed shape into an animal form, or when reference to a wolf's shape was simply added on to those of the more female cats and hares by witnesses or interrogators. If the first two women denounced in 1630 in Oberkirchen, some 60 kilometres north of Dillenburg, provide any evidence of the concept of a female werewolf outside the context of a witch-trial, then their case suggests that it seems to have been independent women who came under suspicion.[70] This was probably also the case in 1590 in Lower Hesse, where a woman was accused of having bewitched a cow. She worked her farm on Sundays and, apparently, had no husband. The neighbours avoided her, because she was said to be 'doing her foul work as a tearing wolf at night with her children'.[71] This woman might not have been called a werewolf, but her behaviour was certainly compared to a wolf. The majority of woman who were accused of being werewolves, however, were considered to be so because the rule of place was applied to them: they had been seen where, just before, a wolf had been spotted. This was one of the recognized shape-shifting mechanisms ascribed to witches, usually in connection with shapes such as cats or hares; notwithstanding a reference to it in one of the Stump pamphlets, there is no evidence, as yet, that it applied to men. The motif was already present in Lucerne in 1489, when a woman appeared in the wrong place at the wrong time.[72] In 1614, a woman was on her way back from the market in Wilz (in the Eifel region of western Germany) where she had sold some cows when she saw one of her neighbours in the moonlight. When she asked her how she had got there and mentioned the name of Jesus, her neighbour had disappeared and a wolf stood in her place and had approached the horses. The woman had driven off and not seen anything further, but later she had become ill. This neighbour had also been encountered as a cat. A similar story was told 40 years later in Sauerland, in the Electorate of Cologne. A horse had been attacked by a wolf, and it was suggested that a woman neighbour had not been far away from it, and was possibly the wolf herself. Again, in 1668, a woman appeared where a wolf had been spotted before, and the woman who saw her was so frightened of the wolf that she miscarried.[73] Yet other women were deemed to have attacked cattle in wolf form.[74]

Overall, however, werewolves only constituted a tiny minority among the witches, and the handful of female werewolves are, in their turn, a tiny minority among the predominantly male werewolves. It might just be possible to scrape together 300 (predominantly male) werewolves in the whole of Europe over a period of 200 years; the suggestion in the 1591 pamphlet that this number of female werewolves would have been prosecuted in one year is absurd. Most of the few female werewolves were accused later, after the male image had become established by the waves of witch-trials between 1590 and 1630. But one should still be aware of regional variation. In Mecklenburg, in the north east of Germany, a different picture emerges. Trials only started there in the second half of the seventeenth century, and the werewolves constituted less than one per cent of all those accused.[75] Here, however, a substantial portion of them were women.

VII

Men such as Stump, Poeck, or Kleikamp might have asserted their own idea of manhood in their sexual exploits and, especially when their behaviour had been more or less tolerated for a while locally (nicknames do need some time to settle),[76] the new trials certainly signalled a tougher regime. Officially, anal sex was not allowed, as it ran counter to the ideas of sexual union for the purposes of reproduction, which could only take place within a sanctioned marriage. The criminalization of female witchcraft expressed similar concerns with productivity, as witches were usually accused of hampering growth (in humans, animals, and crops), and of interfering with processes of maturation.[77] Whereas female witchcraft was seen in terms of negative femininity, which in early modern society amounted to negative female sexuality, male witchcraft was not focused primarily within the sexual domain, but was deemed to run counter to those aspects of masculinity that were defined by honour. Far from being an individual characteristic, honour set out man's relation to the different male communities of which he was part or with which he had dealings. Male witches exercised unnatural power that some considered feminine, but that mainly stood in opposition to communal codes of the distribution of wealth. Sexuality seems to have been absent in male witchcraft, at least in terms of how it was seen on an everyday level.

Apart from the occasional overlap in marginal areas such as the eastern Netherlands (although even there the juxtaposition of the terms for male witch and werewolf did not have to make them synonyms), werewolves and male witches thus occupied different conceptual niches. In short: werewolves usually did not bewitch anything, neither were they accused of enriching themselves in unbecoming ways. It could be argued that werewolves and male witches merely expressed different negative aspects of masculinity; here, I want to suggest that the concept of a werewolf exceeded masculinity and femininity, and constituted a third gender, indicating those humans who had gone beyond humanity and had entered the animal realm.

A detailed discussion of human-animal intersection would obviously make a separate paper, and the possible notion of an 'animal' gender has to remain tentative. A non-man, who did not equal a woman, was possibly too abstract a concept, however; traditionally the wolf image did represent the man – or, more specifically, the sexual criminal – outside society. Someone who was an animal was not part of humanity. The figure of the werewolf also came to combine the animal body and animal sexual behaviour – such as back-riding (as in the Poeck case), or sodomy in general.[78] Putting on a belt separated the upper from the lower half of the body, thereby stressing the sexual. When that belt was made of animal skin (although substitutes were known too), it referred explicitly to bestial sexuality.

Moreover, the conceptual relation between animals and deviant sexuality will have been more current not only in werewolves, but also, for example, in satyrs, another kind of human–animal hybrid who signified excessive sexual lust.[79] Goats had their connotations with the male 'sins of the flesh' as well, in precisely the same intellectual environment in which clerics and sorcerers moved, and where initiates were adorned with goat attributes, for instance.[80] And not only men could become animalized. Stories about dancing cats circulating in the sixteenth-century Netherlands, to mention another instance, pointed at sexually loose women. The notion of animalization of, in this case, incest was also present in the story of the princess who was desired sexually by her father and escaped clad in animal skins – either bear, donkey, or a mixture of different species.[81] In addition to wolves, goats, and men, future research has also to explore similar stories and ideas about shape-changing women. In all these different instances, animal metamorphoses were comprehended as metaphors of sexual deviancy. Possibly, it even concerned more than mere metaphors, since the animal skins indicated that the wearer's body had taken on animal characteristics in an act of animal 'drag' that fused with the wearer's human identity.

Notes

1. For a recent discussion, see F. Klaassen, 'Learning and masculinity in manuscripts of ritual magic of the later Middle Ages and Renaissance', *Sixteenth Century Journal*, 38 (2007), 49–76. For a more balanced view, see N. Cohn, *Europe's Inner Demons: the Demonisation of Christians in Medieval Christendom* (London, 2005; reprint of the revised 1993 edition), 118–43.
2. Cf. W. de Blécourt, 'The Return of the Sabbat: Mental Archaeologies, Conjectural Histories or Political Mythologies?', in J. Barry and O. Davies (eds), *Witchcraft Historiography* (Basingstoke/New York, 2007), 125–45.
3. P.G. Maxwell-Stuart, *Wizards: A History* (Stroud, 2007), 11.
4. For a different slant on the classic children's books by C.S. Lewis, see N. Gaiman, *Fragile Things: Short Fictions and Wonders* (London, 2006), 237–50: 'The Problem of Susan'.
5. Cf. G. Schwerhoff, 'Starke Worte. Blasphemie als theatralische Inszenierung von Männlichkeit an der Wende vom Mittelalter zur Frühen Neuzeit', in M. Dinges (ed.), *Hausväter, Priester, Kastraten. Zur Konstruktion von Männlichkeit in Spätmittelalter und Früher Neuzeit* (Göttingen, 1998), 237–63.
6. For an outdated summary of the scholarship, see P. Dinzelbacher, 'Lycanthropy', in R. M. Golden (ed.), *Encyclopedia of Witchcraft. The Western Tradition*, vol. III (Santa Barbara, CA, 2006), 680–2.
7. Cf. W. de Blécourt, 'A journey to hell: Reconsidering the Livonian "Werewolf"', *Magic, Ritual, and Witchcraft* 2 (2007), 49–67.
8. See R. Briggs, *The Witches of Lorraine* (Oxford, 2007), 123–6.
9. See 'Werwolf', in C. Rose (ed.), *Giants, Monsters and Dragons* (Santa Barbara/Denver/Oxford, 2000), 391; and 'Werewolf', in L. A. Shepard (ed.), *Encyclopedia of Occultism and Parapsychology* (Detroit/New York/London, 1991), 1797. The last quotation is from L. Spence, *An Encyclopedia of Occultism* (London, 1920), 426.
10. C. F. Otten, *A Lycanthropy Reader: Werewolves in Western Culture* (Syracuse, 1986), 51. Otten's approach is literary rather than historical; cf. her latest compilation, *The Literary Werewolf: An Anthology* (Syracuse, 2002).
11. A. Douglas, *The Beast Within: A History of the Werewolf* (London, 1992), 149.
12. See the summaries in R. H. Robbins, *The Encyclopedia of Witchcraft and Demonology* (New York, 1959), 212, 233–5, 324, 489–90, 537–8.
13. M. Summers, *The Werewolf* (London, 1933), 229–30.
14. Summers, *The Werewolf*, 224, 226–7, 230.
15. S. Baring-Gould, *The Book of Were-Wolves* (London, 1865) 73, 81, 78; Summers, *The Werewolf*, 230.
16. Baring-Gould, *The Book of Were-Wolves*, 83–4.

17. On Summers, see J. Wood, 'The Reality of Witch Cults Reasserted: Fertility and Satanism', in Barry and Davies (eds), *Witchcraft Historiography*, 76–85.
18. Baring-Gould, *The Book of Were-Wolves*, 266, 131, 145.
19. Summers, *The Werewolf*, xi, 103.
20. Bodin's influence at the court of Laon, where he was employed, was negligible, on the other hand; cf. C. Opitz-Belakhal, *Das Universum des Jean Bodin. Staatsbildung, Macht und Geschlecht im 16. Jahrhundert*, (Frankfurt am Main and New York, 2006).
21. Summers, *The Werewolf*, 76–7, 98–9.
22. R. Noll, *Vampires, Werewolves and Demons: Twentieth-Century Reports in the Psychiatric Literature* (New York, 1992), 86.
23. Summers, *The Werewolf*, 123.
24. Such as F. Bourquelot, 'Recherches sur la lycanthropie', *Mémoires et dissertations sur les antiquités nationales et étrangères* NS 9 (1849), 193–262; R. Leubuscher, *Über die Wehrwölfe und Thierverwandlungen im Mittelalter. Ein Beitrag zur Geschichte der Psychologie* (Berlin, 1850); W. Hertz, *Der Werwolf. Beitrag zur Sagengeschichte* (Stuttgart, 1862).
25. Baring-Gould, *The Book of Were-Wolves*, 255–60, from *Annales médico-psychologiques*. Cf. C. Crowe, 'The Lycanthropist', reprinted in P. Haining (ed.), *Werewolf: Horror Stories of the Man-Beast* (London, 1987), 13–9.
26. Le Loyer in *Discours des spectres* (1608), 140; cited in Hervé Campangne, '*Arrest memorable contre Gilles Garnier pour avoir en forme de loup-garou devoré plusieurs enfants et commis autres crimes*: Métamorphose et commentaire dans une lettre de Daniel d'Auge', *Nouvelle revue du seizième siècle*, 15 (1997), 343–57, especially 345.
27. Jean Bodin, *On the Demon-Mania of Witches*, translated by Randy A. Scott (Toronto, 1995), 122; Martin Del Rio, *Disquisitionum magicarum libri sex*, (Louvain, 1599), 190 (not included in the English translation), cf. *Investigations into Magic*, edited and translated by P.G. Maxwell-Stuart (Manchester and New York, 2000).
28. H. C. Lea, *Materials towards a History of Witchcraft* (first published in 1939; New York/London, 1957 edn), 941; cf. Hertz, *Der Werwolf*, 71.
29. G. Stein, 'Werewolves', in: *The Encyclopedia of the Paranormal* (Amherst, NY, 1996), 809; K. Roberts, 'Eine Werwolf-Formel. Eine kleine Kulturgeschichte des Werwolfs', in U. Müller and W. Wunderlich (eds), *Dämonen, Monster, Fabelwesen* (St. Gallen, 1999), 565–81, especially 574.
30. E.-D. Güting, 'Michel Beheims Gedicht gegen den Aberglauben und seine lateinische Vorlage', *Forschungen und Berichte zur Volkskunde in Baden-Württenberg*, 3 (1974/1977), 197–220, especially 208 (with thanks to Elmar Lorey).
31. On the werewolf trials there, see R. Schulte, *Man as Witch. Male Witches in Central Europe* (Basingstoke, 2009), 8–18, 23–31.
32. E. M. Lorey, *Henrich der Werwolf. Eine Geschichte aus der Zeit der Hexenprozesse mit Dokumenten und Analysen* (Frankfurt am Main, 1998), 208–9.
33. C. Wilson, *The Occult* (London, 1971), 441.
34. E. Münster-Schröer, 'Hexenverfolgungen in Jülich-Berg und der Einfluß Johann Weyers', *Spee-Jahrbuch*, 7 (2000), 59–102, especially 77.
35. Cf. F. Irsigler and A. Lasotta, *Bettler und Gaukler, Dirnen und Henker. Randgruppen und Außenseiter in Köln 1300–1600* (Cologne, 1984), 152–3; F. W. Siebel, *Die Hexenverfolgung in Köln* (Bonn, 1959), 33–4.

36. Bodin, *On the Demon-Mania* (translated by Scott), 128.
37. Summers, *The Werewolf*, 252, mentions a case at 'Dalheim' in 1581, but this should be Dalem in Lorraine; see Nicolas Rémy, *La Démonolâtrie*, translated by Jean Boës (Nancy, 1998), 210.
38. H. Keussen, 'Die drei Reisen des Utrechters Arnoldus Buchelius nach Deutschland, insbesondere sein Kölner Aufenthalt', *Annalen des Historischen Vereins für den Niederrhein*, 84 (1907), 1–102; 85 (1908), 43–114, especially 85 and 68.
39. Quotes are from the reprint in Summers, *The Werewolf*, 253–6. The edition in Otten, *Lycanthropy Reader*, 69–76, is heavily edited.
40. C. Oates, 'Metamorphosis and Lycanthropy in Franche-Comté, 1521–1643', in M. Feher (ed.), *Fragments for a History of the Human Body*, I (New York, 1989) 304–63, especially 337.
41. Cf. Campangne, *'Arrest memorable'*, 356, where he cites De Lancre's wonder about werewolf names as *Gar*nier and *Gre*nier.
42. Irsigler and Lasotta, *Bettler und Gaukler*, 154.
43. Cf. P. M. Kreuter, 'Paracelsus – und der Werwolf?', *Nova Acta Paracelsica*, NF 20 (2007), 137–46.
44. L. Apps and A. Gow, *Male Witches in Early Modern Europe* (Manchester/New York, 2003), 135–6. This book suffers from a top-down view; cf. Schulte, *Man as Witch*, 4.
45. D. D. Gilmore, *Manhood in the Making: Cultural Concepts of Masculinity* (New Haven/London, 1990), 1.
46. L. Roper, 'Blood and Codpieces: Masculinity in the Early Modern German Town', in *idem*, *Oedipus and the Devil: Witchcraft, Sexuality and Religion in Early Modern Europe* (London/New York, 1994), 107–24.
47. Cf. M. Dinges, '" Hegemoniale Männlichkeit" – Ein Konzept auf dem Prüfstand', in: *idem* (ed.), *Männer – Macht – Körper. Hegemoniale Männlichkeiten vom Mittelalter bis heute* (Frankfurt am Main/New York, 2005), 7–33.
48. Cf. H. R. Schmidt, 'Hausväter vor Gericht. Der Patriarchialismus als zweischneidiges Schwert', in M. Dinges (ed.), *Hausväter, Priester, Kastraten. Zur Konstruktion von Männlichkeit in Spätmittelalter und Früher Neuzeit* (Göttingen, 1998), 213–36.
49. Cf. W. Schmale, *Geschichte der Männlichkeit in Europa (1450–2000)* (Vienna/Cologne/Weimar, 2003). His concept of 'magic' is an extended one, with a main focus on extra-worldly communication; it is also very Catholic.
50. J. Jordan, '*Her*-story Untold; The Absence of Women's Agency in Constructing Concepts of Early Modern Manhood', *Cultural and Social History*, 4 (2007), 575–83.
51. Keussen, 'Die drei Reisen', 52–3.
52. Cf. W. de Blécourt, 'The making of the female witch: Reflections on witchcraft and gender in the early modern period', *Gender & History*, 12 (2000), 287–309, especially 298–9.
53. S. van Leeuwen, *Batavia Illustrata ofte Hollandsche Chronyk* ('s-Gravenhage, 1685), 296–304; cf. Lea, *Materials*, 942.
54. Briggs, *Witches of Lorraine*, 365.
55. The assertion by Klaassen that it is possible to construct a character sketch of the sorcerer on the basis of the appearance of spells to accomplish love magic or good detection and others (see Klaassen, 'Learning and Masculinity', 62)

is wide of the mark. These spells were part of a sorcerer's professional 'toolkit', to be utilized for clients, not intrinsic elements of his character.

56. Especially when they were punished as cunning folk, which usually (according to the *Carolina* and other laws) meant banishment, they should not be confused with male witches, cf. A. Rowlands, *Witchcraft Narratives in Germany: Rothenburg, 1561–1652* (Manchester/New York, 2003), 162–4. The capacity to discover stolen goods involved different techniques from those involved in treasure seeking.
57. For the seventeenth-century eastern Netherlands, see W. de Blécourt, *Termen van toverij. De veranderende betekenis van toverij in Noordoost-Nederland tussen de 16de en de 20ste eeuw* (Nijmegen, 1990), 111–3.
58. On Nassau, see J. Koppenhöfer, *Die mitleidlose Gesellschaft. Studien zu Verdachtsgenese, Ausgrenzungsverhalten und Prozeßproblematik im frühneuzeitlichen Hexenprozeß in der alten Grafschaft Nassau unter Johann VI. und der späteren Teilgrafschaft Nassau-Dillenburg (1559–1687)* (Frankfurt, Berlin, etc., 1995); S. Richter, *Werwölfe und Zaubertänze. Vorchristliche Glaubenvorstellungen in Hexenprozessen der frühen Neuzeit* (Frankfurt, Berlin, etc., 2004). The interpretation in the latter book is insufficient, cf. W. de Blécourt, 'A Journey to Hell: Reconsidering the Livonian "Werewolf"', *Magic, Ritual, and Witchcraft*, 2 (2007), 49–67.
59. L. T. Maes, *Vijf eeuwen stedelijk strafrecht. Bijdragen tot de rechts- en cultuurgeschiedenis der Nederlanden* (Antwerpen/'s-Gravenhage, 1947), 208–9. I owe the information about the reception of the Stump pamphlet to Dries Vanysacker.
60. P.C. Molhuijsen, 'Bijdrage tot de geschiedenis der Heksenprocessen in Gelderland', *Bijdragen voor vaderlandsche geschiedenis en oudheidkunde*, NR 1 (1859), 194–209, especially 202–3.
61. H. Aldieck, 'Akten und Urkunden zur Geschichte des Horster Gerichtswesens', *Vestische Zeitschrift*, 32 (1925), 180–206, especially 193–202. For another werewolf pole, see J. M. Eversen, 'Vonnis en executie wegens weerwolverij in 1607 door de justitie te Maastricht', *De Maasgouw*, 25 (1903), 95–6. Another one was erected in Horst in 1622.
62. B. Niehues, *Zur Geschichte des Hexenglaubens und der Hexenprozesse vornehmlich im ehemaligen Fürstbisthum Münster* (Münster, 1875), 83.
63. [Anonymous] 'Zauber und Gespenstergeschichten', *Alemannia. Zeitschrift für Sprache, Literatur und Volkskunde des Elsasses und Oberrheins*, 4 (1877), 161–81, especially 170.
64. Otten, *Lycanthropy Reader*, 53; Wilson, *The Occult*, 440.
65. On Verjuz, see Schulte, *Man as witch*, 26; cf. B. Rowland, *Animals with Human Faces. A Guide to Animal Symbolism* (London, 1974), 165, who also discusses the medieval sexual symbolism of the werewolf.
66. C. Oates, 'The Trial of a Teenage Werewolf, Bordeaux, 1603', *Criminal Justice History*, 9 (1988), 1–29, especially 10.
67. M. Meurger, 'L'Homme-loup et son témoin. Construction d'une factualité lycanthropique', in J. de Nynauld, *De la lycanthropie* (Préaud & Jacques-Chaquin (eds); Paris, 1990), 143–79, especially 170.
68. Cf. Münster-Schröer, 'Hexenverfolgung', 76–9.
69. See M. Zender, *Sagen und Geschichten aus der Westeifel* (3rd edn, Bonn, 1980), 372 (no. 1134); K. Bartsch, *Sagen, Märchen und Gebrauche aus Mecklenburg* (Vienna, 1879), 149; Hertz, *Der Werwolf*, 80.

70. A. Bruns, 'Die Oberkircher Hexenprotokolle', in A. Bruns (ed.), *Hexen. Gerichtsbarkeit im kurkölnischen Sauerland* (Schmallenberg, 1984), 11–90, especially 52, 57.
71. K. H. Spielmann, *Die Hexenprozesse in Kurhessen* (Marburg, 1932), 67–8.
72. E. Hoffman-Krayer, 'Luzerner Akten zum Hexen- und Zauberwesen', *Schweizerisches Archiv für Volkskunde*, 3 (1899), 22–40, 81–122, 189–224, 291–329, especially 90.
73. H.-P. Pracht, *Täntze, Todt und Teuffel. Die grausame Spur der Hexenverfolgung in der Eifel* (Aachen, 1991), 129–33; W. Dalhoff, 'Zu Rüthener Hexenprozessen', in A. Bruns (ed.), *Hexen. Gerichtsbarkeit im kurkölnischen Sauerland* (Schmallenberg, 1984), 177–88, especially 181–4; W. Niess, *Hexenprozesse in der Grafschaft Büdingen* (Büdingen, 1982), 284.
74. J. Rinscheid, 'Der Hexenwahn im Wildenburger Lande', *Mitteilungen der Westdeutschen Gesellschaft für Familienkunde*, 21 (1963), 203–76, especially 256; Spielmann, *Kurhessen*, 155.
75. K. Moeller, *Dass Willkür über Recht ginge. Hexenverfolgung in Mecklenburg im 16. und 17. Jahrhundert* (Bielefeld, 2007), 191–4.
76. Cf. the Maastricht werewolf of 1607, who simply went by the name of 'le Loup' (see note 61).
77. Cf. I. Ahrendt-Schulte, *Zauberinnen in der Stadt Horn (1554–1603). Magische Kultur und Hexenverfolgung in der Frühen Neuzeit* (Frankfurt/New York, 1997), 213–35.
78. For the nineteenth- and twentieth-century werewolf back rider, see W. de Blécourt, '"I would have eaten you too": Werewolf legends in the Flemish, Dutch and German Area', *Folklore*, 118 (2007), 23–43.
79. Cf. Schmale, *Geschichte der Männlichkeit*, 48.
80. R. M. Karras, *From Boys to Men: Formations of Masculinity in Late Medieval Europe* (Philadelphia, 2003), 100–8. The connection between the figure of the *beanus* and the sabbat-presiding Devil in goat form needs to be further explored.
81. As in the particular werewolf legend, chopped-off hands also play in role in this story cycle, among others presented by Basile, Perrault, and later the Brothers Grimm; cf. J. Zipes, *The Great Fairy Tale Tradition: From Straparola and Basile to the Brothers Grimm* (New York/London, 2001), 26–50.

10
Possession and the Sexes

Sarah Ferber

Demonic possession in Western Christianity is, like witchcraft, a discourse into which questions of gender can be articulated, and often have been articulated historically, with the sex of the possessed seen as relevant to both causes and symptoms. As with witchcraft, too, it is a discourse within which gender can, nonetheless, seem irrelevant at times or, rather, to have no *prima facie* significance: its documentation can be surprisingly gender-neutral. The purpose of this chapter is to assist scholars approaching the analysis of possession from a gender perspective, and particularly those writing about cases of possession among males, by delimiting a few of the questions that need to be asked before the question of gender can be addressed effectively. It begins with some methodological comments, then addresses the gender demographics of possession, and moves to a consideration of the early modern era, with particular reference to the questions of volition and responsibility on the part of the possessed. With these issues in mind, it will address two French cases of possession in adult males from the same period, in order to consider them in the light of the more famous female cases of that time and place. In this context, it will make a personal disclosure of a humbling misreading which (at best) can point to the pitfalls of hasty conclusions about the nature of the gender divide in relation to possessed males and females. The chapter does not provide a complete gender history of possession in the early modern era, but sets out avenues of enquiry that might serve as guidelines for a more sustained examination of the historical phenomenon of adult male possession.

The principal type of possession considered here is what might be termed the 'limelight' cases, those cases in which there is an attempt, either on the part of the possessed or their minders, to make some claim for the condition's wider significance, usually in a way that displays the power of exorcism, or which has some projected polemical or legal outcome. If, as it seems, women, adolescents, or children make up the majority of the high-profile possession cases from the early modern era, we need to ask why adult males did not became possessed in this way as often. And why, in the few cases in which they did become possessed, was that so? These questions can only be answered at present case by case, because there are so few cases of possessed adult males, and because they arise in quite different contexts. We thus need to look for the distinct profiles of the possessed, and for the ways in which particular cases might be read as indices of the changing nature of possession, and its possibly different significance for males and females. As in witchcraft studies, looking for reasons internal to individual cases must take place in a dialectic relationship with the search for generalizations about gender, based on wide-scale statistical analysis. To establish what is 'typical' for an age is always open until all the sources are identified and, even then, re-readings can increase exponentially with changes in historical thinking.

I

Why does the history of possession matter? While possession can still give rise to ironic amusement, and to discussion of such issues as fraud and authenticity, and while it can be considered in the light of medical history, and even modern psychotherapy, many possession cases in early modern Europe also involved the invocation of deeply violent metaphors in a time of religious disharmony. Claims of possession contributed to that disharmony, and saw violence deployed against the possessed themselves and on their behalf. In the contemporary Christian west, claims of demonic possession and the practice of exorcism are widespread, and are apparently on the ascendant in a time of global religious tension.[1] Belief in demonic possession, and in the power of exorcism to relieve it, currently enjoy a credence similar to that granted to it in the early modern era: the Vatican, for example, is currently training 3000 new exorcists.[2] Violence is an issue again: the number of people killed while being submitted to exorcisms performed by lay people, and on occasion by clerics, has reached more than thirty since the 1970s, and most of those killed have been either women or children.[3] Understanding this discourse is, thus, important for historians of the past and present, with gender analysis being one important aspect of this understanding.

Speaking about demonic possession in history brings with it some significant caveats: it is not easy either to qualify or quantify cases of possession. First, the 'epidemiology' of possession is not about the diagnosis of human illness or attempts to heal it but, rather, about the identification of divine action, or at least demonic actions carried out with divine permission. This locates possession in the realms of an ideology, the ultimate goals of which are not the healing of a person but the confirmation and reiteration of the presence, grace, and especially the primacy, of the Christian God. A 'case' of possession, therefore, can be many things, but its ambit is in essence a moral one, fundamentally concerned with questions of authority. Similarly, the curing of the possessed through exorcism is not a stand-alone element of Christian healing: rather, exorcism lies on a continuum with other forms of sacred healing; a great deal of such healing might refer, at least implicitly, to the possible presence of diabolic activity.[4] Theologically, all sacred healing occurs foremost in a moral universe and affects, principally, a moral ledger, and in this framework of orthodoxy it would be simply erroneous to see religious healing as the equivalent of medical healing.

Much therefore depends on the nature of the source of information about possession, and the purpose for which it was written or created. Triumphalist sources, hagiographies and polemical pamphlets account for many of the cases of which we have knowledge, and these can emphasize the role of the immediate healer or his supernatural ally more than they concern themselves with the story of the possessed. When the moral dimension concerns the source of healing, rather than the role of human agency in the affliction, gender might play no role in how cases are understood. The stories of demoniacs in the New Testament were recorded to show Christ's authority over them: discovering the cause of their possession was not the issue. The possessed, described by Peter Brown, who dwelt at shrines in Christian antiquity, were similarly 'seismographs of sanctity' fulfilling a very distinct function, unrelated to the cause of their possession.[5] Thus, when early modern experts, clerics, or physicians were called in to establish an authoritative diagnosis of possession, even when there were questions pertaining to gender or sexuality in the case itself, they applied different models irrespective of the gender of the person they were assessing. As do good case lawyers, experts in possession cases amassed evidence from as wide a spectrum of authoritative sources as possible to help their understanding or representation of a case. Most New Testament demoniacs are male, for example, yet their capacity to know theological truths was regularly attributed to early modern female demoniacs, and the sixteenth-century physician Jean Fernel's story of a young man whose possession took three months to diagnose was a regular feature of discussions of female cases.[6]

Sometimes the sources for diagnosis have been literally canonical, deriving from Christian authorities, such as scripture, the church fathers, and the lives of the saints. Other sources of authentication could be found in texts that described new symptoms within cases of authenticated possession, allowing the proliferation of accounts of cases of possession in early modern Europe to generate, in turn, a proliferation in the criteria for legitimating cases of possession. While new cases always had to have at least some authoritative referent, once authenticated, they were also able to provide evidence of new symptoms that in turn could become authoritative precedents. Exorcists' manuals and other works of demonology in the early modern era also served to assemble a wide range of these authenticating sources to facilitate the rapid and accurate diagnosis of possession.[7] It is important to underline this contingent and discourse-specific process of authentication, because it provides the key to exploring the ways in which different historical junctures can allow for gender stereotypes to break down or re-form in new ways. Even though the truths of demonic possession are supposed to be written in eternity, they are, of course, subject to historic influences, so we need to know what kind of constraints and openings have existed historically in particular times and places for changing the gender profile of possession.

Possession could function, too, as a means to reinforce gender stereotypes, or to undermine them, sometimes even doing both at once.[8] Possessed women acting as demons in the early modern era were given licence to do things that they could not otherwise permissibly do but, at the same time, they were doing them often for gender-defined reasons: because they lived in a convent, for example, or (it has been suggested), as a psychological consequence of having failed to fulfil their family's hopes and expectations.[9]

II

Can gender ever be irrelevant? This is a highly political question. Gender might be deemed irrelevant for the purposes of a particular line of enquiry but, to the extent that gender analysis seeks to illuminate the workings of power, any analysis must surely be diminished if it fails to take gender into account. (The same could be said of both age difference and social standing, in cases of possession: all are critical for a full understanding of the phenomenon.) Even where there is silence on the question of sexual difference, for example, we have learnt – in the wake of commentaries as early as those by Simone de Beauvoir – to realize that silence should not be taken to mean the irrelevance of gender.[10]

In considering the silences of possession cases, one might note, for example, the almost total absence of reference to the bodies of male exorcists in descriptions of exorcism. This particular silence might tell us something about how exorcists saw their own bodies and their own sexuality in relation to the possessed, and in relation to their own minds and spirits. Acting on behalf of a superior, spiritual realm, there is a logic in this silence of exorcists – especially celibate Catholic exorcists – by comparison with their scrupulous attention to the bodies of the possessed. Yet, the bodies of the exorcists are also present in specific ways: the exorcist's holy finger repeatedly made the sign of the cross; some demoniacs were challenged to bite it and, finding themselves unable, reinforced the idea of the exorcist's role as divinely sanctioned.[11] A satirical Dutch-published piece about Jesuit exorcism from 1645 mocks the idea that the exorcist's body contained healing power, saying to the would-be exorcist 'if you wish...with your priestly finger roast the evil spirit as he hides until you make him speak. Stroke every part with you sacred hands'.[12] The bodies of exorcists, then, need to be read as relevant to what might be called a 'gender economy' of exorcism;[13] that is, a framework that looks at the distribution of roles and identities in possession and exorcism, and at broader patterns. If, theologically, anyone can effect an exorcism, until recently the authority of all institutionally sanctioned exorcism had to abide only in male clerics.[14] It is also important to note that, because exorcism in Catholicism is a sacramental, the purity of the exorcist is theologically relevant to whether or not the exorcism might be efficacious.[15]

While gender might not be of capital importance in every case, and while it might also be possible to generate a meaningful analysis without putting gender first, in some early modern cases it was central, notably in cases of possession, as a result of the attempted seduction of a woman. And numerous examples of women 'performing' their sexually fallen state in lascivious displays while undergoing exorcism added to both the fame and the infamy of public exorcisms in this period. In these cases, ideas about the female body – or, rather, the limitations of human morality in relation to the flesh, embodied in the female – were central to the way in which many narratives developed.[16] A female body and a male body in possession cases are, it appears, never present in quite the same way: men were very rarely possessed as a result of an attempt by a female witch to make them respond to her sexual advances, and public displays by female demoniacs were often sexualized in ways that those of males (to my knowledge) were not. In many cases involving women, most notably nuns, possession as a result of male witchcraft only came to prominence because of the premium attached to female virginity. However, female possession was not only meaningful when the women were sexualized: in the French Wars of Religion, two young laywomen, Nicole Obry (1566) and Marthe Brossier (in 1598–99), whose demons proclaimed the power of the Catholic church to confute the French Calvinists (Huguenots), were prized in a time of religious division, their novelty value related to their social class, as well as their lower place in the gender hierarchy.[17]

What arrested the attention of those who saw female demoniacs was not only sometimes sexually suggestive displays, but also those (at least formally) gender-neutral signs, such as a protuberant tongue or bulging eyes, yet these might also be freighted with gendered meaning, and even seen as 'intrinsically sexual', to use James Sharpe's term.[18] It might have been assumed, too, that a flailing female body 'naturally' represented the sign of demonic disorder more than that of a man. (On the other hand, because female disorder was perceived as the 'standard' marker of disorder, a profusion of disordered adult males might ironically have been much more of a shock, much more dissonant, than the many recorded cases of groups of disordered females.) Nancy Caciola, writing about the medieval period, suggests that men's bodies were understood to more closely represent the image of God, and were thus perhaps less likely to be expected to attract the attacks of the Devil. Conversely, the identification of women as the ally of the Devil was a commonplace.[19] Women were seen as more likely to be vulnerable to possession because of sexual temptations, arising for example after the eating of charmed food, sometimes unknowingly, but nonetheless echoing the knowing sin of Eve's seduction. Practicalities, such as the likely greater physical strength of exorcists in relation to females and children, could shade into more ideological aspects: demonic possession was designated as posing a threat to divinely instituted order, thus the 'natural' authority of adult over child and male over female was seen to be reinforced during exorcism as much as that of God over Devil. Almost every generalization, however, seems to be followed by at least one exception: literacy might be relevant in relation to written demonic pacts, for example, as it seems that a signed pact featured more prominently among possessed males, who traded their souls for worldly gain and who were punished by possession.[20] However, the nun Jeanne Féry had a pact that made her more learned than she was supposed to be: under exorcism, she delivered it from her mouth and was reduced to a state of idiocy.[21]

III

Quantification is also fraught: the genre of evidence, for example, can limit or distort detail, or raise questions about the different manifestations of the conditions referred to as possession. A 'case' of possession might occupy as little as a single line in an archive, or as much as a vast collection of published and manuscript works; passing references in medical books or whole medical treatises; polemic tracts; full-blown spiritual autobiographies written by the possessed themselves, and, of course, witch-trial records. Even large numbers available from single-genre sources yield somewhat inconclusive data, and offer a limited capacity for comparison.[22] Artistic representations seem overwhelmingly to depict women under the treatment of exorcists, but is this related to the conventions, traditions and aims of the illustrators, or to some kind of statistical truth? Giovanni Levi uses the testimonials of the rural exorcist and healer Giovan Battista Chiesa, suffragan parish priest of Santena in Italy, who, in a vigorous healing campaign between the end of June and mid-August 1697, treated 225 obsessed or bewitched people as he moved from town to town.[23] Males and females in approximately equal number received his ministrations. Whether or not these people were demoniacs in quite the same way as those described in accounts of witch-trials, or in cases where the possessed became proclaimers of the gospel, is impossible to determine absolutely, but it seems likely that their stories of possession amount to much less, if not in terms of their own suffering, then at least in terms of how far they were in the public eye, and how significant each case was for their healer. Using a large sample of German Reformation-era printed sources, Erik Midelfort identifies a roughly 50–50 split, while the limelight cases he mentions all involved women; David Lederer's research into German baroque 'mental health' shrines shows a strong preponderance of females seeking relief from possession.[24] Based on witch-trial records, William Monter identifies women and children as the most likely demoniacs for the Jura region.[25] For all such sources, questions of the nature of the evidence and the time, place, and religious confessions involved intrude to weaken the possibilities of generalization.

Gender statistics, such as they are, can be read along a variety of axes, including: type of possession, numbers involved, social standing, and age. In cases of adult men, the vast majority are found among the minimally documented cases, usually large-scale possessions, and one would assume that these were more akin to cases of mental illness. If one sets aside, perhaps contentiously, what might be called out-and-out mental illness (such as was apparently the case for the German princes, as described by Midelfort, desperately exorcised when other remedies had failed),[26] and possession as an apparent excuse for moral failings (as in the case of Eric of Lorraine, Bishop of Verdun, who said he had been bewitched by his nun lover),[27] and mixed group possessions, there are not many males left standing. If one sets aside boys and adolescents or, indeed, unmarried men, there are almost none. As Kathleen R. Sands has pointed out, the accepted wisdom about adult male possession is that there was very little of it, and this remains substantially true, but her own illuminating accounts of the case of Robert Brigges attest to the value of looking for more adult male possessions, and of doing more with them.[28] For women, once mental illness is strategically excluded, along with mixed group possessions, the female 'limelight cases' come into view, in which the possessed took on some kind of pubic individual role, and in which the victim's voice is evident, even if it is a voice attributed to the Devil.

Just as in some witchcraft cases a measure of social power might paradoxically render one vulnerable to accusations,[29] there are also such conundrums among the possessed. For some of the female possessed, social weakness was a factor, something that highlighted their elevation as a chosen vessel to display the power of the Church and the presumed paradox of their necessarily diabolical learnedness.[30] For others higher up the social scale, prestige either as a nun or as a member of the lay elite provided a platform from which to project the ambition that could accompany possession, even if such an undertaking ran the risk of an accusation of witchcraft or punishment for fraud. Similarly, it appears that, in most male limelight cases, the possessed came from a position of some social privilege: possessed males of any age were not, in the main, poor or illiterate, and family status might also have meant they were likely to have been more frequently in the company of clerics.[31] For the same reason, though, males might be likely to be fewer in number because of the power of the concept of honour, something that attached in different ways to both males' and females' connections to family. Males carried the family's honour in their name, and in their capacity to marry and produce heirs, while female honour was measured in chastity. Certainly, honour was mentioned more than once in the famous female cases.

The demographics of early modern possession range from solo cases to groups (both mixed and single sex), religious houses, and from young to old. Most, but not all, famous possessed females were either in adolescence or early adulthood. Many were adults in the sense of being professed nuns, but none was old (at least, not at the start of the possession), and the majority of female demoniacs were either outside the governance of, or (depending on the case) without the power base of, the marital home.[32] A large proportion of possessed males were also in their teens or early twenties and unmarried.[33] When we consider single-sex group possessions, either in cases of simpler bewitchment or of full-blown possessions, the preponderance seems to be very strongly female. An exception to this is a case of a group of young boys in Amsterdam;[34] and while the bewitchment of a monastery by one of its members, described by Jean Fraikin, is not, strictly speaking, a possession case, it should nonetheless serve as an indication that single-sex environments of either kind might be seen as vulnerable to the Devil.[35] The preponderance of female group possessions was largely attributable to the predominance of nuns among groups of possessed females, although here, too, there are exceptions. The most famous group of women who were not nuns is, of course, the borderline bewitched/possessed girls in Salem, but there was also a group of lay women in Rome in the 1550s, mentioned by Bodin and others, who were said to have been bewitched by Jews.[36]

It was seen as obvious or logical in the early modern era that the most likely victims of the Devil would be women and children. The French physician Barthélemy Pardoux said, in 1639, that, 'demons especially afflict women and children because of their fragile and infirm condition.'[37] It was so much a cliché that women and children were physically and psychologically more vulnerable to the Devil's attacks that the 1645 parody of Jesuit exorcisms mentioned above claimed to supply the recipe for a successful exorcism beginning, 'first choose someone prone to credulity, a man or (better still) a girl who is delicate and not very strong.'[38] The femaleness of the possessed seemed, too, 'naturally' to highlight certain cultural assumptions or realities about the standing or capacities of women – unnatural strength or uncommon knowledge, such as how to speak (or, as the documentation suggests, at least understand) foreign languages.

Caution is needed, however, in identifying these characteristics exclusively with women. Evidence of learning could have equally gone against assumptions about poor illiterate men: the presumed anomaly of the educated woman is something as much rhetorically constructed by exorcists as it was statistically inevitable. And, indeed, many of the women in question were spending a considerable amount of time with clerics, and a number of famous possessed women themselves belonged to the teaching order of the Ursulines. We are on, perhaps, more solid ground noting that the swearing of women and a penchant to sing 'drinking songs' – theoretically inappropriate because of their social place, and definitely wrong in the Lutheran, Reformed, or Counter-Reformation religious setting – also contrasted with an expected social role.[39] (That is, poor men were expected to be ignorant, but no woman was expected to swear and carouse.) There was a cultural logic in the Devil making people act the opposite of how they were assumed or supposed to act, as, for example, in sexual displays by nuns. The plunging of the possessed female's voice to the register of that of a male (a demon) was a regular feature of possessions, along with bull-like roaring and barking. This led to one ironic situation when one of the demons of a possessed nun had a devil who was said to answer the exorcist with 'a smal (sic) complaining womanish voice'.[40] From the perspective of exorcists, for the purposes of performance, the suffering of women and children might be likely to evince more sympathy, and exorcists pointed to the vulnerability of women in many French cases, referring to them as 'poor things'.

IV

What had changed in the early modern era? While medieval ecstatics could be seen as holy until proven to be captive to the Devil, if identified as inspired by the Devil, they could no longer be credible.[41] Being captive to the Devil in the early modern era, however, took on new possibilities and accrued value in several ways. As fears of witchcraft grew in the sixteenth century, exorcists and other clerics were more likely to imagine witches to be the cause of human afflictions. The possessed victims of alleged witchcraft exposed their human attackers while flattering the power of exorcists to obtain that knowledge. The confessional tensions of the Reformation era, too, affected how exorcists understood and deployed possession. Successful exorcism underscored confessional claims to spiritual superiority, a point reinforced further when the Devil identified an exorcist's confessional opponents as his friends. (Interestingly, however, very few, if any, cases saw devils accuse confessional opponents of witchcraft, an observation that might warrant further 'counterfactual' investigation.)

From the perspective of audiences, those captive to the Devil appear to have been understood as functionally equivalent to those who were divinely inspired. A demoniac might have an ability to respond to curious (and formally forbidden) questions that might equally have been answered by a living saint. Early modern exorcists thus took their charges down an entrepreneurial path already marked out by late-medieval living saints. Celebrity exorcists reinforced that devils could, following biblical models, be compelled to share their superior knowledge, whether it was of a mundane or theological nature: Father

Pierre Coton, a favourite in the court of Henri IV, is said to have asked the demoniac Adrienne Dufresne's demon, for example, whether King James I of England would convert to Catholicism, and the demon of Marthe Brossier relayed news from purgatory to surviving relatives who attended her displays.[42] Sceptics responded to demoniacs in much the same way that they responded to those claiming to be saints, questioning whether demoniacs had welcomed demons into their lives. One way this challenge could be countered was by the possessed demonstrating that their suffering offset any possible elements of worldly benefit: and, here, a heightened premium on female martyrdom – in particular, in the context of affective 'feminized' spirituality – legitimated a greater degree of receptivity to the inner torment of demons.[43]

This deepened moral complexity seems to have been a largely early modern development.[44] Historically, possessions could, to some extent, be divided between those cases for which sufferers are described as morally responsible, and those for which they are not. At one end of this spectrum was that traditional form of bewitchment called 'possession', in which spiritual remedies have been sought when physical remedies have failed, and when there is often a suspicion of witchcraft.[45] In these cases, possession could be a kind of 'last-resort' diagnosis of an innocent victim. Here, would be located those cases of irremediable mania more likely to emerge as part of the healing portfolio of a priest, or to show the acuity of a witch-hunter, than to be seen as of general public or polemical interest, or a source of fame for the possessed. At the other end of the spectrum of responsibility were those cases in which a person caused their own state of possession, as a result of their own sin or malice, or even because they themselves had operated as witches or magicians.[46] Yet, in early modern France some female demoniacs claimed a mixture of personal responsibility and victim-status: external attribution was identified, at the same time as the sufferers saw themselves as possessed because of their own tendency to sinfulness.[47] In such cases, patronage was sometimes the only thing that preserved these bedevilled aspirants from the slur that they might simply be witches, rather than possessed.

The question of volition raises the further question of how much of a role mental illness played in cases of possession. All one can venture with any certainty is that the 'limelight' cases are more likely to have involved some element of volition on the part of the demoniac. Limelight cases in which possession was manifest in the 'demons' preaching, for example, almost by definition cannot be ones of unremitting mania. These are cases where we can speak of at some least capacity for self-control, simply because the exorcists needed something to work with. There had to be some lucidity or insight in the possessed in order for there to be some discernible effect from exorcism and, thence, for the publicity generated to have some power. This is not the place to discuss how far, if at all, exorcism had some adventitious curative effect – modern psychological research debates this intensely – but it remains the case that, if exorcists' charges were totally uncontrollable, we would not generally read about the case – that is, to the (admittedly indeterminate) extent that direct reportage can be believed.

It would be mistaken to assume that the volition levels of the demoniac were necessarily the same throughout the lifespan of the condition: it is quite likely that the possessed embarked on a relationship with an exorcist that entailed far greater demands on them than they might have anticipated. Abusive exorcisms were a regular occurrence, carried out against supposedly uncooperative demons, as in the sideshow exorcism described by Montaigne, where the exorcist slapped his possessed male client.[48] In pointing to the agency of the 'articulate' possessed, therefore, coercion and gratification appear to meet, even if at a different juncture from case to case. Hence, this analysis is largely directed to the limelight cases for which, I suggest, there had to be some element of personal investment in the role.[49] When we consider the two male cases here, this question will be relevant, as they show two quite different developments in terms of the will of the possessed person.

V

Most Jesuits in France in the sixteenth century were relatively indifferent to questions of possession but, around the turn of the century, it came to the fore in the work of some prominent members of the order.[50] The Jesuit theologian Martin Del Rio at Louvain wrote his epic *Disquisitionum magicarum*, one of the most influential works of demonology of the age;[51] Louis Richeome envisaged the entire history of the church through the lens of possession and exorcism, measuring all the church's successes in terms of its historical power to expel demons;[52] and Father Pierre Coton's public dialogues with the demon of Adrienne Dufresne saw him pilloried in a *politique* pamphlet in the early-seventeenth century.[53] Jesuits were the driving force in a 20-year case that started in the 1620s in Lorraine, when Elisabeth de Ranfaing, a possessed widow, charged her doctor with witchcraft, and ended up being herself the focus of a major local cult, following a series of dramatic public exorcisms.[54] Several Jesuit acolytes promoted her sanctity, their enthusiasm only curbed by senior members of the order, who tried to stamp out the cult. In the 1630s, at the confessionally divided town of Loudun, in the most famous case of possession in European history, Jesuits were at the vanguard of the wave of exorcists who came to the Ursuline convent in the wake of the execution in August 1634 of the parish priest Urbain Grandier, who had been convicted of causing the entire convent to be bewitched.

Of the six to eight Jesuits at Loudun up until 1640, none was more prominent or more controversial for his superiors than Father Jean-Joseph Surin.[55] He came to Loudun in December 1634, and became both an exorcist and the spiritual father of the prioress, Mother Jeanne des Anges. Surin trained Jeanne to interpret her experience of possession as something intimately related to her own quest for personal spiritual growth, moving her away from the terrible question of her alleged bedevilment by Grandier, who had been executed principally on her testimony. Surin 'reprogrammed' Jeanne to see her battles with her demons as part of her journey towards spiritual perfection. Through this means, he was largely responsible for turning the cult of public exorcism and witch-hunt at Loudun to the thaumaturgic cult of Jeanne. It was during this transitional phase that Surin, perpetually inclined to depict himself as frail, famously 'caught' Jeanne's possession, when the demons Leviathan and Isaacaron, along with others, jumped directly from her body into his, leaving him intermittently possessed.[56] We encounter in this case a rare example of the very same demons inhabiting a member of each sex at the same time – in a way, the perfect 'control' for consideration of possession and the sexes.

In a 1635 letter to a Jesuit friend, Surin gives the most detailed of several accounts of his possession, declaring 'God has permitted for my sins, I think, something never seen, perhaps, in the Church: that during the exercise of my ministry, the Devil passes from the body of the possessed person, and coming into mine, assaults me and overturns me, shakes me, and visibly travels through me' (357). Surin was deeply gratified by this development, and there is an unexpected glint of vainglory in his claim that he thought his experience was a historical first.[57] Surin makes the meaning of the possession quite explicit: he felt that it signalled God's intimate interest in directly confronting him as a sinner in order to save him, saying his experience of possession was 'in conformity with the conduct of the Providence of God in relation to my soul' and adding, 'You can imagine what a pleasure there is in finding oneself at the mercy of God alone' (356–57).

While it appears to have been a largely early modern phenomenon to associate demonic possession with a divine gift, it continued to be seen as potentially dishonourable, because the condition's origin could lie in one's own sin. For this and related reasons, it seems, Surin walks a fine line between identification as a demoniac and an apparent desire to distance himself from such an identity. He implicitly identifies himself as possessed when he refers to times 'when the other possessed persons see me in this state' (358), yet he uses language to distinguish himself from the demoniacs with whom he had dealt, by referring, for example, to the demon 'visibly possessing me for several hours *like an energumen* [demoniac]'(my emphasis). Similarly, he refers to Jeanne as the 'possessed woman' writing that the demon 'publicly out of the mouth of the Possessed Woman…boasts that he is my master.' He himself appears to have spoken little, if at all, as a demoniac: indeed, at times he was afflicted with mutism. Surin also makes slightly contrary statements in relation to his own desire for exposure. He asks his correspondent, possibly disingenuously, to keep the details he has provided quiet, saying 'I want to tell you something, and I would tell you more of it if you were more close-mouthed' (257). (The letter was subsequently circulated in numerous manuscript copies and printed twice within the year.)[58] He says that people are interpreting his case in different ways, having 'great disputes', so clearly his possession was, even at the time of writing of his letter, a subject of some discussion at Loudun, and probably farther afield. The fact that he also says that he would say more if the reader were not likely to tell others, however, suggests that he anticipated the dissemination of what he did say, at least by word of mouth in the order. And, given that he was exorcized by his Jesuit brothers, with witnesses including the possessed women present, word was bound to get out. There is no sense that he sees himself ultimately as anything other than blessed, although he does intimate that others have more circumspect views of him. And he admits to feeling something akin to possession as a result of sexual thoughts, apparently in relation to Jeanne des Anges, but this is largely separate from his discussion of the experiences for which he underwent exorcism.[59] As his life went on, his experience of possession became part of his spiritual identity, affecting him for decades, and was something about which he wrote extensively. It has been argued, with some validity, that the model of affective spirituality that inspired Surin was regarded as dubious, even by him, because of its association with women: through Jeanne des Anges, certainly, but more because of the highly influential role in this period of the newly canonised St Teresa of Avila.[60] It could be added, however, that were it not for credence given in this period to female demoniacs who claimed they were the victims of witchcraft, there would not have been a possession for Surin to 'catch' at Loudun.

In this case, the discourse of witchcraft played a mediating role, stopping short of directly making Surin possessed, but functioning, it could be suggested, as the prime mover. He wanted to be possessed because he had spiritualized the positive aspects of possession typical of the period to such an extent that he saw possession as morally superior, because it involved an intimate recognition of himself as a sinner. This also might have bought off the possibility of any charge that he might be himself a witch, but while embracing the experience, he had somewhat mixed feelings about seeing himself as no different from a demoniac.

VI

Another case of possession in an adult male comes from the mid-seventeenth century in France. The source is a neatly copied manuscript of 85 folios held in the Bibliothèque Sainte-Geneviève (Paris), dating probably from the late-seventeenth century, but referring to the period 1649–55. It contains four separate accounts describing different stages of this case, the first being entitled *True account of all that happened in an illness that lasted in me from 11 November 1649 to 1655, and which the most able physicians of Paris did not diagnose, and which was in the end found to be possession by a demon, which can be seen by the rest of this discourse.* The accounts are titled in a manner to resemble the many sensational printed accounts of possession from this period in France, but they appear not to have found their way into print.[61] That the manuscript seems to have been a copy suggests others might have circulated in that form. The story the accounts tell is of a layman, identified only as Jerome P., who began to behave strangely on St Martin's Eve 1649, and who soon after began to insist that he was possessed. His case was taken up by three secular priests, Fathers Gervaise, Le Vasseur and Potel, who, helped by others, worked for six years to deliver him through many exorcisms in public and private.

It is important for me to admit at this point that, when I first looked at this account in 1986, I had the impression that it could not be a real case: I misread it entirely and did not realise its significance. All I can hope to do is to try to turn this error to account now, in relation to the question of gender and possession. Even though the seventeenth century was notable for the number of accounts of possession, such texts were usually the proselytizing writings of promoters; self-promoters among the possessed were generally more constrained by the requirements of Christian self-disavowal or, as Surin, tended, at least, to frame their accounts in the context of a spiritual journey, part of a lifelong pilgrimage of suffering to avoid sin. From accounts associated with women's spiritual growth through possession, I had come to expect that the gestures seen by others would be described by the sufferer as torments, not as performances. Women seem to have more of a sense of a purely interior torment – how possession felt, rather than what it looked like. Thus, I allowed myself to be misled by the way in which the man described his own gestures from the outside, rather than from within his experience of them, writing for example, that 'I spun a hundred times around on my hands' (3v-4r); 'I jumped the length of the bed, and banged my head against my bedhead' (4r); 'I turned like a windmill' (4v); 'I stayed on the bed four hours as if I were dead' (1v) and 'it was pitiable to see me' (10v). Assumptions about gender played a further part. Cynical observers in the many French cases of possession satirized the extravagant actions of the female possessed. These cases were the laughing stock of the erudite libertines of the age, the controversial witch-trials they generated causing dissension among senior churchmen, physicians, and jurists. The breathless descriptions in this account, and an explicit reference to the case being even more dramatic and plausible than the cases at Loudun and Louviers, seemed to have the ring of some of the satires I had read, which did not spare the women for their compliance with credulous exorcists. Jerome quotes a physician, M. Guenauet, as saying 'if we believe in the possessed, it would seem that Monsieur would be such. For I assure you that all those at Loudun and Louviers never did postures like those we have just seen' (fol 4r). And, while the title page mentioned events from mid-century, more than one later page featured the date 1686, suggesting that the dates of the alleged events were perhaps fictionalized. As I had found no other references to this case, on the basis of its tone and its supposed date of writing, I was prepared to speculate that it might have been written as a kind of proto-Enlightenment satire on the imagined excesses of a very devout age. As it turns out, going back to the document and examining it more closely, with the question of male possession in mind, I now believe I was wrong.

The first two texts are written in the first person, in the voice of the man himself, amounting to just 19 folios of the 85 total; the second two accounts are written by his exorcists. The man appears to have lived not far from Paris, in a town referred to as Mareil. (There are several Mareils, and it has not been possible yet to identify form which one he came.)[62] His age is hard to determine: he mentions the presence of his mother and, in the one mention of a wife, he also refers to a 'petite fille', which seems here to mean daughter, but could mean granddaughter.

It is possibly an indicator of the class from which the man came, and the dubious honour associated with possession, that his name is not mentioned in full. Indeed, in one section of the document the copyist has started to write the name and crossed it out. The suppression of his name indicates that, even though he appears to have been keen to have the possession diagnosis, someone other than he appears to have wanted to suppress his name. His enthusiasm for his state is indicated early on, when a physician of Queen Henrietta Maria of England was called in and was the first of many commentators – both medical and clerical – who disputed the possession diagnosis.[63] The doctor could find no problem, and said that Jerome's pulse was as strong as his own, to which Jerome responded: 'Oh doctor, if you had as much learning in your head as I have illness [possibly evil? *mal*] in mine (2r) you would be a more knowledgeable and skilful (*habille*) man than you are'.

There is no hint of witchcraft in this case and, in spite of Jerome's enthusiasm about being possessed, no one present suggested that he might have a pact with the Devil, even when other expressions of scepticism are voiced. Neither is there any sense that he is risking the sin of pride by believing in his own possession. Even though Jerome and the priests are keen to attribute his deliverance to the power of Catholic sacramentals – notably, relics of various saints and especially the power of the Virgin Mary – there is here no sense of a personal spiritual journey uncovered and lived through association with demons, as in the Surin case, and as was common for the auto-hagiographical accounts by women demoniacs. Interestingly, however, the fact of his recording something akin to a journal of his experience is paralleled in two other cases of adult male possession, the cases of Robert Brigges in England, who wrote an account of his travails, and the German painter Christoph Haizmann, who kept a diary, as well as making paintings about his experiences.[64] Sexuality only manifests itself in one form in this case, when his demon (named as Robert, Roquebene, Robene and other variants) uses obscene language, and repeatedly calls the Virgin Mary a 'whore', at one point showing true machismo by offering her money, saying 'I pay well'. For this, the account relates, the demon was 'ordered to kiss the feet of each of the company for having scandalized them' (47r). Thus, two of the key features of successful French possession cases – witchcraft and morbid sexuality – are absent here, possibly suggesting why there was relatively little public interest in the case. There is, however, an element of anti-Huguenot sentiment, reminiscent of the propaganda of demoniacs in the French Wars of Religion, as the man refers to the 'Saint Beelzebuth and Saint Calvin' as being the demon's 'good companions' (5r). The further Catholic message to take from the exorcisms, described in increasing detail in the later two accounts, was, according to the words of the demon, that the possession had occurred in order to convince unbelievers.

What is distinctive and troubling about the case is that, as the four accounts unfold, the 'ownership' of the man's condition appears to shift from him to his minders. This is evidenced, for example, in the authorship of the accounts, with the short informative narratives written in the first person being supplanted by lengthy and highly repetitious accounts by the exorcists of the demoniac's displays. Jerome P. appears to have wanted very much to be seen as possessed but, as the documentation develops, he appears either to have had less control of himself, or less control of his circumstances, or both. Whereas the first two accounts have him speaking in his own voice about his experiences, the second two, written by exorcists, only have him speaking as a devil. By the end of the fourth text, Jerome has become merely querulous and cheeky, his words often infantile: at the sight of an image of the Virgin Mary, for example, he says 'voyla la voyla ... bon bon bon pas trop bon bon bon non pas pour moy'. Even the exorcists try to generate a show, urging the uninterested demon to 'show his malice' (49v).

There is a sense that this was a story identified by priests as a potential cult case, which, possibly because of the genuine illness in the protagonist, degenerates into farcical displays in which the demoniac's voice is increasingly submerged. This is a poignant case that seems to show the gradual fragmentation of the mental state of a man whose initial belief in his own possession might or might not have contributed to his further decline, and his diminution at the hands of frustrated exorcists. It might also simply be that he tired of being possessed once he realized what hard work it was to be dragged into church and prayed over, and obliged to do things such as kiss the feet of exorcists or lick the floor of the church in the sign of the cross. Whichever is the case, the priests' journals do not appear to be leading anywhere than to a rather desultory final exorcism, in which the Devil does not want to leave because 'the weather is too bad', and the exorcist replies 'It's not raining where you have to go' (85v).

VII

Perhaps the key observation to make about these two cases is that they either arose (in the case of Surin) or took definition (in both cases) from famous stories of possessed women, at Loudun in both cases, and Louviers for Jerome P. But, in both cases, the element of witchcraft was 'bleached out' as possession took hold, even as both these men found in different ways a touchstone in female possessions that had been caused by diabolical amatory magic. Neither of these cases took off, and Certeau's assertion that the projected death of the accused witch, Urbain Grandier, at Loudun provided a sense of narrative coherence and focus for that case might point to one cause.[65] Possession stories in seventeenth-century France were dominated by tales of alleged witchcraft against women: the fact that the case of Jerome P. appears to have gone nowhere might be, in part, because of its lack of focus on the morality of either the possessed or a witch. Surin, by contrast, appears to have a profound sense of moral coherence in his own narrative of the events that he experienced and the things that he did, with or without his own will. The fuse that runs through his writings belongs to the genre of hagiography. Surin's personality thus held up, if in its own somewhat maverick terms, while Jerome P's appears to have dissolved.

It is useful to consider what elements of the characteristics of the female cases remained once the males had taken on the possessed role. Surin was not bewitched or a victim of seduction; he was able to capitalize on possession in terms of a life narrative; he was possessed and exorcized in public, but appears not to have made anything resembling the speeches of the possessed women; he embraced possession but was committed to doing this entirely on his own terms. Surin distanced himself from the identity of a demoniac, probably because of the association of this role with women, and his performances were not sexualized, as far as we know. He was not favoured uniformly by his order and there was no 'succès de scandale', no witch-trial, or the development of a flamboyant saintly cult. He did not take on the role of a healer, as Jeanne had done: he was more a saint, as it were, for his own sake. For Jerome P., there was also no talk of direct witchcraft and, as a public case, his story was negligible. As with many possessed women, however, Jerome was physically debased, albeit with no sexual overtones, simply in the traditional belief that the body of the possessed was that of the Devil.

These cases did not merely draw strength from female cases: they seem to have been transfigured in the process of 'jumping' from female to male. To what extent did these possessions reflect changes in gender assumptions, or their particularities work as potential media for change? The discourse of possession, or more precisely the flow-on effect of possession among women, helped to provide the ground for authentication of these cases of possession in two men, providing them each in different ways with an idiom through which they could value – or, at least, endure – their own apparent psychological suffering. In considering these cases in relation to broader questions of gender and possession, it seems that even such relatively unspectacular cases can serve to point, by contrast, to the turbulent moral landscapes that were lit up by cases of female possession. Almost the very innocuousness of these cases might take us back to the cultural silences around the idea of the masculine as the human generic.

Notes

1. M. W. Cuneo, *American Exorcism: Expelling Demons in the Land of Plenty* (New York, 2001). In the preparation of this chapter, I acknowledge the advice and aid of Leigh Dale, Robert Mason, and Alison Rowlands.
2. http://www.bild.de/BILD/news/vermischtes/2008/03/07/exorzist/sechsmerkmale-an-denen-sie-den-teufel-erkennen,geo=3953104.html (accessed 17 June 2008).
3. These are preliminary figures based on searches of news reports and legal cases conducted as part of a new research project.
4. See, for example, H. C. E. Midelfort, *Exorcism and Enlightenment: Johann Joseph Gassner and the Demons of Eighteenth-Century Germany* (New Haven, 2005), 59.
5. P. Brown, *Relics and Social Status in the Age of Gregory of Tours* (Reading, 1977), 13.
6. For New Testament demoniacs, see, for example, Mark 1:24–25; Mark 5:7. For the case reported by Fernel, see Jean Fernel, *De Abditis rerum causis libri duo* (Paris, 1548), Book 2, ch. 16, 222–3.
7. On exorcism manuals, see M. R. O'Neil, 'Discerning Superstition: Popular Errors and Orthodox Response in Late Sixteenth Century Italy', (PhD thesis, Stanford University, 1982), 297.
8. This line of argument is also used by Peter Burke and Natalie Zemon Davis in relation to the meaning of the carnivalesque. In both cultural scenarios, the trope of the 'world upside down' allows for the introduction of genuine challenges to tradition as well as its reinforcement. See P. Burke, *Popular Culture in Early Modern Europe* (London, 1978), 178–204; N. Z. Davis, 'The Reasons of Misrule', in *idem*, *Society and Culture in Early Modern France* (Stanford, 1975), 97–123.
9. M. Sluhovsky, *Believe Not Every Spirit: Possession, Mysticism and Discernment in Early Modern Catholicism* (Chicago, 2007), 233–64; E. H. Dickerman and A. M. Walker, '"A woman under the influence": A case of alleged possession in sixteenth-century France', *Sixteenth Century Journal*, 22 (1991), 534–54.
10. S. de Beauvoir, *The Second Sex* (translated and edited by H. M. Parshley, London, 1993), lviii.
11. Exorcists also required the possessed to demonstrate their devil's obedience by making them kiss the hand or foot of an exorcist, or another male official or witness.
12. Anon., 'Elixir Jesuiticum'(1645), in P. Maxwell-Stuart (ed. and trans.), *The Occult in Early Modern Europe: A Documentary History* (Basingstoke, 1999), 50.

13. R. W. Scribner, 'Cosmic Order and Daily Life: Sacred and Secular in Pre-Industrial German Society', in *idem*, *Popular Culture and Popular Movements in Reformation Germany* (London, 1987), 1.
14. There are some records of women acting as exorcists, which was theologically possible but not institutionally approved; see, for example, Sluhovsky, *Believe Not Every Spirit*, 41–2.
15. A sacrament, such as the Mass, will be efficacious regardless of the moral state of an ordained priest. The lesser class of rites known as sacramentals – which includes various kinds of blessing – does not require the cleric to be ordained, but can only work if he is pure of heart.
16. Possession cases such as these were also, of course, one of the principal types of cases in which male witchcraft was an issue.
17. M. Sluhovsky, 'A Divine apparition or demonic possession? Female agency and Church authority in demonic possession in sixteenth-century France', *Sixteenth Century Journal*, 27 (1996), 1039–55.
18. J. Sharpe, *The Bewitching of Anne Gunter: A Horrible and True Story of Football, Witchcraft, Murder, and the King of England* (London, 1999), 160.
19. N. Caciola, *Discerning Spirits: Divine and Demonic Possession in the Middle Ages* (Ithaca, 2003), 137–9.
20. Martin Del Rio, *Disquisitonum*, Book 6, ch. 2, sect. 3, qu. 3, excerpted in Maxwell-Stuart, *The Occult in Early Modern Europe*, 52–7.
21. [*F. Buisseret*], *Histoire admirable et veritable des choses advenves a l'endroict d'vne Religieuse professe du conuent des Soeurs noires, de la ville de Mons en Hainaut, natifue de Sore sur Sambre, aagee de vingt cinq ans, possedee du maling esprit, & depuis deliuree* (Paris, 1586).
22. See D. Lederer, *Madness, Religion and the State in Early Modern Europe: A Bavarian Beacon* (Cambridge and New York, 2006), 149.
23. G. Levi, *Inheriting Power: The Story of an Exorcist*, L. G. Cochrane (trans.) (Chicago, 1988), 12. It is not possible to ascertain from Levi's figures what proportion of this figure, which comprise nearly half of those he treated for a wide range of ailments, were men or women. However, his figures for clients healed overall are more or less equal for the sexes. Many sources make a distinction between possession and obsession. This can refer to a difference between a devil actively inhabiting a personality (possession) and simply besieging the person (to use a common metaphor from the period), for example, by temptations to sin. It is by no means a hard and fast distinction, however, and the use of 'obsession' as a generic term for possession in Latin texts particularly shows it to be somewhat arbitrary. The symptoms of any two cases are also unlikely to be identical: something might resemble possession but not be called possession, while an exorcist such as Chiesa might have been asked to treat physical illness or 'simple' bewitchment.
24. H. C. E. Midelfort, 'The Devil and the German People: Reflections on the Popularity of Demon Possession in Sixteenth-Century Germany', in B. P. Levack (ed.), *Articles on Witchcraft, Magic and Demonology*, vol. 9, 'Possession and Exorcism' (New York and London, 1992), 113–33; Lederer, *Madness, Religion and the State*, 148–52. Five times as many women as men, either obsessed or possessed, presented at one shrine, but the figures move closer to balancing out across other types of mental illness. Another example of a large group in which there were roughly equal numbers of men and women occurred at

Annonay in France, but in this case, too, an individual woman came to prominence: see Claude Caron, *L'antechrist demasque* (Tournon, 1589), 57, 59, 75.

25. E. W. Monter, *Witchcraft in France and Switzerland: The Borderlands During the Reformation* (Ithaca, 1976), 139.
26. H. C. E. Midelfort, *Mad Princes of Renaissance Germany* (Charlottesville, 1994) , 42, 87, 118–121.
27. C. Pfister, *L'énergumène de Nancy, Elisabeth de Ranfaing et le couvent du Refuge* (Nancy, 1901), 25; Joseph d'Orleans, *La Vie du Pere Pierre Coton* (Paris, 1688), 87.
28. K. R. Sands, *An Elizabethan Lawyer's Possession by the Devil: The Story of Robert Brigges* (Westport, 2002), 76; See also *idem, Demon Possession in Elizabethan England* (Westport, 2004), 57–74. On Christoph Haizmann, see H. C. E. Midelfort, 'Catholic and Lutheran Reactions to Demon Possession in the Late Seventeenth Century: Two Case Histories', in Levack (ed.), *Articles on Witchcraft, Magic and Demonology,* vol. 9, 375–400; M. de Certeau, *The Writing of History* (1975), trans. T. Conley (New York, 1988), 289–305.
29. M. Gaskill, 'The Devil in the shape of a man: Witchcraft, conflict and belief in Jacobean England', *Historical Research,* 71 (1998), 142–71; A. Rowlands, 'Witchcraft and old women in early modern Germany', *Past and Present* 173. (2001), 72.
30. On Marthe Brossier, see Dickerman and Walker, '"A woman under the influence"; on Nicole Obry, see Sluhovsky, 'A Divine apparition or demonic possession?'; on Marie des Vallées, the peasant 'saint of Coutances', see S. Ferber, *Demonic Possession and Exorcism in Early Modern France* (London, 2004), 127–35.
31. The story of the witch-trials resulting from the possession of the young teenager Bernard Girault is, in some ways, an exception. N. Jacques-Chaquin and M. Préaud (eds), *Les Sorciers du carroi de Marlou: Un Proces de Sorcellerie en Berry, (1582–1583)* (Grenoble, 1996).
32. See Rowlands, 'Witchcraft and old women', 50–89, at 62; 64.
33. See D. P. Walker, *Unclean Spirits: Possession and Exorcism in France and England in the Late Sixteenth and Early Seventeenth Centuries* (London, 1981); Sands, *An Elizabethan Lawyer's Possession.* In colonial New England, for the period 1620–1725, only one of 75 bewitched people was a married man, see C. F. Karlsen, *The Devil in the Shape of a Woman: Witchcraft in Colonial New England* (New York and London, 1998), 224.
34. Midelfort, 'The Devil and the German People', 110.
35. J. Fraikin, 'Un cas de sorcellerie à la fin du XVIe siècle: l'affaire du moine sorcier de Stavelot', in *Tradition Wallone: Revue Annuelle de la Commission Royale Belge de Folklore, Mélanges Albert Doppagne* 4 (1987), 251–335; Sluhovsky describes a 1671 monastic possession in Sicily, *Believe Not Every Spirit,* 262.
36. Jean Bodin, *De la démonomanie des sorciers* (Paris, 1580), Book 3, ch. 6, fol. 160v.
37. Barthélemy Pardoux, *De Morbis animi* (Lyon, 1649), 34.
38. Elixir Jesuiticum (1645), translated in Maxwell-Stuart (ed.), *The Occult in Early Modern Europe,* 50–1. This satirical poem makes explicit reference to the exorcisms of William Weston in England in 1585–86, but its publication after both the Nancy and Loudun cases suggests it might also have had those cases in mind. Walker, *Unclean Spirits,* 43–4.

39. Jeanne des Anges, *Autobiographie* (Grenoble, 1990), 137; Midelfort, 'The Devil and the German People', 127.
40. Sébastien Michaelis, *The Admirable Historie of the Possession and Conversion of a Penitent woman. Seduced by a magician that made her to become a Witch ... Whereunto is annexed a Pneumology, or Discourse of Spirits*, trans. W.B. (London, 1613), 392. Perhaps conversely, Nathan Johnstone cites the 1574 example of Bishop of Norwich, John Parkhurst, lauding the 'manly fortitude' of a possessed woman, *The Devil and Demonism in Early Modern England* (Cambridge, 2006), 103. Bodin mentions the case of a man who claimed to speak with the voice of a dead woman, the demonic nature of which was revealed when the man was confronted by the recitation of a Miserere; see Bodin, *Démonomanie*, Book 2, ch. 3, fol. 76r.
41. Too great an emphasis should not be placed on the difference between the possible causes of possession in the Middle Ages and early modern era. The idea of the victim status of the possessed as a result of another's curse, for example, was around in the Middle Ages. Rather than imagining that there is something given about the identity of these periods, it might be suggested that, in a small way, the changes in views of possession are among those things that characterize any imagined distinction between 'medieval' and 'early modern'.
42. Bibliothèque Nationale, France, MS Fonds francais, 18453, fol.8v.
43. J. Le Brun, 'Mutations de la notion de martyre au XVIIe siècle d'après les biographies spirituelles féminines', in J. Marx (ed.), *Sainteté et martrye dans les religions du livre* (Brussels, 1989), 77–96; Caciola, *Discerning spirits*, 274–319.
44. Midelfort, 'The Devil and the German People', 111.
45. M. R. O'Neil, '"Sacerdote ovvero strione": Ecclesiastical and Superstitious Remedies in Sixteenth-Century Italy', in S. L. Kaplan (ed.), *Understanding Popular Culture* (Berlin, 1984), 53–83.
46. Many authors acknowledged that both good and evil people could be possessed. See for example Sanson Birette. *Refvtation de l'errevr dv Vvlgaire, tovchant les responses des diables exorcizez* (Rouen, 1618), 246.
47. On Jeanne des Anges, see M. de Certeau, *The Possession at Loudun* (1970), (translated by M. B. Smith, with a foreword by S. Greenblatt, Chicago and London, 2000), 213–26; on Elisabeth de Ranfaing, see E. Delcambre and J. Lhermitte, *Un cas énigmatique de possession diabolique en Lorraine au XVIIe siècle: Elisabeth de Ranfaing, l'énergumène de Nancy* (Nancy, 1956); on Marie des Vallées, see note 30, above.
48. Sluhovsky, *Believe Not Every Spirit*, 47–9; Michel de Montaigne, *Journal de voyage en Italie par la Suisse et l'Allemagne en 1580 et 1581*, C.Dédéyan (ed.) (Paris, 1946), 219–21.
49. None of this is to diminish the role of possible pathology in people becoming possessed, but neither is to suggest that the role of the demoniac was always a calculated off-the-peg identity that attracted simple fraudsters. To consider the role of fraud is not an especially helpful key to understanding possession, not because no one could have ever feigned possession (as early as Caesarius of Heisterbach's writings, the possibility of fraud was allowed for), but because it might seem to take sides with the opponents of possessions, whose goals were more often political than strictly scientific. See

Caesarius von Heisterbach, *The Dialogue on Miracles*, 2 vols, H. von E. Scott and C. S. Bland (trans.), introduction by G. G. Coulton (London, 1929), 333. By implication, too, treating of fraud might import, covertly, the theology that assumes there is such a thing as 'real' demonic possession. Moreover, who is to say that someone party to fraud was not, in any case, acting out some kind of pathology?

50. A. L. Martin, *The Jesuit Mind: The Mentality of an Elite in Early Modern France* (Ithaca, 1988), 135–6.
51. Martin Del Rio, *Disquisitionum magicarum libri sex* (Louvain, 1599–1600).
52. Louis Richeome, *Trois discours pour la religion catholique: des miracles, des saincts etc des images* (Bordeuax, 1598).
53. R. Mandrou, *Magistrats et sorciers en France au XVIIe siècle: une analyse de psychologie historique* (1968; Paris, 1980 edn), 77.
54. Delcambre and Lhermitte, *Un cas énigmatique de possession diabolique*. See also Sarah Ferber, 'Cultivating Charisma: Elisabeth de Ranfaing and the *Médailliste* cult in seventeenth-century Lorraine', in F.W. Kent and C. Zika (eds), *Rituals, Images and Words: Varieties of Cultural Expression in Late Medieval and Early Modern Europe* (Turnhout, 2005), 55–84.
55. M. de Certeau, 'Les aventures de Jean-Joseph Surin', in Jean-Joseph Surin, *Triomphe de l'amour divin sur les puissances de l'Enfer* (Grenoble, 1990), 421–37, at 431.
56. The letter to Father Datichi at Rennes is found in A. C. Kors and E. Peters (eds), *Witchcraft in Europe, 400–1700: A Documentary History*, revised by E. Peters (2nd edn, Philadelphia, 2001), 356–9. A French version is in Jean-Joseph Surin, *Correspondance*, texte établi, présenté et annoté par M. de Certeau (Paris, 1966), 262–8. See also Jean-Joseph Surin, *Triomphe de l'amour divin sur les puissances de l'Enfer* et *Science experimentale des choses de l'autre vie*, 1653–1660 (Grenoble, 1990), 44.
57. 'Thrilled' is the term used by Sluhovsky to describe Surin's reaction: it is well said. *Believe Not Every Spirit*, 162. The case is not unique. Gregory the Great describes a priest 'catching' possession from a possessed woman whom he had tried to help by covering her in an altar cloth, the story relating that he had acted 'beyond his powers'. See *Saint Gregory the Great: Dialogues*, translated by O. J. Zimmerman (Washington, 2002), Dialogue One, 42. I gratefully acknowledge being able to trace this reference through S. Loxton, *Medicine and Healing in Western Europe – Early Middle Ages* (B.A. Honours Thesis, University of Queensland, 2007), note 57.
58. Jean-Joseph Surin, *Correspondance*, 267.
59. Henri-Marie Boudon, *L'homme de Dieu en la personne du R. P. Surin, de la Compagnie de Jesus* (Paris, 1689), 157–8.
60. J. M. Marin, 'A Jesuit Mystic's Feminine Melancholia: Jean-Joseph Surin SJ (1600–1665)', *Journal of Men, Masculinities and Spirituality*, 1 (2007), 65–76.
61. Manuscript BSG T. f. 1033 contains 1. *Recit ueritable de tout ce qui s'est passé en une maladie qui m'a duré depuis le 11e nouembre 1649 iusques en l'année 1655 et dont les plus habiles Médecins de Paris n'ont pût auoir la connoissance, et a la fin s'est troué que c'etoit possession du Demon, ce que l'on voira par la suitte de ce discours* (fols. 1r–8v); 2. *Recit ueritable de tout ce qui s'est passé ensuitte de ma deliurance, et qui est fort considerable, et ou l'on voira la conduitte de Dieu en*

mon endroit, et dont iay eu pareillement commandement de tout ecrire par celuy qui conduisant (sic) mon ame, et par obeissance je l'ay faict, le Seigneur en soit beny ainsy soit il (fols. 9r–10v); 3. *Journal de tout ce qui s'est passé a Mareil dans la neufuaine faitte en l'honneur de la Sainte Vierge par Mr Potel Prestre pour la deliurance de Monsieur* [deletion] *possedé* [sic] *Demon appellé Robene* [?] *suiuant la permission de Mr. le grand Vicaire de Paris* (fols. 11r–18v); 4. *Journal de tout ce qui s'est passé aux exorcismes faits a Mareil depuis le mardy de la pentecoste 6 iuin 1686* [sic] *iusques au lundy 28e aoust de la mesme année par Messieurs Geruaise Potel et le Vasseur en uertu du pouuoir de Mrs les Grands Vicaires de Paris* (fols. 19r–85v).

62. I thank Bronwen Pugsley at CPEDERF for help in tracing this information.
63. This intervention also appears to endorse the view of the man's elite status.
64. See above, note 28.
65. Certeau, *The Possession at Loudun*, 52.

Index

Asterisks* denote individuals either accused of, or denounced as, being harmful and/or Devil-worshipping witches. Individuals accused of being werewolves are denoted with a (w). Possessed individuals are denoted with a (p). Numbers in **bold** denote tables or figures. Titles of books, treatises and pamphlets are in italics.

Adam, Nicolas,* 34
adultery, 33, 88, 151
  see also fornication; homosexuality, acts of; incest; rape; sexuality
Agia, of Ricomagno,* 138, 142
Aitken, Agnes, 151
Aitken, Margaret,* Scottish witch-finder, 152
  see also witch-finders
Alexander VI, Pope, 67
Amersfoort, *see* Dutch Republic, werewolf trials in
Amundsen, Karin, witchcraft historian, 176
Amussen, Susan, gender historian, 182, 184 *passim*
Amsterdam, 86
Anderson, Malcolm,* 160
Angelica, of Radicondoli,* 134–5 *passim*, 142
Anges, Mother Jeanne des,(p) prioress of the Ursuline convent of Loudun, 226–7 *passim*
Antoine, Jean (alias de Socourt),* Lorraine cobbler, 47–9
Antonia, of Monticiano,* 134, 136–7 *passim*
Apotheker, Barbara,* 104
  see also Rabel, Jacob; Rabel, Barbara
Apps, Lara, witchcraft historian, 3, 10, 14, 106, 108, 113 *passim*, 114, 184
  see also feminization theory; Gow, Andrew
Aquinas, Thomas, 159
Argyll, Earl of, 162
Augsburg, Prince-Bishopric of, 21, 65
Augustin, Schneider,* 33
Aulbry, Jean,* 33, 34
Austria, 59

Babey, Jean, *see* Finance, Jean Didier
Badel, Mengin, 46, 47
Baldung Grien, Hans, artist, 114
Balwearie, great witch of, *see* Aitken, Margaret
Balfour, Alison,* 162
Bamberg, city of, 11, 59–62 *passim*, 180
  factional conflict in, 61–2
  see also Bamberg, Prince-Bishopric of; Junius, Johannes
Bamberg, Prince-Bishopric of, 2, 56, 59–62 *passim*, 78
  Counter-Reformation in, 61–2
  witch-trials in, 59–62, 64–5, 75
  see also Bamberg, city of
Baring-Gould, Sabine, historian of werewolves, 193–6 *passim*
Basel, Bishopric of, 1
Baumgartner, Frau,* 111
Baur, Hans,* 100
Bavaria, Duchy of, 100, 116
Beauvoir, Simone de, feminist writer and philosopher, 217
Bedburg, 193, 196, 198
beggars, *see* vagrants
Behringer, Wolfgang, witchcraft historian, 2
Bellarmino, Roberto, Cardinal, 129
Berching, 105, 111
Bergedorf, 52
Bernadino, Saint, of Siena, 143–4 *passim*

bestiality, 33, 88, 109, 177, 198
  in werewolf trials, 204–5, 208
  see also adultery; homosexuality, acts of
Biberach, 21
Bibliotheca sive acta et scripta magica, 196
Binsfeld, Peter, demonologist and Suffragan Bishop of Trier, 67, 77, 81, 83, 85, 89, 93, 94 *passim*
  see also Trier, Electorate of, witch-trials in
Bitburg, 87
Bittelmayr, Margretha,* 105, 107 *passim*, 109 *passim*
Black, Katherine,* 151
blacksmiths
  accused of witchcraft, 15, 41, 44, 64
  as magical practitioners, 39, 64, 128, 130, 140, 172
  see also Didier, Gaspard; Clerget, Claudin; Fei, Giandomenico; male witches
Blécourt, Willem de, witchcraft historian, 7, 8, 155, 156, 158
Bocquet, Jacques,(w) 193
bodies of demoniacs, 218, 232
  female, 218–9
  male, 219
  see also bodies of exorcists; bodies of witches
bodies of exorcists, 218 *passim*, 219, 223–5 *passim*
  see also bodies of demoniacs; bodies of witches; exorcists
bodies of witches
  imagined as boundless, 2, 19
  imagined as conflated with animals, 12, 178
  imagined as maternal, 2, 11–2, 19, 178
  impact of torture on, 91, 92, 115
  physical examination of, 11–2, 175, 179–80
  post-menopausal, 2
  see also bodies of demoniacs; bodies of exorcists; familiar, witches'; werewolves, imagined as human-animal hybrid; witch-prickers
Bodin, Jean, demonologist and French jurist, 67, 222
  on werewolves, 195 *passim*, 197, 199, 203
  see also demonologists; demonology
Boece, Hector, historian of Scotland, 163
Boeufs, Hanriotte de,* 45
Boguet, Henri, demonologist, 21, 195
  see also demonologists; demonology
Bonschab, Lorenz,* 103 *passim*, 112 *passim*
  see also Bonschab, Maria
Bonschab, Maria, 103
  see also Bonschab, Lorenz
Book of Were-Wolves, *see* Baring-Gould, Sabine
books of magic, *see* magic, books of
Borghesi, Aspremio, Sienese noble, 140
Bothwell, Earl of, 160, 162 *passim*
Bouzey, M. de, 44
boy-witches, 2, 5, 16
  new ideas about, 84–5, 93
  see also child-witches; male witches, age of
Brabant, Chrétien, 42
Bragard, Nicolas Noel le,* Lorraine cunning man, 34, 38
  see also clerics, as cunning men; cunning men
Braidhead, Janet,* 153, 157
  see also Taylor, John
Bramford, 175, 177
Brandeston, *see* Lowes, John
Brandt, Lorenz,* 103
Brigges, Robert,(p) 221, 230
Briggs, Robin, witchcraft historian, 87, 102, 151, 184, 202
Brossier, Marthe,(p) 219, 224
Brown, Peter, historian of late antiquity, 216
Buchell, Arnold van, Dutch chronicler, 197, 201
Buckingham, Duke of, 176
Buirmann, Franz, German witch-commissioner, 21, 86–7
  see also Möden, Dr Johann; witch-commissioners; witch-hunters
Burges, Cornelius, 181

Burgh, John,* Scottish charmer, 157 *passim*
Burgot, Pierre,(w), 194
Bürresheim, lordship of, 87
Bury St Edmunds, 176
Bysack, John*, 177

Caciola, Nancy, historian of possession, 219
Caldwell, Christian (alias Dickson, John), Scottish witch-pricker, 152
  see also 'Paterson, Mr'; witch-prickers
Cambridgeshire, 183
Campbell, John, of Ardkinglass, 162
Campbell, John, of Calder, 162
Canon episcopi (9th century), 106
Carinthia, 4, 16, 55, 56–9 *passim*, 90
  beliefs about weather magic in, 57–8
  beliefs about werewolves in, 58
  beliefs about Wolfbanner in, 58
  economic depression in, 58–9
  gendering of witch-persecution within, **57**
  socio-economic profile of male witches in, 58
  witch-trials in, 56–9, 64–5
Carolina code of criminal law (1532), 77
Carre, Henry,* scholar, 179
Caterina, of Ricomagno, Tuscan cunning woman, 141
  see also cunning women
cats, and magical shape-shifting, 201–2 *passim*, 206 *passim*, 208
  see also hares, and magical shape-shifting; werewolves, shape-shifting of
Certeau, M. de, historian of possession, 232
Châlons, tailor of, *see* Damont, Nicolas
Chambers, John,* 175, 177 *passim*
charmers, 158–9
  see also Burgh, John; cunning men; cunning women
Charmes, 47, 49
Châtenois, 45
Cherrie,* accused English male witch and cowherd, 179
  see also herdsmen
Chiesa, Giovanni Battista, priest and exorcist, 220
childbirth, 2, 9, 129
child-witches, 6, 85, 109
  see also boy-witches
Civil War, English, 173, 175, 181, 182 *passim*, 183
  see also familiar, witches', in Civil War propaganda
Clark, Stuart, witchcraft historian, 10, 183
Clarke, Elizabeth,* 179
Claudon, Nicolas,* 34
Clementia, wife of Leonardo, Domenico of, 131–2, 133
Clerc, Jean Demenge le,* 34
Clerget, Claudin,* blacksmith, 34, 44, 44–7
  see also blacksmiths, accused of witchcraft
clerical concubinage, 89
clerics as accused/denounced witches, 13, 15, 16, 82, 88–9, 111–2
  see also clerical concubinage; clerics, as cunning men; Gordet, Dominique; Grandier, Urban; Jesuits; Lowes, John; male witches; Muckenthal, Christoph Otto von; Penman, Gideon; Reichard, Father John; Sempill, George; Welcker, Herr
clerics as cunning men, 37, 89–90, 163
  see also clerics as accused/ denounced witches; cunning men; MacQueen, Patrick
Clermont d'Antraigues, M. de, 44
Cockburn, John, 153
Coeli et terrae, papal bull (1586), 140
Coinsse, Jean,* 33, 36
Colchester, Essex, 175
Colin, Jacquot,* 34
Colin, Jean,* pig-herder, 43, 44
  see also herdsmen
Cologne, city of, 76, 193, 197, 198, 199, 203
Cologne, Electorate of, 21, 31, 86

confessions of witchcraft, 11, 48–9, 52, 84, 85, 92, 104, 113, 157, 174, 175–6, 177, 179 *passim*
conjuration, 125, **126**, 176
Coton, Father Pierre, French Jesuit and exorcist, 223–4, 225
  see also demonic possession; exorcism; exorcists; Jesuits
Cotone, 137
Counter-Reformation, 11, 16, 18, 65
  in Bamberg, 61–2
  in Eichstatt, 110, 112
  in the Rhine-Meuse region, 81, 88–90 *passim*
  in Siena, 129, 140, 143, 144 *passim*
  see also Jesuits, as Counter-Reformation missionaries; Reformation, Protestant
'crisis of confidence' theory, 92
  see also Midelfort, H. C. Erik
Cristofano, Fulvio of, 131, 132
critics of witch-hunts, *see* witch-hunts, critics of
Crooke, Helkiah, 17th-century English physician, 178, 184
cunning men, 15–6, 37, 38–9, 64, 79, 89, 172, 202
  in Scotland, 157–9
  in Siena, New State of, 139–41 *passim*
  see also blacksmiths, as magical practitioners; Bragard, Nicolas Noel le; charmers; clerics, as cunning men; cunning women; Galatrona, the; Giacomo; Grevillon, Antoine; healers; herdsmen, as magical practitioners; indovino; non-harmful magic
cunning women, 16, 38–9, 89, 128
  in Scotland, 158–9
  in Siena, New State of, 139–41 *passim*
  see also Aitken, Margaret; Caterina, of Ricomagno; Gallena, Lisa di; healers; indovina
cursing, 129–30, 157–8

Daemonologie, 154
  see also demonology; James VI
dairy products, 9, 40, 57
Damont, Nicolas,(w) tailor of Châlons, 193 *passim*, 194, 205
Danner, Hans,* 107, 108
Danner, Paulus,* 103 *passim*
Davies, Owen, witchcraft historian, 159
Davis, Natalie Zemon, gender historian, 171
death in custody, of male witches, 52
  see also suicide
De la démonomanie des sorciers, 195
  see also Bodin, Jean; demonology
Del-Rio, Martin, demonologist and Jesuit theologian, 67, 82–3, 87, 94, 225
  see also demonologists; demonology
Demenge, Mongeotte, 43–4
demonic pact, *see* Devil, pact with
demonic possession, 12, 37, 135, 177
  defining cases of, 219–20
  gendering of, 214–5, 217, 220–3, 229, 231–3
  history of, 215–6
  limelight cases of, 214–5, 220, 221 *passim*, 224
  links to religious conflict, 215, 218–9, 223, 230–1
  links to witchcraft of, 221, 222, 223, 224, 225, 226, 228, 229, 230, 231–2
  in men, 216, 220–2
  in relation to age, 221–2
  in women, 216, 217, 218–9, 221–3
  sources about, 216–7, 218, 219–20, 222, 225, 228
  volition in cases of, 224–5, 226, 231, 232
  see also exorcism; exorcists; Lorraine, Duchy of, possession case in; Loudun, possession case in; Louviers, possession case in; mental impairment, in possession cases; named possessed individuals
demonic ritual magic, 114
demonologists, 68, 75, 93
  see also Binsfeld, Peter; Bodin, Jean; Boguet, Henri; Del-Rio, Martin; demonology; James VI; Kramer,

demonologists – *continued*
Heinrich; Lancre, Pierre de; Rémy, Nicolas; witch-trials, critics of
demonology, 173, 181, 217
dual classification system of, 10, 106, 183, 219
on werewolves, 195–6
see also *Daemonologie*; *De la démonomanie des sorciers*; demonologists; *De prestigiis daemonum*; *Discours execrable des sorciers*; *Disquisitionum magicarum*; female witches, in demonological thinking; *Incrédulité et mescréance du sortilege*; *Malleus Maleficarum*
demons, sexual intercourse with, 11, 76, 78, 160, 197
denunciation, by convicted witches, 5–7 *passim*, 33, 37, 43, 45, 47, 59, 61, 64, 78, 82, 87, 150
significance of, in Eichstätt, 100–17 *passim*
Deny, Jeannon, 46
De prestigiis daemonum, 195, 196
see also Weyer, Johann
Devil, the
in folk literature, 163
imagined as an animal, 78, 177, 203–4
imagined as a bearer of authority, 159–60
imagined as a black man, 201
invocation of, 125, **126**, 156
see also Devil's mark; Devil, pact with; demonic possession; demonology
Devil, pact with, 4, 19, 52, 57–8, 104, 154, 160–1, 163, 202, 230
imagined as a covenant, 161, 177, 181
imagined as a marriage, 160
imagined as sexual, 7, 10, 11, 75, 76, 109, 144, 154, 155, 179, 204
imagined as written, 219
see also demons, sexual intercourse with; Devil, the; Devil's mark; seduction into witchcraft
Devil's mark, 90, 152
see also bodies of witches, physical examination of; familiar, witches'; mark, witches'; witch-prickers
Diana (goddess), 106
Dickson, John, *see* Caldwell, Christian
Didier, Gaspard,* blacksmith, 34, 43–4
see also blacksmiths, accused of witchcraft
Diez, Jean,* 34–5
Dirksz, Volkert,* 201
Discours execrable des sorciers, 195
see also Boguet, Henri
Disquisitionum magicarum, 225
see also Del-Rio, Martin
Douglas, Adam, historian of werewolves, 193
Dowsing, William, 183
Dufresne, Adrienne,(p) 224, 225
Duncan, Geillis,* 159
see also North Berwick, witches of
Dürer, Albrecht, German artist, 114
Dutch Republic, 8
werewolf trials in, 200–2, 203–4

East Anglia, witch-trials in, 11, 20, 21, 174–84 *passim*
Easter Ross, 160
Echternach, 90
Eerden, P.C. van der, witchcraft historian, 83
Eichstätt, Prince-Bishopric of, 5, 65, 100–17 *passim*
witch-trials in, 100, 102, 104, 105
Eifel region, 88, 89
see also Manderscheid, Eifel region counties of
Elizabeth I, Queen of England, 175
Ellis, Robert,* 180
Ely, 180, 181
England, 4, 17, 20, 114–5, 123, 124, 149, 152, 159, 171–84 *passim*
see also Civil War, English; English Witchcraft Statute
English Witchcraft Statute
of 1563, 115
of 1604, 181
enigmatical prophecy, 163–4
Entre-deux-Eaux, 35

Erprath, 198
escape from gaol, by male witches, 47, 91
Essex, county of (England), 1, 4, 101–2
  gender of witches in, 175
  see also Colchester; Lambourne; Manningtree
Esslingen, 21
Estonia, 2, 15, 74, 172
Everard, Thomas,* English cooper, 182
executioners, 20, 21, 106
  accused of witchcraft, 90
  as magical practitioners, 37, 90
exorcism, 214–5 passim, 220
  as a form of healing, 216 *passim*, 218 *passim*
  gendering of, 218–9
  by Jesuits, 218, 222, 225–6, 227
  physical abuse during, 215, 225
  see also demonic possession; exorcists; Jesuits
exorcists, 215, 217
  see also bodies of exorcists; Chiesa, Giovanni Battista; Coton, Father Pierre; exorcism; Gervase, Father; Le Vasseur, Father; Potel, Father; Surin, Father Jean-Joseph

factionalism, *see* witch-trials, as tools in power struggles
familiar, witches'
  in animal form, 4, 11–2, 163, 174, 175 *passim*, 177–8 *passim*, 180
  in Civil War propaganda, 182
  see also mark, witches'; searchers, for witches' marks; suckling, by familiars of witches
familiar spirit, witches', 43, 173
fatherhood, *see* masculinity, early modern ideas of
fear, of witches, 121, 142, 145, 164–5, 176
Fei, Antonia of Agapito, 130, 132
Fei, Giandomenico,* Tuscan blacksmith, 9, 121–2 *passim*
  witchcraft case against, 129–33 *passim*, 141–2 *passim*
  see also blacksmiths, accused of witchcraft
female honour, 221
  see also male honour
female werewolves, 205–7
  see also werewolves
female witches, 89
  age of, 2, 6, 32 101–2, **127**
  explanations for the persecution of, 1–2, 7, 9, 75, 102
  in demonological thinking, 10, 143
  historiographical concentration on, 1
  imagined as bad housewives and mothers, 1–2, 11–2, 18, 129, 143, 156
  marital status of, **127**
  sexual abuse of, 104
  shape-shifting of, 206
  socio-economic status of, 2, 80, 101–2, 104–5, **128**
  stereotypes of, 6, 8, 9, 75–6, 83, 101, 102, 114–6 *passim*, 155–8 *passim*
  as victims of patriarchy, 1, 18, 74
  vulnerability to accusation of, 12–3, 14, 84, 100
  see also female witches, trials of; individual named female witches; male witches; maleficium; married couples, imagined as witches; patriarchy; witchcraft beliefs, gendering of; witches, gender-specific terminology for; witch-trials, gendering of
female witches, trials of
  in Bergedorf, 52–3
  in Eichstätt, Prince-Bishopric of, 100–17 *passim*
  in Holstein, Duchy of, 62–3
  in Lorraine, Duchy of, 40–2
  in Luxembourg, Duchy of, 81
  in Siena, New State of, 126–9, 134–42
  in Trier, city of, 81, 82
  see also female witches
feminization theory, of Apps and Gow, 113, 114, 156, 157, 165, 172, 176, 199, 208
  see also Apps, Lara; Gow, Andrew
Fernel, Jean, 16th-century French physician, 216
Ferry, Jean, 44, 45

Féry, Jeanne,(p) 219
Fian, John*, Scottish schoolmaster, 159–60, 161
Finance, Jean Didier (alias Babey),* 34, 35
Finland, 6, 15, 74, 172, 181
Finnmark region (Norway), 15, 16
see also Sami people; shamans
Flade, Dietrich,* high criminal court bailiff in Trier, 13
witchcraft trial against, 82–3, 83, 85, 87, 88
see also Trier, city of; Trier, Electorate of, witch-trials in
fornication, 109, 110, 144, 151
see also adultery; homosexuality, acts of; sexuality
Fouesse, Nicolas, 48
France, 12
werewolf trials in, 193, 196, 197, 205
Franche-Comté, werewolf trials in, *see* France, werewolf trials in
Franchi, Giuseppe, 133
Francis, Richard, witchcraft historian, 21
Frauncis, Elizabeth,* 115
Friuli region, 122

Gabler, Paul,* 107–8 *passim*, 110 *passim*, 111 *passim*
Galatrona, the, Tuscan cunning man, 139
see also cunning men
Gallena, Lisa di, Tuscan cunning woman, 140–1
see also cunning women
Gallier, Margueritte,* 45
Gandillon family,(w) 193
Gardeme, Mengin, 46
Garnier, Gilles,(w), 193 *passim*, 194, 195, 199, 205
Gaskill, Malcolm, witchcraft historian, 9, 21, 158
Gaule, John, cleric and critic of witch-trials, 183
see also witch-trials, critics of
Gauthier, Barbe, 45
Gauthier, Morisot, 45–6
Geiler von Kaisersberg, Johann, 194
Geliat, Jean Pierron,* 42
Gerard, Colas,* 35
Gerardin, Claudon Jean,* 36
Gerardin, Jean Jacques,* 34
Gerardin, Noel, 35
Germany, 75, 172
female werewolves in, 205–7
werewolf trials in, 193, 203, 204–5
see also Stump, Peter
Gervase, Father, exorcist, 228–31 *passim*
see also exorcists
Ghayer, Michael,* 103
see also Khager, Barbara
Giacomo, Tuscan cunning man, 123–4, 139
see also cunning men
Gijswijt-Hofstra, Marijke, witchcraft historian, 121–2
Gilbert, Jean, 44
Ginzburg, Carlo, witchcraft historian, 122
Giovanni, Francesco of, 138
Girtenstihl, Michael,* 109, 110 *passim*
Godfrey, John*, of Lambourne, Essex, 172
Godfrey, John,* of Massachusetts, 19, 172–3
Godfrey, William,* 9, 172
Goeury, Jean,* 33
Gordet, Dominique,* Lorraine cleric, 33
see also clerics, as accused/ denounced witches
Gorge, Barbe la Grosse,* 39
Goudie, Isobel,* 153, 160 *passim*
Gow, Andrew, witchcraft historian, 3, 10, 14, 106, 108, 113 *passim*, 114, 184
see also Apps, Lara; feminization theory
Graham, Richard, Scottish necromancer, 162
Grandier, Urban,* Loudun priest, 226 *passim*, 232
see also clerics, as accused/ denounced witches
Great Waldingfield, 177
Grenier, Jean,(w) 193, 205
Grevillon, Antoine,* 34, 38, 39
see also cunning men
Grieve, Robert,* 160

Grön, Ursula,* 101
Grosseto, 138
Grundy, Jenni, witchcraft historian, 12
Guenauet, M., 17th-century French physician, 229
Gutmann, Catharina,* 109
Gutmann, Enders,* 100, 103, 109
  see also Gutmann, Catharina; Gutmann, Georg; Gutmann, Jacob; Gutmann, Lorenz; Gutmann, Richella; Schiller, Anna
Gutmann, Georg,* 100, 103, 109 *passim*
  see also Gutmann, Catharina; Gutmann, Enders; Gutmann, Jacob; Gutmann, Lorenz; Gutmann, Richella; Schiller, Anna; Spät, Anna
Gutmann, Jacob,* 109
  see also Gutmann, Enders; Gutmann, Georg
Gutmann, Lorenz,* 109
  see also Gutmann, Enders; Gutmann, Georg
Gutmann, Richella,* 109
  see also Gutmann, Enders; Gutmann, Georg

Haan, Dr, Chancellor of the Prince-Bishop of Bamberg,* 61
  see also Bamberg, Prince-Bishopric of; Junius, Johannes
Hagen, Rune, witchcraft historian, 16
Haizmann, Christoph,(p) 230
Halesworth, 182
Hamburg, 52
Hamm, Lord of, 87
hangmen, *see* executioners
Haraucourt, M. d', 36
Harding, Anna,* 103, 105
hares, and magical shape-shifting, 206
  see also cats, and magical shape-shifting; werewolves, shape-shifting of
harmful magic, *see* maleficium
Hastrup, Kirsten, witchcraft historian, 15
Hauff, Daniel, German witch-hunter, 21
  see also witch-hunters
Hault, George de,* 34–5
Hay, John, of Lochloy, 153
Hay, John, of Park, 153
healers, 8, 15, 32, 34, 38–9, 41–2, 49, 157, 158, 160–1, 158
  see also charmers; cunning men; cunning women; herdsmen, as magical practitioners; Lowrie, Patrick; Ratter, Andrew; Ratter, Elizabeth; Ratter, Katherine
healing, 124, 125, **126**, 159
  of maleficium, by witches, 31–2, 39, 42, 48, 123, 127–8, 132, 134–7, 141, 201
  see also exorcism, as a form of healing; healers
Heikkinen, Antero, witchcraft historian, 7
Henri de Valois, 44
Henrietta Maria, Queen of England, 230
Henri IV, King of France, 224
herdsmen
  accused of witchcraft, 15, 16, 32, 33, 41, 43, 58, 64, 103, 172
  as magical practitioners, 37, 39, 64
  see also Cherrie; Colin, Jean; cunning men; healers
heresy, late-medieval, 67
Heuser, Peter Arnold, witchcraft historian, 5, 6, 7
Hexenmeister, 3
  see also Schulte, Rolf
Hexensonderkommando, 102
Hochenschildt, Michael,* 100, 103, 109, 110 *passim*, 112 *passim*
Hochnötige Unterthanige Wemütige Klage der Frommen Unschültigen, 86
  see also Löher, Hermann
Holstein, Duchy of, 15, 56, 62–5 *passim*
  witch-trials in, 62–5, 64–5
Holy Roman Empire, 3, 10, 54, 59, 65, 67, 68, 75, 77, 82, 87, 88, 90, 94
  criminal jurisdiction in, 53
  gendering of witch-trials in, **55**
  regional variation in the persecution of male witches in, **56**, **66**, 68, 79–80
  religious divisions in, 53, 65
  territorial fragmentation of, 53

Holy Roman Emperor, 59
homosexuality, acts of, 177
  in werewolf trials, 204
  see also adultery; bestiality; sexuality; sodomy
honour, *see* female honour; male honour
Hopkins, Matthew, English witch-finder, 11, 20, 21, 154 *passim*; 174 *passim*, 175 *passim*, 176, 179 *passim*, 183–4 *passim*
  see also Phillips, Mary; Stearne, John; witch-hunters
Huillier, Jean, 36
humoral medical theory, 178
Hungary, 1
Huntingdonshire, *see* Molesworth
Hutchison, James, 158

I benandanti, *see* Ginzburg, Carlo
Iceland, 2, 9, 15, 15–6, 74, 172
Imperial Aulic Court, 60
imps, diabolic, *see* familiar, witches'
incest, 33, 88, 193, 197, 198, 204, 205 *passim*, 208
  see also adultery; homosexuality, acts of; sexuality
Incrédulité et mescréance du sortilège, 195
  see also Lancre, Pierre de
indovina, Italian cunning woman, 123, 124, 141
  see also cunning women
indovino, Italian cunning man, 123, 124
  see also cunning men
Institoris, *see* Kramer, Heinrich
Instrumentalisierung (instrumentalization), *see* 'malicious' prosecution
Italy, 121, 124 *passim*, 127, 130, 134, 139, 140, 141, 142 *passim*
  witchcraft studies on, 121–2

James I, King of England, 224
  see also James VI, King of Scotland
James III, King of Scotland, witchcraft conspiracy against, 161
James VI, King of Scotland, 21, 23, 154, 160
  witchcraft conspiracies against, 161
  see also Daemonologie; demonologists; demonology; James I, King of England; North Berwick witches
Jerome P.,(p) possession case of, 228–31, 231–2 *passim*
Jesuits
  as Counter-Reformation missionaries, 81–2, 88–90
  interest in demonic possession of, 225–6
  in the Rhine-Meuse region, 16, 93
  in Trier, city of, 81–2, 84–5
  see also Coton, Father Pierre; exorcism, by Jesuits; Richeome, Louis; Surin, Father Jean-Joseph
Judge Sewall's Apology, 20–1
  see also Francis, Richard
judicial system for trying witches
  in Eichstätt, Prince-Bishopric of, 100, 104–5
  in Lorraine, Duchy of, 31
  in the Rhine-Meuse-Moselle region, 77–8
  in Siena, New State of, 123–4
  in Scotland, 150–2
Junius, Johannes,* mayor of Bamberg, 11, 13, 61, 180
  see also Bamberg, Prince-Bishopric of, witch-trials in; Lauterer, Christoph

Kahk, Juhan, witchcraft historian, 15
Karlsen, Carol, witchcraft historian, 151
Kello, John, Scottish minister and rumoured necromancer, 163
Kent, county of, 172
Kent, Elizabeth, witchcraft historian, 4, 17, 18, 19, 176 *passim*, 184
Kervinen, Timo, witchcraft historian, 7
Khager, Barbara,* 103, 104
  see also Ghayer, Michael
Kidd, John, 157
Kivelson, Valerie, witchcraft historian, 17, 24
Kleikamp, Peter,(w) 204, 207
Knox, John, 162–3

Kramer, Heinrich, Dominican inquisitor and demonologist, 21, 67, 134 *passim*, 137, 139, 141 *passim*
 see also demonologists; demonology; *Malleus Maleficarum*

Labouvie, Eva, witchcraft historian, 8, 9, 17, 32, 33, 37, 87, 124
Ladies from Outside, 101
Lallemand, Jean,* 35
Lambe, Dr John,* 176 *passim*
Lambourne, Essex, 172
Lancre, Pierre de, demonologist, 21, 195
 see also demonologists; demonology; *Incrédulité et mescréance du sortilège*
la Neuveville-sous-Châtenois, 44–7 *passim*
Lanng, Valtin,* 100, 103 *passim*, 109
Larner, Christina, witchcraft historian, 78, 150, 160, 161, 173
Lauterer, Christoph,* mayor of Eichstätt, 103, 107 *passim*
 see also Eichstätt, Prince-Bishopric of, witch-trials in; Junius, Johannes
Lea, Henry Charles, witchcraft historian, 196
Lebenwaldt, Adam Lebaldt von, German physician, 20
Lederer, David, historian of mental health, 220
Leonardo, Domenico of, 131–2, 141
Le Vasseur, Father, exorcist, 228–31 *passim*
 see also exorcists
Levi, Giovanni, historian of possession, 220
Leys, Thomas,* 156–7
 see also Wishart, Janet
Lienard, Barbon, 37
Lienard, Lienard Jean, 36–7
Liermey, Dedier, 45
Lietard, Jean, 45
Livonia, werewolf trials in, 196
Löher, Hermann, juryman and critic of witch-trials, 78, 86–7
 see also witch-trials, critics of
Loos, Cornelius, critic of witch-trials, 78
 see also witch-trials, critics of
Lorenzo de Medici, 139
Lorraine, Duchy of, 6, 14, 79, 80
 beliefs about the sabbath in, 49–50
 gendering of witch-trials in, 31
 possession case in, 225–6
 witch-trials in, 31–50 *passim*, 87
Lorraine, Eric of, Bishop of Verdun, 220
Loudun, possession case in, 226–8, 229 *passim*, 231, 232
Louviers, possession case in, 229 *passim*, 231
love magic, 9, 63, 124, 125, **126**, 133, 159
Lowes, John,* vicar of Brandeston, Suffolk, 13, 181
 witchcraft case against, 175–6, 179
 see also clerics, as accused/denounced witches
Lowrie, Patrick,* 157, 158
 see also healers
Lübeck, 52
Luther, Martin, ideas about witchcraft of, 67–8
Luti, Alberto, Sienese noble, 136
Luxembourg, city of, 81, 88
 see also Luxembourg, Duchy of
Luxembourg, Duchy of, 31, 55, 76, 78, 79, 80, 88, 89, 91
 witch-trials in, 79, 81, 93
lycanthropy, *see* werewolves

Macbeth, King of Scotland, 163–4
MacCalzean, Euphemia,* 153
MacDonald, Stuart, witchcraft historian, 150
Macfarlane, Alan, witchcraft historian, 2, 4, 122 *passim*
MacKenzie, George, of Rosehaugh, Lord Advocate of Scotland, 154
MacQueen, Patrick, Scottish minister and cunning man, 163
 see also clerics, as cunning men
magic, 4
 books of, 43, 90, 131, 133, 142
 gendered beliefs in, 7–12, 37–8, 124–9, 142

magic – *continued*
  gendered practice of, 4, 41–2, **126**, 126
  papal recategorization of, 124, 140–1
  see also cunning men; cunning women; demonic ritual magic; love magic; maleficium; milk magic; non-harmful magic
Maire, Jennon le,* 43
maleficium, 4, 15, 17, 31–2, 36, 52, 60, 67, 76, 78, 82, 89, 104, 106, 113, 123 *passim,* 124 *passim*, 156, 172
  against adults, **40**, 41, 43, 44, 45, 46, 48–9, **128**, 136, 137, 138, 172, 173
  against infants, 9, 37, **40**, 41, 44, 128, 129 *passim*, 130, 134–6 *passim*, 138, 143, 172
  against livestock, 37, **40**, 41, 42, 43, 44, 45, 48, 52, **128**
  gendered beliefs about, 8, 9, 9–10, 37–8, **40**, 62–3, 126, 142
  using substances provided by devils, 37, 42, 48–9
  see also healing, of maleficium by witches; magic; male witches, imagined as workers of maleficium; non-harmful magic; poisoning; Wolfbanner
male honour, 207–8, 221
  negated by possession, 226–7
  negated by torture, 91–2
  see also female honour
male witches
  age of, 48, 52, 64–5, 102, 103, 129, 179
  bodies of, 11–2, 19
  categorised as primary or secondary, 26, 64, 65, 84, 157
  Catholic view of, 66–7
  as contraveners of masculine norms, 17–8, 32, 34–5, 47, 88, 92, 109–10, 176, 178–9, 180–1, 182, 184, 202, 207–8
  defence strategies of, 91
  definitions of, 4–5, 172, 191
  historiography on, 2–3, 113–4, 122
  imagined as bearers of the Devil's authority, 159–60, 161
  imagined as 'kings of the sabbath', 76, 82–3, 88, 92, 93
  imagined as 'patrons of witches', 76, 82–3
  imagined as profit-makers, 8, 9, 17, 34–5, 37, 43, 82
  imagined as sabbath-attenders, 5–6, 45, 68, 81, 159–60
  imagined as workers of maleficium, 9–10, 41, 45, 46, 48, 129–32 *passim*, 172–3 *passim*, 175–6 passim, 179, 201
  key research questions about, 3
  Lutheran view of, 67–8
  marital status of, 44–5, 48, 64–5, 102
  more lenient legal treatment of, 4–5, 62, 92, 111–2, 202
  occupational status of, 15, 16, 33, 58, 61–2, 64–5, 79, 80, 82, 90, 103, 130
  socio-economic status of, 6, 13, 35, 41, 58–9, 61–2, 64–5, 76–7, 79, 80, 82, 91, 93, 102, 103, 104–5, 130, 178–9
  statistical analysis of, 3–7, 53–6, **55**, **56**, **57**, **60**, **63**, **66**, 105, 142, 150
  stereotypes of, 8, 9, 64, 155–61 *passim*, 165, 201, 202
  as 'victims' of patriarchy, 18
  see also blacksmiths, accused of witchcraft; bodies of witches; boy-witches; clerics, accused of witchcraft; death in custody, of male witches; escape from gaol, by male witches; feminization theory; healers; herdsmen, accused of witchcraft; individual named male witches; married couples, imagined as witches; masculinity; patriarchy; vagrants, accused of witchcraft; warlock; witchcraft beliefs, gendering of; witches, gender-specific terminology for; witch-trials, gendering of
Male Witches in Early Modern Europe, 3
  see also Apps, Lara; Gow, Andrew
'malicious' prosecution, 13–4, 22, 35–6, 48, 130–1, 136–7, 153
  see also witch-trials, as tools in power struggles

Malleus Maleficarum, 67, 106, 115 *passim*, 134, 137, 143 *passim*
  see also Kramer, Heinrich
Manderscheid, Eifel region counties of, 76, 78, 88, 89
  witch-trials in, 80, 87, 93
Manderscheid-Blankenheim, Count of, 92
Manderscheid-Blankenheim, court assessor of,* 93
Manderscheid-Keil, Count of, 87
Manfilia, of Cotone,* 137–8, 142 *passim*
Manningtree, Essex, 174, 175, 179
Mar, Earl of, 161
Marchal, François, 45
Marchtal, 21
Maria, of Roccastrada,* midwife, 134, 135–6 *passim*, 142
  see also midwives
Mariastein, 111
Marion, François,* 34
mark, witches', natural causes of, 180
  see also Devil's mark; familiar, witches'; suckling, by familiars of witches
married couples, imagined as witches, 14, 33, 48, 61, 84, 103, 108–9, 157
  see also female witches; male witches; witch family
Martin, Lauren, witchcraft historian, 156, 160–1 *passim*
masculinity, as a category of historical analysis, 171, 180, 192, 199–200
  early modern ideals of, 17–8, 22–3, 88, 92, 173, 182, 184, 200
Massachusetts, 19
Mather, Cotton, New England cleric, 20
Mathis, Demenge,* 35
Mathis, Jean Gregoire,* 34
Mattaincourt, 44
Mattheis, Augustin,* 33
Mayr, Georg, 108–9, 110, 111–2
  see also Mayr, Maria
Mayr, Maria,* 108
  see also Mayr, Georg
Mechelen, werewolf trials in, 203
Mecklenburg, Duchy of, 9, 65
  werewolves in, 207
Mengin, Claudette,* 36
mental impairment, 34, 58
  in possession cases, 220, 221, 224–5, 231
metamorphosis, *see* shape-shifting
Michel, Nicolas Girard, 44
Midelfort, H. C. Erik, witchcraft historian, 6, 75–6, 82, 220 *passim*
  see also 'crisis of confidence' theory
midwives, 20, 41, 128, **128**, 134, 143
  see also Maria, of Roccastrada
milk magic, *see* dairy products
Miller, Joyce, witchcraft historian, 158–9
Möden, Dr Johann, German witch-commissioner, 87
  see also Buirmann, Franz; witch-commissioners; witch-hunters
Moeller, Katrin, witchcraft historian, 9
Molesworth, 178
monocausal explanations, criticisms of, 75, 101–2, 103, 112–3, 176
Montaigne, Michel de, 225
Montepulciano, 121, 129 *passim*, 131, 141
Monter, William, witchcraft historian, 16, 32, 220
Monticiano, 136
Moriviller, 36
Muckenthal, Christoph Otto von, Eichstätt cleric, 107, 108
  see also cleris, as accused/denounced witches
Munro, Hector, 161
Munro, Robert, of Foulis, 161
Murray, Margaret, Egyptologist, 160
Musiel, Claudius, German witch-hunter, 21, 22–3
  see also Omsdorf, Peter; St Maximin, Imperial Abbey of, witch-trials in; witch-hunters; *Witch Register*

Namur, County of, 1
Napier, John, of Merchiston, 163
Nassau, Count of, 201
necromancy, 43, 162 *passim*

necromancy – *continued*
see also Graham, Richard; Kello, John; Knox, John
Neill, John*, 160–1
Newcastle, 158
New England, 4, 17, 74, 151
The Night Battles, *see* Ginzburg, Carlo
night-flying, 2, 8, 106
non-harmful magic, 4, 15, 124–6
recategorized as maleficium, 15–6, 124, 140–1
see also cunning men; cunning women; healers; magic; maleficium
Nördlingen, 21
Normandy, 2, 15, 16, 32, 172
Northamptonshire, *see* Thrapston
North Berwick, witches of, 159–60 *passim*, 161, 162 *passim*
see also Bothwell, Earl of; Duncan, Geillis; Fian, John; Graham, Richard; James VI, King of Scotland
Nynauld, Jean de, 195

Obry, Nicole(p) 219
Odhar, Coinneach (Kenneth),* 160
Omsdorf, Peter, notary and witch-hunter, 81
see also Musiel, Claudius; St Maximin, Imperial Abbey of, witch-trials in; witch-hunters
Orceoli, Father Zaccaria, Sienese General Inquisitor, 129, 130, 131, 133
Orkney, Earl of, 162
Otten, Charlotte, literary scholar, 193, 205

Padelt, Mengin, 46
pagan cult survival, theory of, 160
Pairson, Nicolas,* 34
Palandrana, Antonia la, from Grosseto,* whore, 138, 142 *passim*
pamphlets, *see* witchcraft pamphlets; werewolf pamphlets
Pardoux, Barthélemy, 17th-century French physician, 222
Parisot, Babelon, 43
Pasqui, Agnesa, 144
'Paterson, Mr', female Scottish witch-pricker, 152
see also Caldwell, Christian; witch-prickers
patriarchy, 171–3 *passim*, 182
institutional power of, 1, 18, 19–23, 38, 74, 150–2, 164–5, 199
see also female witches, as victims of patriarchy; male witches, as victims of patriarchy; witch-hunters
Payne,* accused English male witch, 177
Pays de Vaud, 74
Peace of Augsburg (1555), 53
Penman, Gideon,* Scottish minister, 163
see also clerics, as accused/denounced witches
Perlhafter, Verena, witchcraft historian, 20
Perrin, Mengeon Claude,* 35
Persin, M., 47
Petit, Jennon,* 41
Phillips, Mary, English witch-searcher, 175
see also familiar, witches'; Hopkins, Matthew; searching; Stearne, John
physical handicap, 58
Pienza, 129
Piernille, Jean, 43
Pierrat, Didier,* 42
Pierre, Chrétien,* 36–7
Pietenfeld, 103
Poeck, Hans, *see* Steenhuijsen, Johan Martensen van
poisoning
by arsenic, 47
by magic, 62
Poland, 44
Wielkopolska region of, 1
political witch-hunts, *see* James III, King of Scotland; James VI, King of Scotland; Junius, Johannes; witch-trials, as tools in power struggles
Porzin, Peter,* 105, 107 *passim*
possession, *see* demonic possession
Potel, Father, exorcist, 228–31 *passim*
see also exorcists

Pottier, Demenge, 43
pregnancy, as grounds for clemency, 108
prophecy, *see* enigmatical prophecy
prostitutes, *see* whores
Purel, Noel,* 34
Purkiss, Diane, witchcraft historian, 2, 18, 183

Rabel, Barbara,* 104
see also Apotheker, Barbara; Rabel, Jacob
Rabel, Jacob,* 103
see also Apotheker, Barbara; Rabel, Barbara
Radicondoli, 134
Ranfaing, Elisabeth de,(p) 225
Raon, 43
rape, 33, 36, 159, 193
see also adultery; homosexuality, acts of; sexuality
Ratter, Andrew,* Scottish folk-healer, 158
see also healers; healing; Ratter, Elizabeth; Ratter, Katherine
Ratter, Elizabeth,* Scottish folk-healer, 158
see also Ratter, Andrew
Ratter, Katherine,* Scottish folk-healer, 158
see also Ratter, Andrew
Rattlesden, 177, 179
Reformation, Protestant, 15, 18, 143, 172
in England, 179
in Scotland, 151
see also Counter-Reformation
Reckschenkel, Johannes, 76
Reichard, Father John,* Eichstätt cleric, 102, 105
see also clerics, as accused/denounced witches
Remy, Mengin, 36
Rémy, Nicolas, demonologist and jurist, 21, 67
see also demonologists; demonology
reputation, *see* witchcraft, reputation for
Rheinbach, 86
Rhine-Meuse-Moselle region 13, 15, 17, 20, 74–94 *passim*
witch-trials in, 77–80
Richel, Bartholomäus, 103
Richeome, Louis, Jesuit theologian, 225
see also Jesuits
Ricomagno, 138
Roberts, Keith, werewolf historian, 196
Roccastrada, 135–6 *passim*
Roman Inquisition
archives of, 122, 135
in Siena, 121, 122–3, 124 *passim*, 129, 144
see also Siena, New State of, witch-trials in
Roper, Lyndal, witchcraft historian, 2, 21–2, 156, 177
Ross, Katherine, Lady Foulis, 161
Rothenburg ob der Tauber, 9, 13, 173
Rottinger, Michael,* 103 *passim*
Roulet, Jacques,(w) 193, 194 passim
Rowlands, Alison, witchcraft historian, 156, 158, 173
Roy, David,* 159, 162
Rummel, Walter, witchcraft historian, 13
Rupert, Prince, of the Rhine, 182 *passim*
see also Civil War, English
Russia, 2, 15, 17, 172
Rye, 111

Saar region, 8, 17, 32, 33, 87, 124
sabbath, witches', 37, 45, 123, 157
dual-gendered membership of, 10, 68, 79, 202
gender hierarchy of, 93
imagined as a black mass, 78
link to large-scale witch-hunts, 5–7, 61, 78, 104–5
male behaviour at, 110
male musicians at, 5, 84, 93
new ideas about, 5–6, 67–8, 76, 81, 83, 84, 93
scepticism about, 68, 106
see also demonology; denunciation, by convicted witches; male witches, imagined as 'kings of the sabbath'; male witches, imagined

sabbath, witches' – *continued*
as sabbath-attenders; witchcraft beliefs
St Albans, 178
St Bernardino, of Siena, *see* Bernadino, St, of Siena
St Dié, 42
St Maximin, Imperial Abbey of, witch-trials in, 21, 22, 76, 78, 79, 80, 81, 82, 83, 84, 85, 93
see also Musiel, Claudius; Omsdorf, Peter; Trier, Electorate of
Saint-Nicolas-de-Port, 37
St Teresa of Avila, 227
Salem, 20, 21, 85, 222
Salzburg, Prince-Bishopric of, 16, 65, 90
see also Zauberer-Jackl witch-trials
Sami people, 15, 16
see also Finnmark; shamans
Sandaucourt, 45
Sand, Kathleen, R., historian of possession, 221
Santoro, Cardinal Giulio Antonio, 133, 141
Saxony, Electorate of, 65
Saxony-Lauenberg, Duchy of, *see* Duchy of Holstein
Scarfe, John,* 177–8
Schaumburg, County of, 55
Schiller, Anna,* 103, 104
see also Gutnamm, Enders; Gutmann, Georg
Schindler, Norbert, witchcraft historian, 16, 17
Schulte, Rolf, witchcraft historian, 3, 10, 114
Schwarz, Georg,* 107, 108
Schweistal, Johann,* 87–8
Sclater, John McWilliam,* 160
Scotland, 6, 10–1, 20, 23, 149–65 *passim*
decline of witch-trials in, 165
scale of witch persecution in, 149, 150
witchcraft conspiracies in, 161–2
Scott, Joan, gender historian, 171 *passim*, 180
Scott, Sir John, of Scotstarvet, Scottish writer, 164
searchers, for witches' marks, 20
see also bodies of witches, physical examination of; Phillips, Mary
Sebald, Hans, witchcraft historian, 2
seduction into witchcraft, 81, 88, 113
gendering of, 50, 83
sexual, 11, 179
through despair/poverty, 47, 48–9, 177, 178–9
see also Devil, pact with; sexuality
Sempill, George,* Scottish minister, 163
see also clerics, as accused/ denounced witches
Seton, David, bailie of Tranent, Scottish witch-hunter, 153 *passim*
see also witch-hunters
sexuality
of men, 11, 33–4, 83, 88, 109–10, 160–1, 177–8
in possession cases, 218–9, 227, 230, 232
of women, 10, 11, 75, 143–4 *passim*, 155, 160–1, 207
see also adultery; bodies of demoniacs; bodies of exorcists; bodies of witches; Devil, pact with, imagined as sexual; clerical concubinage; seduction into witchcraft, sexual; homosexuality, acts of; werewolves; deviant sexuality of whores
Shakespeare, William, *see* Macbeth
shamans, 2, 16
see also Sami people
shape-shifting, *see* cats, and magical shape-shifting; female witches, shape-shifting of; hares, and magical shape-shifting; werewolves, shape-shifting of
Sharpe, James, witchcraft historian, 219
Shepard, Alexandra, gender historian, 171 *passim*
shepherds, *see* herdsmen
Siena, Archbishopric of, 123, 144
see also Siena, New State of
Siena, New State of 4, 123, 134, 139, 140, 142

Siena, New State of – *continued*
cunning men and women in, 139–41
persecution of magical crime in, 125–6
see also Roman Inquisition, in Siena; Siena, Archbishopric of
Simon, Friar, Tuscan parish priest, 144
Simpson, Cuthbert, 156
slander, 151, 202, 204
sleep deprivation, 152, 174–5
see also torture
Socourt, Jean de, *see* Antoine, Jean
sodomy, 88
in werewolf trials, 204–5, 207, 208
see also homosexuality, acts of
sorcerers, 7, 15
see also cunning men
Spät, Anna,* 103, 104
see also Gutmann, Georg
Spee, Friedrich, critic of witch-trials, 78
see also witch-trials, critics of
St, *see* Saint
Stablo, Bastien,* 34, 36
Stanton, Margery,* 101
Stearne, John, English witch-finder, 11, 20, 21, 174 *passim*, 175 *passim*, 177 *passim*, 178, 179 *passim*, 181, 183–4 *passim*
see also Hopkins, Matthew; witch-hunters
Steenhuijsen, Johan Martensen van, alias Poeck, Hans, (w) 203–4, 207, 208
Stein, Gordon, werewolf historian, 196
stereotypes, *see* female witches, stereotypes of; male witches, stereotypes of; witches, gendered stereotypes of
Stewart, Elizabeth, 164
see also Stewart, James, Earl of Arran
Stewart, Francis, *see* Bothwell, Earl of
Stewart, James, Earl of Arran, 164
Stewart, John, 162
Stigeliz, Hans,* Master of the Hospital, Eichstätt, 103, 105
Stoeckhlin, Chonrad,* 2, 101
strega, harmful female witch (Italian), 124, 141
stregone, harmful male witch (Italian), 124, 131, 141
Stubbe, Peter, *see* Stump, Peter
Stump, Peter,(w), 193, 196 *passim*, 202, 201, 203, 205 *passim*, 206, 207
contemporary accounts of trial of, 197–8
trial of, 196–9
see also A True Discourse Declaring the Damnable Life and Death of One Stubbe Peter; werewolves
suckling, by familiars of witches, 11–2, 175, 177–8, 180
see also bodies of witches; familiar, witches'
Suffolk, 13, 183
gender of witches in, 175
suicide
of accused witches, 92
temptation to, 177
Summers, Montague, werewolf historian, 193–6 *passim*
Surin, Father Jean-Joseph,(p), Jesuit exorcist, possession case of, 226–8, 231–2 *passim*
see also demonic possession; exorcists; Jesuits
Survey of Scottish Witchcraft, 150, 154
Susanna, abbess of the cloister of Mariastein, 111
swimming of witches, *see* water ordeal

Taylor, John, 157
see also Braidhead, Janet
teat, witches', *see* mark, witches'
therapeutic magic, *see* healing
Thiermayr, Regina, 111
Thieriat, Nicolas, 48
Thiery, Demenge, 44
Thiriat, Mengeon Clement,* 34, 35
Thirty Years War, 60, 116
Thomas, Keith, witchcraft historian, 2, 122 *passim*
Thompson, Stith, folklorist, 163
Thrapston, 179

Tirol, 90
torture, 1, 5, 31, 33, 44, 47, 52, 61, 76, 77–8, 90, 104, 113, 115, 123, 133
  criticism of, 52
  female experience of, 92–3, 115
  male experience of, 91–3
  see also sleep deprivation
Tractatus de confessionibus maleficorum et sagarum, 83, 85
  see also Binsfeld, Peter
treasure-seeking, 37, 90, 124, 125
Trier, city of 13, 76, 80, 81, 82, 83, 84, 88
  see also Binsfeld, Peter; Flade, Dietrich
Trier, Elector of, 79, 80, 88
Trier, Electorate of, 87, 89, 91
  witch-trials in, 22, 76, 77, 79–80, 81, 83, 84, 85, 93
  see also Trier, city of; Trier, Elector of; St Maximin
A True Discourse Declaring the Damnable Life and Death of One Stubbe Peter (short title: *Life of Peter Stubbe*) 193, 196, 196–7, 198 *passim*
  see also Stump, Peter
Tuscany, 121, 123, 124, 125

Upper Palatinate, 116
Utchin, Claude, 46
Utrecht, 200–1 *passim*

vagrants, 90
  accused of witchcraft, 16–7, 58–9, 172
  gendering of groups of, 59
  use of magical threats by, 59
  see also boy-witches; male witches, age of; male witches, socio-economic status of; Zauberer-Jackl witch-trials
Valdexey, Anthoine Didier,* 33
Verdun, Bishop of, *see* Lorraine, Eric of
Verjuz,(w), 205
Viney, Bastien Jean,* 34
Voltmer, Rita, witchcraft historian, 13, 21, 22–3
Vomécourt-sur-Madon, 33, 45
Vulgate, 66–7

Wagner, Hans,* 103
Walinski-Kiehl, Robert, witchcraft historian, 11, 17, 78
warlock, use of term, 158, 191, 192
Washington, Sir John, 179
watchers, 175
  see also watching
watching, of suspected witches in England, 177
  see also watchers
water ordeal, 201, 203, 204
weather magic, 40, 45, 57–8, 78, 82, 124, **128**
  see also magic; maleficium
Weinsberg, Hermann, Cologne pastor and diarist, 197
Welcker, Herr ?,* Eichstätt cleric, 112
  see also clerics, as accused/denounced witches
The Werewolf, see Summers, Montague
werewolf pamphlets, 195–6, 196–7, 197–8, 201, 202–3, 205–6, 207
  see also A True Discourse Declaring the Damnable Life and Death of One Stubbe Peter; witchcraft pamphlets
werewolf trials, *see* France, werewolf trials in; Germany, werewolf trials in; Livonia, werewolf trials in; Mechelen, werewolf trials in; Stump, Peter
  see also werewolves
werewolves, 4, 9, 50, 58
  as contravenors of masculine norms, 200
  deviant sexuality of, 198 *passim*, 199, 204 *passim*, 205, 207–9
  difference from male witches of, 208
  dissemination of ideas about, 196–7, 200–1, 202–3
  executions of, 196, 197, 198, 199, 204
  gendering of, 207
  historiography on, 192–6

werewolves – *continued*
imagined as human-animal hybrid, 208–9
invisibility of 198–9
links to cannibalism of, 192, 193–4 *passim*, 197, 198, 199
shape-shifting of, 193, 194, 197, 198 *passim*, 199, 201, 201–2, 203–5 *passim*
total numbers of, 207
see also bodies of witches, imagined as conflated with animals; Bodin, Jean, on werewolves; female werewolves; individual named werewolves; Mecklenburg, Duchy of, werewolves in; Stump, Peter; werewolf pamphlets; werewolf trials; Wolfbanner
Westphalia, Duchy of, 5, 6, 7
wetnurses, 128, **128**, 134, 143
Weyer, Johann, critic of witch-trials, 83, 94, 195, 196
see also witch-trials, critics of
Whitney, Elspeth, witchcraft historian, 180, 183, 184
whores, accused of witchcraft, **128**, 143, 144 *passim*
see also Palandrana, Antonia la; sexuality
Wier, Johann, see Weyer, Johann
Willis, Deborah, witchcraft historian, 11
Willock, John, superintendent of Glasgow, 163
Wilson, Colin, occult historian, 205
Winnick, John*, 178–9
wise women, 128, 134, 143
see also cunning women
Wishart, Janet,* 157
see also Leys, Thomas
witch-commissioners, 5, 20, 21, 86
in Eichstätt, 100–17 *passim*
misogyny of, 114
see also Buirmann, Franz; Möden, Dr Johann; witch-hunters
witchcraft, definition of, 4–5, 123
witchcraft beliefs, 2, 7, 8, 123
confessional differences in, 65–8
dissemination of, 7, 10, 81–2, 85, 87, 94, 115, 116, 143–4
gendering of, 66–8, 76, 106, 114, 126, 143–4, 173, 181
links to heresy of, 67, 76, 104
papal influence on, 124, 140
see also demonologists; demonology; Devil, pact with; enigmatical prophecy; familiar, witches'; female witches, stereotypes of; magic; maleficium; male witches, stereotypes of; sabbath, witches'; witch family
witchcraft confessions, *see* confessions of witchcraft
witchcraft pamphlets, 114–6, 154, 182
see also werewolf pamphlets; *Zwo Hexen Zeitung*
witchcraft, reputation for, 14, 31, 36, 43, 131–2, 151
by association with other witches, *see* married couples, imagined as witches; witch family
witches
age of, 6, 16
gendered stereotypes of, 6, 8, 9–10, 56, 75, 102, 114–6 *passim*, 143, 144, 154–61 *passim*, 201
gender-specific terminology for, 54–5, 124, 158
imagined as bad neighbours, 18–9
socio-economic status of, 2, 6, 13, 41
types of, 7, 128, 134
see also bodies of witches; Devil, pact with; familiar, witches'; female witches; male witches; sabbath, witches'; married couples, imagined as witches; witch family; witch-trials
Witchcraft Special Research Unit, *see* Hexensonderkommando
Witches and Neighbours, 102
see also Briggs, Robin
witch family 8, 14, 32–3, 34, 36, 43, 48–9, 50, 86, 103, 104, 108–9, 156–7, 172, 182, 201, 204

witch family – *continued*
  see also married couples, imagined as witches; female witches, stereotypes of; male witches, stereotypes of; witch household
witch-finders, 79, 89, 90
  see also Aitken, Margaret; cunning men; cunning women; Hopkins, Matthew; Stearne, John
Witchfinders, 21
  see also Gaskill, Malcolm
witch household, 84, 158
  see also witch family
witch-hunters, 13–4, 18, 19–23, 152–4
  motivation of, 21–2, 22–3, 90, 153–4, 183–4
  as victims of witch-trials, 76, 85–7
  see also Hauff, Daniel; Mackenzie, George; Seton, David; witch-commissioners; witch-finders; witch-hunting committees
witch-hunting committees, 13–4, 20, 21, 53, 79, 85–6
  see also witch-trials, popular pressure for
Witch Hunting in Southwestern Germany, 6
  see also Midelfort, H. C. Erik
witch-hunts, *see* witch-trials
witch-prickers, 20, 90, 152
  see also Caldwell, Christian; 'Paterson, Mr'
Witch Register (*Hexenregister*) of Claudius Musiel, 21, 22
  see also Musiel, Claudius
witch-trials
  biblical justification for, 66–8
  chronological dynamics of, 5–7, 32–3, 56, 59–61, 62, 80–3, 104
  from above, 116–7, 150
  gendering of (in early modern Europe), 1, 2, 74, 172
  gendering of (in specific regions of Europe), 1, 2, 5, 6–7, 9, 15, 16, 31, 53, **55, 56, 60, 63, 66**, 79–80, 100, 102, 125–6, 150, 175, 181
  large-scale episodes of, 5–7, 59–62, 65, 76, 77–80, 150
  link to poverty of, 101–2
  non-capital punishments in, 54, 62
  popular pressure for, 52, 53, 88
  regional variation of, 75, 101–2
  as tools in power struggles, 13–4, 22, 61–2, 87, 87–8, 110–2, 161–4, 175–6, 181–2
  see also female witches, trials of; male witches; sabbath, witches'; werewolf trials; witch-finders; witch-hunters; witch-hunting committees; witch-trials, critics of
witch-trials, critics of, 75
  see also demonologists; Gaule, John; Löher, Hermann; Loos, Cornelius; Spee, Friedrich; Weyer, Johann
Witte, Joachim,* 52–3 *passim*
Wolfbanner, 4, 58
  see also werewolves
wolves, *see* Wolfbanner
Würth, Michael,* 9
Würzburg, 21, 75, 116 *passim*

Yeoman, Louise, witchcraft historian, 153
Young, Isobel,* 156
Young, John,* 160

Zauberer-Jackl witch-trials, 16, 65, 90
  see also boy-witches; vagrants
Zedler, J.H., 64
Zwo Hexen Zeitung, 116